Thomas Morris Chester, Black Civil War Correspondent

Thomas Morris Chester, Black Civil War Correspondent

His Dispatches from the Virginia Front

Edited, with a Biographical Essay and Notes,
by R. J. M. BLACKETT

LOUISIANA STATE UNIVERSITY PRESS
Baton Rouge and London

Manufactured in the United States of America
First printing
98 97 96 95 94 93 92 91 90 89   5 4 3 2 1

Designer: Laura Roubique Gleason
Typeface: Palatino
Typesetter: The Composing Room of Michigan, Inc.
Printer: Thomson-Shore, Inc.
Binder: John H. Dekker & Sons, Inc.

Library of Congress Cataloging-in-Publication Data

Chester, Thomas Morris.
    Thomas Morris Chester, Black Civil War correspondent : his
dispatches from the Virginia front / edited, with a biographical
essay and notes by R. J. M. Blackett.
        p.   cm.
    Includes index.
    ISBN 0-8071-1516-9 (alk. paper)
    1. United States—History—Civil War, 1861–1865—Participation,
Afro-American.   2. Virginia—History—Civil War, 1861–1865—
Participation, Afro-American.   3. United States—History—Civil
War, 1861–1865—Campaigns.   4. Virginia—History—Civil War,
1861–1865—Campaigns.   5. Chester, Thomas Morris.   6. United States—
History—Civil War, 1861–1865—Personal narratives.   7. Virginia—
History—Civil War, 1861–1865—Personal narratives.   8. Afro-
Americans—Virginia—History—19th century.   I. Blackett, R. J.
M., 1943–   .   II. Title.
E540.N3C4   1989
973.7'415—dc19   89-30169
                                                        CIP

To Gibbs, for all her understanding and encouragement

Contents

Preface

My first encounter with Thomas Morris Chester occurred years ago while I was doing research in England. He seemed a curiosity then: a captain of a Civil War Pennsylvania regiment! My suspicions were aroused, for I doubted that Pennsylvania would have conferred a captaincy on a black person in 1863. It was possible, I thought, that he was one of a handful of shady characters who operated independently on the fringes of established abolitionist societies and who, as a result, caused British abolitionists considerable anxiety. Louis Chamerovzow, secretary of the British and Foreign Anti-Slavery Society, railed publicly against unattached and unendorsed black lecturers, and wrote privately to American supporters suggesting ways to control such activities, but he was clearly unable to stop the British public's fascination with these black emissaries of oppressed America. But Chester was not one of those who troubled some in organized British abolitionist circles. As I quickly found out, Chester was genuine, a legitimate figure in the effort to win international support for the Union during the Civil War. There were other tantalizing glimpses into his life: claims that he had been a Civil War correspondent, that he had studied at a London Inn of Court, and that he had been received at the court of the czar of Russia. An effort to pursue these leads was the genesis of this study.

It takes an unusual form, in that I combine the reproduction of documents with biography. The latter attempts to trace his life, to account for some of his actions, and to assess what impact he had on nineteenth-century Afro-American history. He provides us with a unique opportunity to evaluate the life of someone who defied the canons of antebellum black thinking by emigrating to Liberia, a creation, many blacks insisted, of white American thinking deranged by racism, and a potential potter's field for all who settled there. One gets the distinct impression that Chester remained suspect in the eyes of many contemporaries even when, in 1870, he returned to America permanently. Chester fueled these suspicions by refusing to either publicly condemn Liberia or relinquish the hope of settling in the country he always called "home." Yet he chose to return to America after completing his legal training in London. I can think of only one other prominent contemporary, Alexander Crummell (interestingly, also a graduate of an English university), who lived in Liberia for any length of time before returning to America. But I have deliberately shied away from making too many comparisons between the two men. Their decisions to settle in Liberia were the result of radically different impulses. Chester seems to have given up on America when he was a teenager; Crummell made his decision as an adult, while in England, removed from the pressures of America and with the comfort and support of friends, after months of agonizing over his future. But their views on Liberia, its role in African development and the succor and the home it offered black Americans denied the rights of full citizenship in America, converge in many instances and provide an important glimpse into the thinking of those who espoused the cause of an exodus to Africa.

Chester is yet another example of those antebellum black men and women who by one means or another defied efforts to impose unfair restrictions on their lives. He came of age in a decade when America seemed bent on sacrificing its soul on the altar of expediency and compromise. The infamous Fugitive Slave Law of 1850 opened a decade that would witness the erosion of pitifully limited black rights and growing northern appeasement of southern demands. Unlike the majority of his father's generation, who had struggled since the 1830s to achieve some limited improvements, and who confronted these new developments with a rededication to the struggle against slavery and racism, Chester chose a future outside the country. Many thought that he had abandoned the cause and gone over to the enemy. Anti-colonizationists were unequivocal in their condemnation of the American Colonization Society and Liberia; it had been created, they insisted, for the express purpose of removing the free black population from America, the easier to consolidate the system of slavery. Yet in spite of his unquestioned dedication to Liberia's development—synonymous in many respects with his hopes for personal advancement—Chester could not bring himself to sever all ties with America. He kept in touch through frequent visits. Later he would boast of crossing the Atlantic more than a dozen times between 1853 and 1870. I hazard only the most limited psychological explanations for his actions. But the contradiction could not have escaped him that the country that denied him rights enshrined in its Declaration of Independence at the same time provided him an opportunity to attend an elite school in the rustic hills of Vermont. That opportunity was not extended, however, to include the right to join his classmates at one of the country's premier colleges; Chester would have to look elsewhere.

All these experiences, including work in Liberia, his reception in Europe, the years spent reading law in London, Chester used to good effect during the final twenty years of his life, which were spent in Louisiana. Like many of his contemporaries, Chester was deeply committed to the idea that Reconstruction presupposed a fundamental reordering of southern society, a new beginning in which both races could compete on an equal footing. That the experiment failed has less to do with the efforts of Chester and others and more to do with the country's refusal to accept and act on the principle of equality for all. He died a disillusioned man, possibly thinking that his youthful instincts to abandon America were right after all. But the country, and especially New Orleans with its cultured, urbane black elite, in 1870 tantalizingly held out the hope of a new order, which Chester could not ignore.

The second section is a reproduction of Chester's dispatches to the Philadelphia *Press* from the James River front. They cover the period August, 1864, to June, 1865, the final critical months of the war. They are an important and unique record of that time and of the uncertainties of life all Richmonders faced after the collapse of the Confederacy. There is no way of knowing exactly why John W. Forney, owner of the *Press*, or John Russell Young, editor, decided to hire Chester for this important assignment. No other daily followed the *Press*'s lead, and there seems to be no obvious reason why the *Press*, which began publication in 1857 as a Democratic newspaper, and which had no record of promoting the interests of blacks, should have decided to hire a black correspondent. Nor does it appear that Forney or Young was trying to make a political statement. Forney was too busy rubbing shoulders with the political gentry of Washington, D.C., to care much about such gestures. But the result is the only sustained eyewitness account of the activities of black soldiers around Richmond and Petersburg.

Chester had a keen eye for detail. His reports, written under the nom de plume Rollin, frequently went beyond the mere reporting of battles to include descriptions of how soldiers survived the ordeals of war. He was particularly empathetic to the suffering soldier. While the propaganda effect of these dispatches cannot be underestimated, Chester's accounts of recently redeemed Union prisoners of war are moving, and paint such lurid pictures of deprivation and starvation that none of his readers could have questioned the enemy's barbarity. His coverage of the treatment of injured and captured white officers and their black troops aimed to do more than praise their bravery, however; it showed the depth to which man could sink in his pursuit of morally indefensible causes. In many respects, Chester's message involved classical abolitionist views of the effects of slavery on American society: freedom for all was threatened by slavery's denial of the inalienable rights of blacks.

These dispatches have an additional value, for they record the efforts of black Richmonders to rebuild their lives in the wake of the war's devastation. Chester was not a disinterested bystander, but an active participant in the struggle to carve out a new order from the ruins. As his reports attest, this was no easy task. The victors, rather than crushing the remnants of the slave order, were falling over themselves to extend the hand of reconciliation. His articles from Richmond and Petersburg, in the days after the surrender, betray an understandable anger at the Union's unnecessarily lenient policies toward those who had actively supported or fought for the Confederacy. These policies were ominous omens, yet Chester's last dispatch from Richmond contained an unexpected element of optimism. The old military commanders either had been removed or had resigned; their replacement, a former commander of black troops, had a history of being sensitive to the needs of his men. The struggle for power between the old order and those who advocated a complete restructuring of southern society and polity were previewed in the weeks after the evacuation of Richmond. Six years later, Chester would return from England to participate in the work of Reconstruction, skeptical of the country's intention toward its black citizens, but nonetheless determined to struggle for a better world for all. His imagery of the piano with its black and white keys, each an independent and equal entity, separate yet playing in harmony, one dependent on the other, attests to his vision of the future and his hopes for America.

Finally a comment on my system—a word I use advisedly—of annotation. The effort, I discovered to my dismay, induces compulsiveness: once the first is done, there is a pressure to do all. I was spared that fate, however, not because of any attempt to be highly selective, but simply because it proved impossible to track down everyone mentioned. Like all correspondents in the heat of war, Chester spelled names as he thought he heard them. Non-Anglicized names caused him considerable difficulty. Some I found by chance, and those I have corrected in the text. Others were more elusive. One example will suffice. In his October 9, 1864, dispatch Chester begins by mentioning a Captain William H. Sigreaves, who in the next paragraph becomes Captain Legreaves and maintains that name for six paragraphs, only to reemerge as Captain Segreaves. And, as if that were not enough, he ends up as Captain Sergreaves. In trying to identify him, I came to despise this man, whoever he was. Chester's handwriting was indecipherable at times. He is the only person I know who lost a job—he was fired by the Justice Department in 1883—because his superiors were driven to distraction by his penmanship. That might account for part of the problem, but Chester should not be held totally responsible for my frustrations. It is very likely that errors were made in typesetting and proofreading. Those I could not identify I was forced to ignore. I have made no annotations for people included in Chester's casualty lists unless he highlighted the person. And where my information on a person could add nothing to Chester's description, I have opted not to include a vignette. I also felt that prominent figures, like Lincoln, Grant, Davis, Lee, and others, would not be slighted if I failed to notice them. In spite of my minimalist approach, this was not an easy task, and a few, alas, have managed to escape my prying.

Acknowledgments

This work is the result of a great deal of assistance from many people who took a keen interest in Chester. Hind Sookdeo performed the almost impossible task of transcribing Chester's dispatches from a nineteenth-century newspaper that seemed to defy modern technology by becoming more indecipherable the more we tried to enlarge the print. In the end, she was forced to revert to a good magnifying glass and infinite patience. Her patience and friendship will always be cherished. Others did all they could to track down obscure information on Chester. Roger Lane brought to my attention a photograph of Chester that Karen C. Humbert, Librarian at Cheyney University in Pennsylvania, kindly reproduced. Svend Holsoe gave copies of letters from the Liberian Archives; George Beyer and Tim Nisen, articles I had missed; Charles Blockson enthusiastically shared his knowledge of Pennsylvania history and located a couple of dispatches; Peter Rachleff and John O'Brien offered pointers on Reconstruction Richmond; the late Tom Shick told me where to look for Liberian documents; Frederick Torrey, Headmaster of Thetford Academy, encouraged my efforts, as did Marian Fiefield of the Thetford Historical Society; Ruth Ziner took time out from vacation to track down information in Vermont; and Matthew Magda and Dan Littlefield entertained me during visits to Harrisburg and Baton Rouge. Rhonda Stone of the Interlibrary Loan Department at Indiana did all she could to fill my requests. So too did Esme Bhan of the Moorland-Spingarn Research Center, Howard University, and E. McNeill, Librarian and Keeper of the Records, Middle Temple, London. My thanks to them and to all the other librarians for their contributions. In the closing stages of the project, a grant from Research and Graduate Development, Indiana University, allowed me to visit archives in Louisiana and Pennsylvania. Allison Blakely, Betty Fladeland, Wilson Moses, and David Thelen read the biographical chapter. I am grateful for their criticism, and a measure of that is the fact that we are still friends. The work has benefited from their sharp comments and suggestions for changes. My daughters have complained bitterly that I never acknowledge the patience and understanding they show whenever I choose to write rather than spend time with them. To Leila and Lavinia a peace offering: my thanks.

PART I

CHAPTER 1

Thomas Morris Chester: A Biographical Essay

It is one of the ironies of American history that the first forces to enter Richmond following its evacuation by the Confederacy were black. Other elements of the Army of the James, poised on the outskirts of the Confederate capital, jostled for the distinction of conquering heroes. Yet that distinction fell to the black 5th Massachusetts Cavalry led by Charles Francis Adams, Jr., followed by troops of the all-black XXV Army Corps under Major General Godfrey Weitzel. Those whose offer to join in the Union's defense, four years earlier, had been spurned because they were black, now found themselves in the vanguard as Union forces marched into Richmond. With them was Thomas Morris Chester, a thirty-year-old black reporter from Harrisburg, Pennsylvania, who had been covering the Army of the James for the Philadelphia *Press* since August, 1864. Sensitive to the significance of these events, Chester—the only black to cover the war for a major daily—began his first report from Richmond: "Seated in the Speaker's chair, so long dedicated to treason, but in future to be consecrated to loyalty, I hasten to give a rapid sketch of the incidents which have occurred since my last despatch." As we shall see, this bit of bravado did not go unchallenged, but his actions offer a glimpse into the life of one of nineteenth-century black America's most versatile individuals. Lauding his accomplishments, a contemporary wrote: "It may be said of him that he was the first negro who appeared in the courts of Dauphin county as a practicing attorney, the first negro admitted to practice before the supreme court of Pennsylvania and the first negro to be called to the courts of England as a barrister."[1] Not all the details were accurate, nor was the list of

1. Dudley T. Cornish, *The Sable Arm: Negro Troops in the Union Army, 1861–1865* (New York, 1956), 282; Philadelphia *Press*, April 6, 1865; Harrisburg *Patriot*, September 13, 1892.

accomplishments complete. A highly motivated person, a dogged
defender of rights, and an avid promoter of black interests, Chester
has left his mark on Afro-American history. Yet little is known of him,
a consequence of both the devaluation of black contributions to
American history and, one suspects, because as a young man Chester
chose to emigrate to Liberia. Supporting Liberia was enough to make
one a pariah, a traitor even.

Thomas was born in Harrisburg, Pennsylvania, on May 11, 1834,
the fourth child of George and Jane Marie Chester. Little is known of
George's life before he settled in Harrisburg in the early 1820s.[2] Jane
was born a slave in Virginia, in 1806. She was sold subsequently and
moved with her new owner to Baltimore, Maryland, and from there
she escaped to York, Pennsylvania, in 1825, long before the organization of the Underground Railroad. It took a particularly bold,
imaginative, and determined person to attempt what was by all
standards a difficult and dangerous journey. Frederick Douglass,
another Maryland fugitive, later recalled the problems he faced
during his escape: "The real distance [between Maryland and Penn-
sylvania] was great enough, but the imagined distance was to our
ignorance, much greater. Slave holders sought to impress their slaves
with a belief in the boundlessness of slave territory, and with their
own limitless power. Our notions of the geography of the country
were vague and indistinct—the nearer the line of the slave state—the
greater the trouble." J. W. C. Pennington recorded similar difficulties
during his escape in 1827. Most fugitive slaves from Maryland
entered Pennsylvania through York, Adams, or Chester counties.[3]
Jane spent only a brief time in York before moving to Harrisburg,
where she went to work as a maid in the home of Alexander

2. Charles L. Blockson, *The Underground Railroad in Pennsylvania* (Jacksonville,
N.C., 1981), 76, points out that George, "the son of an Indian chief on the island of San
Domingo," was whisked away by slave traders and brought to the United States.
Blockson's information came from a descendant of Chester's. An obituary suggests that
George was born in 1784 but gives no place of birth. Harrisburg *Telegraph*, October 17,
1859.

3. Frederick Douglass, *Life and Times of Frederick Douglass* (New York, 1962), 199;
J. W. C. Pennington, *The Fugitive Blacksmith; or Events in the History of J.W.C. Pennington
Pastor of a Presbyterian Church, New York, Formerly a Slave in the State of Maryland, United
States*, in Arna Bontemps (ed.), *Great Slave Narratives* (Boston, 1969), 215; R. C. Smedley,
History of the Underground Railroad in Chester and the Neighboring Counties of Pennsylvania
(1883; rpr. New York, 1968), 31, 45, 208; Wilbur H. Siebert, *The Underground Railroad
from Slavery to Freedom* (New York, 1898), 121.

Graydon, the first prothonotary of Dauphin County, and later took a similar position with Modecai McKinney, a prominent local judge. She met George soon after she settled in Harrisburg, and they were married in April, 1826. They had twelve children, seven of whom survived to adulthood.[4]

An oysterman, George owned a restaurant on Market Street near the courthouse, which also served as a center of social and political activity in the city. Between 1831 and 1834, George was the capital's only agent of William Lloyd Garrison's *Liberator*, which could be purchased at the restaurant. This, fine food, and congenial surroundings soon made the restaurant a hub of local abolitionist activity. Here blacks made plans to protect fugitives from recapture, and organized anti-colonization meetings. The Chesters catered many of the events held in the capital, and on major public holidays it became something of a tradition to dine at their restaurant. Jane continued the tradition after George's death in the late 1850s, when she moved the restaurant to her new home at 305 Chestnut Street. By then, she was considered the town's "principal caterer" and was renowned for her homemade taffy.[5]

The Chesters' abolitionist activities were not always welcomed in a city where colonizationists held considerable sway. The Pennsylvania Colonization Society and its local auxiliary, formed in 1819, were among the strongest in the antebellum period, strong enough to form their own settlement in Liberia and publish a newspaper. Many of their most prominent members, like Elliot Cresson and William Coppinger, later became leading figures in the national organization. But none of this deterred Harrisburg blacks from condemning colonization as a "vicious, nefarious and peace-disturbing domination," whose sole purpose was to "drain the country of the most enlightened part of our colored brethren, so that they may be more able to hold their slaves in bondage and ignorance."[6]

4. Luther Reily Kelker, *History of Dauphin County, Pennsylvania* (2 vols.; Chicago, 1907), I, 128–29; W. H. Egle, *Commemorative Biographical Encyclopedia of Dauphin County, Pennsylvania* (Chambersburg, Pa., 1896), 188, 423; *Oracle of Dauphin*, April 29, 1826; United States Population Schedules, Dauphin County, Pa., 1850.

5. H. Napey, *The Harrisburg Business Directory and Stranger's Guide with a Sketch of its First Early Settlement 1842* (Harrisburg, 1842); Harrisburg *Telegraph*, October 17, 1859, January 16, July 3, 1862; Harrisburg *Patriot and Union*, October 18, 1859; Harrisburg *State Journal*, December 6, 1884, January 24, 1885.

6. *Liberator*, October 15, 1831; William Lloyd Garrison, *Thoughts on African Colonization* (1832; rpr. New York, 1969), Pt. II, 41–42.

Although small by the standards of Philadelphia and New York, the Harrisburg community was proud of its accomplishments. Most of the city's five hundred blacks owned their own homes in 1830. The African Methodist Society, formed in 1817, ran a successful school. Years later, Douglass spoke of the black Methodist church's "order, neatness and gentility" exceeding "any congregation of our oppressed brethren I have seen for a long time." He was particularly impressed by the women who had established a number of benevolent societies to promote "the general improvement and elevation of our long abused race." Blacks protected fugitives who had settled in the city. In 1825, about the time Jane came to Harrisburg, a group of blacks armed with "clubs and cudgels" attacked a handful of Maryland slave catchers on the courthouse steps in an unsuccessful effort to free a fugitive. Of the nineteen indicted, six were sentenced to one year, and five received six months in jail; the rest were acquitted. In 1842, it was rumored that a group of blacks had "united to resist and punish slave hunters." Twelve years later, a local paper observed that after their arrival in the city, "the fugitives became invisible. They are as hard to find as the Know Nothings. Nobody knows nothing about their whereabouts." The failure to punish slave catchers in 1825 was a rare defeat for the community, a result, one suspects, more of its ability to defend those fugitives who had settled in the capital, than a lack of escaped slaves, for the city lay on a major escape route for fugitives from Maryland, Delaware, and Virginia.[7]

Life for blacks in Harrisburg was no bed of roses; in this, their experiences were no different from those of blacks in other northern cities. Their lives were circumscribed by laws and traditions that severely limited opportunities and barred them from the right to full participation as citizens. To economic and social restrictions were added political proscription in 1838, when a constitutional amendment took away their right to vote. Petitions to the state legislature calling for the removal of all voting restrictions were consistently

7. *Pennsylvania Freeman*, September 2, 1847, August 19, December 5, 1850; *Pennsylvania Intelligencer*, April 22, 1825; Edward Raymond Turner, "The Underground Railroad in Pennsylvania," *Pennsylvania Magazine of History and Biography*, XXXVI (1912), 315; Harrisburg *Herald*, June 15, 1854; Mary D. Houts, "Black Harrisburg's Resistance to Slavery," *Pennsylvania Heritage*, IV (1977), 9–13; Anne Bustill Smith, "The Bustill Family," *Journal of Negro History*, X (1925), 641.

Mrs. Charlotte Weaver (*left*), Chester's eldest sister, became the first black teacher in Harrisburg. His mother, Jane (*right*), worked among Confederate prisoners held in that city.

Courtesy of Yvonne Martin

ignored. Violence was not unheard of. When Douglass attempted to speak at a public meeting in 1848, he was attacked with "brickbats, fire-crackers and other missiles" by a mob trying to silence what Garrison sarcastically called this "unparalleled audacity." Rather than succumb to such intimidation, the community organized a second meeting in the safety of one of its churches and invited white supporters to participate. On occasion, blacks openly defied the system. For example, they formed a committee to resist enforcement of the Fugitive Slave Law, "believing it better to suffer for the cause of righteousness than to submit to a law which tramples under foot the laws of the Most High God." Denied the political influence that comes with the right to vote, they organized informal groups to pressure local authorities when it mattered. Such activities would lead to a slow but perceptible improvement in educational opportunities and create a tradition of community-inspired action. They also built their own churches and organized benevolent, temperance, and literary societies, as well as Masonic and Odd Fellow lodges. Here George and Jane carved out a relatively economically independent and secure niche for themselves and their growing family.[8]

Nothing is known of Thomas' early life. He later recalled developing a passionate commitment to education and, with the encouragement of Modecai McKinney, a determination to become a lawyer. But his parents appear to have been the dominant influence. They did everything within their means to educate all their children. Charlotte, the oldest surviving daughter, became a teacher in Harrisburg. Jane carried on this commitment after George's death. Whenever Thomas needed assistance, he could count on his mother's total support—no mean accomplishment, considering he spent the better part of forty years educating himself. But most of Thomas' drive to attain an education was self-induced. That seems the only adequate explanation for the decision of a young man of sixteen "in the midst of winter, before the Pennsylvania railway had leveled the Allegheny Mountains" to leave home to attend Allegheny Institute in Allegheny City across the river from Pittsburgh.[9]

The institute, later Avery College, was built with a bequest from the philanthropist Charles Avery as "a college for the education of colored Americans in the various branches of science, literature and ancient and modern languages." Opened in April, 1850, the institute was little more than a preparatory school during its early years. Entry requirements were minimal: a student had to be at least fourteen years of age, able to read, write, and do multiplication, and possess a certificate attesting to good moral character. Its principal, Philotus Dean, a graduate of Yale, was already a recognized proponent of improved instruction in mathematics and languages. By 1855, commencement addresses were being delivered in French. Dean initiated most of the institute's early developments, ably assisted by Martin H. Freeman, a recent black graduate of Middlebury College in Vermont. Twenty years later, Chester recalled that he arrived at the institute with "all the vanity . . . which illiterateness had implanted and conceit had strengthened," but that by the time he left two years later, he had begun Greek and Latin. More important, because of its

8. *Pennsylvania Freeman,* December 21, 1848, October 31, 1850; Walter M. Merrill (ed.), *The Letters of William Lloyd Garrison,* Vol. III, *No Union With Slave Holders, 1841–1849* (Cambridge, Mass., 1973), 507–508.

9. Harrisburg *Telegraph,* September 30, 1892.

lasting impression, "this fountain of learning," Chester claimed, provided him with "those moral and intellectual impressions" that sustained him throughout his life.[10]

While a dedication to his studies and a determination to succeed are evident in all that Chester did, developments outside the walls of the institute were also influential. These were particularly trying times for black Americans. The Federal government seemed determined to crush all their aspirations in a desperate effort to appease the South. The Fugitive Slave Law, under which the Federal government committed itself to facilitating the return of fugitive slaves to their owners, was the keystone of this policy. Just nine months after Chester's arrival in Pittsburgh, the city's black population, according to one observer, was almost decimated in the wake of this "ungodly antirepublican law." Within one month, three hundred blacks had fled Pittsburgh and Allegheny City, and Sandy Lake, a fugitive slave settlement fifty miles to the north, ceased to exist when its inhabitants decamped for the safety of Canada. But some blacks stood their ground in open defiance of the law. At a public meeting in late September, 1850, Martin R. Delany, Pittsburgh's most prominent black, called on all concerned to resist. Turning to the mayor, he said, "[W]hatever ideas of liberty I may have, have been received from reading the lives of your revolutionary fathers. I have learned that a man has a right to defend his castle with his life, even unto the taking of life. Sir, my house is my castle; in that castle are none but my wife and my children. . . . If any man approaches that house in search of a slave . . . if he crosses the threshold of my door, and I do not lay him a lifeless corpse at my feet, I hope the grave may refuse my body a resting place, and righteous Heaven my spirit a home."[11] The sanctity of the home became a metaphor for the protection of the community. The city lost just one slave to the South during the next five years.

But this organized resistance to the law was, for some, tempered by a gnawing uncertainty that America was, after all, a white man's country in which blacks had no future. That, of course, had been the

10. Victor Ullman, *Martin R. Delany: The Beginnings of Black Nationalism* (Boston, 1971), 70; Ann Wilmoth, "Pittsburgh and the Blacks: A Short History, 1780–1875" (Ph.D. dissertation, Pennsylvania State University, 1975), 181–83; Harrisburg *Telegraph*, July 16, 1870.

11. R. J. M. Blackett, "Freedom or the Martyr's Grave: Black Pittsburgh's Aid to the Fugitive Slave," *Western Pennsylvania Historical Magazine*, LXI (1978), 127–28; Ullman, *Martin R. Delany*, 112.

position of the American Colonization Society (ACS). But few blacks
who came of age in the 1830s were willing to accept the Society's
reasoning or its solution of settling blacks in Liberia. Pittsburgh
blacks, for example, had denounced as traitors those who accepted
the Society's solution. While others were more restrained, all dismissed the Society's plans as anathema to black interests, which, they
insisted, were predicated on a future in a free America. Yet the fact
remained that, in 1850, blacks had little to show for twenty years of
political agitation. The Fugitive Slave Law was not only a weak-kneed
and myopic effort at appeasement, it was also an unequivocal
rejection of black demands for equality. Not surprisingly, there were
some who sought solutions outside the ambit of both the colonizationists and the abolitionists. The period saw the emergence of a
nationalist emigrationist movement led by Delany and others. Its
manifesto, published in 1852, called in part for blacks to explore the
possibilities of establishing a home outside the United States.[12]

Under these circumstances, Liberia increasingly assumed center
stage as the issue of independent settlement came to dominate debate
among blacks. In the anti-colonizationists' view, it was, as it had
always been, a leper house where blacks were consigned to certain
death. And for those, like Delany, who advocated an alternative
home in Africa, its reputed shortcomings became the yardstick by
which their own plans could be measured. Attending Allegheny
Institute, in the midst of a community dominated by these issues,
Chester would likely have joined the debate on the merits of staying
in or leaving America. He might have arrived in Allegheny City
already partial to Liberia, though that seems unlikely, given his
father's staunch anti-colonization position. But Harrisburg and Philadelphia colonizationists were so well organized that they managed to
maintain a measure of influence in spite of opposition from blacks
and white abolitionists. Their fortunes improved dramatically, in the
early 1850s, sparked by a program to win public and government
support. Annual receipts increased from $29,000 in 1847, to $97,000 in
1851. In 1850 the Virginia legislature appropriated $35,000 for five
years to encourage emigration. Other state legislatures, including
Pennsylvania's, quickly followed Virginia's lead. In light of these

12. Garrison, *Thoughts on African Colonization*, Pt. II, 35; Martin R. Delany, *The
Condition, Elevation, Emigration and Destiny of the Colored People of the United States* (1852;
rpr. New York, 1969), 212.

developments, some black Pennsylvanians began exploring the possibilities of settling in Liberia. One of these was the Reverend Samuel
Williams of Johnstown. The combination of disfranchisement, the
Fugitive Slave Law, palpable evidence of growing discrimination
everywhere, he wrote, prompted him and a handful of others to visit
Liberia in 1852. The party returned impressed and soon after organized the "Liberian Enterprise Company," to promote the emigration
of black Pennsylvanians and "to engage in the iron and lumber
business" in Liberia.[13]

The state Society was on the verge of an impressive breakthrough
in 1853, the result of a sustained public campaign begun some years
before. Legislators were lobbied, ministers preached sermons on the
merits of colonization, and the Society's corresponding secretary,
J. Morris Pease, traveled the state promoting the cause through public
lectures and debates. For a month, in early 1853, Harrisburg blacks
conducted a series of weekly debates on the topic "Which offers the
greatest inducements for a permanent home for the colored man,
Africa or America?" Chester argued in favor of colonization, rivaling,
one sympathetic editor wrote, "the great guns on the Hill." In the
midst of the debate, Pease organized a public meeting attended by
local dignitaries including the governor and state senators, all of
whom endorsed colonization. Days later, Chester announced his
decision to emigrate.[14]

The confluence of these developments and Chester's plan to
emigrate suggest that he must have been impressed by colonizationist
arguments. But nothing was further from the truth, he declared in a
letter to Freeman. "[P]ure and preconcerted convictions" concerning
the future of the "aliens of Africa" in America, not colonizationists,
had led him to his decision. His passion for liberty could no longer
"submit to the insolent indignities and contemptuous conduct to
which it has almost become natural for the colored people dishonorably to submit themselves." The alternative was life in another country
where freedom was guaranteed. But Chester's protestations, fueled,
one suspects, by a desire to demonstrate an unyielding indepen-

13. P. J. Staudenraus, *The African Colonization Movement 1816–1865* (New York, 1961),
242–44; Samuel Williams, *Four Years in Liberia: A Sketch of the Life of Rev. Samuel Williams,*
in *Two Black Views of Liberia* (New York, 1969), 6–7; *African Repository*, November, 1853;
Colonization Herald, August, 1857.
14. Harrisburg *Borough Item*, February 10, 15, 23, 28, March 10, 22, 31, April 6, 1853.

dence, could not mask the fact that his decision rested heavily on the traditional colonizationist rationale. Like them, he argued that Liberia was a land set aside by God for the African and his descendants, a land rich in natural resources where talents freed from the shackles of oppression could reclaim Africa's glorious past, rid the country of the slave trade, develop legitimate commerce, and spread Christianity. Unlike colonizationists, however, he never assumed that emancipation should depend on the removal of freedmen from the United States. He also predicted that Liberia was destined to become a proud and independent nation. "Do not for a moment think that Liberia will always be depending upon other countries to promote her interests, but her own sons will arise from that dormant state in which their genius has been slumbering, and make discoveries to the world, to whom she will be as much indebted, as she was for the learning of science which were born in Egypt."[15]

Yet this could not have been an easy decision for young Chester. Emigration under the auspices of the ACS had never been accepted as a moral or practical solution to American racism, and though, by 1853, it appeared that some blacks were going over to the enemy, anti-colonizationists refused to give ground. When, for example, a group of blacks in New York, led by Lewis Putnam, organized the "Liberian Agricultural and Emigration Association" to promote Liberian colonization, opponents rallied, held public meetings, and organized a "Committee of Thirteen" to lead the fight against the new society.[16] Similar efforts were made in Pennsylvania to discredit this new wave of interest in colonization. It was led in the west by Delany and in the east by Robert Purvis and others. Delany's opposition was unequivocating. Liberia, he wrote some years later, that "miserable hovel of emancipated and superannuated slaves," had been "knowingly and designedly established a national Potter's Field, into which the carcass of every emigrant who ventured there, would most assuredly moulder in death." Colonizationists grew wary of these attacks, some even suggesting that opponents had infiltrated their ranks in an effort to subvert the movement. These suspicions were

15. *Colonization Herald,* September, 1854. See Floyd J. Miller, *The Search for a Black Nationality: Black Colonization and Emigration 1787–1863* (Urbana, 1975), 82–90.
16. *African Repository,* September, November, 1851, January, 1852; *Anti Slavery Standard,* January 22, 1852.

confirmed with the publication of William Nesbit's vituperative anti-colonization tract in 1855. Colonizationists who were generally inured to the criticism of disappointed emigrants were totally unprepared for Nesbit's vitriol. He was one of the party of thirty-two Pennsylvanians organized by Williams' Liberian Enterprise Company. The pamphlet, with an introduction by Delany, had nothing good to say about Liberia. Led by a "cod-fish aristocracy," this "burlesque of a free country" could never succeed, Nesbit warned. "It is now only a fraud; and as soon as the American and English people withdraw their support it will irresistably fall back to its native heathenism."[17]

The decision to emigrate, in the face of such widespread condemnation of the movement and opposition from Freeman and, one suspects, his parents, says something about Chester's sense of independence and the manner in which he pursued his goals. The single-mindedness, which some found admirable in one so young, would be the source of many difficulties in the future. Back in Harrisburg, in early 1853, he held a series of private meetings with Pease, which put him in contact with the Pennsylvania and New York societies. While committed to settling in Liberia, Chester suggested that colonizationists first finance the completion of his education in America. The proposal was understandable; an educated person stood a better chance of making his mark in the growing settlement. But Pease and others demurred, suggesting that he stood a better chance of achieving his objectives in Liberia. Pease was impressed with the young man, whom he considered of "much more than ordinary character." In this he was not alone; one local editor, clearly partial to colonization, consistently referred to Chester as "our distinguished friend," and predicted that he would one day become "President of the Republic."[18]

Chester set sail from Baltimore on the barque *Banshee* in late April, his passage paid by the Pennsylvania Society with pledges of support from New York, to attend Alexander High School in Monrovia. Pease must have known that the promise of an education, at least some-

17. *African Repository*, December, 1853, March, 1854; *Pennsylvania Freeman*, September 8, 1853; William Nesbit, *Four Months in Liberia Or, African Colonization Exposed*, in *Two Black Views of Liberia*, 5–8, 15, 29, 53.

18. J. Morris Pease to William McLain, February 18, March 9, 1853, both in American Colonization Society (ACS) Papers, Library of Congress; Harrisburg *Borough Item*, April 14, 1853.

thing beyond what Chester had received at Allegheny Institute, could not be realized at Alexander High School, which, in 1853, was a high school in name only. Under the leadership of the Princeton-trained Reverend D. A. Wilson, students took a series of courses including orthography, geography, Latin, arithmetic, and theology, at levels that Chester had mastered. The curriculum had little to offer the ambitious young man who entertained lofty ideas about his potential contributions to his adopted home, goals that did not include joining the ranks of the unskilled emigrants, becoming simply a "hewer of wood and drawer of water." Those were the standards prescribed for his race in America; in Liberia, he insisted, things must be different.[19]

Frustrated by conditions at the school, Chester left Liberia in September, 1854, to attend Thetford Academy in Vermont, supported by New York colonizationists. Located in the quiet village of Thetford, on the Connecticut River, ten miles from Dartmouth College, the academy offered the type of advanced education Chester thought he deserved. Divided into three departments, English, Classical, and Normal, students were taught the "higher branches" by college-educated teachers. Exempted from the first year, Chester enrolled in the Classical Department in December, 1854. By the end of the first year, he had successfully completed a course of study in Latin and Greek grammar, translation, and literature, ancient Greek and Roman history, and ancient geography. The final year was devoted, almost exclusively, to the study of Cicero and Homer, Greek and algebra. Chester obviously enjoyed himself at Thetford, though life at the school was limited almost entirely to academics. There were no organized sports, so the only distractions were periodic rambles over the hills, swimming during the summer, or frequent acts of mischief against village people. Somewhat older than his peers, and the only black at the school, Chester probably avoided participating in too many pranks. Instead, he was actively involved in the school's many societies, especially the debating society, where he developed the forensic skills for which he later became famous. One classmate later

19. "Minutes of the Executive Committee of the Young Men's Colonization Society of Pennsylvania," Lincoln University, Oxford, Pa.; Pease to McLain, April 13, 22, 1853, McLain to H. W. Dennis, April 28, 1853, all in ACS Papers; Harrisburg *Borough Item*, April 26, 1853; *African Repository*, June, 1854; Hollis R. Lynch (ed.), *Black Spokesman: Selected Published Writings of Edward Wilmot Blyden* (London, 1971), xii, 217; *Colonization Herald*, September, 1860.

commented on Chester's superior debating skills, calling him "as smart a fellow as I ever saw."[20]

It had always been Chester's ambition to read law, and classmates expected him to join them at one of the major eastern colleges or universities. Thetford had a proud history in this respect. One hundred thirty-three of the 2,500 students who attended the academy during the thirteen years of Hiram Orcutt's tenure as principal went on to institutions such as Yale, Harvard, Dartmouth, Williams, Amherst, and Brown. Chester, however, could not afford the cost of a university education. Most of his expenses at Thetford had been met by New York colonizationists and what little his parents could contribute. The combined pressure of supporters to return to Monrovia and his inability to raise sufficient funds forced Chester to abandon any immediate plans he had of joining his classmates at college. "With what acquired ability I now have I intend to return to Liberia during the coming fall for certain," he wrote R. R. Gurley of the ACS, "unless an opportunity presents for me to go through college which opportunity I think is doubtful."[21]

Attending college at this time might also have had wider ramifications in the long-standing struggle between colonizationists and their opponents in Pennsylvania. Like Nesbit's, Chester's return in 1854 had been construed by some as another example of an emigrant's disaffection with Liberia; to have stayed in America after graduation, therefore, would have lent credence to this position. The publication of Nesbit's scathing, sometimes scurrilous work the previous year had given anti-colonizationists additional ammunition for a sustained attack, and had set colonizationists on a desperate search for adequate refutations. In this setting, Chester's return was symbolically important to the cause. "The position which my parents have occupied among the colored people," he wrote William McLain of the ACS, "has given me almost universal notoriety since my connection with Liberia." His return to America in 1854 had been greeted "with

20. Chester to R. R. Gurley, July 7, 1856, in ACS Papers; *Catalogue of the Officers and Students of Thetford Academy, Thetford, Vt., For the Academical Year 1853* (Concord, N.H., n.d.); *Catalogue of the Officers and Students of Thetford Academy, Thetford, Vt., For the Academical Year 1856* (Hanover, N.H., 1856); Mary B. Slade, *Thetford Academy's First Century 1819–1919* (Thetford, N.H., 1941[?]), 100–101.

21. Slade, *Thetford Academy's First Century*, 111; Hiram Orcutt, *Reminiscences of School Life: An Autobiography* (Cambridge, Mass., 1898), 91; *Catalogue of the Officers . . . 1856*; Chester to Gurley, July 7, 1856, in ACS Papers.

mingled feelings of joy and malice" by blacks, many of whom believed that he had permanently spurned Liberia. "Prompted by feelings of jealousy at the success of African colonization and the obvious superiority of Liberians in a national and individual capacity, they seized upon the absurdities of the most ignorant of the returned emigrants when they are in accordance with their own views, and with presumptive impudence contrast their misapprehensions with the true state of affairs which knowledge and experience brings to arouse them from their delusion." Many, he concluded, were anxious to see if he would return.[22]

If this decision to return frustrated his cherished hopes of attending college, it also improved Chester's standing with colonizationists at the national and state levels. He may have couched his desire to return in terms of racial advancement and the promotion of Liberia, but his personal welfare was never far removed from consideration. An opportunity to forge a secure future presented itself with the founding of Robertsport, Grand Cape Mount, in 1855 and the decision of the ACS to open a Receptacle in which "recaptive slaves" and emigrants could be more safely acclimated. In May, Chester wrote offering his services as a teacher. But the Society was still debating the merits of a permanent school at Tracy Receptacle. As a result, they could offer Chester only free passage in steerage if he agreed to devote some time each day, during the crossing, to teaching the settlers, and four days a week, for six months, once they were in Liberia. Gurley considered the offer "highly honorable and useful," one that would allow Chester time to seek out "more permanent and profitable employment." Aware of his importance, Chester, however, insisted on a more settled relationship, suggesting that he be put in charge of the Receptacle with sufficient land on which to conduct an effective manual labor school, one that would not only increase educational opportunities for emigrants but also, in the produce grown, save the Society a considerable amount of money.[23]

For someone as convinced of his importance to the movement and deeply committed to the building of the new nation as Chester was,

22. Chester to McLain, August 13, 1856, in ACS Papers.
23. Chester to McLain, May 13, 1856, Gurley to Chester, October 16, 18, 1856, all in ACS Papers; Chester to Joseph Tracy, August 18, October 17, 1856, Tracy to Chester, October 20, 1856, all in Liberia College Papers, Massachusetts Historical Society, Boston.

traveling steerage seemed undignified. This, and the rather offhanded offer of employment, stuck in his craw. He wrote Coppinger requesting an advance on the support usually allowed emigrants after arrival in Liberia. This he intended to combine with the stipend from the national office and purchase a cabin. Unsatisfied with Gurley's offer and reasoning, he continued to badger the national office to establish a permanent school and put him in charge. While rejecting Chester's "double shuffle" device to procure a cabin, McLain nonetheless recognized the wisdom of establishing a permanent school. The Executive Committee finally adopted Chester's plan for the school, in early November, and appointed him its teacher. But in doing so, McLain was not completely honest with Chester. The Executive Committee had earmarked $300 for the teacher's annual salary; but unwilling to "pay that much if we can get good teachers for less," McLain, with the approval of the committee, offered Chester $250. Immediately thereafter, Chester sailed on the *Mary Caroline Stevens* from Baltimore in late November.[24] It was not a very auspicious beginning. Such naked and cynical exploitation of someone so deeply committed to the cause would inevitably lead to open conflict between Chester and the Society.

Chester's positive reactions to the expectedly unsettled conditions at the Receptacle delighted McLain and Gurley. But there were some ominous signs. Since independence in 1847, some ardent nationalists in Monrovia had been questioning the need to rely on or follow the dictates of the Society in Washington, D.C. The fact that Liberia could not sever its ties with the Society completely and hope to survive only increased frustration and exacerbated existing tensions. Chester spent his first three weeks in Monrovia before going on to Robertsport, where ninety of the *Mary Caroline Stevens'* two hundred emigrants were to be settled. The time in Monrovia was spent in a futile attempt to convince H. W. Dennis, the Society's agent, that he was entitled to the support customarily granted new immigrants. But Dennis would not budge without explicit instructions from McLain. In addition, there were delays in naming the Board of Trustees to supervise

24. William Coppinger to McLain, October 23, November 3, 1856, Chester to Gurley, October 27, November 3, 1856, Chester to McLain, November 12, 1856, McLain to Coppinger, October 30, 1856, McLain to Chester, November 12, December 3, 1856, McLain to J. Pinney, November 15, 1856, McLain to John Seys, November 15, 1856, all in ACS Papers; "Minutes of the Executive Committee of the Young Men's Colonization Society of Pennsylvania"; Harrisburg *Herald*, November 25, 1856.

operations at the Receptacle. Neither problem affected the beginning of school, however. Dr. Henry Roberts wrote in mid-March that Chester had started school one week after his arrival and that it had "progressed unremittingly ever since, with the exception of two or three days caused by indisposition on his part."[25]

Although Chester had some reservations abut the Receptacle's location and the type of buildings that had been put up, he and the immigrants were enthusiastic about their new home. They were all "delighted with the romantic scenery of the place [and] the richness of the soil," so much so that Chester predicted that Robertsport would eventually become "the great metropolis of Liberia." In spite of his enthusiasm and rosy predictions, there were all the usual problems associated with new settlements in the tropics: acclimation was long, enervating, and sometimes deadly; expectations were always high, inflated, one suspects, as a device to maintain morale in trying circumstances; relations with the native population were not always cordial; and throughout was intrigue that sometimes bordered on the theatrical as individuals jockeyed for position. There were the handful of "lazy" and "indolent" immigrants, Chester wrote the national office, who failed to attend school or work the land, and whose actions threatened the experiment at Grand Cape Mount. "There are some persons who loiter about the receptacle in good health who are unwilling to attend school, refuse to work on the society's grounds and manifest no disposition to provide for them-selves." Cultivating the Receptacle's two acres proved difficult at first because of an inadequate supply of seed and labor, depredations by wild animals, and "loafing thieves who avail themselves of every privilege to plunder." Chester suggested building a sturdy fence to keep the animals out, and tighter security among settlers, he be-lieved, would ultimately curtail the larcenous activities. In July he reported a bumper crop of cassavas, sweet potatoes, plantains, and some coffee. In spite of all these problems, it seemed that Chester would make good his promise to save the Society hundreds of dollars usually expended on provisions.[26]

25. *Liberian Herald*, February 4, 1857; *African Repository*, June, 1857; Chester to McLain, March 13, June 17, July 22, 1857, McLain to Coppinger, July 23, 1857, Henry Roberts to McLain, March 19, 1857, all in ACS Papers.

26. Chester to McLain, March 13, April 4, March 21, 1857, all in ACS Papers; *African Repository*, July, 1857; *Colonization Herald*, July, 1857, August, 1857.

Running the school proved much more problematic than its organization. Teaching in "the passage-way up stairs" of the Receptacle was not what Chester had in mind. Immediately, he began pressuring McLain for a "good thatch house" in which to conduct classes. Although the surroundings left a great deal to be desired, and pupils did not always attend classes, Chester's first report spoke glowingly of his accomplishments. He had also organized a Sabbath school, which recent arrivals attended regularly: "The silver-haired mother, the venerable father, the middle aged and all the youths were present with an anxiety which evinced their appreciation of [the] Sabbath school." Not so others who, Chester insisted in some of his more florid prose, were deterred by "the languid imbecility from the febrile." With a regular supply of books, a restructuring of the school year into terms of three months, and the authority to compel students to attend classes, Chester predicted continued success. In customary fashion, he lapsed into grandiloquence when describing the future: "Standing as I do upon a soil which is consecrated to liberty and to learning, all the vicious scenes of their illiterate impiousness in the past crowding around me, and the bright future guaranteed by the efficatious operations of the present, I can cherish no brighter hope that the day will soon dawn upon a secular resurrection of these dry bones which are now stupefied by their indulgent repose in pagan barbarity and that education and christianity will lower to the summit of their gratifying perfection."[27] Such effusiveness probably elicited wry smiles in Washington and, more important for Chester's relationship with the Society, raised expectations unnaturally.

Optimism could not mask the fact that Chester was embroiled in a power struggle for the Receptacle. He had never reconciled himself to simply teaching in a school conducted in a passageway. His penchant for inflating the importance of his work, and a genuine commitment to Liberia aside, Chester could not have failed to compare his position with that of contemporaries at Thetford or, for that matter, with less well educated immigrants who had already made their mark in Liberia either in business or politics. Not surprisingly, on many occasions his perception of reality was warped by these frustrations and disappointments. While he worked to improve conditions at the Receptacle, Chester kept up a constant barrage of criticism against

27. Chester to McLain, March 13, 21, 1857, Chester to Gurley, May 4, 1857, "The First Semi-Annual Report," all in ACS Papers.

Ralph Moore, the steward and his superior. There were demands for greater authority to force immigrants to attend school. There were also frequent hints that dissatisfied immigrants were on the verge of rebellion and that only his intervention had prevented a "serious eruption." Moore's overindulgence in "ardent spirits" and his incompetence, Chester maintained, were at the root of these problems. Were it not for Mrs. Moore, who "does more than her part," there would have been serious conflicts in the settlement. The only reasonable solution to this dangerous situation, Chester advised, was Moore's dismissal and his assumption of the steward's responsibilities, which, he rather sheepishly informed Gurley, could be added to his present duties and so save the Society at least $150 per year. If something was not done soon, he predicted ominously, "another Washington will rise up to furnish the enemies of Liberia with prejudicial arguments which have a tendency to confirm the erroneous conceptions of our people."[28]

Chester got his way. Moore was dismissed in June, and Chester appointed to his position; Mrs. Moore, however, was retained. Chester was authorized to submit an estimate for a stone fence around the Receptacle, encouraged to build a log schoolhouse, and empowered to "enforce authority and require all the emigrants during their stay in the receptacle, either to attend school or to work in your garden, . . . or on their own land unless they have excuse from the Physician." But Chester's was a pyrrhic victory. Attacks on Moore, based on half-truths and innuendos, soon backfired. Throughout the entire controversy, Chester expressed an abiding concern for the welfare of the immigrants, and there is no doubt that he was popular with the majority of them. But his frequent warnings of possible rebellion by disaffected immigrants did not comport with earlier glowing reports of a striving, vibrant community. Back of this contradiction was an apparent vendetta against Moore that stemmed from an event during Chester's first visit to Monrovia. Evidently, Moore had testified against Chester and others in a case involving keys stolen from a government building. Chester's attack, some suggested, was a thinly disguised effort to get even with Moore.[29]

28. Chester to McLain, March 21, April 10, May 2, 1857, Chester to Gurley, May 4, 1857, all in ACS Papers.
29. McLain to Chester, June 16, 1857, Chester to McLain, July 7, 1857, Richard Stryker to Seys, August 20, 1857, Stryker to McLain, August 20, 1857, all in ACS Papers.

Chester's problems began with the arrival of McLain's letter announcing his new appointment. Moore simply would not comply without a fight, and his hand was strengthened by the support of Richard Stryker, the Society's recently appointed agent in Robertsport. It is clear that Stryker felt threatened by Chester's popularity among the immigrants. Although Chester initially welcomed Stryker's appointment and offered to support his efforts, Stryker remained suspicious of Chester's motives. Was Chester angling to become agent? Stryker and others thought so. Having attained the position of steward, he might logically want that job. In spite of declarations to the contrary, Chester periodically hinted that he was the obvious person for the post. "As I am in the receptacle and have more communication with the immigrants than either the agent, or physician and they bring in general all their complaints to me, I have often regretted," he told McLain, "that it was out of my power to promote their comfort." But Stryker was also opposed to the manner in which Moore was dismissed; McLain had made his decision solely on evidence provided by Chester and had not given Moore a chance to defend himself. In letters to John Seys, the Society's senior agent in Monrovia, and McLain, Stryker called for an impartial hearing and announced that he would retain Moore as steward until a final disposition of the case. Chester stormed against such high-handed usurpation of authority and utter disregard of an Executive Committee mandate. How, he asked, could Stryker ignore Washington's order to dismiss Moore and still retain his position? Concerns for Moore's rights were "a subterfuge on the part of your agent which neither meets the approbation of the citizens or the immigrants." Such "presumptuous arrogance" should not be tolerated. By August, Chester could do little more than resurrect the specter of rebellion, threaten to have Moore removed by the courts, and repeat the proven charge that Moore was fond of drink.[30]

Encouraged by Stryker's decision to retain him, Moore struck back. He was simply defending himself, he told superiors, against the efforts of an "unprincipled, indolent and mischievous" man to usurp his position. Chester's method was first to sow dissension among immigrants and then exploit the chaos to his benefit. With letters of support from his wife and a few immigrants, Moore accused Chester

30. Chester to McLain, August 20, July 7, 1857, Chester to Gurley, August 15, 1857, Chester to Seys, August 21, 1857, Stryker to Seys, August 20, 1857, Stryker to McLain, August 20, 1857, all in ACS Papers.

of misusing the Society's rations and of immorality. "Mr. Chester's conduct was such, as caused me to interfere with him several times, his familiarity with the females about the house, his carelessness in his dress by going through the house with his gown flying open and showing his nakedness"—more than enough, Moore implied, to warrant dismissal. While difficult to prove, the charge of immorality was virtually impossible to refute, and all Chester's fulminations against Stryker and Moore "consorting together" had no effect. His letters to officials in Washington suggesting names of people who could vouch for his moral character were equally unavailing.[31]

There was no immediate response from Washington. Having acted without first canvassing the views of his agent, McLain could do little. He chose to bide his time, hoping that relations between Chester and Stryker would improve. But the situation only grew progressively worse. Moore repeated his accusation of immorality, adding that Chester was in the habit of having both American and African women in his quarters late at night. For his part, Chester kept up a steady stream of letters to McLain, insisting that the impasse be resolved. Conditions were deteriorating rapidly, he claimed. Rations were inadequate when available, with the result that immigrants, rather than going through the necessary seasoning process in the Receptacle, hurried to clear their land and build homes. This affected both the school, where attendance was down, and his agricultural effort (cultivation was slowed by an irregular supply of labor). More important, the effect on the health of the settlement was deleterious. Chester estimated that at least one-third of those who died during the first year could "live to enjoy the land of their adoption, if they had proper attention and nourishment." He could not condone these conditions. "My regard for right and justice often prompts me [to] speak in behalf of the sufferers and on the unpopular side of the question, but my too sensitive feeling cannot always brook the invectives which a disordered head and a corrupt heart expectorate with galling bitterness."[32]

In spite of efforts to paint himself as the victim of injustice, it is clear that Chester's designs on the position of steward and even

31. Ralph Moore to McLain, August 25, 1857, Chester to Gurley, August 21, 1857, both in ACS Papers.
32. Moore to McLain, October 3, 1857, Chester to McLain, September 21, 1857, both in ACS Papers.

possibly that of agent in Robertsport contributed both to the initial
problem and to the consequent impasse. Offers to transfer to another
Receptacle and suggestions for promotion fell on deaf ears. When
these failed, he urged that his duties be placed "entirely under my
control and hold me responsible for their faithful performance." He
also considered resigning but was dissuaded by Dr. Roberts, who
sympathized with his predicament. Gurley even wrote an encouraging letter, at the end of October, which must have raised Chester's
expectation for a favorable resolution of the conflict. "Some reports
have . . . come to Mr. McLain unfavorable to your character," he
confided, "but I am unwilling to believe there is any just foundation
for them. They, my young friend, prove the many temptations that
may surround you, and show your strength of purpose in the service
of your country and your God."[33]

Whatever encouragement the beleaguered Chester took from
Gurley's faith in his character was soon dashed by a stinging rebuke
from McLain. Having acted on Chester's recommendation, McLain
could not now admit to his error. Instead, he chose to vent his spleen
on someone he considered "overbearing and disposed to assume
what does not belong to the office" he holds. Chester was admittedly
very ambitious and envisaged a future more substantial than the one
assigned him by the Society. Earlier he had suggested to McLain a
partnership that would control trade in the settlement; McLain would
supply the goods and he would dispose of them. McLain never took
up the offer, partly because he questioned Chester's motives, but also,
one suspects, because he had never been honest and open with
Chester. The issue of the teacher's salary is a case in point. Rather
than dealing with the problem equitably, McLain chose to ignore the
decision to fire Moore and to side with Stryker, exhorting Chester "to
gentleness, to conciliation and to peace!" To Stryker, he wrote, "I
have told Mr. Chester that he is responsible for the school, literacy
and agriculture, but that all our business matters are entrusted to you
and that we hold you bound to take the government of all our
affairs."[34]

Chester had no alternative but to resign; Stryker had carried the

33. Chester to McLain, September 21, 1857, Gurley to Chester, October 29, 1857,
both in ACS Papers.
34. McLain to Chester, November 3, 1857, McLain to Stryker, November 6, 1857,
Chester to McLain, August 10, 1857, all in ACS Papers.

day both in Robertsport and in Washington. From Monrovia, Dennis wrote that the Board of Trustees was considering firing Chester when he resigned. "My impression," he informed McLain, "is that he has not been very faithful in his position as teacher, and that he has meddled rather too much with matters and things that did not claim his attention." Chester would have disagreed strenuously with this assessment of his brief tenure at the Tracy Receptacle. All the expected difficulties of forging a new settlement, and his own ambitions aside, Chester's dedication and hard work should have been enough proof of his commitment. He worked tirelessly to make the school and garden a success in the face of inadequate accommodations and supplies, and settlers more concerned with establishing their own homes than with education. Where he could, he attempted to increase interest in education by organizing a Sabbath school and a lecture series. Yet McLain, who was well aware of all these problems, deeply distrusted Chester.[35]

Chester returned to America, in February, under a cloud of suspicion, disappointed and understandably bitter about the treatment he had received from McLain, but still unalterably committed to Liberia. His experiences could conceivably have resulted in an open break with the Society. After all, others with less ammunition to support their case had left Liberia totally disillusioned, issuing, in some instances, stinging indictments of the Society's policies. Not Chester. He always managed to maintain a positive public posture. Even at the height of these trials, his articles in the *Colonization Herald*, organ of the Pennsylvania Society, were enthusiastic about the future. Liberia, he maintained, "has wealth enough within herself to be a flourishing country, but as yet wants the proper elements necessary to develop her resources. We have minds, but we lack capital; we have comparative means, but we need economy; we have industry, but we require system; we have a prolific country, but we are deficient in numerical strength that will develop its resources, and give character and dignity to our people."[36]

His return coincided with a resurgence in the debate over the

35. Dennis to McLain, January 30, 1858, Chester to McLain, August 28, 1857, Chester to Gurley, October 28, 1857, McLain to Chester, November 3, 1857, all in ACS Papers.

36. Stryker to McLain, February 3, 1858, Roberts to McLain, February 5, 1858, both in ACS Papers; *African Repository*, April, 1858; *Colonization Herald*, December, 1857, May, 1858.

competing merits of emigration and colonization. There were those, like Delany and Henry Highland Garnet, who, in rejecting colonizationists' insistence on total expatriation, advocated a limited voluntary emigration of skilled blacks to a colony where their talents could be put to productive use. The existence of Delany's Niger Valley Exploring Party, and Garnet's African Civilization Society, both promoting emigration to Yorubaland, raised the temperature of the debate. In New York, Pennsylvania, Massachusetts, and Ohio, those blacks who opposed all forms of emigration launched a series of concerted attacks in 1858 and 1859. Chester kept his distance from these disputes, not because of any lowered expectations about Liberia's future, but because of a reluctance to become embroiled in what he considered internecine conflicts. Years earlier, he had learned the futility of engaging opponents. But one also suspects that Chester's measured and balanced views of Liberia's prospects to some extent defused potential opposition. Although he maintained that the "social condition of the colored people in Liberia" was far better than in the United States, and that the new country had a "mission as palpable as it is transcendent," Chester never flinched from discussing its weaknesses. "Liberia would never be a great commercial country," he told a meeting of the New York Colonization Society, "as it had no navigable rivers and capacious harbors, but it was a most productive agricultural country." It was also the "only place and the only means which has ever elevated our race by its own exertions."[37]

Rather than exacerbate differences through public disputes, Chester chose to work behind the scenes, quietly supporting blacks who were considering emigrating to Liberia. In this he had the support of John Pinney and Joseph Tracy of the New York and Boston societies, who arranged Chester's lecture tour of New England during the summer. In May, he moved to Boston to work with a group planning to emigrate to Liberia. This was no easy task, given Boston's strong abolitionist and anti-colonizationist traditions. Chester was circumspect, limiting himself to discussions of conditions in Liberia and encouraging the recently formed "Cambridge Liberian Emigrant Association." The time had come, the association declared, for Africa to join the comity of nations and "like the Pilgrim Fathers, seek to establish the institutions of civil and religious liberty, the blessing of

37. *New York Colonization Journal,* June, 1858; New York *Herald,* May 13, 1858; *African Repository,* June, 1858.

education and the full enjoyment derived from mechanical, mercantile and agricultural pursuits." Led by Enoch Lewis, Superintendent of Rooms at Harvard University, the association planned to take one hundred emigrants overseas in the fall. Excited by the prospect, Chester was, however, skeptical of the association's chances of success. There was not enough "intellectual stamina . . . in the company to direct its movement and forward it to completion," he told Gurley. Although he predicted that some would emigrate, the company needed a more enterprising leader than Lewis. With this in mind, Chester tried to persuade Dr. John DeGrasse to join the association. From all accounts, he almost succeeded. DeGrasse had studied at Bowdoin College, had spent two years in London and Paris hospitals, and had been a ship's surgeon on several transatlantic voyages before settling in Boston and marrying into one of the city's influential black families. DeGrasse considered the idea seriously, but eventually declined when the ACS failed to offer him an acceptable position. In the end, only twenty emigrated to Liberia.[38]

Having failed in earlier efforts to persuade McLain to join his trading scheme, Chester used his visit to win support for his plans to establish a newspaper in Monrovia. The capital was without a newspaper since the *Liberian Herald* suspended publication. Chester hoped to fill the void with the *Star of Liberia.* Publishing a newspaper was a risky business under the most favorable circumstances; it required substantial investments and guarantees of continued revenue beyond that generated by subscriptions, neither of which was forthcoming in Monrovia. While everyone agreed that the city needed a newspaper, no one could assure Chester of regular financial support. The alternative, he told Pinney, was a job with the Society, the income from which would subsidize publication. Nothing came of the suggestion, but a few days later, Chester contacted McLain, requesting a cabin aboard one of the Society's ships, "for which I shall consider your committee as subscribing for fifty copies of the Star." McLain could hardly contain his anger at this effrontery. He had written Coppinger in March, condemning Chester for his actions

38. Coppinger to Gurley, July 6, 1858, Pinney to McLain, July 3, 1858, Chester to Gurley, September 8, 1858, Tracy to Gurley, July 22, 1858, Tracy to McLain, October 9, 1858, all in ACS Papers; Harrisburg *Herald*, June 2, 1858; *African Repository,* August, October, December, 1858; *Colonization Herald,* November, 1859; Benjamin Quarles, *Black Abolitionists* (New York, 1969), 35.

in Robertsport and insisting that the Pennsylvania Society stop supporting him. "I think enough has been done for him and we had better reserve what little money we can get to send out some more useful people." Now he responded to Chester testily. "I do not think that our Executive Committee will do anything great to assist you." McLain's anger was unmistakable, yet Chester persisted. He was not requesting the usual support given emigrants, he responded, only that the Society enter a subscription for twenty-five copies of the *Star* and advance him the money, which he would then use to pay his passage. Chester had a knack for contriving schemes that annoyed McLain, but that for some reason the Society usually considered. In the end, they agreed that if Chester advanced $60 toward the cost of the passage, they would accept an annual subscription for twenty-five copies of the *Star* as payment for the remaining $50. He returned to Liberia in November, traveling cabin class in a manner befitting his status.[39]

McLain must have cringed when word arrived from Liberia that Chester had been named one of two teachers at the Brewster Receptacle in Monrovia. Faced with a massive influx of "recaptive slaves" at the end of the decade, the Monrovia authorities were desperate for qualified teachers. Chester's contract lasted only a few months; but during that time, his salary provided him enough security to launch his newspaper. The success he had anticipated— being the only newspaper in the capital—was not realized, however, because of the reappearance of the *Liberian Herald*.[40]

In the highly charged political climate of Monrovia, the existence for the first time of an independent newspaper provided the opposition a medium in which government policies could be assailed. By early May, the *Star* was embroiled in an unseemly and bitter dispute with the government. Evidently, Chester had published an anonymous letter castigating President Stephen Benson's administration. Suspecting that former president J. J. Roberts was the author, Benson

39. Pinney to McLain, October 8, 1858, McLain to Coppinger, March 26, 1858, Coppinger to McLain, October 11, 1858, McLain to Chester, October 13, 16, 1858, Chester to McLain, October 14, 1858, all in ACS Papers; *African Repository*, September, December, 1858.
40. Dennis to McLain, February 23, May 14, 1859, both in ACS Papers; Tom W. Shick, *Behold the Promised Land: A History of Afro-American Settler Society in Nineteenth-Century Liberia* (Baltimore, 1980), 67–69; *New York Colonization Journal*, July, 1859; *African Repository*, July, 1859.

replied with a scathing denunciation of his opponents in the *Liberian Herald*, organ of the government. Angered by his inability to confirm authorship of the letter or silence his critics, Benson did the next best thing and launched a campaign of vilification against Chester. It was clear, at least to Dennis, that accusations of sexual impropriety between Chester and Mrs. Ruth Brown, the other teacher at Brewster, were politically motivated. Although Dennis intervened to stop publication of an anonymous letter about Chester and Brown in the *Herald*, the rumors persisted, fueled by the accusations of Brown's daughter that her mother and Chester were frequently caught in each other's rooms "with the door fastened." Although Chester's contract to teach ended in May, Benson's supporters were determined to get even with Brown, whom they suspected of assisting Chester "in preparing his editorials."[41]

The Board of Trustees was deadlocked when it met in late June to consider the accusations against Brown. Some, like Daniel Laing, insisted that they had found Brown guilty and had voted to terminate her services immediately; others, Dennis and Dr. Roberts among them, disagreed. Using his authority as agent, Dennis refused to fire Brown. That and his continued insistence on Chester's and Brown's innocence put him on a collision course with Benson. The situation rapidly deteriorated when Benson used the full weight of his office to pressure the courts to investigate conditions at the Receptacle. A grand jury was empaneled in September, but was promptly dismissed because of a lack of sufficient evidence. Angered by this result, Benson sued to have the foreman of the grand jury removed for incompetence and, according to Dennis, forced the judge to swear in a new grand jury. Again the grand jury failed to find a true bill. As the "strange trial" continued, the criticism of Benson's actions intensified. Only growing public hostility forced Benson to abandon his vendetta. McLain did what he could from Washington to pacify both protagonists, suggesting to Dennis that it was in the Society's interest to terminate its connection with Brown. But by then she had left.[42]

Chester departed for America in the midst of the dispute, leaving

41. Dennis to McLain, August 4, 1859, Daniel Laing to McLain, August 25, 1859, both in ACS Papers.
42. Laing to McLain, August 25, 1859, Roberts to McLain, August 28, 1859, Dennis to McLain, October 11, 1859, Benson to Gurley, October 20, 1859, McLain to Dennis, December 29, 1859, all in ACS Papers.

the *Star* in the hands of supporters. It is quite possible that his going away also helped to defuse tensions. He would later lament his attacks on Benson, attributing them to misplaced ambition and youthful exuberance, but for the moment, Chester felt exceedingly bitter about this treatment by a group he considered devious and conniving. His sense of alienation must have been increased by lingering questions about his moral rectitude. There is no way of judging the veracity of these accusations, but this was the second time in the space of two years that his behavior had been questioned. There is no doubt that Chester was a lady's man. Tall and muscular, always dapper, and proud of his "pure African origin, a splendid looking man, with manners highly cultivated," Chester enjoyed the company of women. Later letters to his close associate Jacob White, Jr., of Philadelphia spoke longingly of two young women he had met. There were even rumors of marriage to someone at the Tracy Receptacle in 1857, but they were apparently unfounded.[43] What is certain is that these accusations of philandering had the desired effect of temporarily silencing Chester in Liberia. Not so in America, where, surprisingly, the issue never affected relationships with Pennsylvania colonizationists. One suspects that his importance to the cause far outweighed his moral foibles; Chester was, after all, the most prominent black supporter in the state at a time of open competition between colonizationists and emigrationists.

The Pennsylvania Society employed Chester in late 1859 to work "among the colored population of Pennsylvania." Chester held the position until the following summer, during which time he toured central and eastern Pennsylvania promoting Liberian colonization. It is difficult to determine how successful he was, but in April, thirty-nine emigrants sailed for Liberia. By October, an additional fifty-nine, including Chester's nephew, were ready to embark on the *Mary Caroline Stevens.*[44] Chester returned to Liberia in September, 1860,

43. Chester to Coppinger, March 28, 1868, Chester to McLain, August 20, 1857, both in ACS Papers; Charles Carleton Coffin, *Four Years of Fighting: A Volume of Personal Observation With the Army and Navy, From the First Battle of Bull Run to the Fall of Richmond* (1866; rpr. New York, 1970), 519; William Wells Brown, *The Rising Son; or the Antecedents and Advancement of the Colored Race* (1874; rpr. Miami, 1969), 528; Chester to Jacob White, Jr., September 25, 1860, in Jacob C. White Jr. Papers, Moorland-Spingarn Collection, Howard University, Washington, D.C.; *Louisianan*, September 24, 1871.

44. "Minutes of the Pennsylvania Colonization Society, July 15, 1856 to October 10, 1864," Lincoln University; *Colonization Herald*, April, June, October, 1860.

anxious to recommence publication of the *Star*, which had been
suspended during his absence. The paper was back in circulation in
early 1861. As in the past, Chester saw his paper as the principal
vehicle of antigovernment sentiment in the capital. With an election
imminent, he wrote White almost gleefully, "I am in the thickest of
the fight and shall lose no effort to hurl from power the present
administration."[45] He failed miserably, and with Benson's return to
office, Chester once again began making plans for another visit to
America.

Pennsylvania, like other northern states, was buzzing with competing emigration schemes in the summer of 1861. Delany's success in
negotiating a "treaty" with the Alake of Abeokuta gave a boost to his
plans to settle a select group of black Americans among the Yoruba.
The Haitian authorities' promise of land generated considerable
interest among blacks, even among traditionally staunch anti-
emigrationists. Some black Pennsylvanians took up the Haitian offer.
The "Industrial Regiment," a group of two hundred Harrisburgers,
planned to leave for the island in May, 1862. It is impossible to
determine exactly how many Pennsylvanians finally joined the exodus of roughly two thousand blacks who settled in Haiti during 1861
and 1862. Liberian colonizationists were not inactive in the face of this
growing competition. Two of its most articulate advocates, Alexander
Crummell and Edward Wilmot Blyden, visited America during this
period. Both spent some time in Pennsylvania, Crummell as a
temporary agent of the state Society and Blyden on an extensive
lecture tour. Their message was unabashedly partisan: schemes like
Delany's were a mistake, Crummell told New York colonizationists.
He saw the hand of Providence at work preparing different fields for
workers with varying talents. While Abeokuta had been earmarked
for emigrants "raised up and prepared by the English at Sierra
Leone," Liberia had been set aside for black Americans.[46]

Chester had nothing to do with either mission. Disputes in Liberia,
particularly those surrounding the last election, might account for this
lack of cooperation. But Chester was not inactive. He did what he

45. *Colonization Herald*, October, 1860; Chester to White, February 18, 1861, in White
Papers.
46. Harrisburg *Telegraph*, March 4, June 21, 1862; "Minutes of the Pennsylvania
Colonization Society, July 15, 1856 to October 10, 1864"; Alexander Crummell, *The
Future of Africa: Being Addresses, Sermons, Delivered in the Republic of Liberia* (New York,
1862), 147.

could to promote Liberian colonization, though there is no evidence of coordination with colonizationists in either Philadelphia or Washington. This is particularly surprising, in view of the interest among blacks and the Federal government's plan to tie limited emancipation to expatriation. President Lincoln had suggested such a policy in his message to Congress in December, 1861: contraband slaves entering Union lines and free blacks who wished to emigrate should be encouraged to leave the country. Although the plan was condemned by both blacks and white abolitionists for the same reason that they had always opposed the ACS, Lincoln persisted, anxious to appease certain sectors of the South, but also convinced that there were enough blacks who were eager, as one Haitian emigrant put it, to "escape from the miasmatic influences of prejudice." Congress appropriated $100,000, in April, 1862, to finance the emigration of slaves freed by the District of Columbia Emancipation Act. Within a week, Chester contacted Simon Cameron, the dominant political figure in Pennsylvania and Lincoln's former secretary of war, suggesting ways to implement the president's colonization plan. They were based on those traditional colonizationist premises that never failed to fire the indignation of black opponents. Continued prejudice, he wrote, had always worked against the advancement of blacks, and there was no reason to expect anything different in the wake of the new emancipation law. "Being relieved from service and labor, the Negro in this country attains a certain standard, not very high, not even availing themselves of the few privileges which they enjoy nor elevating themselves to that standard of respectability which all are capable of attaining." There were, he conceded, cultivated and refined Negroes, but the masses were "profoundly ignorant, morally degraded, and not a few of them desperately vicious." Given this fact, and aware of the merits of competing colonization schemes, Chester pleaded for emigration to Liberia, "the only true and natural home of our race." Playing on widespread white fears of amalgamation, Chester added a wrinkle reminiscent of "nationalist" concerns about race purity: "There [Liberia] a great destiny awaits us, and the Negro, returning to his untarnished color which slavery had bleached, will kindle a generous enthusiasm to rear an empire to the glory of our race."[47]

47. James M. McPherson, "Abolitionist and Negro Opposition to Colonization During the Civil War," *Phylon,* XXVI (1965), 392–94; Chester to Simon Cameron, April 23, 1862, in Simon Cameron Papers, Dauphin County Historical Society, Harrisburg.

While Chester's racial pride was well known, these views were
nonetheless so uncharacteristic that one suspects him of pandering to
conventional prejudices in a rather transparent attempt to curry favor
with Cameron. The fact that he had run afoul of colonizationists like
McLain and had alienated the dominant political figures in Liberia
might help to explain Chester's actions. Gaining Cameron's support
would both outflank detractors and put him in a position to influence
policy in Washington. But Chester not only overestimated his powers
of persuasion, he failed to take into account the reaction of black anti-
colonizationists to Lincoln's plan. They roundly condemned the
president's proposal. At a meeting in Philadelphia, they demanded to
know why blacks should abandon their property, forsake their
birthplace, and move to a strange country just "to appease the anger
and prejudice of the traitors now in arms against the Government."
No one but the enemy favored such a scheme. Give "four millions of
slaves their freedom, and the lands now possessed by their master,"
and the Union would reap the rewards. Although Lincoln persisted,
colonizing blacks in Central America or the Caribbean failed to elicit
support from the one group it was meant to benefit. Two additional
factors worked against Chester: none of Lincoln's proposals included
Liberia; and Cameron had, by April, fallen from grace among
important elements in the administration.[48]

For blacks, at least, Lincoln's provisional emancipation act in
September effectively pulled the rug from under proponents of
emigration, even if the president continued to hold to the belief that
voluntary expatriation was in the nation's best interest. Caught up in
the wave of heightened expectations brought on by developments in
early 1863, and frustrated by his failures in Monrovia, Chester
abandoned plans to return to Liberia. There had been perceptible, if
minor, shifts in policy both by the Federal government and by the
state administrations. Yet the reluctance of some northern states to
endorse these changes tempered the hopes of blacks. In Pennsylvania, for example, Governor Andrew Curtin adamantly refused to
recruit blacks to fill the state's quota under the military draft.
Northern intransigence was best illustrated by Ohio governor David
Tod's response to John Mercer Langston's plea for black recruitment:

48. Herbert Aptheker, *A Documentary History of the Negro People in the United States* (2
vols.; New York, 1951), I, 474–75; McPherson, "Abolitionist and Negro Opposition to
Colonization During the Civil War," 396–98.

"Do you not know Mr. Langston, that this is a white man's government; that white men are able to defend and protect it? . . . When we want you colored men we will notify you."[49]

Governor John Andrew of Massachusetts broke the cycle of intransigence when, after months of pleading with officials in Washington, he was authorized by Secretary of War Edwin Stanton in January, 1863, to organize a black volunteer regiment. Andrew named abolitionist George L. Stearns to head a committee of prominent citizens to conduct recruitment. Stearns selected a number of black agents, including Douglass, Delany, and Charles Lennox Remond, to canvass the northern states for black recruits. Their call to arms was not always enthusiastically received, for too many questions concerning the assigned role of blacks in these regiments remained unanswered. Not that blacks were unwilling to volunteer their services; they had frequently offered to contribute to the war effort since Fort Sumter.

At a meeting in Harrisburg, presided over by Chester, blacks made their position abundantly clear. They would not shrink from meeting in battle "desperate men who are struggling to destroy free institutions upon this continent," including "secession sympathizers in the north, who have been industriously attempting to reason themselves into the belief that black men will not fight." But they would do so only "when legitimately called upon by the proper authorities, that will not involve our self-respect." If, as one New Yorker insisted, the government wanted their services, then blacks should be guaranteed all the rights of citizens and soldiers. The demands were revolutionary, and no one in Washington was willing to take that leap. All Douglass could do in answer to these demands was plead the potential: "Remember Denmark Vesey of Charleston; remember Nathaniel Turner of Southampton; remember Shields Green and Copeland, who followed noble John Brown, and fell as glorious martyrs for the cause of the slave. Remember that in a context with oppression, the Almighty has no attribute which can take sides with oppressors." While few questioned Douglass' assessment of the war's ultimate consequences, many were determined to seize the opportunity to wrest concessions from the government. But the authorities

49. James M. McPherson, *The Negro's Civil War: How American Negroes Felt and Acted During the War for the Union* (New York, 1965), 180. Tod later became a proponent of admitting blacks to the military.

resisted, and such demands as black officers for black regiments were systematically denied. Andrew was able, however, to do something about matters of pay and bounty. In February he sent one of his representatives to consult with the black "Philadelphia Committee to Recruit Colored Troops." Douglass visited a few weeks later. By April, there were reports of increased recruitment in the state. Chester headed the drive in Harrisburg. In early June, 135 recruits left the city, 45 from Harrisburg, the rest from neighboring towns and Cumberland County, to join the 55th Massachusetts Regiment.[50]

Even before the black recruits left for Massachusetts, Harrisburg was bracing itself for a possible attack by Lee's Confederate forces. There was a fair amount of apprehension about the city's ability to repulse such an onslaught. Two years earlier, engineers in the Pennsylvania Home Guard had warned that Harrisburg was "the weakest and most assailable position" should an attack be mounted from the south. By June, Lee's vanguard, under Richard Ewell, was in Pennsylvania. Chambersburg, Carlisle, Gettysburg, York, and Wrightsville fell in rapid succession, and at month's end, his forces were bivouacked on Harrisburg's fringes on the west bank of the Susquehanna River. Governor Curtin issued a proclamation calling on Pennsylvanians to enlist, and two days later, Lincoln requested militias in the mid-Atlantic states to defend Harrisburg. There was mass confusion in the capital. Uniformed units of untrained soldiers were hastily commissioned in a desperate effort to stem Ewell's advance. Officers were selected almost entirely on the basis of the number of men they had persuaded to enlist in thirty days: captaincies for forty men, lieutenancies for twenty-five or fifteen.[51]

Curtin's problems were exacerbated by the reluctance of locals to enlist and by his equivocation on the issue of black recruitment. Only 60 of the 25,000 defending the capital were from Harrisburg. With black refugees pouring into the city in advance of Ewell's forces, some effort was made to employ them as laborers on defenses along the

50. Harrisburg *Telegraph*, February 4, 19, April 25, June 8, 9, 1863; *Pacific Appeal*, March 23, 1863; McPherson, *The Negro's Civil War*, 177; Douglass, *Life and Times*, 341; Frederick M. Binder, "Pennsylvania Negro Regiments in the Civil War," *Journal of Negro History*, XXXVII (1952), 385–86; "Documents," *Journal of Negro History*, XI (1926), 83.

51. Harrisburg *Telegraph*, June 18, 1863; Harrisburg *Patriot*, June 16, 1863; Robert Grant Crist, "Highwater 1863: The Confederate Approach to Harrisburg," *Pennsylvania History*, XXX (1963), 160, 168; Philip S. Klein and Ari Hoogenboom, *A History of Pennsylvania* (University Park, Pa., 1980), 283.

river. But that was as far as the authorities were willing to go. Responding to Curtin's proclamation, a group of 90 black Philadelphia volunteers arrived on July 17, only to be unceremoniously snubbed by the governor and General Darius Crouch, the commanding officer. One observer later recalled Curtin pleading with those volunteers "to keep very quiet, lest a democratic convention, then in session, should have its attention drawn to the fact of black soldiers being in town." Rather than accept such ignominious conditions, they returned to Philadelphia. Stearns, who was in Philadelphia at the time, wired Stanton for clarification, and the war secretary informed Crouch that he was to accept volunteers "without regard to color." Yet Stanton hedged on the issue: "[I]f there is likely to be any dispute about the matter," he wrote Stearns, "it will be better to send no more. It is well to avoid all controversy in the present juncture as the troops can be well used elsewhere." Unaware of Stanton's qualifiers, blacks responded positively to this apparent change of policy. Many of those who had returned to Philadelphia offered their services again; so did blacks in Harrisburg. By month's end, city recruits had been formed into two companies; one was captained by Chester, the other by Henry Bradley, a barber. Neither company was pressed into service, for in early July, the emergency was lifted when Ewell's forces withdrew to prepare for the bloody and decisive encounter at Gettysburg.[52]

The decision to enlist was based on a whole complex of reasons. One, of course, was a determination to defend their families and property. Another was the hope that participation in the state's defense would lead to a dismantling of local systems of discrimination. It unfortunately was a hope based on flimsy foundations, for war had done little to change white attitudes toward blacks. Although there were no race riots to compare with those in New York in 1863, blacks lived in constant fear of attacks from whites. One observer reported in August, 1862, that it was "dangerous for colored people to walk the streets after night." One year later, a white mob, aware of the mayor's sympathies with their actions, assaulted blacks, "tearing down their homes and breaking their windows." Even Henry Bradley was not immune from intimidation and assault. Less than two weeks

---

52. *Christian Recorder,* November 11, 1865; Harrisburg *Telegraph,* June 25, 26, 1863, October 7, 1870; Harrisburg *Patriot,* June 29, 1863; *North American and U.S. Gazette,* June 20, 1863; Crist, "Highwater 1863," 183.

after Ewell's retreat, Bradley was accosted by a group of white soldiers wielding bayonets. The soldiers were acting under orders to impress all able-bodied men who were not engaged in "respectable business." This was not a case of mistaken identity. When challenged, Bradley identified himself, only to have a bayonet stuck in his face; and when he resisted, he was subdued by additional soldiers who fortuitously arrived on the scene. The commanding officer, aware of the possibility of retaliation from the black community, moved quickly to defuse the situation by imprisoning those who had made the arrest.[53]

Although he had recruited for the Massachusetts regiments and the state militia, in the end Chester's racial pride could brook no limits on the rights of blacks to fully participate in the armed forces. In fact, he might have stopped recruiting for Massachusetts when it became clear that Andrew would not entertain the idea of black officers. Things were not much better in Pennsylvania. Although he and Bradley were given captaincies in the state militia (the first time that had occurred in the state), General Crouch and state and federal authorities did little to expedite black recruitment. If Chester ever harbored any misapprehensions on this score, then Bradley's arrest confirmed that many whites were still adamantly opposed to the legitimate demands of blacks for equality. This may help explain why he decided to leave the country for Britain in the fall of 1863. While one should not underestimate the deep sense of revulsion these acts of racism produced, they may also have been responsible for reactivating Chester's wanderlust.

Although he had turned his back on America when he was a young man of eighteen, preferring to gamble on a future in Liberia, Chester found it impossible to sever the emotional umbilical cord to his birthplace. It was not only a need to keep in touch with his family in Harrisburg or, as in the case of other emigrants, to raise money for particular projects in Liberia. It was more, one feels, the result of an imperceptible yearning to leave his mark on a country whose revolutionary principles he admired, but whose society, steeped in racism, he detested with a passion. Although he continued to call Liberia "home," at least until 1870, one gets the distinct impression that by the early 1860s, it had become little more than a refuge from

53. "Documents," *Journal of Negro History,* XI (1926), 83; *Christian Recorder,* May 20, 1863; Harrisburg *Telegraph,* July 13, 1863.

the enervation and emasculation caused by American racism. But Chester's determination to attend college also contributed to his decision to leave America. Britain was an obvious choice. Many other black Americans, James McCune Smith and Alexander Crummell among them, had successfully completed their college training at British universities after being denied entry into American schools. But a college education required substantial personal resources or, as in the case of Crummell, subsidies from wealthy patrons, neither of which Chester possessed. His plan, it appears, was to use contacts in London, particularly Gerard Ralston, long Liberia's consul general in England, to raise sufficient money to attend one of the Inns of Courts.

While pursuing this goal, Chester lent his support to the cause of the Union. Ever since the outbreak of the war, Britain had been besieged by emissaries from both sides of the conflict. Lincoln's temporizing on emancipation, Confederate victories, and Britain's reliance on cotton turned many, including some with impeccable abolitionist credentials, against the Union. Southern emissaries recorded impressive victories as the Union blockade of southern ports cut off the flow of cotton to Britain, devastating Lancashire and other manufacturing districts. Britain's declaration of neutrality not only raised questions about its objectives but also tipped the balance in favor of those advocating southern claims. Union supporters, reinforced by a large contingent of Americans, rose to the challenge. There were Henry Ward Beecher, J. Sella Martin, Moncure D. Conway, William and Ellen Craft, William G. Allen, the Reverend W. Mitchell, and William Jackson, Jefferson Davis' coachman, to mention a few.

Chester gave a series of lectures in late 1863 on the American crisis and its effect on the Negro, under the auspices of the British and Foreign Anti-Slavery Society (BFASS). Charles Francis Adams, the American minister to the Court of St. James's, supported Chester's effort with a contribution of $25, and Benjamin Moran, the legation's secretary, a rather irascible man not given to lavishing praise on others, confided in his diary that Chester had "few superiors, white or black, in the command of language and its appropriate use." He was also warmly received by many of Britain's leading individuals and, as he reported home, "some of the nobility." Such support, if marshaled properly, could be important in the battle to win public opinion. Some suggested that he shift his field of operations to

Lancashire, where, because of the cotton famine, there was greater need for Union advocates. But that was easier said than done. Not only did an agency of this sort require a substantial treasury and months of careful planning, its chances of success also rested on the endorsement of the country's abolitionist societies. Even if Chester could raise sufficient money to finance such an agency, he first had to win support from the BFASS, the London Emancipation Society, or the Manchester Union and Emancipation Society. His association with the ACS, which British abolitionists viewed with considerable distrust, limited his chances of success. But more significantly, the Union's position was now more than adequately represented, at a time when the tide of war was apparently turning against the Confederacy following Union victories at Gettysburg and Vicksburg.[54]

The alternative to British abolitionist endorsement, Chester thought, was an official commission from Washington. Again he turned to his old Harrisburg acquaintance, Simon Cameron, suggesting he use his influence in Washington to that end. But Cameron, who was no longer in office, could do nothing for Chester.[55] An official agency would undoubtedly have proven personally beneficial, bringing Chester to the attention of a wider public and increasing his chances of raising support for his legal training. Frustrated, Chester left for home in the spring of 1864. But all was not totally lost, for the contacts made would be useful when he returned to London two years later. The trip did have an immediate impact on Chester's life, however; it seemed to enhance his reputation in Pennsylvania. Not long after his return, John Russell Young, the youthful editor of and former war correspondent for John W. Forney's Philadelphia *Press*, engaged Chester as one of his war correspondents attached to the Army of the James.[56]

There is no way of knowing why Young took this unusual course, for the *Press* had a decidedly mixed record in its attitudes toward blacks. By the fall of 1865, it was a staunch supporter of Lincoln's

54. *Anti Slavery Reporter*, November 2, 1863, January 1, 1864; Sarah Agnes Wallace and Frances Elma Gillespie (eds.), *The Journal of Benjamin Moran 1857–1865* (2 vols.; Chicago, 1948), II, 1245; *Louisianan*, September 24, 1871.

55. Chester to Simon Cameron, December 12, 1863, in Cameron Papers.

56. Fragment of Chester to Young, n.d., in John Russell Young Papers, Library of Congress; Emmet Crozier, *Yankee Reporters 1861–65* (New York, 1956), 99; J. Cutler Andrews, *The North Reports the Civil War* (Pittsburgh, 1955), 26.

policies—a marked change from its earlier Democratic inclinations—
and Young might have seized the opportunity to hire as a symbol of
that support the first and only black correspondent of a major daily
during the war. But some in the black community suspected the
publisher and the editor of trimming their sails. These suspicions
were confirmed when in 1865 the paper endorsed President Johnson's
policy on Negro suffrage. The *Christian Recorder*, organ of the African
Methodist Episcopal (AME) church, condemned such inconsistency:
"It [the *Press*] awakes suddenly from its tortoise-like apathy and turns
from the humane and Christian course which it has been pursuing till
last fall and winter, and becomes a bona fide weather-cock, turning
with the strongest current." All the more surprising that Young
would have decided to employ Chester in such a sensitive and visible
post. There is no doubt that Young was taking a gamble; a black
correspondent might have affected sales negatively. Chester's experience as editor of the *Star of Liberia* and his knowing shorthand proved
invaluable when he prepared his dispatches.[57]

The *Press* and other major dailies had shown little interest in the
activities of black troops prior to 1864. There were a few scattered
brief reports, but no sustained coverage of black contributions to the
war effort. This was left almost exclusively to two black weeklies, the
Anglo-African, published in New York, and the *Christian Recorder.*
Chester was commissioned in August, 1864, and for the next eight
months sent the *Press* the most exhaustive accounts of black troop
activity around Petersburg and the Confederate capital. The war had
wrought significant changes in the image of newspaper correspondents as the public hankered for news from the front. No longer were
they just busybodies prying into people's private lives, they had
become, with the unexpected length of the war and the new
technology that speeded up the transmission of news, the most
reliable sources of information about developments on the battlefield.
These were hardy men. One day in the field was sufficient to test the
mettle of the bravest. Chester's introduction to the war, for example,
was a literal baptism of fire. Just after his arrival in Virginia, a massive

57. *Christian Recorder*, July 22, 1865. The *Press* subsequently abandoned Johnson in
his fight with the Radicals, which seems to confirm the *Recorder*'s criticism. It is not
known precisely when Chester learned shorthand. He had written McLain from Liberia
as early as 1857, promising to send verbatim reports of speeches. Chester to McLain,
October 5, 1857, in ACS Papers.

explosion at Grant's headquarters at City Point left scores dead and dismembered. It was a horrible carnage; "[f]ragments of humanity were scattered around in the immediate vicinity of the tragedy in frightful profusion." There was also the constant danger of being caught in the line of fire as he followed the armies. In late January, Chester was lucky to escape when a shell exploded nearby. He cushioned himself against these experiences with a barbed sense of the absurd. "Such reflections," he wrote of the incident, "are by no means the most agreeable to your correspondent, who, in the darkness of night before last, came near losing the top of his quarters by a Brooks shell, which went into the ground but a few feet beyond. In going into the earth it put out its fuse, and the nervous system of 'Yours truly' did not receive a serious shock." He was fond of the humorous metaphor to describe events. For instance, he frequently referred to the bombardment of the opposing armies as the fireworks displays of "the enterprising managers of the firm of Grant & Lee."[58]

These light touches enchanced his coverage of the war and gave added meaning to the message he conveyed. Like other northern correspondents, Chester consistently reiterated the inevitability of Union victory. In January and February, 1865, as both armies were dug in around Richmond and Petersburg, Chester's dispatches sought to assure readers that the winter inactivity was only the lull before the storm, that Grant was slowly tightening the noose, that enemy desertions were on the increase, that Confederate defenders were facing starvation, and that the spirit of the Union army was high. But unlike other correspondents, Chester in his reports paid specific attention to the actions of black soldiers in the field. They highlighted and repeated accounts of bravery and dedication to the cause, for Chester was determined to dispel the myth that blacks would not fight. When, for instance, he felt that their efforts at New Market Heights in late September, 1864, had not been given adequate coverage, Chester wrote glowingly of their assault on Confederate defenses. He frequently criticized white commanders of black troops who refused to treat "a negro patriot as a man" and lavished praise on those who did. One month after his arrival, he wrote: "It seems

58. Louis M. Starr, *Bohemian Brigade: Civil War Newsmen in Action* (New York, 1954), 5–6; Philadelphia *Press*, August 18, 19, 1864, January 27, 1865. In order to avoid confusion, I have chosen to use dates of publication rather than dates on which Chester wrote his dispatches.

that the disposition to treat colored persons as if they were human is hard for even some loyal men to acquire. The wrongs which they have suffered in this department would, if ventilated, exhibit a disgraceful depth of depravity, practiced by dishonest men, in the name of the Government."[59] Chester never wavered in his determination to keep the issue before the public.

On only one occasion did Chester's coverage of the war take him beyond Virginia. In December, 1864, he accompanied the ill-fated Union expedition sent against Fort Fisher, North Carolina. The fort with its walls nine feet high and twenty feet thick guarded the mouth of the Cape Fear River, the South's last remaining trading artery. Its fall, Union strategists calculated, would complete the blockade of Confederate ports and cut off vital supplies to the enemy. The simplicity of the plan seemed to guarantee a quick surrender: a barge loaded with nearly 250 tons of powder would be floated down to the base of the fort and detonated. In the carnage and confusion caused by the explosion, overwhelmingly superior Union forces would gain easy access to the fort and subdue the survivors. The plan proved much more difficult to carry out. The explosion, heard miles away in Wilmington, failed to breach the walls and the assault had to be called off. The expeditionary force retreated, weighed anchor, and returned to Virginia.[60] Chester did not return with the second, and this time successful, assault force sent against the fort a month later. He spent the rest of the war covering the bloody and protracted battles leading up to the fall of Petersburg and Richmond.

He was one of the first reporters to enter the Confederate capital with the victorious Union forces led by black troops of the XXV Army Corps under Major General Godfrey Weitzel. The fact that black troops were the first to enter Richmond, in spite of efforts by some to deny them that distinction, struck Chester as symbolically significant. Blacks, who had first been rejected as soldiers, and only later accepted when the North seemed on the brink of defeat, and who throughout the conflict had been vilified and demeaned, had won the laurels of conquering heroes as black Richmonders, free and slave, poured into the streets to welcome them. "There may be others," he reported, "who may claim the distinction of being the first to enter

59. Philadelphia *Press*, August 25, September 27, 1864.
60. Philadelphia *Press*, December 30, 1864; Shelby Foote, *The Civil War: A Narrative. Red River to Appomattox* (New York, 1974), 715–20.

the city, but as I was ahead of every part of the force but the cavalry, which of necessity must lead the advance, I know whereof I affirm when I announce that General Draper's brigade was the first organization to enter the city limits."[61] Aware of the irony and eager to thumb his nose at the Confederacy, that ultimate expression of oppression, exploitation, and human misery, Chester deliberately chose to write his first dispatch at the desk of the Speaker of the Confederate House. Charles Carleton Coffin of the Boston *Journal* and Charles A. Page of the New York *Tribune* later recalled what transpired when a paroled Confederate officer entered the chamber and found Chester seated in the Speaker's chair. Flying into a rage, he ordered Chester to leave the room. Unperturbed, Chester looked up briefly, then continued writing. The irate officer rushed Chester but was greeted by a well-placed punch that sent him tumbling. Chester adjusted his sleeves and returned to the desk. The Rebel demanded a sword from a Union officer who was standing nearby. The officer refused but offered to clear a space for a fair fistfight, which the chagrined southerner declined. Looking around for a moment and obviously savoring the situation, Chester commented cryptically, "I thought I would exercise my rights as a belligerent," before returning to his writing.[62]

Chester remained in Richmond until June, 1865, reporting on efforts to rebuild the city ravaged by retreating Confederate soldiers, and supporting the black community's activities. Predictably, Richmond was a city in chaos; businesses were destroyed, large numbers of blacks, many from other parts of the state, descended on the city, either fleeing former masters or searching for relatives, and thousands of destitute whites (the Relief Commission estimated as many as fifteen thousand) had to be fed. Black Richmond had a long and enviable record of providing for itself through an efficient network of societies. In a petition to President Johnson, they asserted proudly: "None of our people are in the Alms-House, and when we were slaves the aged and infirm who were turned away from the homes of hard masters, who had been enriched by their toil, our benevolent societies supported while they lived, and buried when they died, and

61. Philadelphia *Press*, April 6, 1865.
62. Coffin, *Four Years of Fighting*, 519; Charles A. Page, *Letters of a War Correspondent* (Boston, 1899), 326–27; Andrews, *The North Reports the Civil War*, 635; *New National Era and Citizen*, March 24, 1870.

comparatively few of us have found it necessary to ask for government rations, which have been so bountifully bestowed upon the unrepentant Rebels of Richmond."[63] That was no empty boast, and all the evidence suggests that the community could have continued to take care of itself. Although Chester commended the military authorities for their overall balanced approach to solving the city's problems, he was utterly bewildered by the leniency shown Confederate leaders, who, he believed, should have been tried and punished for treason. Those who had "defied the powers of the Government to the extent of their endurance" should not be "readmitted to the privileges of American citizens," he declared. His suspicions of Union intentions were aroused when Rebel soldiers were imprisoned while their officers were allowed to move about freely. What galled Chester most was the fact that these men were permitted to wear their uniforms, to "sport their best suits of gray with a degree of arrogance which should not be tolerated—more with the bearing of conquerors than routed vandals, as they are."[64]

The appointment of General Henry Halleck to the post of senior military officer in the department raised concerns in the black community. Halleck had enraged blacks and white abolitionists when, as commander in Missouri, he issued an order excluding fugitive slaves from his lines. Halleck was one of a triumvirate of military leaders in Richmond; the others were General Edward Ord, commanding the Army of the James, and General Marsena Patrick, who was in charge of the police and the relief agencies. None of these men evinced any interest in problems facing blacks. But more important, they were committed to the notion that the city's interests would be best served if freedmen were compelled to return to plantations as wage laborers, and if leniency was shown former Confederates. In early May, Ord issued a proclamation forcing those freedmen who attempted to enter Richmond to return to their plantations, and a week later, Patrick instituted a pass system for blacks. These passes, which had to be signed by a white person, contained names, showed if their owners were employed, and who their employers were. Chester roundly denounced the policy as inhumane and a cynical

63. John T. O'Brien, "Reconstruction in Richmond: White Restoration and Black Protest, April–June 1865," *Virginia Magazine of History and Biography,* LXXXIX (1981), 269, 276; Philadelphia *Press,* June 17, 1865.
64. Philadelphia *Press,* April 12, 22, 26, 1865.

attempt to rehabilitate the enemy. "The loyal men of Virginia," he wrote, "with more magnanimity than the rebels ever thought of extending to them, are industriously engaged in smoothing the way for their misguided brethren to return to the full enjoyment of their political rights."[65]

Then came the reappointment of Joseph Mayo as mayor. Mayo had served as the city's mayor since 1853, backed by a dreaded police force notorious for its treatment of blacks. "Without any evidence of repentance," Chester thundered, "and with nothing to recommend them but the oath of allegiance—which they have taken with a mental reservation—and with four years of vindictive hate, and hands covered with blood of patriots, the good sense of the American people has been shocked by the elevation to trust and power of this old public sinner and his satellites whose treason in this city before the occupation was regarded as the standard for the Richmond rebels."[66] Mayo and his police approached the job with renewed enthusiasm, anxious to exploit this opportunity to reassert their authority and at the same time return the city to some semblance of traditional order. The police took over where the military left off, arresting and imprisoning any black person caught without a pass. Two weeks after the pass system was introduced, eight hundred blacks, children among them, had been arrested.

The local media were united in support of the new policy. But the black community had other ideas. Unable to find an outlet for their protest, a group penned a letter to the New York *Tribune* on June 7, condemning the new policy. "All that is needed to restore slavery in full," they concluded pointedly, "is the auction block as it used to be." Another group met the following day and appointed a committee of four to conduct hearings and compile depositions from those who had been harassed. The stories that told of unnecessary assaults and intimidation should have been enough to win the attention of local Union officials. Instead, complaints only angered Patrick, and Halleck simply refused to grant the committee an audience. Faced with such insensitivity and hostility, they called a public meeting for June 10. More than three thousand jammed into the First Baptist Church. The meeting endorsed the investigation committee's findings, approved a protest memorial, and named a committee of ten, headed by Fields

65. Philadelphia *Press*, May 23, 1865.
66. Philadelphia *Press*, June 15, 1865.

Cook and including Chester, to take their case to the president. Two days earlier, Chester had been insulted and pushed around by a group of provost guards on his way to mail a dispatch to the *Press*. Money was collected at the meeting and at local churches the following Sunday to defray the delegation's expenses.[67]

Such unity and determination forced local authorities to reexamine their policies. Before leaving for Washington, the delegation presented evidence of extensive intimidation to Governor Francis Pierpoint, who agreed to dismiss Mayo and the city council. In Washington they met with General O. O. Howard of the Freedmen's Bureau, who promised to investigate conditions in Richmond and report his findings to the president. Johnson, in turn, committed himself "to do all in his power to protect them and their rights." As Cook later reported, the delegation left Washington pleasantly surprised by their success. By the end of June, blacks were savoring their victory. Ord and Halleck had been reassigned, and Patrick had resigned in disgust over what he considered Johnson's partiality for the freedmen. More to the point, the new military commander of Virginia, General Alfred Terry, seemed disposed to treat blacks more equitably.[68]

After the meeting with Johnson, Chester left for Harrisburg rather than return to Richmond. It is not known exactly why he decided to leave a community in which he had become so deeply involved. Richmond, in 1865, stood on the brink of a new era, exciting and full of challenge. The community's unified resistance to efforts to reimpose the ancien régime won Chester's admiration, yet this need for united action presaged even greater struggles against the virulence of both Union and former Confederate officials. In spite of all that blacks had done to ensure the defeat of the South, the question of their future in Virginia and the other former Confederate states remained largely unanswered. In fact, Chester was convinced that this uncertainty provided colonizationists with a unique opportunity to attract settlers to Liberia, though he showed no interest in returning

67. New York *Tribune*, June 12, 17, 1865; O'Brien, "Reconstruction in Richmond," 276–79; Peter J. Rachleff, *Black Labor in the South: Richmond, Virginia, 1865–1890* (Philadelphia, 1984), 36–37.

68. New York *Tribune*, June 27, 1865; O'Brien, "Reconstruction in Richmond," 276–79; Rachleff, *Black Labor in the South*, 37; David S. Sparks (ed.), *Inside Lincoln's Army: The Diary of Marsena Rudolph Patrick, Provost Marshal General, Army of the Potomac* (New York, 1964), 514–15.

immediately.[69] He planned instead to move to Britain in the fall, but developments in Harrisburg delayed him temporarily.

Prior to Chester's return from Richmond in July, 1865, black Pennsylvanians had launched a sustained campaign against a broad range of racial inequities, from the denial of the vote to segregation on public transportation. This new effort had its genesis in the October, 1864, Syracuse meeting of the National Convention of Colored Men, out of which came a new organization, the "National Equal Rights League," to "encourage sound morality, education, temperance, frugality, industry, and promote everything that pertains to a well-ordered and dignified life" for blacks. Pennsylvanians met within a week to form the Pennsylvania State Equal Rights League (PSERL). Its foundation was a network of local societies large enough to sustain activities in their communities. Although many of these auxiliaries were short-lived, the PSERL reported forty-three affiliates in early 1866. The Harrisburg society, the Garnet Equal Rights League (GL), was formed in August, 1865. There is no record of why it was named in honor of Henry Highland Garnet, though it is very likely that many of its founders were also members of the Henry Highland Garnet Guards, a private militia company, formed six years earlier.[70]

The GL articulated a broad range of interests. It was organized, its president, the Reverend John E. Price, observed, "to promote the interest of our people at home, to encourage mental improvement and moral rectitude, and to defend our race when assaulted in the person of any colored man and woman." When, for instance, the School Board delayed opening a school for blacks in the city's Fourth Ward, the GL organized a protest and won an agreement from the board to supply fuel and pay the teacher's salary if the community provided an appropriate room, furnished it, and found someone to run the school. The school was opened within a few weeks in the basement of a church on South Street.[71] The GL also protected the

69. Chester to Coppinger, July 4, 15, 17, 1865, Coppinger to Chester, July 7, 1865, all in ACS Papers.

70. "Proceedings of the National Convention of Colored Men, held in the City of Syracuse, New York, October 4, 5, 6, and 7, 1864," in Howard H. Bell (ed.), *Minutes of the Proceedings of the National Negro Conventions, 1830–1864* (New York, 1969), 3–7, 36; *Christian Recorder*, March 31, 1866; Jane H. Pease and William H. Pease, *They Who Would Be Free: Blacks' Search for Freedom, 1830–1861* (New York, 1974), 158–60.

71. *Christian Recorder*, December 23, 1865, February 10, 1866; Harrisburg *Telegraph*, January 3, 1866.

community against assault. Its response to an attack on William Bush, a veteran, in late 1865 was typical. Bush was assaulted and shot at by a gang of whites who later claimed he was drunk and dangerous. The GL set up a committee to investigate the incident, won Bush's release, and prosecuted his attackers. It opened a reading room at its headquarters on South Street in April, 1866, which also became a meeting place for its literary and dramatic associations. Finally, it provided the services of an employment agency, an "intelligence office," one local newspaper called it, where black women seeking jobs as maids could register and families needing their services could apply. "Great care," they announced, "will be taken to prevent families from being imposed upon by improper servants, and it will be made the business of those in charge of the office to see that none but reliable colored people are recommended."[72]

Chester joined the League soon after his return to Harrisburg, acting first as "Solicitor and Literary Critic" and subsequently as "Corresponding Secretary." He might even have delayed his trip to England for a few months at the behest of the League, whose leaders recognized his usefulness and the potential prestige of having the *Press* war correspondent as an officer. The GL initiated a series of paid public lectures in October, which exploited the presence of prominent black individuals in the city to pressure state legislators to grant blacks the full rights of citizens. The first was given by the Reverend J. J. Clinton, bishop of the AME Zion church and president of the Freedmen's American and British Commission, successor of the American Freedmen's Friend Society, a black organization that worked with other associations collecting clothes for the needy and recommending teachers for schools in the South. Clinton was followed by William Howard Day, Garnet, J. J. Wright, and others.[73] But by far the largest event organized by the League was the three-day celebration in November, 1865, to honor the state's black veterans. The tribute was all the more significant because blacks were determined to use their defense of the Union as a lever to pry all the rights of citizenship from the grasp of a vulnerable nation wracked by doubt

72. Harrisburg *Telegraph*, November 15, 18, December 19, 1865, March 26, 28, 29, April 4, 28, 1866; Harrisburg *Patriot*, November 15, 18, 1865; *Christian Recorder*, December 23, 1865.

73. Harrisburg *Telegraph*, October 7, 9, 12, 14, 1865, January 1, February 16, March 30, April 17, May 21, 1866; *Christian Recorder*, October 21, 1865, March 31, 1866.

following the self-inflicted carnage of the war. In earlier wars, at Boston, Lake Champlain, and Chalmette Plains, blacks had contributed as much to the nation's defense as the country permitted. Now black Pennsylvania had sent ten thousand men—over one thousand from Harrisburg and adjoining counties—to battle the enemy. The GL's motto, "He Who Defends Freedom is Worthy of All its Franchise," expressed their determination to achieve full citizenship. The League appealed to all Harrisburgers to demonstrate their "gratitude to the living as well as respect for the memory of the dead who fell in the cause of the Union." The effect of such a celebration, they insisted, would be twofold. It would pay homage to those blacks who served the nation, and it "would have a salutary effect in removing for once, and perhaps, permanently, the crude and vulgar ideas of the colored citizens' inferiority to whites." It did no such thing. But there were some signs of imminent change. Governor Curtin, who earlier had refused to accept blacks in the state militia, now endorsed the celebration and agreed to review the soldiers. The fact that illness prevented him from participating does not diminish the significance of his support.[74]

Chester headed the celebration's organizing committee, which commissioned Day to deliver the main address. Most of the state's leading black figures—including William Nesbit of Altoona, PSERL president Joseph G. Bustill, Professor E. D. Bassett of the Institute for Colored Youth and William D. Forten of Philadelphia, Aaron L. Still of Reading, and George B. Vashon of Pittsburgh—were in attendance. Veterans from all sectors of the commonwealth attended, their numbers swollen because the railroad companies serving the capital decided to carry passengers at half the regular fare. Chester headed the procession as chief marshal and served as chairman of the many public meetings. The final meeting appealed to the legislature to repeal the 1838 constitutional amendment, that "mighty wrong done to the colored freemen of Pennsylvania," which disfranchised blacks, and declared that "this land of our birth is, if possible, more endeared to us, and rendered ours more rightfully by the courage of the colored soldiers in its defence." Although the soldiers were warmly received, there were some, like the editor of the Harrisburg *Patriot*, organ of the Democratic party, who would brook no changes. They ridiculed the "Darkies Jubilee" and, in what must rank as one of the

74. Harrisburg *Telegraph*, October 12, November 1, 1865, April 27, 1870; *Christian Recorder*, November 11, 1865.

most perverse bits of reporting, wrote that Day in his speech "wanted the niggers to vote, to hold office, to intermarry with whites, in fact, to rule America."[75] Any hope that the success of the celebration could be translated into enlarged rights for blacks was shattered by the sort of virulence exhibited by the *Patriot,* which unfortunately spoke for a significant portion of the white electorate.

Such views were instrumental in delaying the dismantling of the state's edifice of racial laws. Achieving the GL's and PSERL's objective of a racially neutral franchise would take another four years. But removal of the restrictions on the right to vote was not necessarily synonymous in the eyes of some blacks with acceptance of the principle of universal franchise. Many held to the position that the franchise should be exercised only by those elevated enough by education and culture. It was accepted almost axiomatically that "equality of privilege" rested on the intellectual improvement and elevation of the overwhelming majority of blacks. Otherwise, detractors would always construe individual achievements as exceptions to the rule. Aiming to combat this predicament, the GL broadened its interests to include "the moral and educational improvement of the freedmen and the assistance of those whose condition entitles them to charity, the encouragement of all purely philanthropic movements, calculated to promote the material interests of the colored people, and the stimulation of a higher standard of literature, and a more cultivated civilization, and the organization of auxiliaries, either upon this continent, or elsewhere, to advance the prosperity of the freedmen, by sending among them, as numerous as possible their own kith and kin as teachers and ministers, to instruct them in all the moral and religious duties pertaining to civilized communities." While its goals were similar to those of other freedmen's societies, there is no evidence that the GL ever established schools in the South or even, as in the case of the Freedmen's American and British Commission, recommended teachers for the schools of other associations. The GL did win the endorsement of a broad cross section of people in central and eastern Pennsylvania, including the "pastors of every church in Harrisburg."[76]

75. Harrisburg *Telegraph,* November 1, 2, 7, 13, 14, 15, 1865; *Christian Recorder,* November 18, 1865; Harrisburg *Patriot,* November 11, 1865.

76. For an earlier articulation of this position on the franchise, see Sterling Stuckey (ed.), *The Ideological Origins of Black Nationalism* (Boston, 1972), 119; *Laws of the General Assembly of the State of Pennsylvania, Passed at the Session of 1866* (Harrisburg, 1866), 803; Harrisburg *Telegraph,* March 27, 21, April 10, 27, 1866.

In an effort to expand its sources of support, the League commissioned Chester to undertake a fund-raising tour of England and the Continent in 1866. He was a logical choice, given the many contacts he had made during his earlier visit. Chester began in England, in August, with the endorsement of the National Freedmen's Aid Union of Great Britain and Ireland. Unfortunately, it was a decidedly inauspicious time to begin an agency in England. British freedmen's associations were deeply divided over what policies to adopt in response to the October, 1865, peasant uprising at Morant Bay, Jamaica. Shock waves from the rebellion reverberated throughout Britain. There were those who condemned Governor Edward John Eyre's brutal suppression of the revolt. For others, however, the uprising was nothing more than the predictable response of ungrateful freedmen to British philanthropy. The rebellion, and the furor created in its aftermath, directly affected efforts to raise money for American freedmen. Meetings were canceled, and when they were not, donations dropped precipitously. J. Sella Martin, who had only recently returned to England as agent of the American Missionary Association, also discerned a marked increase in antiblack sentiments. "It makes one's heart ache," he lamented, "to find these fallacies and inconsistent fooleries more rife in England than they are now in America." Although Martin placed the blame for this turn of events on the aristocracy, America's traditional enemies, the fact remained that these conditions effectively undermined Chester's ability to raise money in Britain.[77]

Chester left England in the fall for a tour of the Continent and Russia. In early February, Cassius M. Clay, an antislavery supporter and U.S. minister to Russia, introduced Chester to the Russian court in St. Petersburg. Chester was invited by the czar to join the annual review of the imperial guard and to dine with the royal family.[78] He was impressed by both the pageant and the fanfare of the review and the hospitality of the royal family. The irony of a person from

77. *Freedmen's Aid Reporter*, September, 1866; Christine Bolt, *The Anti-Slavery Movement and Reconstruction: A Study of Anglo-American Co-operation 1833–1877* (London, 1969), 41–42; London *Daily News*, September 4, 17, 1866.

78. Cassius M. Clay to William H. Seward, February 9, 1867, in U.S. State Department Dispatches from U.S. Ministers to Russia, 1808–1906, National Archives; Harrisburg *Telegraph*, June 15, 1869; Chester to Coppinger, July 5, 1867, in ACS Papers; Allison Blakely, *Russia and the Negro: Blacks in Russian History and Thought* (Washington, D.C., 1986), 42–44.

democratic America, where the future of blacks was still very much in doubt, being warmly received at the Russian imperial court was palpable. Yet, surprisingly, Chester rarely employed this cachet to taunt, embarrass, or pressure America to live up to its principles of equality as so many of his contemporaries did. Only indirectly was his treatment in Russia held up as a mirror to America; a person invited to the royal household, he sometimes implied, surely was qualified to be admitted to all of American society.

One suspects that this reluctance to berate his white countrymen while he was abroad was due almost entirely to Chester's uncertainty about the future of blacks in America. His was not an unrequited love for his native land. There is little to suggest that Chester saw America in these terms. On the contrary, his position was unequivocal. Even before going to Allegheny Institute, he had committed himself to a future in Liberia, the one country where blacks could develop their potential unrestrained by racism. At no time did he publicly express a fondness for America. Garnet's lament, "I hate nothing in America but Slavery and its associated evils. Even to me my country is lively— how much more so it must be for those of her sons around whom she throws her arms of protection," would have mystified Chester. In fact, he was utterly contemptuous of those who refused to entertain a future beyond America. When, in 1869, for example, J. J. Roberts, former president of Liberia, was snubbed by a number of blacks, Douglass among them, Chester was so incensed that he launched into a tirade that rivaled some of the worst examples of colonizationist disdain. He castigated Roberts for meeting with "servants or the associates of servants." Liberia, he insisted, should reject black American ambassadors, not because of their color, but because they were "personally objectionable." Their "condition is such in the United States that we would be warranted in declining to receive [them], and thereby master our sense of the degradation to which [they] submit. The only thing I admire about the American negro is his color, but that is not sufficient in itself to rescue him as a minister." Only when blacks are treated as equals in America, he concluded, should Liberia receive them as representatives.[79]

If that sounded like blaming the victim, Chester would have

79. *Non Slaveholder*, October, 11, 1850; Chester to Coppinger, August 12, June 9, 1869, Coppinger to Chester, June 29, 1869, all in ACS Papers; New Orleans *Republican*, October 6, 1871.

replied that blacks had developed a fatal fascination with America, one that blinded them to the availability of alternatives. Blacks, in other words, had been accessories to their own oppression. Yet even here one can discern traces of ambivalence in Chester's views of America that go beyond merely missing the company of his family or the camaraderie of friends. There were times when events, as in the apparent insult to Roberts, drove him to speak of America as "your country" and of Liberia as "home." And there is no doubt that he was passionately committed to Liberia's development and longed to be part of that, in a role commensurate with his talents. Yet Chester always managed to drift back to Harrisburg. Later in life, he would boast of the number of times he had crossed the Atlantic, but not once could he bring himself to admit to the emotional pull of his native land.

Before his audience with the czar, Chester had been actively promoting the GL in St. Petersburg. He held a series of meetings in December at which he discussed conditions in the South and the needs of the freedmen, who, he insisted, had taken the initiative in building schools and working the land, and who were now appealing to the benevolent to lend support. The appeal was rooted in the theme of international solidarity, long a feature of the Anglo-American abolitionist movement. The deliverance of American slaves from oppression, as well as aid to the freedmen, he wrote, is "a task which befits not only Americans but in general Christians of each country and nation, and I firmly hope that Russians show themselves to be the best friends of America in its hard times, not only keeping up with other countries, for example France, England and others, but also surpassing them in wishing to further the rebirth of so many unfortunates." In response to Chester's appeal, Tedor Seminoff, a "peasant landholder," sent six rubles: "Belonging, in my own great country—Russia—to the number of twenty three millions of former serfs set free by the kindness of our great Alexander II," Seminoff wrote, "I consider the new citizens of America as brothers not merely on account of the principle that all men are brethren, but by the force of those feelings which must unite the freedmen of one land to those of another."[80]

80. *Golos*, No. 35 (1867). My thanks to Allison Blakely for sending me a copy of this Russian newspaper and to Carmen Storella for his thorough translation. Harrisburg *Telegraph*, May 30, 1867.

There is no way to determine either the success of Chester's tour or the amount of money he raised for the GL. His mission completed in May, 1867, he returned to England, where he planned to enroll in one of the Inns of Court. This desire for professional training had become, by now, something of an obsession with Chester. He never forgot those in his graduating class at Thetford Academy who had gone on to New England's most prestigious universities and colleges. Although the passage of time might have persuaded others to lower their sights, Chester seemed to draw strength from the impediments he encountered. One also gets the impression that Chester compensated for his frustrations by means of an exaggerated sense of his personal worth that bordered on the arrogant. When he first applied to the Pennsylvania Colonization Society for assistance to emigrate in 1853, his cockiness took Coppinger by surprise. But it was a brashness born of a singular determination to surmount the invidious distinctions and limitations imposed by American racism. Such a talent, if properly nurtured, as Chester himself put it, through "perseverance [and] stability of character," could redound to Liberia's benefit. Although his actions in Liberia raised serious doubts among some colonizationists, Chester saw in them what, with benefit of hindsight, he called "a regular chain of connecting links."[81]

Those links, considered by many to be totally disjointed and pointless, the actions of a frustrated individual, were forged together, in Chester's mind, by the attributes of "self-respect and pride of race." He was, he proudly asserted, descended from a long line of gifted black men and women who had consistently resisted oppression. "In direct opposition to the wishes of prejudice of our oppressors, to public sentiment and the laws of the land," he told a meeting of the Philadelphia Literary Company in 1862, "we have come up from the house of bondage where every effort was made to brutalize and corrupt us; and as we advanced along the track of time, uncheered by the quickening beacons of good schools and pure churches, we were nerved on by nothing else under Heaven but the transcendent superiority of our nature." Given this history, the race's future could be assured only if blacks made a concerted effort to develop and nurture a sense of pride, one predicated on what, in another context, he called the "utility of learning." Ignorance was

81. Coppinger to Chester, July 25, 1867, Chester to Coppinger, March 28, 1868, both in ACS Papers.

analogous to the "inextricable confusion" of an untended garden or a pawnbroker's shop. The mind, "nourished by study and garnished by culture" in the "crucible of an institution of learning," provided the most efficient means to unravel the confusion and establish order. With well-trained intellects, blacks had a greater chance of improving their position in society. Yet in spite of this abiding commitment to education, Chester was not above advocating the burning of books that denigrated blacks or rejecting versions of the Bible that portrayed the devil as black and God as white. In the end, he called on his black listeners to remove the pictures of Washington, Jefferson, Webster, and other famous white statesmen and military figures from their walls and replace them with black heroes, like Toussaint L'Ouverture, Douglass, and Garnet.[82]

This commitment to the elevation of the race, which some saw as synonymous with civilization, fueled Chester's personal objectives. Individual achievement and racial advancement were not mutually antagonistic goals; on the contrary, they were an indispensable tandem. When dreams of attending college after Thetford were dashed, Chester did not despair. There were times in Liberia when he even saw college as a respite from interminable political strife. But he could not muster sufficient resources to attend, nor could he per-suade friends to sponsor him. Never one to accept defeat, Chester began reading law under a Liberian lawyer while editing the *Star of Liberia*.[83] But he saw this as an interim measure only, a prelude to enrolling in an accredited school of law.

The resources of an editor, even when supplemented by a tempo-rary teacher's salary, were barely enough to live decently in Monrovia. Not until he was hired by the *Press* was Chester able to save enough to continue his legal training. His agency for the GL also enabled him to increase his savings. Yet in the three years he spent at Middle Temple in London, Chester had to rely on periodic lecture tours and an appointment as Liberia's roving ambassador in Europe, to meet the cost of his education, which in the first year alone totaled in excess of "seven hundred dollars in gold." Chester's years there were rewarding ones and in April, 1870, he became the first black American to be called to the English bar. He argued his first case a

82. T. Morris Chester, *Negro Self-Respect and Pride of Race* (1863; rpr. Philadelphia, n.d.), 3–7; Harrisburg *Telegraph*, July 16, 1870.
    83. *Colonization Herald*, April, 1860.

few weeks later in the hallowed halls of the Old Bailey, defending a shoemaker charged with murder. It was a rather unusual case, if only because the judge was so convinced of the defendant's guilt that he never concealed the black cap worn when pronouncing a sentence of death. By "sharp cross-examination," Moncure D. Conway reported, Chester "managed to so shake the evidence regarding malice and deliberation as to save his client from the gallows." The accused was sentenced instead to ten years' penal servitude.[84]

By this time, Chester had become something of a celebrity in London and other European capitals. His reception in St. Petersburg in 1866 opened a number of doors that he used to good effect as "aide-de-camp of the President of Liberia." Chester was appointed by President James Spriggs Payne sometime in 1868, when Liberia was attempting to expand trading and political ties with Europe. Most of his official duties were performed during term breaks. His 1868 tour, for example, lasted four months and took him to Brussels, Bremen, Hamburg, Copenhagen, Gothenburg, Stockholm, and Christiania. In each of these cities, Chester was introduced to the royal court and held meetings with major political figures to discuss the needs of Liberia. In early 1869 he and Ralston were appointed commissioners to negotiate a "treaty of Amity, Commerce and Navigation" with Russia. The Russian ambassador to London balked at the notion of negotiating a treaty that would put Liberia in the company of such favored nations as Great Britain, France, and the United States of America. He offered instead a more limited treaty of commerce, which Ralston and Chester rejected. No further negotiations were conducted during Chester's stay in London.[85]

Even before completing his dinners and being called to the bar, Chester had been considering his future. He hoped to hang out his

84. Chester to Coppinger, July 5, 1867, August 3, 1868, Gerard Ralston to Coppinger, May 25, 1869, all in ACS Papers; "Certificate of Attendance at two Courses of Public Lectures and Private Classes," Middle Temple, London; Harrisburg *Telegraph*, October 5, 1870; New York *Sun*, January 7, 1871; *Louisianan*, September 24, 1871.

85. Chester to Coppinger, August 3, 1868, February 10, 1869, Ralston to Coppinger, May 25, 1869, all in ACS Papers; Charles Goedelt to John W. Lewis, April 20, 1868, W. A. Johnson to Ralston, January [?], 1869, May 19[?], 1869, Chester to Edward James Roye, February 23, 1870, Lewis to Chester, April 7, 1870, all in Executive Department of State, Foreign Correspondence, 1868–1872, Bureau of Archives, Ministry of Foreign Affairs, Monrovia, Liberia. My thanks to Svend Holsoe for providing me with copies of these letters. *African Repository*, September, 1869; *New National Era and Citizen*, March 24, 1870; New Orleans *Republican*, October 6, 1871.

shingles in Monrovia. As a young man, he had spoken of "taking the helm of affairs" in the new republic, but his experiences quickly disabused him of such exalted notions. Becoming a lawyer, especially a graduate of one of London's Inns of Court, the appointment as Payne's aide-de-camp, and his reception at the royal courts of Europe seemed to point to a future in politics. But the dispute with Benson had made him understandably wary, even contemptuous of Liberian politics. Furthermore, he insisted on assuming a position commensurae with his superior qualifications and experience. He pointedly suggested to Coppinger that an appointment at the College of Liberia would be appropriate for a person of his attainments. Of the college's faculty, Crummell was a graduate of Cambridge University and Freeman held a diploma from Middlebury College; only Blyden had not received any college training. Chester abandoned the idea, however, when Coppinger ignored his suggestions. In place of specific proposals, he reiterated vague assertions of his commitment to work for "the improvement of our aboriginal inhabitants." There were also proposals for establishing another newspaper, which Payne, locked in a heated race for the presidency with Edward James Roye, endorsed. Victory for Payne would facilitate Chester's return; defeat, he told Coppinger, "would indeed be a misfortune."[86]

Roye's victory forced Chester to cancel any plans he had of returning to Liberia immediately. Instead, he left London for Harrisburg sometime during the summer of 1870. Pennsylvania had undergone dramatic political change during his absence. Locally, the GL had given way to a new organization, the "Lincoln Industrial Protective Union of Colored Men." While both organizations were pledged to improving relations between the races, procuring jobs for blacks, and protecting blacks from "privation, suffering and imposition," most of the Lincoln Union's interest and energies were devoted to the removal of voting restrictions. The PSERL and its local affiliate had conducted a sustained drive for black enfranchisement since 1868. But state legislators—Democrats who generally opposed granting the vote to blacks, and Republicans who were aware that the issue could redound to the benefit of their opponents, as it undoubtedly did in 1867—proceeded very cautiously, unwilling to take an active lead on the issue. Blacks would have to wait until the passage of the

86. Chester to Coppinger, March 28, 1868, August 12, 1869, Ralston to Coppinger, May 25, 1869, all in ACS Papers.

Fifteenth Amendment in 1870. Two months before Chester's return, Harrisburg blacks held a massive ratification celebration reminiscent of the welcome given black veterans in 1865.[87]

Black Pennsylvanians were poised on the edge of a new age full of both promise and foreboding. Problems in Liberia aside, the promise of the Fifteenth Amendment prompted Chester to look to America as his future home. Not that this one act was enough to allay his skepticism about white America's true intentions, but developments since 1865 had provided a narrow vein of opportunity that, if effectively mined, could herald a new era in American history. He returned to Allegheny City in July to deliver the commencement address at his old school. Both the setting and his speech seemed to reflect a new optimism. Garnet, Avery College's president, had also invited Senator Hiram Revels of Mississippi and South Carolina Supreme Court Justice J. J. Wright to participate, bringing together, across the divide of the Civil War, those who had fought for change and those, the students, who were the beneficiaries of those changes. Not surprisingly, Chester was buoyed by the occasion. "In a country like this, which has so many resources to develop—which respects a man only for his individual worth and not for the greatness of his ancestors—which is everywhere recognizing merit irrespective of complexion and which by its fundamental law has proclaimed the equality of all men—it especially becomes a people whose mental improvement circumstances have retarded to fully appreciate the utility of learning."[88]

Chester had not suddenly become enamored of America; his knowledge and experience of racism militated against too rosy a view of the future. Yet he discerned perceptible changes that he believed blacks should position themselves to exploit. With rights, however, came responsibilities. The right to vote, for example, assumed a responsibility to act judiciously and intelligently when exercising it. In this respect, Chester was no different from the majority of his contemporaries. But why this compulsion to demonstrate that blacks could act intelligently? There was no evidence, after all, to suggest that American democracy had ever depended on an electorate acting intelligently. Part of the answer, as we have seen, is to be found in

87. Harrisburg *Telegraph*, November 14, 17, 1869, April 26, 27, 1870.
88. Harrisburg *Telegraph*, July 16, 1870; Pittsburgh *Post*, July 8, 1870; Pittsburgh *Gazette*, July 8, 1870.

traditional black approaches to the problems of racial exclusion. Denial of the right to vote was protested on a variety of grounds, many premised on the demonstrated fact that blacks were solid, law-abiding members of their community. Petitions spoke of property ownership, number of churches, community provision for the needy, and efforts to eradicate the problems of intemperance and other social evils. But there was also the understandable fear that the limited advances made since the war could be easily reversed by a white backlash. Some, like J. Sella Martin, even predicted a possible return to the status quo ante in twenty-five years. In this atmosphere of hope and uncertainty, Chester suggested two approaches to safe-guard gains already made: blacks must act intelligently in exercising the franchise, and their votes must go to keep the party of Lincoln in power. The first required an educated electorate. "The elective franchise, while it confers a high privilege, can never crystalize ignorance, dignify inactivity nor propitiate impurity. . . . Should you improve your opportunities," he told a Harrisburg meeting, "by study and associating yourselves into societies for your mutual benefit, there is no doubt of your becoming worthy of the glorious act of enfranchisement." The second was articulated in terms that defied all the pragmatism of electoral politics. To vote for a Democrat was not only an act of ingratitude, it was tantamount to "moral and political turpitude." Reverting to biblical imagery, he warned: "If there be such an ingrate in Pennsylvania, let him be marked by your displeasure, spurned from your associations, despised wherever he puts in an appearance, and especially point him out with the unerring finger of scorn to the orphan children of lamented soldiers, that they may early learn to execrate him while living and curse his memory when he is dead."[89] Both seemed an unnecessary burden for the newly enfranchised to carry. But these were the heady days of 1870 when many were determined to march in solid phalanx behind the Republican party.

Chester reiterated this message throughout a lecture tour of Kentucky and Louisiana in the summer of 1871. Large crowds greeted him at each stop. He was particularly impressed by the hospitality of his New Orleans hosts. His lectures there were sponsored by the Louisiana Progressive Club, whose membership included many of

89. Harrisburg *Telegraph*, October 5, 7, 1870.

the state's leading black political figures. Oscar Dunn, C. C. Antoine, and William G. Brown demonstrated the sophistication, self-respect, and pride of race that Chester maintained were prerequisites for full participation in the economic, social, and political life of any society. "There are many things which we as colored men must accomplish," he told one meeting, "and though we have the power, we will never effect our object unless the spirit of self-respect, which has been weakened by circumstances for which we are in no way responsible, becomes as prevalent all over this land as it is here manifested, which will enable us to move in one solid column in advancing the best interest of our people."[90] That, as we have seen, did not preclude the fulfillment of personal ambitions. In Louisiana, unlike Pennsylvania, blacks were a dominant force in state politics, a fact that did not escape Chester. In spite of earlier laments about the destructive nature of politics, he was excited by the chance to participate in the reconstruction of Louisiana. "Experience teaches me," he once wrote Coppinger dismissively, "that in republics politics degenerate into trade, while partisan rancour spares neither age nor sex in its vindictive fury." He found political parties generally "ignorant . . . and as capricious as the weather in April. They raise up idols one day for admiration and the next they . . . crucify them."[91]

Chester should have heeded his own words, for while his concerns in this case were with Liberia, there was no more fitting description of Louisiana politics in 1871. Quite possibly, that very similarity drew him to New Orleans. By late 1871, Louisiana politics had degenerated into a series of internecine squabbles between Governor Henry Clay Warmoth and more radical members of the Republican party, headed by Lieutenant Governor Dunn, and what its opponents called the Customs House clique. Most of the conflict centered on Warmoth's vetoing, or refusing to sign into law, bills considered by blacks and white radicals the centerpieces of Reconstruction policy. The social equality bill of 1868 and the public education and civil rights bills of 1870 were viewed as important guarantees of black equality. Conditions worsened when Warmoth pushed through the legislature a law allowing him to continue in office for another term. Opponents

90. Louisville *Commercial*, July 11, 1871; *Louisianan*, September 10, 24, 28 (quotation), October 1, 8, 1871; New Orleans *Republican*, October 6, 1871; New Orleans *Times*, October 6, 1871.
91. Chester to Coppinger, March 28, 1868, in ACS Papers.

attempted to isolate the governor from the party but without much success.

By the time of Chester's arrival in New Orleans, the Republicans were almost immobilized by factionalism. Some of Warmoth's staunchest opponents were members of the Progressive Club. It therefore came as no surprise that Chester would join their ranks after accepting a clerkship in the Customs House. Things began to unravel following Dunn's mysterious death in November, 1871. Warmoth recalled the senate in December to find a successor to Dunn, convinced that his candidate, P. B. S. Pinchback, inheritor of Dunn's mantle as the leading black political figure in the state, would carry the day. But the governor underestimated his opponents and, in the end, was forced to pull a number of strings to ensure Pinchback's election. Even then, the margin of victory was one vote, and that, many believed, was achieved by fraudulent means. Chester literally got caught in the line of fire between those the *Louisianan*, Pinchback's newspaper, called "the low snails" who leave "a trail of filth" behind them, and "manhood [who] walks erect and spurns the earth on which they tread." He was shot in the head and dangerously wounded on January 1, 1872, during an altercation with a group of Pinchback supporters.[92]

The incident became something of a *cause célèbre*, providing all factions with a convenient opportunity to attack opponents. Democrats saw it as another example of Republican machinations, and Customs House supporters accused Pinchback, and indirectly his mentor, Warmoth, of being accessories to the assault. Pinchback, who was at the scene of the shooting, denied any involvement. He and a large party of legislators had been making the customary New Year's social rounds when, he said, some of them accosted Chester. Pinchback attempted to intervene but was spurned by Chester. He turned to enter his carriage and heard a loud bang that he mistook for a firecracker. Chester's screams brought Pinchback back to the scene, but Pinchback did nothing to help the injured. His account ends, "This is all I know of the circumstances." Not a word of remorse, nor

92. Althea D. Pitre, "The Collapse of the Warmoth Regime, 1870–1872," *Louisiana History*, VI (1965), 162–65; *Edwards' Annual Directory to the Inhabitants, Institutions, Incorporated Companies in the City of New Orleans for 1872* (New Orleans, 1872); *Louisianan*, November 26, December 10, 24, 1871; New Orleans *Times*, November 24, 1871; New Orleans *Picayune*, January 2, 1872.

for that matter an expression of concern. Pinchback might have been simply inured to the violence that had become an everyday occurrence in the city, yet the suspicion lingers that the shooting was a botched attempt by his supporters to get rid of Chester.[93]

While reaction to the assault seemed to take Pinchback by surprise, such an astute politician could not have doubted for a moment that opponents would use the incident to maximum effect. This "gang of political rowdies" should be promptly arrested, the *Times* insisted, but doubted that would occur, since the lieutenant governor was president of the Board of Police. "When such disturbances break out it is obvious that the present police, being controlled by one of the belligerent factions, cannot be depended on to maintain order. It can only be used to protect and aid one of these factions in any deeds of outrage against the other." Pinchback's protestations of innocence fell on deaf ears. The crisis and the concern over politically motivated violence were heightened with the assassination of Walter H. Wheyland on January 9. According to Warmoth, Wheyland, a Sabine Parish representative, was killed when he resisted arrest by the sergeants at arms sent out by Speaker George Carter, head of the Customs House clique, to find those who had deliberately absented themselves from the legislature in an attempt to deny him a quorum. Democrats tried to exploit these two incidents to increase Republican factionalism. In the lead was Judge Edmund Abell, a "reactionary Unionist" with a long history of hatred for blacks. When he summoned the grand jury on January 11 and discovered that it had already taken action on the Wheyland but not the Chester case, he launched into a vituperative condemnation of its actions, accusing its members of being the governor's quislings. Abell promptly dismissed the grand jury. Some, like the *Times*, hailed Abell's actions; others, the *Picayune* surprisingly among them, flatly condemned him for a decision "bearing the shadow of political bias." Republicans in the house moved quickly to silence him. A special committee was empaneled to investigate his dismissal of the grand jury and his charges of political tampering. Abell appeared before the committee

93. New Orleans *Times*, January 3, 1872. Pinchback had a reputation, much of it justified, as a man who easily resorted to violence. In 1862 his brother-in-law attacked him on a New Orleans street but got the worst of it. There were also many threats on his life during his political career in Louisiana. James Haskins, *Pinckney Benton Stewart Pinchback* (New York, 1973), 21–22, 123–24.

on four occasions, but there is no evidence that he was silenced. A reconstituted grand jury "found true bills" against Pinchback and three others for shooting "with intent to kill, and slightly wounding one Chester." Bond of $1,500 was posted, and then the case surprisingly disappeared from the political stage.[94]

Chester had recovered sufficiently, by the end of January, to return to the fray. His first speech, and the reaction of Pinchback and his supporters to it, demonstrates the political nature of the entire incident. In an apparent show of unity, blacks called a meeting in St. James Chapel to express support for Charles Sumner's supplementary civil rights bill then before Congress. The chairman, J. Henri Burch, in a gesture of reconciliation, called on Chester to make a few introductory remarks. Chester seized the opportunity, and what followed was a two-hour tirade against Warmoth's failure to enforce existing laws. All rights acquired so far, he thundered, were the direct consequence of Federal intervention. "We owe nothing to Louisiana but what she was compelled to give under pressure from Washington. The late black code of this State which was swept from the statute books by the National Government is an evidence of the enmity which the pro-slavery whites entertain for us; and though we endured its accumulated wrongs, accompanied by crushing indignities, without any manifestation of corresponding vindictiveness, yet the time is coming, if it has not already arrived, when humanity under the inspiration of self respect, might give hate for hate." Pinchback and others were stunned. They condemned the criticism of Warmoth and, by extension, their implied collusion in his policies, and wondered why Chester had not castigated President Grant for similar failures. Chester's warning of retaliation caused even deeper concern; it was the sort of bravado that whites could use to justify lawlessness. The *Louisianan* attempted to distance itself from such inflammatory rhetoric. If the title of Chester's speech was "Law is Accepted to be a Rule of Civil Conduct," then the editor concluded that Chester "must be an outlaw." That observation contained an unmistakable warning: outlaws against the established order were guaranteed swift and

94. Henry Clay Warmoth, *War, Politics and Reconstruction: Stormy Days in Louisiana* (New York, 1930), 131, 135; Ted Tunnell, *Crucible of Reconstruction: War, Radicalism, and Race in Louisiana, 1862–1877* (Baton Rouge, 1984), 59; New Orleans *Times*, January 4, 5, 12, 13, 17, 1872; *Louisianan*, January 4, 14, 1872; New Orleans *Picayune*, January 12, 17, 1872; New Orleans *Republican*, January 17, 21, February 9, 1872.

partial justice. Chester may have taken the hint. Soon after, he left for Harrisburg, ostensibly to recuperate, but clearly concerned for his safety.[95]

Chester was not easily intimidated either by the assault or by threats from opponents. Experiences in Liberia inured him to the cut and thrust of politics, and one gets the distinct impression that he almost relished the thought of returning. He was back in New Orleans in May as Pennsylvania's representative to the "Colored Convention." Some, like J. Sella Martin, questioned the wisdom of meeting there, especially in light of the state's political turmoil and violence. In spite of gallant efforts by the organizers and by Douglass, the convention's president, local and national disputes threatened to disrupt the proceedings on a number of occasions. It was rumored that Charles Sumner, considered the premier white champion of the cause, was seriously contemplating joining the ranks of the Liberal Republicans opposed to Grant. The issue centered on the Federal government's failure to enforce existing laws that guaranteed the rights of blacks. Grant's conservative approach, many insisted, was grist for the mill of local opponents to black advancement. Whereas Chester had argued earlier that the Federal government had been the sole protector of black freedom, Martin wondered why "even though there is a Republican majority of white men in both houses of Congress, we are not yet allowed all the rights that we are entitled to as citizens of the United States." The Federal government's tardiness only widened existing divisions in Louisiana. While Douglass called on the meeting to remain faithful to the party of Lincoln, some, like Pinchback, seemed determined to follow Sumner's lead. The fact that Warmoth, Pinchback's major political benefactor, was at loggerheads with Grant and on the verge of declaring for the Liberal Republicans, further complicated the situation. In the end, the convention managed to maintain a semblance of unity only by skirting these divisive issues. Chester played an active role at the meeting, serving on a number of important committees while at the same time avoiding becoming embroiled in the heated political disputes. When, however, the *Times* accused the convention of promoting forced social equality, Chester's racial pride would not allow him to remain silent. He submitted a series of resolutions that the convention unanimously

95. New Orleans *Republican*, February 2, 1872; *Pacific Appeal*, March 9, 1872; *Louisianan*, February 4, 1872.

adopted, opposing social equality as repugnant, condemning those whites who "preach against social equality in the day and practice it at night," and trumpeting their preference for "our ladies to any white women in the land both for their beauty and purity, which have ever remained as an ornament to the sex when beyond the control of our white fellow-citizens."[96]

Martin crossed to the Liberal Republicans in June, disillusioned with the glacial pace of reform. "The [Stephen B.] Packard corruption, conspiracy and tyranny has triumphed over the will of the colored people," he wrote Pinchback. "By keeping Republicans divided they have driven thousands from the ranks and organized a defeat. The only hope of the negro in the State rests in the Liberal Republican party. Henceforth I am one of them." Chester remained faithful, however, supporting William Pitt Kellogg, the Republican candidate for governor. The issue was not whether Republicans had abandoned blacks, or even if they were taking black support for granted, but what was the best mechanism for achieving economic and political transformation in Louisiana. Democrats, as a party, remained intransigent in their opposition to black political aspirations. Liberal Republicans, while holding out the promise of greater freedom for blacks, were nothing but a fragile coalition of disgruntled and disaffected Republicans and Democrats. Warmoth's decision to throw in his lot with the Liberal Republicans and Pinchback's late endorsement of Grant and Kellogg, in September, effected a reconciliation of sorts between contending Republican factions in New Orleans. Chester spoke at a number of meetings in support of Kellogg, but spent most of his time in the weeks leading up to the elections working for Republican candidates in Mobile, Alabama.[97]

The elections failed to resolve any outstanding issues. In the end, both the fusionist Liberal Republican/Democratic and the Republican tickets claimed victory and promptly went about establishing separate governments, the former under John McEnery, the latter led by Kellogg. On December 10, just two days before Grant recognized the Republican government, McEnery supporters led by Warmoth staged a massive public rally in New Orleans and named a committee of one hundred to petition the president and visit Washington to confer with Congress. A smaller committee spent the rest of the month in

96. *Louisianan,* April 11, 14, 18, 1872; *New National Era and Citizen,* May 2, 1872.
97. *Louisianan,* June 25, 1872; New Orleans *Republican,* November 1, 21, 1872.

Washington, meeting with Grant, Supreme Court justices, and both houses of Congress in a futile attempt to win recognition for McEnery. A congressional committee that met in January to hear accusations of voter intimidation, electoral fraud, and judicial deception did nothing to resolve the impasse. While the committee's reports denounced the actions of both factions and verified claims of voter intimidation and questionable judicial decisions, it nonetheless called for new elections under Federal supervision, something no Republican in Louisiana was willing to accept.[98]

Blacks were not disinterested onlookers during these developments. One month prior to the McEnery meeting, they formed a committee of fifteen to investigate the abridgment of black rights during the elections. The committee reported its findings in early January. Not surprisingly, it found massive fraud and intimidation of black voters. Over 34,000 blacks had been denied the vote by a series of deceptions including, *inter alia*, the destruction of registration and record books, the appointment of only Democratic commissioners of elections, and the refusal to open an adequate number of voting places. The principal purveyor of this fraud, the committee concluded unreservedly, was Warmoth, who "corruptly made a free use of his vast appointing power and joined in the machinations of wily, reckless and unscrupulous Democrats, and fostered the prejudice of the wicked, hereditary, negro-hating portion of the community."[99]

Blacks were determined not to concede any ground to their opponents in Louisiana and to challenge the legitimacy of the so-called sorehead committee in Washington. But their position was weakened by the inability to translate an electoral plurality into political power in the state. In addition, while Kellogg's victory was due to massive black support, it did not result in commensurate power or, for that matter, political preferment. Blacks did receive some important state offices, including that of lieutenant governor and superintendent of education, and a significant number were elected to both the house and the senate. For most, however, these were small rewards for their electoral majority. When Pinchback was denied his senatorial seat in Washington, suspicions of Republican insincerity increased. The die was cast when the Republican-

98. See *Senate Reports*, 42nd Cong., 3rd Sess., No. 457; New York *Daily Tribune*, December 20, 24, 25, 30, 1872.
99. New Orleans *Republican*, November 19, 1872, January 5, 1873.

controlled Senate investigation committee voted in favor of new elections.

During a visit to New Orleans in May, Senator Matt Carpenter of Wisconsin, chairman of the committee, argued for new elections in meetings with a group of blacks. In response to questions from Chester, Burch, James Ingraham, and others, Carpenter defended the committee's conclusions: "[W]e came to the conclusion that Kellogg would have been elected if there had been a fair election, but that in the way the election was in fact conducted, he was not elected, and McEnery was." But what mattered most to Chester and the others was the Federal government's inability or reluctance to protect blacks against escalating violence. It seemed absurd to call for new elections in a state where close to 5,000 Republicans, most of them black, had been slaughtered since 1865—unless the government was willing to garrison every polling station. Just a few weeks earlier, on Easter Sunday, 103 blacks had been butchered in a cold-blooded massacre by McEnery supporters in Colfax in Grant Parish. In this context, the senator's suggestion that blacks cease bringing their troubles to Congress and instead defend themselves, baffled Chester. In a speech denouncing the massacre, he lamented: "[W]hen we reflect how our blood has crimsoned nearly every parish in the State, and with the full facts of this Grant massacre before us, we solemnly ask how long, oh! Lord, holy and true, dost Thou not judge and avenge our blood on them that dwell on the earth?" The answer, resounding and apparently unequivocal, was that no amount of blacks' blood would be sufficient to appease the gods or purify the state of its racism. The fact that it occurred on the weekend Christians celebrate the crucifixion and ascendancy of Jesus Christ heightened the event's significance.[100]

In spite of repeated veiled threats of imminent black vengeance by Chester and others, black leaders in New Orleans confronted this wave of terror indirectly by putting an almost desperate effort into ensuring the survival of the Kellogg administration. Carpenter's suggestion of greater self-defense, while acceptable to most, did not,

100. New Orleans *Republican*, May 21, April 23, 1873; *Horrible Massacre in Grant Parish, Louisiana. Two Hundred Men Killed. Details of the Occurrence. Meeting of the Colored Men in New Orleans. Address and Speeches* (New Orleans, 1873), 4; Tunnell, *Crucible of Reconstruction*, 189–93; Donald E. Reynolds, "The New Orleans Riot of 1866, Reconsidered," *Louisiana History*, V (1964), 13; Melinda Meek Hennessey, "Race and Violence in Reconstruction New Orleans: The 1868 Riot," *Louisiana History*, XX (1979), 89.

Chester insisted, absolve the Federal government of its responsibility to protect black citizens. But they all knew that guarantees of Federal protection, even if forthcoming, were directly related to the state's ability to maintain a measure of political stability, and, in 1873, Louisiana was on the brink of anarchy. Caught in a vise of rising violence and the Federal government's unwillingness to act concertedly, the New Orleans group could only stake their immediate future on Kellogg. In turn, that required above all else endorsements from Grant and Congress. But northern public opinion, as Carpenter made clear, had grown weary of Louisiana politics and seemed on the verge of bringing down the plague on both Republican and fusionist houses. An extensive public campaign highlighting all the grisly details of mayhem and political machinations struck blacks like Chester as the best method for increasing Kellogg's stock. A meeting in June named Chester to a committee of ten to "place our party and race in Louisiana properly before the American people, and also to be in readiness to meet our vilifiers and persecutors at the bar of public opinion at the North and the American Congress." It was wicked and criminal, Burch told the meeting, for blacks "to sit down and leave the white Republicans to fight our political battles for us."[101]

Chester provided the delegation's philosophical underpinnings. The "car of progress," he argued, was now at full speed, taking the state from the darkness of slavery, with all its attendant evils, into the sunlight of liberty. White Louisianians, therefore, were faced with the choice of either impeding the irresistible motion of progress, in which case they would be "politically crushed," or joining forces with the black majority and working for fundamental changes. Like so many of his contemporaries, Chester subscribed to the notion that certain immutable laws governed the pace of history. Civilizations, their governments and people, like a giant wheel, rose and fell with predictable logic. Delany and Garnet, among others, found confirmation in the biblical declaration, "Ethiopia Shall Soon Stretch Forth her hand Unto God." Chester, however, located it elsewhere. While the "pursuit of knowledge and the qualities of logical perfection" were first manifested in Africa and then transmitted to Greece and Rome, all three civilizations ultimately collapsed because of their failure "to be governed by public virtue and impartial justice." Emancipation,

101. New Orleans *Republican*, June 1, 1873.

justice, and the emergence of a black majority in Louisiana following
the Civil War provided the motive force for the "car of progress."
Although the black majority had no intention of "Africanizing" the
state, the offer of cooperation could not be extended indefinitely. "[A]
union of your means with our muscle, an association of your capital
with our labor, a combination of your cultivated brains with our
brawny bodies, the time may come when under a more advanced
civilization and the inspiration of a higher degree of self-respect, the
union which we are now so anxious to cement would be rejected
through our independence of your elements of progress." While
Chester's prescription for development differed little from those of
other black leaders of the period, his insistence that the opportunities
for cooperation between the races were finite and were limited by the
speed and sincerity of white responses, set him apart from many of
his contemporaries. Either whites rode the "wave of civilization" or
risked being swamped by an advancing black majority no longer
dependent on their skills and money. The principle of majority rule
was irreducible. In Louisiana that meant black political power, yet for
Chester, that fact in no way assumed an eventual tyranny of the
majority. "Let us be like the black and white keys of a piano,
independent in their construction, but intended for combination,
where mutual reliance and association when blended together under
an accomplished execution, compass an admirable and thrilling
degree of musical perfection; so will the black and white man, equally
and impartially utilized in developing the best interests of the nation,
under the inspiration of justice, virtue and religion, attain that degree
of righteousness which exalteth a nation." Unlike Booker T. Washington's analogy of separate but equal, which eschewed political
involvement, Chester's spoke of cooperation between equals and
insisted on the competence of blacks to rule. In fact, he saw a future
in which blacks, as the majority, would assume political ascendancy
in the state.[102]

It is no wonder that Chester was skeptical of the unification plan
floated by concerned whites in spring, 1873. The unifiers, as they
were called, were shaken by the state's drift toward anarchy following the elections, and their manifesto, presented in June, exploited
the theme of cooperation, which, they insisted, was the only means

102. New Orleans *Republican*, March 26, June 1, May 24, 1873.

of returning Louisiana to some semblance of order. Behind all of this
lay the belief that the state's problems were directly attributable to
carpetbag political dominance. Its proposals, which recognized the
principles of free speech, total desegregation in public places and on
conveyances, integration in education, and thoroughly condemned
all acts of violence, therefore, were aimed at returning the reins of
political power to Louisianians. For blacks interested in the movement, however, the iron fist in the velvet glove was political control.
Here the manifesto was less forthright. Given the "numerical equality
between the white and colored elements of our population," it stated,
"we shall advocate an equal distribution of the offices of trust and
emolument in our State, demanding as the only conditions of our
suffrage, honesty, diligence and ability." Black supporters of the plan,
particularly those anxious to eliminate carpetbagger influences, actively trumpeted the cause. James Lewis, New Orleans' administrator
of public improvements, for example, thought that Democrats involved were sincere and anxious to rally the people "to the support
and revival of its drooping resources."[103] Many blacks were distinctly
uncomfortable with this newfound willingness to accept the principle
of equality. More to the point, this was a predominantly New Orleans
movement, with little or no support in the hinterland. In fact, some
white opponents outside the capital saw the handiwork of the devil
and the socialists in this "repulsive commingling of antagonistic
races." Chester would have nothing to do with it. The issue, he
insisted, remained one of political control. Responding to the manifesto, he told a reporter: "Suppose we should join in the new
movement, what then? Next year they might give us a majority of the
Congressmen. That would be a good bait. At the next gubernatorial
election one of their number would lead the ticket for Governor; we
would have the Lieut. Governor, and so on. At the next state election
they would control the registration, which means the control of the
State, and if there is a colored man in Louisiana who imagines he
would get a nomination or secure his election when they are in
power, he is either an ass or a fool." No doubt, as a northerner,
Chester was reacting in part to the movement's antipathy toward
carpetbaggers. But he also questioned their sincerity, insisting that

103. T. Harry Williams, "The Louisiana Unification Movement of 1873," *Journal of
Southern History*, XI (1945), 360–61, 363–64.

the offer of cooperation was nothing more than "a device to influence Northern opinion."[104]

The speed with which the movement collapsed, in late summer, 1873, confirmed Chester's suspicions. Events and attitudes militated against success because, as Chester observed, whites were generally unwilling to forget the past and look to the future. Meaningful and lasting change would occur only "when they . . . cease in their efforts to govern by means of their color, rather than by their merits; when they . . . not merely tolerate but recognize the rights and citizenship of all men, irrespective of color, and when mankind shall be known, respected and honored for patriotism and virtue." Few questioned the wisdom of this observation, but it was a rare reformer indeed who was willing to act upon its principles.[105]

The delegation left the scene of "Machiavellian complication, commotion, sedition and massacre" in late July, for a two-and-one-half-month whirlwind tour of the Northeast, Maryland, Kentucky, and Missouri. All the reports suggest that Chester was the principal spokesman, providing the most thorough analysis of conditions in Louisiana since 1865. The villain of the piece, he told a New York meeting, was Warmoth, a man in whom blacks had placed considerable trust, but who, as soon as he assumed power, ignored his constituents in a quest for absolute power. The delegation's objective was not to defend Kellogg, who all impartial observers agreed was the lawfully elected governor, but to protect the right of Louisianians to elect the government of their choice. That right had been nearly usurped by the fraudulent practices of the Warmoth machine through the intimidation of voters, stuffing of ballot boxes, and encouraging supporters to vote "early and often." Only intervention by the courts, enjoining the returns, prevented Warmoth and his supporters from gaining control. In this atmosphere, it was the height of naïveté for anyone to assume that blacks would voluntarily relinquish gains made, or enter into coalitions with those who only months earlier were promoting a return to the old order. "We have persistently refused to entrust our old oppressors with the control of public affairs, unless they become converted to the gospel of freedom; and if they think they can defraud us, when we are in the majority, they

104. New Orleans *Republican*, July, 23, August 13, 1873.
105. New Orleans *Republican*, September 29, 1873.

little know our sagacity or the inflexibility of our purpose." The message was received enthusiastically by the large meetings they addressed, but, not surprisingly, was rejected contemptuously by Democrats. One disgruntled Democrat wrote that members of the delegation were to a man Warmoth's co-conspirators until he fell from favor. And in Harrisburg the *Patriot* gleefully reminded Chester of that bloody day in New Orleans when there was "a formidable display of razors and pistols," and wondered if he ever turned his back on Republicans like Pinchback.[106]

By the time the delegation reached Louisville, Kentucky, Chester was ill and confined to bed. For all the venom of northern Democrats, it appeared that the delegation had recorded some successes. There were numerous resolutions of support from both black and white Republicans for Kellogg. Yet one gets the distinct impression that throughout the trip the delegation's litany of Democratic depredations and Republican innocence strained credulity. While partisans rushed to their defense, there were many who had grown weary of all the violence and charges of corruption, and were interested only in a return to order. That attitude, which probably represented the views of the majority of northern Republicans, placed additional burdens on Louisiana blacks. Reversing this skepticism of Louisiana's future required above all else the unchallenged assertion of power by Kellogg and control of violence and corruption, neither of which seemed imminent. But blacks had not gotten this far to unceremoniously abandon the field to the enemies of progress. Soon after the delegation's return, a series of meetings was organized to report on the mission and to elect two new delegations; one to attend a National Colored Men's Convention in Washington, and the other, composed of blacks and whites, to lobby Congress during its investigation of political turmoil in the state. But true to form, the meeting in November almost degenerated into a free-for-all between representatives from rural parishes and those from New Orleans, over the composition of the delegation to lobby Congress. Speaking for the rural delegates, Burch chastised New Orleanians for their un-

106. New Orleans *Republican*, July 27, August 8, 12, 13, 21, 26, 28, 30, September 7, 29, October 5, 19, 1873; Harrisburg *Telegraph*, July 7, August 1, September 25, 1873; Newark *Daily Advertiser*, September 4, 1873; New York *Times*, September 10, 1873; New York *Herald*, September 10, 1873; Pittsburgh *Evening Telegraph*, October 2, 1873; New Orleans *Picayune*, September 12, 1873; Harrisburg *Patriot*, September 8, 1873.

disguised attempts to dominate the proceedings. "Some of those composing a faction here would rather rule in Hell than serve in Heaven. They opposed and scoffed at the country and if it were not for the votes of the country for Kellogg those men couldn't have a bone to pick." When he threatened to withdraw, a resolution was offered that gave Lieutenant Governor Antoine, president of the meeting, power to select members of the delegation. Antoine moved quickly to defuse tensions by naming slates of delegates and alternates made up of whites and blacks, New Orleanians and rural representatives.[107]

In the attempt to address Burch's demand for equitable representation, Chester was placed on the list of alternates. There is no way of knowing how he reacted to this compromise. Although he kept his own counsel, there is no doubt that the exclusion, coming so soon after the recent tour, rankled. But Chester could take solace from the fact that his talents were needed elsewhere in the city. He was, without doubt, a recognized figure among local lawyers. Few if any of his contemporaries, white or black, could match his legal education, since most acquired their training as apprentices in the offices of practicing lawyers. Sometime in 1873, Chester became the first black to be admitted to the Louisiana bar.[108] The courtroom provided him with a forum in which he could demonstrate his extensive forensic skills, and, like Moncure D. Conway at the Old Bailey, many observers in New Orleans were favorably impressed. The editor of the *Republican*, for instance, took the unusual step of publishing verbatim Chester's closing remarks to the jury at the murder trial of Beauregard Jamison, Richard Brown, and Robert West. The summation, the editor observed, was ample "evidence of an education which should be the envy and emulation of every member of the bar." Chester devoted a fair amount of time defending poor black clients, like Jamison, Brown, and West, who, he consistently reiterated, were discriminated against by the system. "That they are poor is their misfortune; that they have been accused of this crime is not their fault, and the responsibility of being black is assumed by Him who created them after His own image; and it would not only be a

107. New Orleans *Republican*, October 7, 10, November 18, 19, 20, 1873.
108. New Orleans *Republican*, May 4, 1873; *Soards New Orleans City Directory for 1874* (New Orleans, 1874).

violation of your oaths, if you permitted either of these circumstances to influence your judgement against the accused, but it would be an everlasting disgrace upon the administration of public justice in Louisiana." Chester compiled an impressive record of victories during this period. In the case of Joseph Macmillan, accused of murdering Ulysses Jacob, a planter in St. John the Baptist Parish, for instance, Chester appealed against a verdict of guilty without capital punishment and moved for a new trial, which was granted. The new jury found Macmillan innocent.[109]

But Chester was also a central figure in legal disputes involving important constitutional issues. If virtue and impartial justice were the hallmarks of advanced civilizations, as Chester maintained, then there were many whites in Louisiana who were determined to impede the "car of progress" by denying blacks their rights. Ever since the passage of anti-discrimination accommodation laws in 1869, blacks in New Orleans had sued for the right to be served or accommodated in public places. Chester was an active participant in many of the fourteen suits brought by blacks between 1869 and 1875. Corporations that discriminate against blacks, he had told a meeting of the Louisiana Progressive Club on his first visit to New Orleans, should be taught a "judicial lesson that will put an end to the infamous treatment to which we are now subjected." When Charles Lewis was denied a glass of soda water at Hugh McCloskey's soda shop, he sued, claiming damages of $500, and hired Chester to argue his case. Such denials, Chester remarked, which violated rights guaranteed by both federal and state constitutions, and by the organic law of the state, flew in the face of the "wisdom and economy of God's government" and deliberately impeded the state's progress toward civilization. It was unacceptable, in these circumstances, to claim, as McCloskey did, that custom was the arbiter of policy. "It is fatal to liberty," Chester continued, "when the color of a man's skin, deepened by the sun of heaven in its fructifying influence in the land of their fathers, ostracizes him by violation of organic law, from the public places, and outlaws him in public estimation." Lewis won, as did William Smith and Emily Lobre, both of whom brought similar suits against soda shop proprietors. Lobre had won an earlier

109. New Orleans *Republican*, May 4, December 19, 1873, January 25, 1874; *Louisianan*, May 23, 29, 1875.

judgment for $250 in a suit against Loper, a confectioner, for denying her a glass of soda. Smith was not denied service, but was charged $1 for a glass of soda that normally sold for $0.05.[110]

The struggle to desegregate public places was unrelenting, and while there were some successes, foes of integration remained implacable. Although these litigations affected the lives of only a small group of the city's black elite, Chester saw them as one facet of a larger effort to eliminate the vestiges of the old order. In this he was largely correct, for white intransigence showed little sign of abating during Kellogg's administration; if anything, it reached new heights of virulence. There were those, both Republicans and Democrats, who were convinced that Kellogg's authority rested solely on the presence of Federal troops and the hated state militia. Of the two the former was clearly more important to Kellogg's survival, yet it is hatred of the latter, known derisively as the Negro State Militia, that provided grist for the governor's opponents' mills.

Kellogg commissioned Chester a brigadier general in the 4th Brigade, 1st Division, of the state militia, in May, 1873. His first posting, however, was to the 1st Brigade, where he filled in intermittently until November for A. E. Barber, then on a leave of absence. The *Republican* hailed the appointment, praising Kellogg for "bringing about him in trustworthy positions men of ability and experience." Under normal circumstances, Chester's captaincy in the Pennsylvania company might have qualified him for the position, but the militia was in such deep trouble in 1873 that one wonders why Chester accepted the post. It was clearly a political appointment; in fact, everything about this and other state militias smacked of politics. They were formed by Republicans to fill the void left by departing Federal troops following the formal reentry of southern states into the Union. In the days after Appomattox, these states had mustered in all-white militias with the express purpose of denying freedmen their rights and ensuring the political ascendancy of the old order. Not surprisingly, these became early casualties of Reconstruction. Only when Republican governments were firmly entrenched were states again permitted to organize militias. The party in power had always considered militias the necessary guardians of political survival.

110. John Blassingame, *Black New Orleans 1860–1880* (Chicago, 1973), 182–86; *Louisianan*, September 28, 1871, April 3, 1875; New Orleans *Republican*, May 24, June 25, 1874.

Chester was appointed brigadier general of the Louisiana State Militia in 1873.

Courtesy of Yvonne Martin

Warmoth had organized the militia in June, 1870, supported by an appropriation of $100,000 from the legislature, and in an astute gesture of reconciliation had placed General James Longstreet, the Confederate war hero, in command. The initial force consisted of an equal number of whites and blacks, supplemented by the old metropolitan police. But that kind of equitable racial balance impressed few of the governor's opponents. James Gordon Bennett, editor of the New York *Herald*, venting all the spleen for which he was famous, spoke for the opponents of the militia: "The fact is inevitable that bloodshed will follow. Reconstructed governments are bad enough with negro legislators, negro magistrates, negro police, and negro Commissioners of Education and other matters; but when armed negroes appear as military forces to keep white men in order . . . the spirit . . . must revolt."[111]

Unfortunately for Kellogg, when the expected revolt occurred in September, 1874, the militia was totally unprepared to handle it. Adjutant General Henry Street had reported earlier on a marked improvement in morale, arms, and uniforms, but the militia was beset with problems. Promised appropriations rarely materialized, the men were not paid promptly, and the officer corps was by and large unqualified. "A great obstruction and hinderance to the success of our military organization," Street observed, "has been heretofore and previously experienced in consequence of the appointment and election of officers in the State militia of persons entirely incompetent and unfit for such a position." His solution, which required staff officers to pass tests conducted by qualified examining boards, seemed reasonable. But these were not reasonable times, nor were the politics of Louisiana susceptible to balanced suggestions for reform. One year later, Street was still trying to persuade the administration to adopt his suggestions. "I regret to say that the encouragement that I had received previous to making my last annual report, of reorganizing a good and efficient division of National Guard during the past year, has been entirely overthrown." By then, organized armed opposition had challenged Kellogg and found his first line of defense wanting. There were few criticisms of Chester's brigades, at least in Street's reports. Both Barber's 1st and Chester's 4th seemed to function capably; others, however, left a great deal to be desired. Even supporters of the administration, like the *Republican*, questioned the utility and effectiveness of the militia, and doubted that Street could "muster militiamen enough to suppress a mob of one hundred armed men without calling on the police or U.S. troops."[112]

111. New Orleans *Republican*, June 1, 1873; "Annual Report of the Adjutant General of the State of Louisiana, 1873" (Typescript in Hill Memorial Library, Louisiana State University, Baton Rouge); "Historical Militia Data on Louisiana Militia, January 5, 1872 to December 3, 1873" (WPA Typescript, 1938, in Hill Memorial Library); Otis A. Singletary, *Negro Militia and Reconstruction* (Austin, 1957), 13–15, 67, 70, quotation on 30–31.

112. "Annual Report of the Adjutant General of the State of Louisiana, 1873"; "Annual Report of the Adjutant General of the State of Louisiana, 1874" (Typescript in Hill Memorial Library); New Orleans *Republican*, March 27, April 28, 29, 30, May 1, 2, 1874.

The test soon came. In late June, the New Orleans *Picayune* published a virulent article replete with the customary phobias of slaveholders. It was rumored that the militia was planning, under cover of the July 4 celebrations, to enter all those businesses that denied service to blacks and demand that they be served. If refused, these "outrageous communes" planned to "kill the proprietor and as many white men as possible, and then, supported by the other colored people who would rally to their support, and, as was expressed, take it for themselves, kill all the men and *keep all the women*." Such responses were typical of the hysteria that greeted black court challenges to social inequities. The *Picayune*'s call to vigilance was answered a few days later with the formation of the White League in the city, committed to the restoration of a white order. Rumors of imminent clashes between Leaguers and the militia persisted throughout the summer. The clash finally came late in the afternoon of September 14 in a short, bloody encounter. By the time the militia was forced to retreat, and Kellogg to take refuge in the Customs House, an estimated 27 were dead and 104 wounded. A triumphant public meeting selected a committee to call on Kellogg to resign, but the governor spurned the overture. Angered, the committee called on whites to make the city an armed camp and to expel Kellogg and his hirelings. With forces loyal to Kellogg bottled up in the St. Louis Hotel, the Third Precinct Station, and the Customs House, the rebels were in control of the city. The Third Precinct Station fell the following day, and with the occupation of the State House, the *Picayune* joyously proclaimed the end of the Kellogg regime. But their celebrations were premature. Responding to calls for assistance from Kellogg, President Grant issued a proclamation calling on the Leaguers to disperse and ordering Federal troops to take control of the capital. Kellogg was back in control five days after that assault.[113]

Fortunately for Chester, he was away in Harrisburg when the attack occurred. He returned only after Federal troops had restored order. Although he was critical of Kellogg's hasty and unceremonious retreat to the Customs House, which he believed demoralized the

113. New Orleans *Picayune* quoted in Stuart Omer Landry, *The Battle of Liberty Place: The Overthrow of Carpet-Bag Rule in New Orleans, September 14, 1874* (New Orleans, 1955), 70, 57; New Orleans *Republican*, August 21, 1874; New Orleans *Picayune*, September 22, 1874; Singletary, *Negro Militia*, 66, 79.

militia, Chester remained a staunch supporter of the governor and retained his post until 1876 when the Democrats assumed power. This was the militia's only major encounter during Reconstruction, and its miserable performance confirmed Street's worst fears. For the next two years, Chester's brigade was limited to guard duty as Federal troops took responsibility for maintaining order in the capital.[114] Both the September assault and continued League depredations in New Orleans and other parts of the state ultimately undermined blacks' confidence in the Kellogg administration and raised considerable doubts about continued Federal support. But what were blacks to do? In a situation in which Republicans cynically waved the "bloody shirt" and welcomed their votes, yet made few concessions, and in which Democrats were for the most part opposed to equal black participation, the choices were limited. One could join the Liberal Republicans as Martin had in 1872, with results that were very discouraging, or follow the example of some northern blacks and cross over to the Democrats. But neither alternative held out much hope in a state where Liberal Republicans had been decimated and where Democrats and White Leaguers were synonymous. In such a setting, political independence seemed an empty gesture. The dilemma was debilitating.

In the wake of the September assault, a group of prominent blacks issued a public address on union, peace, and reconciliation, which embodied, in the starkest terms possible, the problems they faced. The group, which surprisingly included Chester, placed their hopes almost exclusively on the numerical superiority of the black electorate. Majority rule in a democratic society, they declared, was a shield against frauds, massacres, and armed attacks. But appeals to the principles of democracy in such circumstances struck even the most uninformed observer as hollow. The address chastised Kellogg for his failure to include blacks in decision making: "There is a species of mystery, so far as we are concerned, about the plans of campaign and the policy of the State Administration, which denies to every colored man in this commonwealth, party and government." Yet, in the end, they reaffirmed an abiding commitment to the national party. "Our homes may be destroyed, our school houses wrapt in flames, our churches desecrated, and our people massacred, but as long as the

114. New Orleans *Picayune*, September 22, 1874; Singletary, *Negro Militia*, 80.

national Republican party shall be as true to our liberties in the future as it has been in the past, we shall neither be seduced nor coerced from our partizan fealty." Reiterations of support for the party, which in some sections of the address bordered on the obsequious, were in direct proportion to a lack of perceived alternatives. "We have been wronged, outraged and massacred by the whites, without cause or provocation, until the air is heavy with our sighs and the waters of Louisiana are reddened with our blood," they concluded with customary hyperbole, "but as citizens, we cannot retaliate, and as Christians we bear our afflictions as becomes our faith." When St. F. Cassanave wondered why blacks could not declare themselves to be "Independent Republicans," he was roundly denounced.[115]

While some found the committee's counsel acceptably moderate and predicted that sooner or later blacks would "obtain that important share in the management of party interests to which their worth and intelligence, as well as their race's influence entitled them," Chester was too hardened a politician to be that sanguine about the future.[116] Yet he could not sever his ties with the Kellogg administration. In spite of all Kellogg's shortcomings, he had appointed a number of blacks, including Chester, to important offices, more, by comparison, than Republican administrations in his home state. And Chester continued to be the recipient of Kellogg's political largesse. In early 1875 he was appointed superintendent of public education for the First Division, to fill the unexpired term of P. M. Williams. The division was made up of parishes to the southeast, north, and northeast of New Orleans, covering an area from Baton Rouge southeast to the Gulf of Mexico. Despite a cut in appropriations of close to one-third in 1875, William G. Brown, the state superintendent of public education and a leader in black New Orleans society, reported substantial improvements in the system. But public education in Louisiana was in a sorry state. Its teachers were poorly paid, and the number of superintendents was abysmally low—6 compared to 65 in Mississippi, 114 in Missouri, and 102 in Illinois—supervising 56 school boards, 1,032 schools, and 74,876 students over an area of 40,000 square miles. Williams faced similar problems in the First Division. When Chester took over, he was forced to defer appoint-

115. *Louisianan*, October 3, 1874; New Orleans *Republican*, October 9, 28, 29, 30, 1874.
116. New Orleans *Republican*, October 10, 1874.

ments of teachers and even to recommend to several school boards the closing of schools until conditions improved. That was not an easy decision for someone who put such emphasis on education's potential to elevate the backward. "Mind in the majesty of its cultivated power, utilizes the elements, quickens progress, and advances science. The great object of education is to inspire man with thought and communities with intelligence, so that each member of society may have an appreciable conception of duties and responsibilities." If this were so, Chester wondered why the state appropriated more to punishing ignorance and suppressing crime than fostering education.[117]

One year after his appointment to the First Division, Chester was named superintendent of the Fifth Division with offices in Delta, Madison Parish. The appointment apparently met with some local resistance, which as late as July had not been appeased and which threatened to lead to his ouster. But Jacque Gla, the black state senator from East Carroll Parish, came to Chester's defense. The superintendent's opponents, Gla insisted, were motivated solely by a desire to remove the only black superintendent on the board. They could find no other cause, for Chester managed his office "with more propriety and regularity than any of his predecessors, and his appointment is looked to with pride by the colored people all over his district." Gla's support was enough to allay any doubts Brown might have harbored about Chester's performance. Chester retained the position until the end of Kellogg's term of office.[118]

The defeat of the Republicans in 1876, and the "compromise" of 1877 that returned the Democrats to power, brought to an end Chester's involvement in state government. His warnings about the consequences of a Republican defeat now were confirmed. It is ironic that those, like Chester, who, in the wake of the 1874 slaughter, had

117. *Louisianan*, March 13, 6, 1875; New Orleans *Republican*, May 11, 1875; *Annual Report of the State Superintendent of Public Education, William G. Brown, to the General Assembly of Louisiana, for the Year 1875* (New Orleans, 1876), 4, 6, 29–31, 36, 94–95, 237, 259; Chester to M. C. Cole, New Orleans, September 25, 1875, in State Board of Education Correspondence, 1863–1879, Louisiana State Archives, Baton Rouge.

118. New Orleans *Republican*, April 29, May 9, August 29, 1876; Jacque Gla to William G. Brown, July 7, 1876, in William P. Kellogg Papers, Hill Memorial Library; T. A. Routon to M. C. Cole, July 13, 1876, in State Board of Education Correspondence, 1863–1879.

reaffirmed their "partizan fealty" to the national Republican party, three years later could do nothing to forestall the party's undignified abandonment of Reconstruction. Not that blacks were taken totally by surprise, for the Senate's refusal to seat Pinchback, its unusual nonpartisan report on electoral fraud, and general northern disdain for Louisiana politics were indicators of things to come. Yet Chester dared to hope that in this state governed by Republicans, where blacks held an electoral majority, and which produced some of the most gifted and educated blacks, he could play a role in molding a future in which talent, freed finally from the restraints of racism, would flourish. But he had invested too much in New Orleans to abandon it now that it had come under Democratic control. Nor could he think of returning to Liberia, for sophisticated New Orleans with its black elite was too much to his liking. He relied instead on periodic extended retreats to Harrisburg.

With the loss of state appointments, Chester turned to his Harrisburg connections, particularly the Camerons, in search of a Federal position. He was named U.S. Commissioner for New Orleans in late 1878 and held the position for roughly two years. Nothing is known of his activities as a commissioner. A year later, he was appointed special assistant to the U.S. Attorney for the Eastern District of Texas, with responsibilities to investigate "grave offenses against the law." Because of the sensitive nature of the job, and the very real chance of violence, it was recommended that he assume a fictitious name. After reporting for duty in Galveston, Chester was sent to Texarkana to investigate voter fraud and violence. But Chester was dismissed before he completed his assignment. There were disputes over Washington's refusal to pay some of his expenses. There was also dissatisfaction with his reports from the field. His first, an extensive coverage of events, was rejected as unsatisfactory and illegible, and he was informed, rather arrogantly, that "a report of your duties should be a plain, brief statement of the facts. There is no one here who has the time to read a long rambling letter like this." When subsequent reimbursement claims for expenses were signed so illegibly that they could not be read by the accounting officer, and were not supported by appropriate vouchers, Chester was dismissed. The grounds for dismissal appear trivial, considering the reasons for the appointment and the gravity of the situation in Texas. At a time when

blacks were being intimidated and laws openly defied, poor penmanship and sloppy accounting should have been the least of the
attorney general's concerns.[119]

The Texas experience of violence and death was replicated
throughout the South in the 1870s. Redemption had been achieved by
means of naked violence and intimidation. While it is impossible to
determine with any accuracy the exact number of blacks killed in
Louisiana since 1865—some put the total as high as six thousand—
there is no doubt that scores had lost their lives every year since the
surrender of the Confederacy. The formation of the White League in
1874 gave organizational legitimacy to these acts. Blacks resisted
where they could, refusing to give ground in the face of indiscriminate attacks. As early as 1870, a group of mustered soldiers led by
Henry Adams had formed an organization of laborers in Shreveport
to investigate the condition of blacks in the South. Its membership
increased dramatically in the following years, reflecting a growing
disillusionment with conditions in the state. By the end of 1875, they
were discussing the merits of emigrating to either Liberia or other
parts of the country. Warnings of large-scale emigration, and its
consequences for the state's economy, were generally dismissed as
the railings of misguided and politically ambitious black leaders.
Following the Colfax massacre, Pinchback had appealed to whites to
turn from violence and allow blacks the free expression of their
constitutional rights or face either a "frightful exodus of colored
people to other localities" or the establishment of a "military government." Most Republicans agreed. There was a pressing need to
reconcile white capital and black labor if the state's agricultural
economy was to recover its antebellum vibrancy. Employing an
interesting labor theory of value, the *Republican* argued that "it is
labor that, like the blood, flows through, strengthens and animates
the industrial system." The lost black labor could not be replaced
immediately by an infusion of European immigrants who were not
inclined to settle in a state notorious for its violence. The solution, the

119. *Soards New Orleans City Directory for 1879* (New Orleans, 1879); *Louisianan*,
December 14, 21, 1878, August 9, 1879; U.S. General Accounting Office, warrants 2407,
536, 1827, Record Group 217, Benjamin H. Brewster to Chester, December 22, 1882,
Brewster to Edward Guthridge, December 27, 1882, Instruction Book, Vol. M, Cameron
to Chester, January 3, 30, February 24, 1883, Chester to Cameron, January 26, March 9,
1883, Records of the General Agent, 60, Brewster to Chester, March 8, 10, 29, 1883,
Instruction Book, Vol. N, all in U.S. Department of Justice, National Archives.

editor concluded, was a strong government willing and able to protect blacks.[120]

Both the Warmoth and Kellogg administrations were incapable of providing that protection. The alternative under these conditions, some insisted, was emigration. As a result, interest in Liberian emigration showed a marked increase in 1877. One expedition sailed in April, 1878, carrying 206 emigrants. But most black Louisianians interested in emigration opted for Kansas as their future home. By March, 1879, an estimated 10,000 had joined the exodus of southern black labor to Kansas. The following month, a state convention of blacks met in New Orleans to consider the issue of emigration. As in the past, the issue generated heated disputes between proponents and opponents. Given his long-standing interest in emigration, it is not surprising that Chester became an active supporter of the movement. Others, like Pinchback, worried that the movement would result in the destruction of an important economic and political base. Whereas in the past he had called for strong government protection, now he appealed directly to white landowners. "Do away with the country store," his newspaper editorialized just before the convention, "encourage thrift and economy in the laborers, not in a missionary and philanthropic spirit, but as a matter of sound policy. Sell land to such of the laborers who are most industrious and give promise of being successful planters." When J. D. Kennedy, editor of the *Louisianan*, rose to oppose resolutions encouraging emigration, he was roundly denounced. Pinchback came to his defense, accusing pro-emigrationists of demagoguery, but could do little to stem the tide. Chester harbored none of Pinchback's and Kennedy's concerns about the movement. A people once denied political rights and economic opportunities, he insisted, should seek their fortune elsewhere. He had been one of the convention's organizers and played a prominent role throughout the meeting, fending off opponents and serving on most of the major committees. He served, for instance, on the Business Committee, chaired by George T. Ruby, which prepared the convention's "Address" and "Appeal." Since blacks were threatened with peonage by whites determined to reduce "the laborer and his interests to the minimum of advantages as freemen, and to

120. Nell Irvin Painter, *Exodusters: Black Migration to Kansas After Reconstruction* (New York, 1976), 76, 82–83; New Orleans *Republican*, September 23, 1872, April 21, 24, October 1, 1873; *Horrible Massacre in Grant Parish, Louisiana*, 16.

absolutely none as citizens," the exodus was a "flight from present sufferings and the wrongs to come," the "Address" declared in its endorsement of emigration. It called on the Exodusters to effect an efficient organization that would facilitate their departure, recommended going out in companies, and called for a pattern of emigration from those areas with a history of violence—first from bulldozed areas, then from sugar-growing parishes. The convention concluded its deliberations by appointing a committee on emigration and relief.[121]

The committee had little opportunity to function. The massive movement of black labor, caught up in what Nell Painter calls the "Kansas fever idea," threatened the state's economy and therefore had to be curtailed. Planter interests responded by calling a convention in Vicksburg in May, and invited blacks to attend. In fact, David Young, the black state senator from Concordia, had tried unsuccessfully to persuade the New Orleans convention to send a delegation to Vicksburg. Although he was denounced by the convention for endorsing the Vicksburg meeting, Young almost single-handedly undermined the movement in Concordia, where he dissuaded an estimated thirteen thousand blacks from becoming Exodusters. The following year the Democrats repaid his support by expelling him from the legislature. The Vicksburg meeting was just one expression of white landowners' opposition to the Exodus. The *Picayune* saw the hand of disgruntled black politicians at work in the movement. Most whites, it claimed, now recognized the rights guaranteed blacks during Reconstruction. "Protection in industry and the enjoyment of educational advantages and religious liberty are facts conceded. There is no agricultural peasantry in all the wide world so highly blessed in those particulars." Calls for emigration, therefore, were actuated by a desire for black supremacy, something that would never be tolerated in Louisiana. "The experiment has been tried, and the record of its failure is the foulest and bloodiest chapter in the history of the State." Those who claimed that blacks were leaving because of violence were being disingenuous and were ignorant of the fact that the movement of labor has historically been governed by the simple law of supply and demand. The Exodus was fueled by nothing more than "the commercial and industrial depression of the last five years." When

121. *Louisianan,* April 5, 26, 1879; New Orleans *Picayune,* April 18, 19, 20, 22, 1879; Painter, *Exodusters,* 89–93.

the New Orleans meeting chronicled the history of violence against blacks, the *Picayune* resorted to *ad hominem* attacks on its leaders. "We could say, and we could say with truth, that there never has been a prominent negro killed in this State for so-called political causes who was not a scoundrel by profession and by practice. If there is an exception to this rule, let him be named. We challenge the Republican party of the country to produce the example. We have already said that during the reign of negroism, and carpet-baggery in this State, there never was a negro official, from high or low, from first to last, that did not sell his public functions for money."[122]

The *Picayune* reserved most of its vitriol for Chester, "whose chief claim to distinction rests on the incidents of a European tour, during which he was, as he alleges, the favorite partner of Grand Duchesses and Princesses in the mazy intricacies of the quadrille or the dreamy circles of the waltz." The sexual innuendos were transparent. Chester, the editor continued, was a frustrated politician unable to translate "his tender alliances with the royal white trash of the Old World" into political power in Louisiana. Chester denounced the "crabbed uncharitableness" of the editorial and challenged the *Picayune* to furnish an instance in which he sold his "public functions for money." While understandably concerned to maintain his reputation, Chester entirely missed the point of the editorial. Nothing he could have said would have influenced those of the *Picayune*'s persuasion; Louisianians, as far as they were concerned, would never accept black political parity. History—nature, even—had consigned blacks to a position of permanent inferiority. Given the circumstances, Chester would have been well advised to remain silent, for a defense of his personal integrity only opened the way for the editor to substantiate his general claims. The error in this particular, he chortled, was the exception that proved the rule. "We are glad to give him [Chester] the full benefit of his disclaimer. He has been an honest negro official. Very well, where is the next one." The issue for the *Picayune* was larger than trivia concerning minor players like Chester; it had to do with control of the state's economic and political apparatus, which demanded both defeating the Republican party and stemming the flow of black labor. The first had been attained in 1876; the second, in

122. Painter, *Exodusters*, 216, 220; William Ivy Hair, *Bourbonism and Agrarian Protest: Louisiana Politics, 1877–1900* (Baton Rouge, 1969), 96; New Orleans *Picayune*, April 19, 23, 24, 25, 1879.

the weeks following the New Orleans convention. The Exodus showed signs of abating in May, because of murder, boat captains' refusing to pick up blacks waiting on the banks of the Mississippi and Red rivers for transportation to St. Louis, and starvation among migrants stranded along the rivers.[123]

While the political ascendancy of the Democrats, with all its consequences for blacks in the state, deeply distressed Chester, he could not bring himself to sever all ties with the South. In spite of its history of violence and bloodshed, the South not the North, he observed years later, was the place "where the triumph of negro manhood and prosperity under the material elements of life will be most successful." His own experience in Louisiana should have challenged this conviction. That it did not could be attributed to his lifelong ambition to create a sanctuary where blacks could develop their talents, an ambition that sometimes distorted Chester's perceptions of reality. He had, in effect, transferred the emigrant's vision from Liberia to the South. Echoing earlier views about Liberia, Chester informed a Harrisburg journalist that he "would rather live in the South with the pleasant intercourse between whites and blacks than in the North, for the Southern men are not afraid of the color rubbing off. They are in all matters outside of politics just and generous to the blacks."[124]

Yet Chester spent an inordinate amount of time away from New Orleans at the comfortable home of his mother. Harrisburg held an additional appeal after 1879. He had recently married, and his bride, Florence Johnson, lived part of the time with her mother-in-law. Twenty-one years Chester's junior, Florence was born in Natchez, Mississippi, and had moved to New Orleans after the war. She attended Straight University in the early 1870s, graduating with the first class in 1875. Following graduation she taught school in Tangipahoa Parish, one of the districts under Chester's superintendency. Her school was described as "among the most flourishing" in the division, the result of her dedication and commitment. Marriage in no way affected her determination to pursue a career in teaching. She attended Peabody Normal School and took courses at Tuskegee Institute and Cheyney State Teachers' College. When she retired in

123. New Orleans *Picayune*, April 24, 25, 1879; Painter, *Exodusters*, 190.
124. Harrisburg *Patriot*, September 13, 1892.

1927, Johnson had been a teacher and school principal for almost fifty years. Fifteen years after her death in 1944, the Orleans Parish School Board dedicated an elementary school for blacks in her honor.[125]

In the years after his marriage, Chester was a regular commuter between Harrisburg, New Orleans, and Delta, where he lived briefly between 1881 and 1882. The *Louisianan* pleaded with him on many occasions to come home from the "regions of bliss," where he lingered too long.[126] But more than just conjugal attraction was responsible for Chester's constant movement; necessity played an important part. Once he had been dismissed from his Federal post in March, 1883, Chester had to rely almost exclusively on income from his law practice, and a successful practice required considerable travel. It also required a clientele of means. In spite of a full docket of cases in Louisiana, Washington, D.C., and Pennsylvania, Chester's clients were generally black and poor.[127]

This might explain why he accepted the presidency of the North Carolina "Wilmington, Wrightsville and Onslow Railroad" in January, 1884. The company, owned by blacks, was chartered in 1883 after acquiring the rights to construct a line between the three towns. The charter was granted by the state legislature in 1869 and later transferred to the company, with the provision that construction commence within one year. Construction did begin within the allotted time, but was suspended because of insufficient capital. Although one-quarter of an estimated capital stock of $100,000 had already been subscribed, the company was unable to attract enough shareholders. Chester limited his duties almost exclusively to selling stock. Soon after his appointment, he set out on an extensive tour of the Northeast and the Midwest. His message was a call to racial solidarity and self-reliance, in keeping with his commitment to race pride and self-respect, though he did encourage whites to support the company. The Board of Bishops of the AME church endorsed the company's plan as "conducive to a practical solution of the negro problem on this continent" and purchased a number of shares. The

125. New Orleans Health Department, "Register of Marriages as Kept by the Recorder of Births, Marriages and Deaths," New Orleans Public Library; *Louisianan*, September 6, 1879; Robert Meyer, Jr., *Names Over New Orleans Public Schools* (New Orleans, 1975), 38; New Orleans *Times-Picayune*, December 18, 1959.

126. *Louisianan*, April 10, 17, 24, 1880, January 22, August 6, 1881.

127. Harrisburg *Patriot*, November 25, 27, 29, 1882.

"Inter-State Convention of Colored Men of the Northern States," meeting in Pittsburgh, momentarily papered over its differences to unanimously endorse the railroad, hailing it as "a new departure fraught with incalculable results, in developing business capacity and industrial pursuits worthy of favorable consideration, and identifying us with the material interests and important industries of the country."[128]

While this was indeed the first railroad project undertaken by blacks—a worthy and important event, according to Douglass—and while Chester praised it as the "first great organized effort of colored men," enthusiasm and pride were not enough to overcome the many obstacles to construction. A project of this nature required substantial capital outlays. Bishops of the AME church and Douglass could subscribe, but $25 shares were, by and large, well beyond the means of most blacks. White financial support, therefore, was critical, but there is no evidence that such support was forthcoming. In fact, whites in Wilmington and Onslow were actively promoting competing companies. Most agreed that a railroad linking the three towns would have a positive impact on the local economy, facilitating the transportation of farm produce and opening vital links to Virginia and other states to the north. It was something, a local paper observed, that "Wilmington *must have*, and the sooner it is built the better for all concerned." The company that constructed this line stood to reap enormous profits. The black company opened offices in March, and in May announced that work on the road would begin before July. It was reported that T. Thomas Fortune, editor of the New York *Globe*, had agreed to act as an agent, and that a "Northern syndicate" had offered to build the first stretch of road to Wrightsville Sound. But nothing came of the proposal. The announcement might even have been a device to forestall local white competition. There were calls by some whites for cooperation in the weeks following the announcement of the offer from the "Northern syndicate," but these soon gave way to plans for a line under the control of whites. C. W. McClammy spoke for the group: "[I]f the colored people were going to build the road, all well and good; but if they cannot build it, which seems to be

128. Wilmington *Morning Star*, January 1, 18, April 2, July 8, 1884; New York *Globe*, January 26, May 31, 1884; Cleveland *Gazette*, February 16, May 10, 1884; Harrisburg *State Journal*, January 19, March 8, 1884; Harrisburg *Telegraph*, February 5, 1884; Pittsburgh *Commercial Gazette*, May 2, 1884.

the case, let them step aside." A meeting of whites commissioned a survey between Wilmington, New River, and Fayetteville that summer, but it is unclear when construction actually began. The "Wilmington, Wrightsville and Onslow Railroad Co." was out of business by the end of the year, a casualty no doubt of local competition and lack of adequate capital.[129]

Chester returned to his practice following the failure of the railroad company. His inability to generate support for construction of the line seems to have finally sapped the spirit of this determined man; his involvement was the final public act in a distinguished if checkered career. The rest of his life is a complete mystery. He and his wife returned to New Orleans in 1888; he to his practice, she as a teacher at Robinson School, one of twelve schools for blacks in the city.[130] The fires of ambition that had burned so fiercely, stoked by both a profound sense of racial pride and a singular determination to succeed, seem to have abated now that Chester had turned fifty. Gone was the feistiness and arrogance that Coppinger first tried to tame and, when he could not, to harness for the benefit of Liberia thirty years before. By the end of his life, Chester was much more content—willing, even—to accept existing conditions. Louisiana, in the late 1880s, had undergone dramatic changes from the days when he had made his first public address in New Orleans. Not even the most detached observer could have avoided the conclusion that conditions for blacks had deteriorated markedly in the intervening years. The ancien régime under Bourbon hegemony had destroyed many of the major accomplishments of Reconstruction. Yet Chester, who earlier had spoken of the sagacity and determination of blacks to resist all efforts to reinstate the old order, by the end of his life seems to have overlooked the reality of oppression and hailed the South as a place of "pleasant intercourse between whites and blacks." Although the denial of political rights rankled, he painted a relatively rosy picture in which white southerners were proud of black accomplishments and respected "those who have been conservative in the positions they have held." The *Picayune* was vindicated.[131]

Was Chester a conservative, and were these views of the South

129. New York *Globe*, May 31, 1884; Wilmington *Morning Star*, May 18, 20, 22, 29, June 11, 13, 18, July 9, August 15, 1884.

130. *Soards New Orleans City Directory for 1889* (New Orleans, 1889).

131. Harrisburg *Patriot*, September 13, 1892.

logically those of a conservative mind? Coming of age in the late antebellum period, Chester undoubtedly subscribed to the belief that blacks would acquit themselves capably under conditions of fair and open competition. That required shattering the shackles of slavery, and its handmaiden racism, the unnecessarily unfair restraints to black participation in the system. Yet, as a young man, he was not willing to wait for America to live up to the principles of equal opportunity. Liberia seemed the only logical alternative for someone who, in the 1850s, saw his native land sliding irreversibly toward a future dominated by the slaveholding South. But there were unforeseen pitfalls in Liberia, many of them the result of Chester's frustrated ambitions, which worked against the achievement of his personal goals. In the end, he sought a future in the new America, where emancipation and Reconstruction promised a new beginning. Yet the enduring reality of racism tempered any hopes for immediate and fundamental change. For the oppressed, race pride and self-respect were the antidote, Chester insisted, for this peculiarly American sickness. These were not, however, naturally induced; they were attained only through education and training, which instilled a profound sense of one's worth. This is why he so doggedly pursued his education, logging thousands of miles between Harrisburg, Pittsburgh, Monrovia, Thetford, and London. There was no doubt in his mind, or in the minds of most observers, that he epitomized the best of nineteenth-century culture and civilization. "Cultivated genius and virtue are the irresistible elements of progress," Chester insisted when speaking of the late judge A. A. Atocha in 1875, "the stars of our social and political sphere, the hope of humanity, and the glory of the State."[132] Chester might have been something of a star in the European firmament, but as the *Picayune* reminded him, neither America nor the South was willing to accept him, or any other black, educated or uneducated, cultivated or untutored, into society on grounds of perfect equality.

In the face of such intransigence, Chester seems to have lost the will to fight, his hopes for the race squelched by a more virulent racism poised to implement harsher forms of segregation and exclusion than anything he had known. It is no wonder that he and some of his contemporaries took refuge in a "conservatism" that found

132. *Louisianan*, April 17, 1875.

hope in even the most distressing conditions. He returned—almost symbolically, it appears—to his mother's home in April, 1892, suffering from what one newspaper called a "complication of diseases in which dropsy and heart trouble figured prominently." He never recovered and died from an apparent heart attack on September 30. He was interred, three days later, in the segregated Lincoln Cemetery in Harrisburg. It seems ironic that a person who had struggled so valiantly against racial restrictions should be buried in a segregated cemetery in his hometown. Chester's epitaph for Judge Atocha seems the most apt summation of his own life: "In his death, the bar has lost a shining ornament . . . the State an eminent citizen, and the spirit of progress and reform an earnest and enthusiastic advocate. As mourners we bow with afflicted hearts over his coffined remains, lamenting his departure, cherishing his virtues, and resolving to emulate his example."[133]

133. Harrisburg *Patriot*, September 13, October 1, 4, 1892; Harrisburg *Telegraph*, September 30, 1892; *Louisianan*, April 17, 1875.

PART II

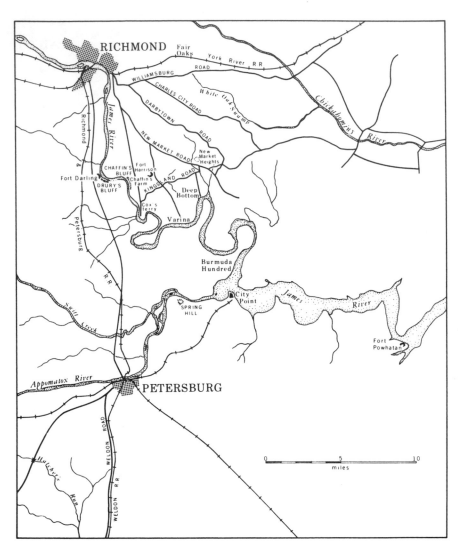

The Virginia front

CHAPTER 2

A Baptism of Fire

HEADQUARTERS 2D BRIG., 3D DIV., 18TH A[RMY] C[ORPS]
IN FRONT OF PETERSBURG, AUG. 14, 1864

The latest sensation in this army[1] is the explosion which happened at City Point on the 9th inst.[2] Presuming that your correspondent at that point has furnished you with all necessary details, with the due proportion of speculation as to the cause of the accident, I shall do nothing more than describe the scene, as it appeared about one mile distant. With eyes turned in that direction, my attention was attracted by a huge volume of smoke, through the center of which like flames from the center of a volcano, a terrible blaze suddenly ascended, intermingled with dark objects which were thrown in every conceivable direction. Then followed a tremendous report and a spherical body of smoke which seemingly curled up to the clouds—all presenting a spectacle of more than ordinary grandeur. The dust now rose in darkening confusion, and literally obscured everything within a half

1. The 3rd Division, composed entirely of blacks, was led by Brigadier General Charles J. Paine; the XVIII Corps was under the command of Edward O. C. Ord. The other all-black division in the Army of the James was the 3rd Division, X Corps. Both were discontinued in December, 1864, when General Butler amalgamated all the black units in the Army of the James to form the XXV Corps, comprising three divisions of thirty-two regiments, the largest black outfit formed during the war. Dudley T. Cornish, *The Sable Arm: Negro Troops in the Union Army, 1861–1865* (New York, 1956), 266, 279; Patricia L. Faust (ed.), *Historical Times Illustrated Encyclopedia of the Civil War* (New York, 1986), 181.

2. Soon after Grant returned from Washington to his headquarters at City Point, an ammunition barge containing twenty thousand artillery projectiles exploded, killing all aboard and forty-three along the docks. The explosion brought back horrible memories of the fiasco outside Petersburg nine days earlier, known as the Battle of the Crater. Shelby Foote, *The Civil War: A Narrative. Red River to Appomattox* (New York, 1974), 543; *The War of the Rebellion: A Compilation of the Official Records of the Union and Confederate Armies* (128 vols.; Washington, D.C., 1880–1901), Ser. I, Vol. XLI, Pt. 2, pp. 94–96, hereinafter cited as *OR*.

mile of the scene. Then came toward me hundreds and thousands of civilians and soldiers, rushing from a terrible danger which, on account of its mystery, seemed to quicken their speed and their fears.

For several hundred yards the ground was thickly strewn with debris. The million of property destroyed was but little thought of in the midst of the immense loss of life. Fragments of humanity were scattered around in the immediate vicinity of the tragedy in frightful profusion. Sorrow was depicted in every countenance that gazed on the ruins, but those loudest in their grief were the contrabands who mourned their relatives and comrades. Being employed in great numbers where the accident occurred, more of them were killed and wounded than any other class of individuals.

The Venom of the Enemy Along the Lines

The incessant fire of the enemy along his lines during the past few days has been of the most malignant character. A disposition on the part of the Union soldiers to cease this murderous proceeding has been met by the rebels with increased spitefulness and rage, in consequence of which an unbroken fire is exchanged between the pickets of both armies. Everywhere an Union soldier exposes the least part of his person to the sight of the pickets, or even those behind the enemy's breastworks, he is fired on with a suddenness which at once manifests the deadly venom of the rebels. Shells and round shot are continually being thrown inside of our breastworks, occasionally wounding some one. Explosive bullets are incidentally flying through one's quarters, and falling about in a variety of directions. Whenever such proceeding becomes annoying, our guns along the line immediately in front of these headquarters are opened, which has the effect of silencing, for a time, the heavy firing of the enemy. The unceremonious argument of artillery is the only influence that he heeds, or the only reason that he respects.

Dismissed from the Service

Lieutenant John O'Brien, of the 36th United States Colored Troops,[3] had the misfortune to undergo an examination before

3. Formerly the 2nd North Carolina Colored Infantry, the 36th was organized in February, 1864, and served at Norfolk and Portsmouth before becoming part of the 3rd

General Butler[4] on the following charges: First, Disobedience of orders. Second, Drunkenness on duty. Third, Conduct unbecoming an officer. Fourth, Breach of arrest. The Lieutenant confessed guilt enough to justify the General in immediately dismissing him from the service, with a forfeiture of all pay and emoluments. The examination was on the 9th instant. Too much credit cannot be given to Colonel A. G. Draper,[5] of the 36th United States Troops, acting brigadier general of the 2d Brigade, for the prompt manner in which he brought Lieutenant O'Brien's unbecoming deportment to the notice of the military authorities. No officer will retain a place in his command unless he conducts himself within the bounds of discipline. The 36th is a model regiment, and, wherever it has operated, it has been distinguished by the undaunted bravery of the men and the gallantry of its officers.

AN OFFICER KILLED

Yesterday Lieutenant E. R. Smith,[6] of the 5th United States Colored Troops,[7] was mortally wounded in the trenches while in the performance of his duty as the officer of the day, and he died a few hours after. He was undoubtedly picked off by a sharpshooter. The

---

Division, XVIII Corps, and, later under reorganization, the XXV Corps. Frederick H. Dyer, *Compendium of the War of the Rebellion* (Des Moines, Iowa, 1908), 249; Cornish, *The Sable Arm*, 244.

4. Benjamin Franklin Butler (1818–1893). Best-known for declaring slaves to be contraband, Butler was a prominent figure in the war until his recall following the fiasco at Fort Fisher in December, 1864. Prior to that, he had led the land forces against New Orleans and after its fall became administrator until December, 1862. The following month he was put in command of the Army of the James. *DAB*, II, 358.

5. Alonzo Granville Draper (1835–1865) entered the war as captain, 1st Massachusetts. He assumed command of the 2nd North Carolina Colored Infantry in December, 1863, and in April, 1864, was put in command of the district of St. Mary, Maryland. He was subsequently brevetted brigadier general and headed the 1st Brigade, 3rd Division, XXV Corps. *OR*, Ser. I, Vol. XLI, Pt. 2, p. 622, Ser. I, Vol. XXXIII, p. 1057, Ser. I, Vol. XXIX, Pt. 1, pp. 910–13, Ser. I, Vol. XLII, Pt. 3, p. 1126; Mark Mayo Boatner III, *The Civil War Dictionary* (New York, 1959), 246.

6. Edwin R. Smith (1835–1864) joined Company H as a second lieutenant in July, 1863, and was promoted to first lieutenant five months later. *Official Roster of the Soldiers of the State of Ohio in the War of the Rebellion, 1861–1865* (12 vols.; Akron, 1893–95), I, 615.

7. Raised in Ohio during 1863 and 1864, the 5th USCT served at Portsmouth, Norfolk, and Yorktown, later becoming part of the XVIII Corps. The regiment suffered heavy losses during the assault on Fort Gilmer and Fort Harrison near New Market Heights at the end of September: 28 killed, 185 wounded, and 23 missing or captured. Cornish, *The Sable Arm*, 279; Dyer, *Compendium of the War of the Rebellion*, 248.

ball entered his right side, and came out of the left about one inch from the spine. Lieut. Smith is a native of New York, but his parents are now residing in Illinois. He was attending college, at Oberlin, at the commencement of the war, and was among the first to shoulder a musket. He enlisted in the 7th Ohio volunteer service in the spring of 1861, with which regiment he was connected until he received his commission in the 5th United States Colored Regiment, about year since. In saying that Lieut. Smith was a patriot and a soldier, it is but adding a just tribute to the memory of departed worth.

HEADQUARTERS 2D BRIGADE, 3D DIVISION, 18TH ARMY CORPS

BEFORE PETERSBURG, SUNDAY AUGUST 14, 1864—7 P.M.

Nothing of importance has occurred to-day to mar the monotony of camp life. The Sabbath has been spent as appropriately as possible. Religious services were held at division headquarters and by the different regiments which were not under fire.

THE GRAND FIREWORKS

The enterprising managers of the firm of Grant & Lee take pleasure in announcing to the public in and around Petersburg that they are now prepared, and will continue until further notice, to give every evening a grand exhibition of fireworks for the benefit of their respective employees. The past experience of the firm has enabled it to acquire a success in this direction which it feels satisfied a liberal-minded public will concede. The managers will not in any case hold themselves responsible for any accidents which may occur to those who may be attracted, from curiosity or otherwise, to witness their exhibition. The managers promise nothing on their part shall be wanting to increase the interest of the display, or be unworthy of the firm which has gained such a world wide reputation. Being the largest company that has ever undertaken a display of fireworks on so grand a scale, it is confident in its ability to surpass all other exhibitions of its kind, and increase the wonder, if not the admiration, of all spectators. The heads of this grand firm take this method of inviting all able-bodied males in the United States to witness their brilliant displays. Special care will be taken to accommodate all who patronize it; and in order that association may be agreeable, all those from the South will be continued together as far as practicable whose conveniences will be especially consulted by the junior member of the firm, while those from the North will be provided with the most favorable arrangement that circumstances will admit, with the supervision of which the senior member is charged. The managers would inform all who have not witnessed their grand exhibitions that it would be best to avail themselves of the first favorable opportunity, as they are considering the propriety of bringing their engagement on a large scale to a speedy close. Two of the most brilliant displays the world has ever witnessed are expected to terminate the grand series, speedily, in front of Petersburg and Richmond. Due notice, however, can only be given to those in the immediate vicinity.

REORGANIZATION OF COLORED TROOPS

The following order has been promulgated for the reorganization of all colored troops in General Butler's department:

HEADQUARTERS DEPARTMENT OF VA AND N.C.

IN THE FIELD, VA., JULY 29, 1864.

ORDERED: Brigadier General C. J. Paine[8] is hereby ordered to the command of the 3d Division 18th Army Corps.

First Brigade—1st U.S. Colored Troops,[9] Col. J. H. Holman[10]

8. Charles Jackson Paine (1833–1916). A Harvard graduate and a lawyer, Paine entered the war as captain, 22nd Massachusetts. In early 1863 he was a colonel in the 2nd Louisiana under Banks in the Department of the Gulf and fought at Vicksburg as a lieutenant of the 9th Louisiana, part of the "African Brigade." He later commanded the 3rd Division, XXV Corps, under Weitzel. In January, 1865, Terry put him in command of forces occupying the line of defenses facing Wilmington. Boatner, *The Civil War Dictionary*, 615; *OR*, Ser. I, Vol. XV, p. 254, Ser. I, Vol. XXIV, Pt. 2, p. 158, Ser. I, Vol. XLVI, Pt. 2, p. 174.

9. Organized in Washington in June, 1863, the 1st USCT served at Norfolk, Portsmouth, and Yorktown. It later became part of the 3rd Division, XVIII Corps, and the XXV Corps. Dyer, *Compendium of the War of the Rebellion*, 248.

10. John H. Holman (d. 1883) commanded the 26th Missouri in Mississippi during 1862 and was severely wounded at Corinth. The following year he led the 1st USCT in campaigns in Virginia. He was promoted to colonel of the "African Brigade" under Brigadier General Edward A. Wild and subsequently served as commander of the 1st Brigade, 3rd Division, XVIII Corps, and was wounded at Darbytown Road in October, 1864. Boatner, *The Civil War Dictionary*, 406; *OR*, Ser. I, Vol. XVII, Pt. 1, p. 207, Ser. I, Vol. XXXIII, p. 483, Ser. I, Vol. XL, Pt. 1, p. 266, Ser. I, Vol. XLII, Pt. 1, p. 151.

commanding; 22d do.,[11] Col. J. B. Kiddoo[12] commanding; 37th do.,[13] Lieut. Col. A. G. Chamberlain.[14]

Second Brigade—30th U.S. Colored Troops,[15] Col. A. G. Draper commanding; 5th do., Col. J. W. Conine[16] commanding; 38th do.,[17] Lieut. Col. D. E. Clapp[18] commanding.

Third Brigade,—4th U.S. Colored Troops,[19] Col. S. A. Duncan[20]

11. Raised in Pennsylvania in 1864, the 22nd USCT took part in the assault on Petersburg in June, 1864. Indecision by commanders failed to sustain the initial advantages, allowing the Confederates time to bring up reinforcements, with the result that Union forces could do no more than settle in for a siege. It also participated in the capture of Fort Gregg outside Petersburg toward the end of the war. Frederick M. Binder, "Pennsylvania Negro Regiments in the Civil War," *Journal of Negro History,* XXXVII (1952), 411–12, 414; George Washington Williams, *A History of the Negro Troops in the War of the Rebellion, 1861–1865* (New York, 1888), 298.

12. Joseph Barr Kiddoo (1840–1880) enlisted in the 12th Pennsylvania and served also in the 63rd and 137th Pennsylvania. He was promoted to colonel of the 22nd USCT in January, 1864. Samuel P. Bates, *History of Pennsylvania Volunteers, 1861–1865* (5 vols.; Harrisburg, 1869–71), V, 943, 945; Boatner, *The Civil War Dictionary,* 458; *OR,* Ser. I, Vol. XXI, p. 925.

13. Formerly the 3rd North Carolina, recruited in January, 1864, the 37th USCT served at Norfolk and Portsmouth before being transferred to the XVIII Corps and subsequently the XXV Corps. Dyer, *Compendium of the War of the Rebellion,* 200, 249.

14. Abial G. Chamberlain (?–?) was in command of the 1st Brigade, 3rd Division, XVIII Corps, in October, 1864. Prior to that, he commanded the 3rd North Carolina, part of Holman's "African Brigade." *OR,* Ser. I, Vol. XLII, Pt. 3, p. 467, Ser. I, Vol. XXXIII, pp. 482, 1054.

15. Organized in Maryland in 1864, the 30th USCT was first part of the Army of the Potomac and then was transferred to the XXV Corps, Army of the James. Dyer, *Compendium of the War of the Rebellion,* 249.

16. James W. Conine (?–?). Born in the North, Conine lived in Lexington, Kentucky, before the war and was supposedly sympathetic to secession. Yet he left for Cincinnati, where he was mustered in as a lieutenant, 2nd Kentucky. He was made a colonel of the 5th USCT in late 1863. Cornish, *The Sable Arm,* 223; *Official Roster of the Soldiers of Ohio,* I, 593.

17. Organized in Virginia in 1864, the 38th USCT served in Norfolk and Portsmouth before becoming part of the XVIII Corps and then the XXV Corps. Dyer, *Compendium of the War of the Rebellion,* 249.

18. Dexter E. Clapp (1830–1882). A captain, Company C, 148th New York Infantry, between September, 1862, and March, 1864, Clapp became lieutenant colonel of the 38th USCT in March, 1864. He was made a brigadier general by brevet, for gallant and meritorious service in March, 1865. Frederick Phisterer (comp.), *New York in the War of the Rebellion, 1861 to 1865* (5 vols.; New York, 1912), I, 377–78, V, 3721, 3723; Boatner, *The Civil War Dictionary,* 156.

19. Recruited in Baltimore in September, 1863, the 4th USCT was first assigned to Yorktown before joining General Edward Ward Hinks's division of the XVIII Corps. It became part of the XXV Corps following reorganization. Dyer, *Compendium of the War of the Rebellion,* 248.

20. Samuel Augustus Duncan (1836–1895). Formerly a major, 14th New Hampshire Volunteers, Duncan was commissioned a colonel, 4th USCT, in late 1863. He was

commanding; 6th do.,[21] Col. J. W. Ames[22] commanding; 10th do.,[23] Col. Elias Wright[24] commanding.

Col. Holman is acting brigadier general of the 1st, Col. Draper of the 2d, and Col. Duncan of the 3d brigade.

WOUNDED

The following persons were wounded yesterday by the firing of the enemy, all of whom belong to the 36th U.S. Colored Troops:

Washington Darley, Company G, slightly.

John Saunders, Company G, slightly.

Wm. Babley, Company F, slightly in the head.

Henry Jones, Company F, leg amputated.

Hardy Ebon, Company F, leg amputated.

Toby Cornich, Company F, flesh wound in leg.

Nathaniel Watkins, Company F, hand and head, severely.

---

promoted to command the 2nd Brigade, 3rd Division, XVIII Corps. He was severely wounded in the assault on Fort Harrison near New Market Heights in September, 1864. William H. Powell, *Officers of the Army and Navy* (Philadelphia, 1893), 213; Horace Montgomery, "A Union Officer's Recollections of the Negro as a Soldier," *Pennsylvania History*, XXVIII (1961), 165; Boatner, *The Civil War Dictionary*, 251.

21. Raised in Pennsylvania in 1863, the 6th USCT left for Virginia in October to join the Army of the James. Its duties involved building fortifications at Yorktown, foraging and garrison assignments on the James River. In May, 1864, the 6th and the 22nd repulsed Confederate cavalry charges at Wilson's Wharf, Spring Hill, and Powhatan. In August, Butler assigned it the task of dredging the canal at Dutch Gap. Binder, "Pennsylvania Negro Regiments," 410–11; Benjamin Franklin Butler, *Autobiography and Personal Reminiscences of Major-General Benj. F. Butler—BUTLER'S BOOK. A Review of His Legal, Political and Military Career* (Boston, 1892), 744–52; Dyer, *Compendium of the War of the Rebellion*, 248. For an account of the 6th, see Montgomery, "A Union Officer's Recollections," 156–86.

22. John Worthington Ames (d. 1878) served as captain, 11th Pennsylvania Regular Infantry, before joining the 6th USCT, which he led until he was injured during the attack on Fort Harrison, September, 1864. He became commander of the 3rd Brigade, 3rd Division, XXV Corps, and was subsequently moved to the command of the 2nd Brigade. Montgomery, "A Union Officer's Recollections," 180; Cornish, *The Sable Arm*, 259–60; Bates, *History of Pennsylvania Volunteers*, V, 943, 945; Boatner, *The Civil War Dictionary*, 12.

23. Recruited in Maryland and Virginia, the 10th USCT served at Drummondstown before being transferred to the XVIII Corps and then the XXV Corps. Dyer, *Compendium of the War of the Rebellion*, 248.

24. Elias Wright (d. 1901). Mustered in as a second lieutenant, 4th New Jersey, Wright became commander of the 2nd Brigade, 3rd Division, X Corps, in October, 1864. He subsequently assumed command of the 3rd Brigade, XXV Corps. Boatner, *The Civil War Dictionary*, 949; *OR*, Ser. I, Vol. XLII, Pt. 3, pp. 465, 1126.

HEADQUARTERS 10TH ARMY CORPS
TEN MILES FROM RICHMOND, AUGUST 18, 1864.

Another step has been taken toward the rebel capital. Another warning has again disturbed the heavily-burdened consciences of the arch conspirators. Lieut. Gen. Grant is rapidly negotiating peace "on this line," and is daily despatching messengers towards Richmond, and into Petersburg, whose powerful reasonings even Jeff Davis will not be able to resist much longer.

Another battle has been fought, and a decided advantage has been gained. The troops, white and black, covered themselves with undying fame. Their conduct could not have been surpassed. The colored troops fully sustained the most exalted opinion which their ardent friends could possibly entertain. Major General Birney,[25] commanding the 10th Army Corps remarked yesterday, without, however, wishing to do any injustice to the whites, that his colored soldiers had done handsomely. There was neither wavering nor straggling; but presenting a fearless front to the enemy, their conduct elicited especial remark, and excited admiration. A few more exhibitions of loyalty and bravery, as evinced during the past few days in this Corps, will soon eradicate the last vestige of prejudice and oppression from the grand Army of the Potomac. The circumstances which gave the colored troops, in conjunction with the others, the opportunity of a passage into public favor, are as follows; On the night of the 13th inst., in accordance with the masterly strategy of General Grant, a part of the 10th Corps crossed the James river at Deep Bottom,[26] and on the 14th moved out on the Darbytown road, and, as a necessary precaution, indulged in skirmishing during the day. About 4 P.M., Brigadier General Wm. Birney,[27] commanding a

25. David Bell Birney (1825–1864). Younger brother of William Birney, David practiced law before the war. He was mustered in as a lieutenant colonel and saw action in West Virginia. He was promoted to brigadier general in 1862 and held a command in the Army of the Potomac, seeing action at Second Bull Run and in the Peninsula campaign. He was promoted to major general following Chancellorsville. He also fought at Gettysburg and took part in the first assault against Richmond in mid-1864, rising to the command of the X Corps. He was stricken with malaria, from which he never recovered. *DAB*, I, 290–91.

26. In the attack on Deep Bottom Run, the Union ran into stiff resistance from Confederate veterans, suffering close to three thousand casualties. Foote, *The Civil War . . . Red River to Appomattox*, 545.

27. William G. Birney (1819–1907). Son of the abolitionist James Gillespie Birney, Birney raised a volunteer company in New Jersey at the outbreak of the war. In 1863 he

division, sent seven companies of the 7th U. S. C. T.,[28] supported by a part of the 9th Regiment U. S. C. T.,[29] to retake a line of rifle pits on our left, which had been captured by Brigadier General Terry[30] in the morning, and afterwards abandoned voluntarily by a mistake and reoccupied by the enemy. They sent up a shout of confidence, and, under the inspiration of their beloved commander, General Wm. Birney, the colored troops charged through a corn field and drove the rebels out of the rifle-pits. The enemy poured a heavy fire upon them, but was obliged to yield to their bravery. He was driven out, and we occupied them as a part of our defences. In this assault our loss was between fifty and sixty killed and wounded.

That night our forces moved from Deep Bottom, and took the position which they now occupy. It is an onward to Richmond movement, and thus far is regarded as a success. As speculations always tend to acquaint the enemy with our movements, I will add nothing more than the cheering prospect which now animated this grand army. The crowning act of the Commander-in-Chief may be the reduction of Richmond and Petersburg at the same time.

On the 16th, General Terry was directed to attack the line of the enemy's works on our left, and to drive him from his position. Brigadier General Birney was ordered to hold his division as a support to Brigadier General Terry. General Terry advanced, and drove the enemy out of the first line of rifle-pits, and then stormed the strong line of breastworks, suffering severe loss, but driving the enemy from his position. The rebs rallied, however, in overpowering numbers, to force General Terry to retreat in confusion. Finding

---

was named a superintendent of enlistment for black troops and organized seven regiments. He was promoted to brigadier general of volunteers in May, 1863, and to brevet major general of volunteers in March, 1865. *DAB*, I, 294.

28. Recruited in Baltimore in 1863, the 7th USCT served in Jacksonville, Florida, and Hilton Head, South Carolina, before it was transferred to the X Corps and then the XXV Corps. The regiment suffered heavy losses during the assault against Fort Gilmer, New Market Heights, in September, 1864. Joseph Mark Califf, *Record of the Services of the Seventh Regiment, U.S. Colored Troops* (1878; rpr. Freeport, N.Y., 1971), 7, 34–50; Cornish, *The Sable Arm*, 280; Dyer, *Compendium of the War of the Rebellion*, 248.

29. Organized in Maryland in 1863, the 9th USCT served at Hilton Head, South Carolina, and in Florida, becoming part of the X Corps in December, 1864, and the XXV Corps under Butler's reorganization. Dyer, *Compendium of the War of the Rebellion*, 248.

30. Alfred Howe Terry (1827–1890) participated in the Georgia and South Carolina campaigns during the first two years of the war. He was transferred to the Army of the James in late 1863 and brevetted brigadier general of volunteers in August, 1864. He led the expeditionary force that captured Fort Fisher, North Carolina, in January, 1865. *DAB*, IX, 378.

himself gradually driven back by a greatly superior force his men acquitting themselves grandly amid a galling fire, Brigadier General Birney moved forward to his support, and with his troops, which consisted of the 2d and 3d Brigades of the 10th Corps, and the 9th U.S. colored troops, he advanced to the enemy's breastworks. The rebels then appeared in great numbers, advancing upon Gens. Birney's and Terry's forces, and a brisk fire was opened and continued on both sides. The enemy in attempting to take the breast works were repeatedly driven back with severe loss. The rebels finally succeeded, however, by moving their troops to our left; a portion of the breast works which had extended beyond our lines, and had not been carried by our forces. By this manoeuvre, they were enabled to pour a galling fire upon our flank and rear, and under which the men on the left were obliged to withdraw, not because they were whipped, but that the position was, under the circumstances, untenable.

General William Birney, after having twice filled the gaps caused by the giving way on the left, was unable to do so again without exposing his lines at other and more vital points. He gave the order to fall back to the first line of rifle-pits, which were captured from the enemy, which was accomplished in good order and without any confusion. The colored troops were the last to retire, which they did with unwavering firmness and in obedience to orders; not, however, before they gave three cheers, which evinced their dauntless spirit.

During this fighting the 3d Brigade, 21 Division, 10th A. C., lost one hundred and forty-eight men and officers, killed, wounded, and missing.

Colonel F. A. Osborn, 21th Massachusetts, was slightly wounded; Major Walroth, 115th New York, wounded in the side; Captain F. W. Parker, 4th N. H., wounded in the face. These officers were wounded while each was temporary commander of the 3d Brigade.

The 4th Regiment N. H. Volunteers lost three killed, thirty-two wounded, and fourteen missing. The killed are Corp. David W. Knox, Joseph Appleyard, and First Sergt. Edmund T. McNell.

The 115th N. Y. Volunteers lost four killed: Sergt. Frank M. Conner, Co. D.; Corp. Abott C. Meisgrove, Corp. J. H. Haynes, and First Sergt. F. W. Francisco; forty wounded, and fifteen missing.

The whole loss in this brigade is thirteen killed, ninety-one wounded, and forty-four missing, making a total of one hundred and forty-eight.

TROPHIES

The 10th Army Corps has captured during this flanking campaign four 8-inch siege guns, six colors, and over five hundred prisoners.

FLAG OF TRUCE

Major General Birney requested, yesterday, a cessation of hostilities to allow him to recover his wounded and bury his dead, which were near the enemy's breastworks. It was conceded, and the time was fixed from four to six o'clock P.M. Major J. C. Briscoe[31] and Captain Sweet, aide-de-camp to Major General Birney, and Lieut. Pancoast, ambulance officer, carried the flag of truce. It was received by Captain Rand, aide to General Ewell.[32] Major Briscoe delivered the body of the rebel Gen. Chambliss,[33] killed and remaining within our lines. The Major received our dead. During the existence of the flag of truce the rebel officers manifested no inclination to communicate with our officers. Their countenances wore an aspect of anxiety, not unmingled with chagrin and disappointment. The interchanging was of that formal nature which convinced the Union officers that the enemy was not in the enjoyment of good spirits, or were indulging in pleasing prospects.

STRIPPING THE UNION DEAD

As the hour approached for the cessation of hostilities, I mounted and advanced to the outer line of our works, to witness the bearing in

31. James C. Briscoe (d. 1869) rose through the ranks from private to major. He was brevetted brigadier general and commanded brigades in the X and XXIV Corps. Boatner, *The Civil War Dictionary,* 86–87.

32. Richard Stoddert Ewell (1817–1872). A veteran of the Mexican War, Ewell was appointed brigadier of the Confederate army in June, 1861. He fought at First Bull Run, Winchester, Cross Keys, and Groveton, where he lost a leg. He later assumed command of the 2nd Corps, Army of Northern Virginia. Ewell's forces menaced Harrisburg, Pennsylvania, before being withdrawn to Gettysburg. There he was wounded, yet continued to fight, strapped to his saddle. Later he saw action in the Wilderness and at Spotsylvania, and commanded the Department of Henrico during the final assault on Richmond. *DAB,* III, 229–30; Jon L. Wakelyn, *Biographical Dictionary of the Confederacy* (Westport, Conn., 1977), 181–82.

33. John Randolph Chambliss (d. 1864) entered the war as a colonel in the 13th Virginia Cavalry and fought at Rappahannock and Fredericksburg. He commanded the 5th Virginia Cavalry at Chancellorsville and Gettysburg. He was killed at Deep Bottom. Boatner, *The Civil War Dictionary,* 136.

of our honored dead. Two rows of men, several deep, extending far into the dense forest, formed a passage through which their comrades were now borne on stretchers. As each fallen hero was carried along this passage of brave men, even the solemnity of the scene could not restrain the indignation of the soldiers, as they witnessed the Union dead returned to them stripped of their shoes, coats, pants, and, in some instances, of their shirts. Those who were returned in their pants gave unmistakable evidence of having their pockets rifled—the pockets of which were turned inside out. The mutterings of the men were deep, and their feelings emphatically expressed on witnessing the respected dead dishonored. This act of ineffable meanness has nerved the hearts and strengthened the arms of the defenders of the Union, who will sweep from existence these enemies of God and civilization.

THE ENEMY REPULSED

Last evening, just after the flag of truce returned, the enemy advanced in line of battle, and made a vigorous effort to turn our left flank, but were forced to retire. Later in the evening an effort was made to drive in our skirmishers, but without success. The firing was so severe for a few minutes that it much resembled the opening of a grand battle.

SLAVE MANACLES

The hurried manner in which the worshippers of the patriarchal institution were obliged to leave these parts for Richmond, compelled them to leave behind several articles which illustrate their character and their humanity. I am, through their haste, able to add to some one's collection two pair of manacles for the wrists, and one iron collar for the neck, which is fastened with a padlock, to which are several links of a chain to be attached, if necessary, to a similar necklace on an individual, by which means quite a number of men and women could be yoked together, single file, for any desirable length.

HEADQUARTERS 2D BRIGADE, 3D DIVISION, 18TH ARMY CORPS

BEFORE PETERSBURG, AUGUST 22, 1864

The hearts of the colored soldiers in this vicinity have been gladdened by the good news from the extreme left of the Army of the Potomac. Yesterday, about the time the church bells were inviting the inhabitants of your city to renew the assurances of their Christianity, the loud report of cannon announced that once more the defenders of the Union had met its enemies in mortal combat.

THE ENEMY MOVING TO THE LEFT

As soon as the attack began, the enemy, plainly visible to the vigilant black troops in our front, began to hurry off troops to support the attempt which he had undertaken on our left. This information was, no doubt, duly attended to by the authorities.

THE ATTACK

The Weldon railroad[34] having been severed, the enemy, finding an important advantage was gained by the commander-in-chief, sought, by a desperate assault, to drive him from his position, and permit, as heretofore, uninterrupted supplies to reach his army in and around Richmond and Petersburg. The enemy, by a well-conceived piece of strategy, manoeuvered to advance on our flank and rear. Insomuch they had gained an advantage, but the 5th Corps, under the immediate supervision of General Warren,[35] fought with an unwavering firmness that withstood the several assaults of the enemy, and

34. The railroad was a vital supply line connecting the besieged Petersburg and Weldon, North Carolina. The line was severed four miles south of Petersburg by a Union assault on August 18. Confederate forces counterattacked unsuccessfully in a bloody battle lasting two days. When they withdrew, there were 4,500 Union and 1,600 Confederate casualties. Montgomery, "A Union Officer's Recollections," 175; Foote, *The Civil War . . . Red River to Appomattox*, 545–56.

35. Gouverneur Kemble Warren (1830–1882). A graduate of the United States Military Academy and a teacher at West Point, Warren saw action in the Peninsular campaign of 1862, at Second Bull Run, and at Fredericksburg. He is best known for leading the defense of Little Round Top at Gettysburg. He assumed command of the V Corps in March, 1864. *DAB*, X, 473–74.

drove him into his jungle to mourn over his disaster—not, however, before three stand of colors and six hundred prisoners were captured.

Another attempt was made last night with renewed vigor, to force our army from its gained position, and in order that the enemy might obtain possession of the important rail communication which he lost. He was repulsed with severer loss than in the morning. Several stand of colors and one brigade were captured.

The rebels during Sunday morning and night fought desperately and furiously, and were only checked by the stubborn resistance which they encountered. General Grant, without weakening any part of his lines, has sent forward sufficient reinforcements to hold his position, and advance when he deems it necessary. A division of negro troops has also been given a position where the enemy will have an opportunity of testing their mettle, should he attempt again to recapture the Weldon railroad. Our losses in the engagements of yesterday were comparatively small, as later dates will corroborate.

THE NEGRO TROOPS BEFORE PETERSBURG

In General Butler's army there are many regiments of colored troops,[36] who, thus far, have inspired confidence in their officers by the discipline and bearing which they have evinced under the incessant fire of the enemy, along the lines, and the handsome manner in which they have borne themselves whenever opportunity placed them in front of the rebels. It would not be extravagant to predict that they will yet accomplish more brilliant achievements. Their success will depend much on the character of the officers in immediate command. If the men are attached to them for their kindness and consideration on their behalf there is no doubt but what they will follow wherever their superiors may lead. So long as they are commanded by such accomplished gentlemen as Col. A. G. Draper, 36th U.S. Colored Troops, Lieut. Colonel Pratt,[37] of the same

36. There were fifteen black regiments in the XVIII Corps and a total of twenty-five in the Army of the James during the winter of 1864–65. Cornish, *The Sable Arm*, 266; Williams, *A History of Negro Troops*, 291.

37. Benjamin F. Pratt (d. 1890). In late 1863, Pratt led the 2nd North Carolina (a command later taken over by Draper). He commanded the 36th USCT under Draper in Maryland in April, 1864. Boatner, *The Civil War Dictionary*, 667; *OR*, Ser. I, Vol. XXIX, Pt. 1, p. 911, Ser. I, Vol. XXXIII, p. 1057.

regiment, and many other excellent officers whom I will credit when I
shall speak of the regiments separately, there is not the least doubt
but what they will fully meet public expectation.

In this connection it may not be inappropriate to speak, for the
guidance of others, of the enthusiastic admiration of the colored
troops under Gen. Wm. Birney for that gallant officer. They are all
from Maryland, and were taken from the plantations of their former
owners by the General, whom they regard as their deliverer. The
General has implicit confidence in their fighting qualities. The highest
praise that can be bestowed upon them is, that he prefers them rather
than white troops. This is not a mental preference, for he has had the
opportunity of electing, and chose to command colored soldiers. The
secret of Gen. Birney's success is, that he treats his men as any other
gallant officer would regard the defenders of the Union.

There are other colored troops from Maryland, obtained in the
same way, but under a different class of officers, in the Army of the
Potomac. I trust they will do all that is expected of them, but fear that
the kind of men who command them has tended to demoralize rather
than to inspire them. What Gen. Birney has done others may
accomplish, if they do not regard it as humiliating to treat a negro
patriot as a man, who offers himself a willing sacrifice upon his
country's altar.

Those before Petersburg have the good fortune to be commanded
by good men—though there are some black sheep among them—
who are laboring to bring this branch of the service to the highest
state of perfection. The kindness of the officers is reflected in the
unflinching mettle of the men in the trying positions where duty calls
them. There is not a day but what some brave black defender of the
Union is made to bite the dust by a rebel sharpshooter or picket, but
his place is immediately and cheerfully filled by another under the
inspiring glance of such commanders as Colonels Wright, Pratt, and
Acting Brigadier General A. G. Draper. They are ever on the alert to
catch a glimpse of a rebel, to whom they send their compliments by
means of a leaden messenger. Between the negroes and the enemy it
is war to the death. The colored troops have cheerfully accepted the
conditions of the Confederate Government, that between them no
quarter is to be shown. Those here have not the least idea of living
after they fall into the hands of the enemy, and the rebels act very

much as if they entertained similar sentiments with reference to the blacks. Even deserters fear to come into our lines where colored troops may be stationed. Not unfrequently have they asked if there are any black troops near, and if there were the rebs have entreated that they should not be permitted to harm them. Such has been the effect of Jeff Davis' proclamation[38] for the wholesale massacre of our colored troops, and such will it continue to be until the rebels shall treat all the defenders of the Union as prescribed by the rules of civilized warfare.

The military situation never was more encouraging. The Army of the Potomac during the past few days has successfully performed several strategic movements, which surprised the enemy and gave to us many important advantages. The successful "onward to Richmond," the severing of the Weldon railroad, by means of which the enemy has received all his supplies from the South, and the threatening demonstrations against Petersburg, each one of which is a grand campaign in itself, can be regarded as nothing less than the successful accomplishment of a masterly mind. When or where next the commander-in-chief will suddenly appear is a matter which, under the circumstances, should be left to the development of his strategy. Advancing on several points at the same time will effectually checkmate the enemy. One of his principal means of maintaining his position in different parts of the country has been the celerity with which he has been able to move great bodies of troops to places which our army was about to attack. Everything betokens success. The army is in the best of spirits. The colored soldiers are not only ready, but are anxious to meet the rebels.

38. The "proclamation" was that captured slaves should be returned to masters. Among black troops was the belief that blacks would be slaughtered if taken. The issue of how to treat blacks captured in battle remained a vexing problem for the Confederacy. There were those who insisted that no quarter be given black soldiers and their white officers, convinced that harsh measures had to be employed to stop what one Mississippian called "the inhuman, and to us dangerous practice" of arming blacks. There were rumors in 1863 that captured black soldiers and their officers were executed, and in some instances, captured blacks were sold into slavery. Lincoln pledged retaliation. The problem led to the suspension of agreements on prisoner exchanges. In 1864 the South agreed to recognize captured free blacks as prisoners of war and eligible for exchange, but would not budge on the issue of captured slaves. Exchanges were suspended in the spring of 1864. Black prisoners were not returned until the end of the war. Cornish, *The Sable Arm*, 162–73; Benjamin Quarles, *The Negro in the Civil War* (Boston, 1953), 207–208; Williams, *A History of Negro Troops*, 307–19.

Casualties in the 9th U. S. Colored Troops, August 14th

Wounded.

Corporal Robert Cole. Co. C, slightly.

Stephen Russell, Co. D, severely.

Corporal Daniel H. Carroll, Co. H, severely.

Joseph Chase, Co. H, slightly.

William Thomas, Co. H, slightly.

Elijah Trailor, Co. H, seriously.

Daniel Wright, Co. H, seriously.

Levi Boyer, Co. H, seriously.

James Stout, Co. H, slightly.

Killed and Wounded on August 15th

Killed.

John Williams, Co. E.

George Roxbury, Co. E.

Wounded.

L. Jones, Co. B, seriously.

Jesse Jacobs, Co. B, seriously.

Henry Ashley, Co. B, seriously.

Henry Watts, Co. B, seriously.

James Lindsey, Co. C, slightly.

Henry Irrideil, Co. D, slightly.

Solomon Gunter, Co. D, slightly.

George Killim, Co. D, slightly.

George Collin, Co. E, slightly.

Killed and Wounded on August 16th

Killed.

Captain Edwin Post, Co. C.

Daniel Brises, Co. A.

Robert Ennels, Co. B.

John F. Barnes, Co. C.

Moses Cottman, Co. C.

Edward Morris, Co. C.

Robert Missill, Co. C.

Elijah Johnson, Co. I.

Corporal William Shipley, Co. K.

Wounded.

Second Lieutenant Austin Wismall, seriously.

Sergeant John Dennis, Co. A, severely.

Corporal John L. Dennis, Co. A, slightly.

Isaac Ballard, Co. A, slightly.

Franklin Barclay, Co. A, slightly.

Philip Dorsey, Co. A, slightly.

Henry Smith, Co. A, slightly.

George E. Taylor, Co. A, slightly.

Henry F. Thompson, Co. A, slightly.

Sergeant Stephen Wallace, Co. B, seriously.

Andrew Campier, Co. B, slightly.

John Clark, Co. B, seriously.

Lewis Miller, Co. B, slightly.
George Britts, Co. C, seriously.
Henry A. Wise, Co. C, slightly.
Henry Allen, Co. C, seriously.
John Brough, Co. C, seriously.
John Chandler, Co. C, seriously.
John Hargus, Co. C, seriously.
William Roach, Co. C, seriously.
Robert Smith, Co. C, seriously.
Leon Shamell, Co. C, seriously.
Joseph Taylor, Co. C, seriously.
John Toadmine, Co. C, slightly.
Henry H. Wright, Co. C,
   slightly.
Solomon Wise, Co. C, slightly.
Perry Henry, Co. D, slightly.
Riley Fasset, Co. D, seriously.
Sergeant Lewis Major, Co. E,
   seriously.
George Showell, Co. G, slightly.

Sergeant Leonard Parsons, Co.
   H, slightly.
Corporal George Collins, Co. H,
   seriously.
Robert Grey, Co. H, slightly.
Albert Fringel, Co. H, seriously.
James Baily, Co. H, slightly.
Frederick A. Bunell, Co. H,
   slightly.
Sergeant John Pullet, Co. I,
   seriously.
William Pinket, Co. I, seriously.
Mitchell Leonard, Co. I, slightly.
George Evens, Co. I, slightly.
Joseph Johnson, Co. I, slightly.
John Shelton, Co. K, seriously.
Henry Carr, Co. K, slightly.
William Curtis, Co. K, seriously.
William Careful, Co. K, slightly.

Missing.

Joseph Atkinson, Co. A.
Benjamin Seby, Co. A.
Samuel Waller, Co. A.
Benjamin Hancy, Co. B.
Eli Wright, Co. B.
James Young, Co. C.

Arthur Baily, Co. H.
Corporal Edward Taylor, Co. I.
Joseph Pullett, Co. I.
Robert Rinhet, Co. K.
William Johnson, Co. K.

BEFORE PETERSBURG, AUGUST 30, 1864.

Nothing of marked importance is transpiring in front of Petersburg, excepting always the artillery compliments so frequently exchanged, which are sometimes disagreeably impressive. Yesterday the shelling was continued nearly all day, and, with a view to afford mutual amusement, it was prolonged during the evening, with a display of meteoric flashes not altogether unattended with danger. The "Petersburg Express" was actively engaged in conveying leaden despatches to our Southern brethren, insomuch as there is a great gulf which we may not pass until Gen. Grant shall bridge it. It is peculiarly gratifying to witness with what pleasure our soldiers give the enemy an indisputable proof of the quality of their powder. They recognize but one way of dealing with him, and that is by the means now so vigorously employed.

Occasionally we are called to mourn the death of a soldier under very extraordinary circumstances. Yesterday, one of these cases happened. A private in the 7th U. S. C. T. got a sight on a rebel sharpshooter and fired through one of the rifle-holes on the breast-works, merely large enough to enable him to put the muzzle of his musket through and sight his object. Having fired he withdrew his weapon to observe what effect he had made, when, from a distance of about three hundred yards, a ball passed through the rifle-hole, entering the head of this colored defender and killing him instantly. This is the second instance of the kind which has come under my notice, and may be regarded as either wonderfully expert or surprisingly accidental. This unfortunate soldier's name was Stanley,[39] and was a member of Company B.

In the battle north of the James river, in the vicinity of Deep Bottom, one of those unfortunate mistakes was made which was attended with melancholy results. While the engagement was raging fearfully, the 7th U. S. Colored Troops were hardpressed by the rebels, and, through a mistake, the 4th New Hampshire, thinking them Confederates, also opened a galling fire upon them. With the black soldiers it now became a question of life and death. Fully impressed that no quarter would be shown them if captured, and with the recollection of Fort Pillow[40] to quicken their impulses, they

39. Alexander W. Stanley was from Dorchester County, Maryland. Califf, *Record of the Seventh Regiment, U.S. Colored Troops*, 109.

40. Located on the Mississippi River north of Memphis, the fort was defended by 295 whites and 262 blacks. The Confederates' successful assault on the fort in April, 1864, is one of the most controversial battles of the war. When the besieged Union forces refused to surrender, Forrest ordered Confederates to attack. There is considerable dispute about exactly what occurred as Union forces retreated. There is little doubt, however, that the black soldiers of the 11th USCT and of Battery F, 4th U.S. Colored Light Artillery, fell victim, in some measure, to southern rage. Only 58 of the black troops were taken prisoner. The incident became known in the North as the Massacre of Fort Pillow. Among black soldiers, the massacre confirmed southern barbarity, warned of the treatment that awaited them as prisoners, and became a rallying cry for revenge in subsequent battles. Williams, *A History of Negro Troops*, Chap. 12; James M. McPherson, *The Negro's Civil War: How American Negroes Felt and Acted During the War for the Union* (New York, 1965), 216–23; Faust (ed.), *Historical Times Illustrated Encyclopedia*, 277–78.

charged desperately upon the rebels and drove them a short distance from their position. Flushed by this success, the colored soldiers now turned their attention to the 4th New Hampshire, whom they supposed to be "graybacks," especially as they had been firing severely into the black troops for some time, under a similar mistaken apprehension. The regiment and the division to which it was attached now prepared to charge, when the mistake was suddenly discovered, which, if it had been a moment later, would have swept the entire colored regiment from existence. As it was, many valuable lives were lost, which, under the circumstances, is extremely painful. The affair is one of those unfortunate occurrences which could scarcely be avoided.

The 7th Regiment was raised in Maryland by Colonel, now Brigadier General Wm. Birney, and its splendid fighting now is to be attributed to the spirit which he has been enabled to infuse into his entire command.

HEADQUARTERS 2D BRIGADE, 3D DIVISION, 18TH ARMY CORPS

DEEP BOTTOM, SEPT. 1, 1864.

The 10th and 18th Corps having changed locations, I find myself now very pleasantly situated on the north bank of the James river, about ten miles from Richmond. I visited the front of Petersburg yesterday and the day before. There is less enmity than usual manifested against our pickets. Yesterday there was scarcely any artillery firing. This occasioned a great deal of remark, especially as the day previous had been noted for an almost unceasing cannonading. Some argued from this suggestive quiet that the rebels were contemplating a strategic movement, but others jocosely asserted that it was the respect for the day on which the Chicago Convention[41] would

41. With the Union apparently unable to force a successful conclusion of the war, its troops stalled around Richmond and Atlanta, Lincoln was under serious political threat. Some Republicans were calling for a "more vigorous" candidate, and Democrats were determined to nominate a "peace man" to contest the upcoming elections. Their convention met in Chicago on August 29 and, convinced that public opinion supported their position, nominated General George B. McClellan. Two days later, Atlanta fell to the Union, destroying any chances the Democrats had of winning the White House.

probably nominate a candidate for the Presidency. The rebels therefore put themselves on their best behavior.

The rebel authorities are gradually improving in manners, if not in morals. Immediately in our front, an arrangement has been entered into, in which the enemy has agreed to discontinue firing on this part of the picket line. The rebels and our colored soldiers now converse together on apparently very friendly terms, and exchange such luxuries as apples, tobacco, and hard tack, by throwing them to each other. It was hardly deemed possible that the enemy could be induced to refrain from firing on black troops wherever they could be seen, but this concession on their part is another evidence that the barbarous position assumed by the rebel President, with reference to our colored defenders, could not be sustained in application. It is gratifying to record this fact, especially so as the rebs were aware that the 36th U. S. Colored Troops, recruited in North Carolina, are among those whom they know would enjoy its benefit. Of course, it is a mutual arrangement, conferring no more favors than it receives.

This part of the army was startled on the 29th ultimo by the intelligence that Private Spencer Brown,[42] Co. H, 5th U. S. C. T., had deserted to the rebels. This being the first instance of the kind that has occurred in this corps which has come under observation, it very naturally excited wonder and amazement. As no cause can now be satisfactorily assigned, it is necessary to indulge in conjecture to find a mitigation, if possible, for this unfortunate man's conduct. He was heard to remark by several of his comrades, previous to his desertion, that he was considering the matter, under the plea that he was no better treated in the army than he was by his former master.

Silas Holly, Co. G, 36th U. S. C. T., was shot a few days ago, by Lieut. Francis A. Bichinel, for alleged stubbornness, disobedience of orders, and manifesting a mutinous spirit. The 36th was recruited in North Carolina. The soldier is still living, though but faint hopes are entertained of his recovery.

John Williams, of the 36th U. S. C. T., was accidentally shot on the 29th inst., by James Williams, of the same regiment. He is not expected to survive.

Foote, *The Civil War . . . Red River to Appomattox,* 549–52; J. G. Randall and David Donald, *The Civil War and Reconstruction* (Boston, 1969), 473–75.

42. According to the records, Brown had enrolled for three years in Company H in May, 1864, at age twenty. *Official Roster of the Soldiers of Ohio,* I, 616.

BEFORE PETERSBURG, SEPT. 2, 1864.

In my despatch of yesterday I mentioned the growing good-feeling
which was manifested for the colored soldiers by the rebels on our
extreme right, north of the James river, in front of Richmond. I have
also to add that the enemy before Petersburg is also giving evidence
of kindred inclination. Here is where we were accustomed to see
nothing but the most vindictive manifestations on the part of the Rebs
against all Union soldiers, and especially the colored ones; but now it
appears that a change has been made in the rebel programme, and
the graybacks and the blacks are daily exchanging such articles as
they possess, and such civilities as the nature of the case may admit.
These courtesies are believed to be the outcroppings of some undeveloped purpose on the part of the Davis Government. As the chief
conspirator was not successful in frightening by threatening instant
death to all colored men captured in the uniform of the United States
Government, he is probably attempting a new dodge, with a view to
encourage desertion, or throw these troops off their guard for the
purpose of surprise at some vital point. However, General Paine,
commanding the 3d division, 18th Army Corps, has issued orders
that any one detected in holding communication of any character
with the enemy will be instantly shot.

BUILDING A RAILROAD

Yesterday afternoon I called to see an officer on business promising
to return in an hour, which I did, when, to my surprise, I saw an
engine and several cars passing before his quarters. Sixty minutes
previous there were neither spade, rail, nor ties, or any indication
that such an improvement was contemplated, and you may judge of
my astonishment and the rapidity of the work, when I inform you
that nearly a mile of track was laid and the train was passing over it.
As it is a part of the Commander-in-chief's strategy, I will not say
which way it is proposed to run, but merely assure you that it will be
a benefit to the army, and that in a few days, at the rate at which it
commenced, it will soon be completed.

Lieutenant McDonald, Co. K., 20th Colored Troops,[43] raised in

43. There is some mix-up here, for the 20th USCT was raised in New York in early
1864 and, throughout the war, served in the Department of the Gulf. It is likely that
Chester meant the 29th Connecticut, mustered in April, 1864, and sent first to Hilton

Connecticut, who has been acting as assistant inspector general on General William Birney's staff, went out to post some pickets yesterday, and has not been heard from since. It is supposed that he was killed by a sharpshooter.

General William Birney is now confined to his quarters by an indisposition which is by no means dangerous at present. General Birney is now in command of the 3d division, 18th Army Corps.

HEADQUARTERS 2D BRIGADE, 3D DIVISION, 18TH ARMY CORPS

SEPTEMBER 4, 1864.

Everything is as quiet as one could wish in this part of the Army of the James. The troops are enjoying, without any fear of being struck by a passing bullet, the satisfaction of an improved healthy state in camp. Sunday morning has dawned, with as much observance for the day as is possible in camp. The colored troops are nearly all professors of religion, and during the week manifest their faith in those animating prayer meetings so peculiar to the race.

FIRING ALONG THE LINE

About sundown last evening a heavy firing was heard in the direction of Petersburg, and continued until a late hour, when everything seemed to subside to its usual quietude. It was probably nothing more than the usual artillery exchanges, yet it was more rapid than such communications generally are. In and about those regions it generally rains lead, done up in the most disagreeable packages, which are attended on both sides with many serious and fatal results.

Head, South Carolina. It was transferred to the Army of the James that summer and saw action in the siege of Richmond and Petersburg. There is no record of a Lieutenant McDonald. However, Company K has a Second Lieutenant R. McDonough who was mustered in January, 1864. Cornish, *The Sable Arm*, 253–54; Dyer, *Compendium of the War of the Rebellion*, 248; W. A. Croffut and John M. Morris, *The Military and Civil History of Connecticut During the War of 1861–65* (New York, 1868), 637, 648; Joseph T. Wilson, *The Black Phalanx: A History of Negro Soldiers of the United States in the Wars of 1775–1812, 1861–65* (Hartford, 1888), 519–24; *Catalogue of Connecticut Volunteer Organizations* (Hartford, 1869), 915. Note that Chester, in his September 5, 1864, dispatch, identifies the 29th as a regiment raised in Connecticut.

How the News from Atlanta Was Received

Day before yesterday this part of the army was officially informed that Atlanta was captured[44] and a great victory had been gained. The cheers of the colored defenders about division headquarters (it should be remembered that the 3d Division is entirely composed of negro troops) were loud and prolonged. The different regiments in camp were soon electrified with the news, and caught up the subsiding cheers from headquarters and made the welkin ring with rejoicings and congratulations, until the spirit of enthusiasm reached the outermost pickets, who joined in the shout of exultation. The rebels in the woods opposite to our pickets rushed out inquiring what was the matter with the Yankees, and when informed that it was owing to the fall of Atlanta they forgot to return thanks for a courteous reply to their question.

Fatal Accident

One of those accidents proceeding from carelessness, or, perhaps, in this instance, recklessness, occurred in the camp of the 38th United States Colored Troops on the 2d, and resulted in the death of two men and slightly wounding three others. It appears that an unexploded shell was found near the camp of the 38th, which in some way excited the curiosity of some of the men. They were warned against it, and in order to prevent danger, a sergeant unscrewed the fuse plug and threw it away. Isaiah Wilson looked for and found it, and foolishly began to refit it, when the shell exploded, killing Wilson and Philip Woodland, and slightly wounding Frederick Fenwick, Fred. Cole, and Denson White, all of Company B.

Desertion of Colored Soldiers

Joseph Haskins and Robert Beasely,[45] members of the 5th U. S. C. T., deserted to the enemy on the morning of the 2d inst. The 5th was recruited in Ohio, and to the credit of the loyal colored population of that State, it should be understood that these deserters

44. Atlanta fell to Sherman after Confederate forces evacuated the city on September 1, following a two-month siege. Foote, *The Civil War . . . Red River to Appomattox*, 530; Randall and Donald, *The Civil War*, 427.

45. Joseph Haskins and Robert Beasely (along with Spencer Brown) were members of Company H. Haskins, age thirty-six, and Beasely, twenty-five, were mustered in at the same time. *Official Roster of the Soldiers of Ohio*, I, 616–17.

did not come from that State, but were enlisted at City Point, together with several other contrabands, while the regiment was located at that place. These two, with Spencer Brown, whom I announced in a former despatch, the first desertions which have occurred among the colored troops to the enemy, have very naturally suggested many conjectures as to the cause, but as they are all speculation, I will mention but two, in no way holding myself responsible for their correctness: Some say it was the bad treatment of company commanders, while others affirm that it is the result of placing contrabands in a regiment of free colored men. There are regiments in this division, the men of which are so firmly attached to their officers that not the slightest fear is entertained that they will desert. There must be a cause, though by no means a justification, for such a vile act, which the authorities will learn, if they deem the matter worthy of an investigation.

Along the Picket Lines

Through official courtesy I rode along our vidette lines, yesterday, in full view of the enemy's pickets, many of whom—some of them officers—waved papers with a view to invite an exchange of news. Our troops are forbidden to hold any communication with the enemy, which, of course, deprives the rebels of their usual supply of Northern papers. Occasionally, however, there are some whose anxiety for Southern news rises above their love for obedience. A white non-commissioned officer of cavalry was caught in the act of exchanging papers, day before yesterday, and was immediately put under arrest by the officer of the day. The great desire of the enemy for Northern news, at this juncture, is to be attributed to their interest in the late Chicago Convention, and to learn whether they have gained a victory there.

The absence of all firing between the pickets along this part of the line is owing to an arrangement made upon an overture from the enemy to our colored pickets.

BEFORE PETERSBURG, SEPT. 5, 1864—6 A.M.

We have been speculating in camp to-day as to the result of the shot and shell which were poured in copious showers during last night and quite early this morning, among the inhabitants of Secessia.

Yesterday was the quietest Sunday we have had along this part of the line for some time. The absence of the usual cannonading produced the impression that it was caused by the mutual respect which the belligerents entertain for the day. During the night, however, the artillery duel was severe.

There must be some object in the incessant artillery and musket firing by the enemy in front of Petersburg. Every inducement possible has been made, on the part of our troops, to cease this barbarous practice, but the overtures have been met by renewed malignity and vindictive bitterness. When it is known that the enemy is especially anxious to discontinue this murderous propensity everywhere else but in front of Petersburg, it gives cause for suspicion that the rebels are endeavoring, by the report of cannonading, to conceal some terrible purpose. The future can only develop the mystery of the present.

The new railroad which is in progress of construction is rapidly advancing to completion. It begins at the terminus of the road from City Point, which runs to nearly the limits of Petersburg, and will run along the line to connect with the Weldon road. The rapid manner in which it is being laid gives assurance that but a few days will be required to complete it. This looks very much like overcoming the usual objections and obstructions to prosecuting a winter campaign.

Brigadier General Birney, commanding the 3d Division, 10th Army Corps is now quite ill with the dysentery, and, with a view to assist in his recovery, he has been removed to the Chesapeake Hospital at Fortress Monroe. The absence of this gallant officer is a source of serious regret to the colored troops, who have the most implicit confidence in God and General Birney. Colonel Howell,[46] of the 85th Pennsylvania Volunteers,[47] is the temporary commander of the division.

Casualties Among the Colored Troops

Dennis Portlong, Company C, 22d United States Colored Troops, was killed on the 1st, and Daniel Wilson, Company K, on the 2d, in

46. Joshua B. Howell (d. 1864). A colonel, 85th Pennsylvania, Howell was placed in charge of the black division in early September. He died on September 14 from injuries sustained when he fell from his horse two days earlier. Bates, *History of Pennsylvania Volunteers*, III, 1–7.

47. Organized in Uniontown in November, 1861, the 85th was attached to the Army of the Potomac. It was later moved to North Carolina and South Carolina and participated in the assault on Fort Wagner. By May, 1864, it was part of the Army of the James. Dyer, *Compendium of the War of the Rebellion*, 1602–1603.

the trenches before Petersburg. The following persons, of the same regiment, have been wounded recently:

Sergeant William H. Mathews, Charles Middleworth, Isaac Young, Company C; James Harris, Co. I; James Murry, Joseph Wilson, and Samuel Leaton.

The 22d was raised in Pennsylvania. John Wilson, Co. A; John Ford, Co. C; William Jones, Co. K; and Charles Shortes, have recently died in the hospital. Shortes died from the effects of a wound received at Fort Powhatan on the 31st of May.

In the 7th United States Colored Troops, recruited in Maryland, George Young, Co. E, was wounded slightly in the left shoulder; Sergeant John H. Bundick, Company K, on the 2d; E. Mooney, Company D; and on the 3d Sergeant John Gross, left hip, and Samuel Mander, Co. G. side of the foot.

Samuel Burton, Co. K, and Henry Parker, Co. I, 29th (Connecticut) U. S. C. T., were killed on the 1st inst., and on the 3d Chas. D. Ennings. The following persons were wounded during the last day or two: Dennis Williams, Co. E, knee; Abraham Johnson, Co. H, flesh wound in the cheek; William Lambert, Co. G, back, a contusion; Geo. F. Porter, Co. D, shoulder; George Odell, Co. E, toe, and Theodore Anderson, thigh.

REGIMENTAL BANDS

The colored bands attached to the 22d and 8th U. S. C. T. were discoursing excellent music yesterday evening till dark. The band of the 8th,[48] under the instruction of Captain Joseph Anderson, the leader of Frank Johnson's[49] famous band, has progressed to an

---

48. Recruited in Pennsylvania, the 8th USCT suffered heavy casualties at Deep Bottom in August, 1864. It participated in the attack on Chaffin's Farm, part of the Confederates' defenses outside Richmond, and a few days later saw action at Darbytown Road. It was involved in the final assault on Petersburg and was the first infantry regiment to enter the city after its fall, followed by the 45th, 41st, and 127th, three black Pennsylvania regiments. Binder, "Pennsylvania Negro Regiments," 414–15; Dyer, *Compendium of the War of the Rebellion,* 248.

49. Francis Johnson (1792–1844). Born in Martinique, Johnson emigrated to Philadelphia in 1809. Ten years later, his band was considered one of the finest in the city. He gave a series of promenade concerts in London in 1837. Later he played a number of engagements sponsored by the Philadelphia Museum. Following Johnson's death, his band was taken over by one of its members, Joseph G. Anderson (*ca.* 1816–1873). Anderson conducted a music studio in Philadelphia. He was employed by the government to train brass bands for black regiments at Camp William Penn. Eileen

efficiency in music which has endeared it to the officers and men of that excellent regiment, and is calculated to surpass in correct playing any of the similar institutions which have had their existence in this rebellion. Captain Anderson is still instructing them, though they can execute, to the satisfaction of competent judges, some forty pieces of scientific music. He will probably visit Philadelphia in a day or two, from which city he has been absent since the 8th Regiment left Camp Penn, about nine months ago.

HEADQUARTERS 2D BRIG., 3D DIV., 18TH A. C.

NORTH OF THE JAMES RIVER, SEPT. 7, 1864.

Intelligence from Richmond of yesterday and the day before acknowledges the capture of Atlanta by General Sherman, and ascribes it to the removal of General Johnston from command of the Army of Tennessee.

Day before yesterday the enemy's pickets in front of this corps engaged in a variety of fancy and other dances opposite our outposts. The dancing itself would scarcely have been noticed, but having ladies, relatives, and friends for partners within speaking distances of our videttes, attracted some attention, and afforded no little amusement.

There are sure evidences of a scarcity of food just now among the rebels. They are continually soliciting to exchange tobacco and their papers for hard tack, sugar and coffee, which are regarded by them as luxuries. The great desire to obtain these eatables, since the capture of the Weldon Railroad, has somewhat shortened their supplies; of course, in itself, sufficient to reflect the exhausted condition of their supplies. The men acknowledge that they receive far below the usual quantity allowed to them, in consequence of its great scarcity, and as yesterday was spent by their pickets in gaming for squirrels and other things, to be obtained by shooting, we may very correctly infer that they are in a very hungry condition.

One of the rebel pickets a day or two ago advanced, unarmed, of

Southern, *Biographical Dictionary of Afro-American Musicians* (Westport, Conn., 1982), 205–206, 12–13; Nicholas B. Wainwright (ed.), *A Philadelphia Perspective: The Diary of Sidney George Fisher Covering the Years 1834–1871* (Philadelphia, 1967), 70.

course, to the post of a colored sentinel. He immediately hauled out a large piece of tobacco, which would cost in this army about two dollars, and begged that the darkskinned soldier would give him one biscuit, or hard tack, as it is known here, to eat. He merely informed the reb that it was against orders to make exchanges with their enemy, and to the persistent and repeated entreaties of this hungry Confederate he turned a deaf ear. After Johnny found he could not persuade this colored soldier to furnish him with a biscuit, he went away cursing him for refusing to meet his wishes. It is very difficult, in fact, generally impossible, to induce a colored soldier to swerve one iota from the instructions he may receive towards awakening the inhabitants of Jeffdom to a fearful realization of their assumed position.

One of the best evidences of confidence in the valor of colored troops is manifest in the fact that they are entrusted with holding the right of our line, which is the nearest point we possess to Richmond. Their character for fighting and discipline is established, and henceforth they may be expected to take a part in all the grand engagements along this line. They are anxiously waiting for the opportunity to meet the enemy, as, independent of the affair of Government, many of them have a private account which they are determined to settle at the first opportunity.

DEEP BOTTOM, VA., SEPT. 9, 1864.

Last evening we were favored with one of those cool, chilling rains which herald the approach of bracing weather. This morning we are in the enjoyment of an invigorating climate, feeling considerably refreshed by a comfortable night's rest. Blankets were indeed serviceable and appreciated last evening. Any improvement on the present state of the weather, tending towards zero, will suggest the propriety of the troops making themselves as comfortable as possible while in the field. In a short time we expect to be in Petersburg or Richmond, or both—certainly by the first of January, where, for the first time, the grand emancipation proclamation of freedom will be commemorated in these strongholds of the enemy.

We have the pleasure of greeting many of the prodigal sons of Father Abraham, who, having repented, are returning honorably to worship at the shrine of their former devotion. Several came in yesterday, and were surprised at the kind manner in which they were received and treated. Knowing the exhausted state of the enemy's commissariat, a good meal was prepared, to which they did ample justice. On the cup of coffee alone, one of them declared that he could travel fifty miles. That drink is quite a luxury in the South at present, and its delicious taste awakened no doubt former reminiscences which smote their guilty consciences, and called to their remembrance how much suffering they had entailed upon themselves by deserting the flag of their fathers. These deserters affirm that it is the impression in the rebel army that all who come over to our lines will be unfriendly dealt with, and forced to perform military service, and that if the truth could be circulated it would soon be depleted. The light, it is to be hoped, will soon dawn upon their darkened minds, and that they will accept the proffered mercy of General Grant before it is too late.

The canal at Dutch Gap,[50] by which Gen. Butler hopes to avoid some seven or eight miles of the James river, and the obstructions placed there, is grandly progressing to a satisfactory completion. To the labors of the colored troops, who, amid the showers of shot and shell, are industriously prosecuting this great enterprise, will be ascribed the glory of its accomplishment. Though batteries, forts, and a ram are continually hurling their messengers of death to interrupt the work and drive them off, our black troops, who have become seasoned to this kind of exercise, which they regard as sport, continue on in their operations as cheerfully as if nothing was happening. Yesterday I saw a shell explode in the camp of the 6th (Penna.) U. S. C. T., and expected to see some uneasiness manifest at the close proximity of these ugly customers, but was surprised to observe no more commotion than if the occurrence had been one of the most ordinary circumstances. It will be gratifying to the people of

50. Beaten back by the defenders of Petersburg and bottled up around Bermuda Hundred, Butler decided to dig a canal at Dutch Gap, a 175-yard spit of land in a bend on the James River. It was the only way, he concluded, to avoid the obstructions placed in the river and the constant enemy fire. The canal could open the way for an assault on Richmond. The black troops building the canal were under constant fire, and though casualties were low, the effort took much longer than anticipated. In the end, it had little effect on the final assault on Richmond. Butler, *Autobiography,* 743–52; Faust (ed.), *Historical Times Illustrated Encyclopedia,* 231–32.

Pennsylvania to learn that this gallant regiment, raised near Phila-delphia, is doing a service, under trying circumstances, in connection with others equally as brave, that commends it to the consideration of the country. That colored troops should be selected to perform such an arduous duty, exposed as they are to the raking fire of the enemy from several batteries, is an evidence of their high standard in the estimation of their military chieftain.

This canal, constructed for some purpose best known to the commander-in-chief, will shortly be completed, when the colored troops, who have labored so faithfully for its execution, will be ready to respond to "Forward!" whenever it may be passed along the line.

CORRESPONDENCE BETWEEN GENERALS LEE AND FORREST AND GENERAL WASHBURN ON THE TREATMENT OF PRISONERS, NEGRO TROOPS, ETC.—THE MASSACRES AT FORT PILLOW AND BRYLE'S CROSS ROADS—THE BLACK FLAG

Enclosed I forward you a long correspondence between General Washburn[51] and the rebel Generals Lee[52] and Forrest[53] as to how they regard colored persons captured in the uniform of the United States Government. The correspondence is interesting, and should be read as an evidence of Southern barbarism and inhumanity, coupled with prevarication to shrink from the consequences which their infamy has entailed upon them. The rebels can raise the black flag as soon as they please in reference to colored troops, by whom they will be met with a corresponding determination. They ask neither favors nor

51. Cadwallader Colden Washburn (1818–1882) entered the war as a colonel, 2nd Wisconsin Volunteer Cavalry, which he had raised, and was promoted to major general in 1862. His forces saw action west of the Mississippi River. Later he was placed in command of the Department of West Tennessee. *DAB*, X, 496.

52. Stephen Dill Lee (1833–1903). A graduate of West Point, Lee was the youngest lieutenant general in the Confederate army. He saw action at Sharpsburg, Second Manassas, and Vicksburg, where he was captured and later exchanged. He succeeded Hood as commander of the Army of Tennessee. *DAB*, VI, 130–31; Wakelyn, *Biographical Dictionary of the Confederacy*, 282.

53. Nathan Bedford Forrest (1821–1877) is best known for his cavalry raids against Union communications and behind enemy lines. He is generally held responsible for the slaughter of black troops at Fort Pillow. *DAB*, III, 532; Wakelyn, *Biographical Dictionary of the Confederacy*, 189–90; Cornish, *The Sable Arm*, 173–76.

quarter from them, and are willing to meet them in whatever manner they propose to fight them—"only let the rebs come along."

The correspondence, as published in full in the Richmond *Sentinel*, is very long. It opens with a letter to General Washburn by the butcher Forrest, asserting his civilized character, and asking if captured rebels are to be treated as prisoners of war, and proposing an exchange of wounded officers and men of Sturgis'[54] command. A letter, dated June 17th, from Washburn to Lee, declares that if it is intended to raise the black flag, the black troops will cheerfully accept the issue. "Up to this time no troops have fought more gallantly, and none have conducted themselves with greater propriety." In reply to General Forrest, General Washburn does not accept his arrogation of being "civilized," but receives with satisfaction the intimation "that the recent slaughter of colored troops at the battle of Tishomingo Creek[55] resulted rather from the desperation from which they fought than a predetermination to give them no quarter"—(a curious confession from the chivalry!) Following this General Washburn directs his attention to the murder of Major Bradford:

"Among the prisoners captured at Fort Pillow was Major Bradford,[56] who had charge of the fort after the fall of Major Booth.[57]

54. Samuel Davis Sturgis (1822–1889). A graduate of West Point and a Mexican War veteran, Sturgis was in command of Fort Smith, Arkansas, when all his officers resigned to join the Confederacy at the outbreak of the war. He briefly held a command in Kansas and later led the defenses of Washington, D.C. He was transferred to the West after Antietam and held commands in Tennessee and Mississippi. *DAB*, IX, 182–83; Ezra J. Warner, *Generals in Blue: Lives of the Union Commanders* (Baton Rouge, 1964), 486–87.

55. Sherman had ordered Sturgis from Memphis to protect the vulnerable single-track railroad that supplied his forces in northwest Georgia. On June 10, 1864, Sturgis was routed by Forrest at Tishomingo Creek and Brice's Cross Roads. There were 223 dead, 394 wounded, and 1,623 missing. The defeat saw the end of Sturgis' military career. Faust (ed.), *Historical Times Illustrated Encyclopedia*, 79.

56. William F. Bradford (*ca.* 1832–1864). A Tennessee lawyer, Bradford raised a cavalry regiment that served in Kentucky. He was transferred to Fort Pillow in February, 1864, where he was second in command under Major Lionel Booth. Stewart Sifakis, *Who Was Who in the Civil War* (New York, 1988), 67.

57. Lionel F. Booth (1838–1864). A Philadelphia clerk, Booth joined the army before the outbreak of hostilities. In mid-1863 he moved from quartermaster sergeant to captain of a company of black soldiers. He was promoted to major and transferred to Fort Pillow in March, 1864. Booth was killed by a sharpshooter during the Confederates' first assault. Sifakis, *Who Was Who in the Civil War*, 63; Faust (ed.), *Historical Times Illustrated Encyclopedia*, 277; Williams, *A History of Negro Troops*, 257.

After being taken prisoner, he was started with the prisoners, in charge of Colonel Duckworth,[58] for Jackson. At Brownsville they rested over night.

"The following morning two companies were detailed by Colonel Duckworth to proceed to Jackson with the prisoners. After they had started and proceeded a very short distance, five soldiers were recalled by Colonel Duckworth, and were conferred with by him.

"They then rejoined the column, and after proceeding about five miles from Brownsville, the column was halted, and Major Bradford taken about fifty yards from the roadside and deliberately shot by the five men who had been recalled by Colonel Duckworth, and the body left unburied upon the ground where it fell. He now lies buried near the spot, and if you desire you can easily satisfy yourself of the truth of what I assert."

The following letter of Forrest is, in the light of facts well known to our military authorities, a blustering and clumsy attempt to shuffle off the charges against him. General Lee's letter, it will be seen, labors to palliate rather than excuse. But, on the whole, it is very evident that the Southern authorities do not wish to rest under the odium of the inhuman massacres in the West:

GENERAL FORREST TO GENERAL WASHBURN

HEADQUARTERS FORREST'S CAVALRY, IN THE FIELD, JUNE 23, 1864.

Major General C. C. Washburn, Commanding U. S. Forces, Memphis, Tenn.:

GENERAL: Your communication of the 19th inst. is received, in which you say you are left "in doubt as to the course the Confederate Government intends to pursue in regard to colored troops."

My Government is in possession of all the facts as regards my official conduct and the operations of my command since I entered the service, and if you desire a proper discussion and decision, I refer you again to the President of the Confederate States.

I would not have you understand, however, that, in a matter of so much importance, I am indisposed to place at your command and disposal any facts desired, when applied for in a manner becoming an

---

58. William L. Duckworth (?–?) was in command of the 7th Tennessee Cavalry, 1st Brigade, Chalmers' division, under Leonidas Polk. *OR*, Ser. I, Vol. XXXII, Pt. 1, p. 334.

officer holding your rank and position, for it is certainly desirable to every one occupying a public position to be placed right before the world, and there has been no time since the capture of Fort Pillow that I would not have furnished all the facts connected with its capture, had they been properly applied for. But now the matter rests with the two Governments.

I have, however, for your information, enclosed you copies of the official correspondence between the commanding officers at Fort Pillow and myself. Also, copies of a statement of Captain Young,[59] the senior officer of that garrison, together with (sufficient) extracts from a report of the affair, by my A. D. C., Captain Charles W. Anderson, which I approve and endorse as correct.

As to the death of Major Bradford, I knew nothing of it until eight or ten days after it is said to have occurred. On the 13th (the day after the capture of Fort Pillow) I went to Jackson, and the report I had of the affair was this: Major Bradford was, with other officers, sent to the headquarters of Colonel McCulloch,[60] and all the prisoners were in charge of one of McCulloch's regiments. Bradford requested the privilege of attending the burial of his brother, which was granted, he giving his parole to return. Instead of returning he changed his clothing and started for Memphis. Some of my men were hunting deserters, and came on Bradford just as he had landed on the south side of the Hatchie, and arrested him. When arrested he claimed to be a Confederate soldier, belonging to Bragg's army;[61] that he had been home on furlough, and was then on his way to join his command. As he could show no papers, he was believed to be a deserter, and was taken to Covington, and not until he was recognized and spoken to by the citizens did the guard know that he was

59. John T. Young (?–?), provost marshal of the post, was taken prisoner by the Confederates. Williams, *A History of Negro Troops*, Chap. 12.

60. Robert McCulloch (?–?) commanded the 2nd Brigade of Cavalry, Chalmers' division, under the command of Polk in Tennessee. He was wounded during the Meridian Expedition in March, 1864. *OR*, Ser. I, Vol. XXXII, Pt. 1, pp. 198, 258, 334.

61. Braxton Bragg (1817–1876). A graduate of West Point, Bragg became a commander of Confederate forces in the Army of Tennessee. He suffered a number of defeats in 1862 and 1863 before turning the tables on Union forces at Chickamauga in mid-September, 1863. Unable to follow up this victory, Bragg's army was defeated by Grant in November. *DAB*, I, 585–87; Wakelyn, *Biographical Dictionary of the Confederacy*, 105–106.

Bradford. He was sent to Col. Duckworth, or taken by him to Brownsville. All of Chalmers' command[62] went south from Brownsville via Lagrange; and as all the other prisoners had been gone some time ago, and there was no chance for them to catch up and place Bradford with them, he was ordered by Col. Duckworth or Gen. Chalmers to be sent to me at Jackson.

I knew nothing of the matter until eight or ten days afterwards, when I heard that his body was found near Brownsville. I understand that he attempted to escape and was shot.

If he was improperly killed, nothing would afford me more pleasure than to punish the perpetrators to the full extent of the law; and to show you how I regard such transactions, I can refer you to my demand upon Major General Hurlbut[63] (no doubt upon file in your office), for the delivery to the Confederate authorities of Col. Fielding Hurst[64] and others of his regiment, who deliberately took out and killed seven Confederate soldiers, one of whom they left to die after cutting off his tongue, punching out his eyes, splitting his mouth on each side, to his ears. I have mentioned and given you these facts in order that you may have no further excuse or apology for referring to these matters in connection with myself, and evince to you my determination to do all in my power to avoid the responsibility of causing the adoption of the policy which you seem determined to press.

The negroes have our sympathy, and, so far as consistent with safety, we will spare them at the expense of those who are alone responsible for the inauguration of a worse than savage warfare.

Now, in conclusion, I demand a plain, unqualified answer to two

62. James Ronald Chalmers (1831–1898). A lawyer, Chalmers rose rapidly through the ranks to brigadier general in the Confederate army. He was transferred to the cavalry service in 1863 and saw action at Munfordville and Murfreesboro while in command of the Department of Alabama, Mississippi and Eastern Louisiana under Forrest. *DAB*, II, 593; Wakelyn, *Biographical Dictionary of the Confederacy*, 127.

63. Stephen Augustus Hurlbut (1815–1882) saw action with Grant's Army of Tennessee, at Shiloh (after which he was promoted to major general) and Corinth. He assumed command of Memphis in September, 1863. Powell, *Officers of the Army and Navy*, 351; Cornish, *The Sable Arm*, 258–59.

64. Fielding Hurst (?–?) commanded two companies of the 1st West Tennessee Cavalry at Corinth in 1862. Two years later, he was in command of the 6th Tennessee, 2nd Brigade, 7th Division, Army of Tennessee. *OR*, Ser. I, Vol. XVII, pp. 367, 372, Ser. I, Vol. XLV, Pt. 1, p. 96.

questions, and then I have done with further correspondence with you on this subject. This matter must be settled:

In battle, and on the battle-field, do you intend to slaughter my men who fall into your hands?

If you do not intend to do so, will they be treated as prisoners of war?

I have over two thousand of Sturgis' command prisoners, and will hold every officer and private as a hostage until I receive your declaration, and am satisfied that you carry out in good faith the answers you make and until I am assured that no Confederate soldier has been foully dealt with from the day of the battle of Tishomingo Creek to this time. It is not yet too late for you to retrace your steps and arrest the storm.

Relying, as I do, upon that Divine Power which in wisdom disposes of all things, relying also upon the support and approval of my Government and countrymen, and the unflinching bravery and endurance of my troops, and with a consciousness that I have done nothing to produce, but all in my power consistent with honor and the personal safety of myself and command to prevent it, I leave with you the responsibility of bringing about, to use your own language, a "state of affairs too fearful for contemplation."

I am, sir, very respectfully yours,
N. B. FORREST, Maj. General.
official: P. ELLIS, JR., A. A. G.

[Enclosures in the foregoing.]

CAHABA HOSPITAL

CAHABA, ALA., MAY 11, 1864.

Col. H. G. Davis,[65] Commanding Post Cahaba:

COLONEL: I herewith transmit you as near as my memory serves me, according to promise, the demand made by Major General Forrest, C. S. A., for the surrender of Fort Pillow, Tenn:

Major Booth, Commanding U. S. Forces, Fort Pillow, Tenn:

65. Henry Gee Davis (b. 1819) raised a number of companies in Indiana in the first year of the war. He saw action at Shiloh, Corinth, and Chattanooga. In 1864 he was put in command of the 101st USCT, which fought at Nashville. Powell, *Officers of the Army and Navy,* 302.

I have force sufficient to take your works by assault. I, therefore, demand an unconditional surrender of all your forces. Your heroic defence will entitle you to be treated as prisoners of war; but the surrender must be unconditional. I await your answer.

FORREST,
Major General Commanding.

HEADQUARTERS U. S. FORCES

FORT PILLOW, TENN., APRIL 12, 1864.

Maj. Gen. Forrest, Commanding Confederate Forces:

GENERAL: Your demand for the surrender of United States forces under my command received. I ask one hour for consultation with my officers and the commander of Gunboat No. 7, at this place.

I have the honor to be, your obedient servant,
L. F. BOOTH,
Major Commanding U. S. Forces.

Major L. F. Booth, Commanding United States Forces:

I do not demand the surrender of the gunboat No. 7. I ask only for the surrender of Fort Pillow, with men and munitions of war. You have twenty minutes for consideration. At the expiration of that time, if you do not capitulate, I will assault your works.

Your obedient servant,
FORREST,
Major General Commanding.

HEADQUARTERS U. S. FORCES

FORT PILLOW, TENN., APRIL 12, 1864.

Major General Forrest, Commanding Confederate Forces:

GENERAL: Your second demand for the surrender of my forces received. The demand will not be complied with.

Your obedient servant,
L. F. BOOTH,
Major Commanding U. S. Forces, Fort Pillow.

Col. H. G. Davis: I give you the above, for your own satisfaction, from memory. I think it is true in substance. My present condition would preclude the idea of this being an official statement.

> I am, Colonel, your obedient servant,
> JOHN T. YOUNG,
> Captain Company A, 24th Mo. Inf. Vols.

GEN. LEE TO GEN. WASHBURN

HEADQUARTERS DEP'T ALA., MISS., AND E. LA., MERIDIAN, JUNE 28, 1864.

Major General C. C. Washburn, commanding U. S. forces, Memphis, Tenn.:

GENERAL: I am in receipt of your letter of the 17th inst., and have also before me the reply of Major Gen. Forrest thereto.

Though that reply is approved by me, yet I deem it proper to communicate with you upon a subject so seriously affecting our future conduct and that of the troops under our respective commands. Your communication is by no means respectful to me, and is, by implication, insulting to Major General Forrest. This, however, is overlooked, in consideration of the important character of its contents. You assume as correct an exaggerated statement of the circumstances attending the capture of Fort Pillow, relying solely upon the evidence of those who would naturally give a distorted history of the affair.

.   .   .   .

As commanding officer of this department, I desire to make the following statement concerning the capture of Fort Pillow—a statement supported in a great measure by the evidence of one of your own officers captured at that place: The version given by you and your Government is untrue, and not sustained by the facts, to the extent that you indicate. The garrison was summoned in the usual manner, and its commanding officer assumed the responsibility of refusing to surrender, after having been informed by General Forrest of his ability to take the fort, and of his fears as to what the result would be in case the demand was not complied with. The assault was made under a heavy fire and with considerable loss to the attacking party. Your colors were never lowered and your garrison never surrendered, but retreated under cover of a gunboat, with arms in their hands and constantly using them. This was true particularly of your colored troops, who had been firmly convinced by your teachings of the certainty of slaughter in case of capture. Even under these circumstances many of your men—white and black—were taken prisoners. I respectfully refer you to history for numerous cases of indiscriminate slaughter after successful assault, even under less aggravated circumstances.

It is generally conceded by all military precedent that where the issue had been fairly presented and the ability displayed, fearful results are expected to follow a refusal to surrender. The case under consideration is almost an extreme one. You had a servile race armed against their masters, and in a country which had been desolated by almost unprecedented outrages.

I assert that our officers, with all the circumstances against them, endeavored to prevent the effusion of blood, and, as an evidence of this, I refer you to the fact that both white and colored prisoners were taken, and are now in our hands. As regards the battle of Tishomingo Creek, the statements of your negro witnesses are not to be relied on. In their panic they acted as might have been expected from their previous impressions. I do not think most of them were killed—they are yet wandering over the country, attempting to return to their masters. With reference to the status of those captured at Tishomingo Creek and Fort Pillow, I will state that, unless otherwise ordered by my Government, they will not be regarded as prisoners of war, but will be retained, and humanely treated, subject to such future instructions as may be indicated.

Your letter contains many implied threats; these, of course, you can make, and you are fully entitled to any satisfaction that you may feel from having made them.

It is my intention, and that also of my subordinate officers, to conduct this war upon civilized principles, provided you permit us to do so, and I take this occasion to state that we will not shrink from any responsibility that your actions may force upon us. We are engaged in a struggle for the protection of our homes and firesides, for the maintenance of our national existence and liberty; we have counted the cost, and are prepared to go to any extremes; and though it is far from our wish to fight under a black flag, still if you drive us to it, we will accept the issue. Your troops virtually fought under it at the battle of Tishomingo Creek, and the prisoners taken there state that they went into battle under the impression that they would receive no quarter, and, I suppose, with the determination to give none.

I will further remark, that if it is raised, so far as your soldiers are concerned, there can be no distinction, for the unfortunate people whom you pretend to be aiding are not considered entirely responsible for their acts, influenced, as they are, by the superior intellect of their white brothers. I enclose for your consideration certain papers touching the Fort Pillow affair, which were procured from the writer after the exaggerated statements of your press were seen.

I am, General, yours, respectfully,
S. D. Lee, Lieut. General.
Official: T. Ellis, Jr., A. A. G.

CHAPTER 3

Encircling Richmond and Petersburg

DEEP BOTTOM, VA., SEPT. 11, 1864.

There is nothing of any special interest to communicate at this date. The two armies—Union and rebel—are confronting each other with fretful impatience. The enemy is mystified by the operations of Gen. Grant, and, from his movements, is unable to conjecture where or when he proposes to crush them. He would be considerably relieved if he could only suppose at what point the Lieutenant General intends to hurl his hosts; but what increases the anxiety of the rebels is the fear that our Commander-in-chief will attack them at different points, and prevent them, as has been their custom, from concentrating their forces. If the devotees of the imperilled Confederacy are ignorant of the intentions of our master mind, we here are no less so, but with little better opportunities of judging what is most probable.

Everything is progressing as rapidly as the circumstances will admit, to the completion of our grand plans for the destruction of Lee's army, and the capture of the enemy's strongholds. Never has there been so much uneasiness manifested in the rebels' department, and in the sentiments of their journals, as there has been since Gen. Grant, with his unbending will, grasped the very core of the rebellion, which he holds with a tenacity that fully exhibits the paroxysm of fear and grief of the Davis concern.

There is nothing new or interesting from the exciting point in front of Petersburg, which I visited yesterday, but the continual artillery and picket firing. Shot and shell are daily thrown into Petersburg with a view of impressing the Johnnies of what they may reasonably expect. One of the most dreaded features about here is the certain shooting of any of our men who exhibits the least part of his head where the enemy may see it. With a view of trying the expertness of his sharpshooters, caps are frequently raised on a ramrod just above the breastworks, when immediately a ball passes through, to the amusement of the troops. Many of those persons who are shot in the trenches by muskets may attribute their misfortunes to carelessness or a foolish display of courage. But there is no dodging whenever the pieces of shell explode in one's immediate vicinity. This kind of life rather hardens our troops for the service, and, by its frequency, renders them insensible to any emotions of fear. It was hardly to be expected that men, having no previous experience in martial affairs, would present such an undaunted and unwavering front as has been exhibited by the colored troops in front of Petersburg.

CASUALTIES AMONG THE COLORED TROOPS

The following casualties have occurred during the last week in front of Petersburg in the 7th United States Colored Troops:

Captain A. R. Walker, Company I, killed. Perry Richardson, Company B, wounded with a shell in the right wrist, and Stephen W. White, Company F, wounded in the forehead, slight.

8th U. S. C. T.—Calvin Vonhazel, Company B, killed.

9th U. S. C. T.—Hirst Coston, Company C, gunshot wound in the throat; George Jervis, Company H, shell wound in the right leg and right fore finger, slight; John Wesley, Company K, gunshot wound third finger of left hand; Jesse Elsey, Company H, shell wound in left foot, slight.

22d U. S. C. T.—Thomas Ringold, Company B, and Daniel Wilson, Company K, killed.

29th U. S. C. T.—Theodore Anderson, Company H, gunshot wound, thigh, slight; George Carl, Company C, contusion of the thigh; Joseph Demony, Company E, gunshot wound in the hand.

DEEP BOTTOM, VA., SEPT. 24, 1864.

Late last night, the welcome intelligence that General Sheridan[1] had attacked and gained another victory in the Shenandoah Valley

1. Philip Henry Sheridan (1831–1888). A graduate of the United States Military Academy, Sheridan entered the war as a captain. His successes in the West led to his promotion to major general in December, 1862. After victories at Chickamauga and Chattanooga, he was put in command of the cavalry in the Army of the Potomac. He

reached acting Brigadier General Draper's headquarters, exciting
mingled feelings of rejoicing and gratitude. When the good tidings
were received by General Grant, he ordered a shotted-salute to be
fired at daylight this morning along the entire line, but Gen. Butler
requested that the Army of the James delay its firing until 8 o'clock,
which was granted, with the view of making it more effectual. About
half past seven, the camps in this vicinity presented quite a lively
appearance. The different regiments, all of them colored, marched
out with solemn aspect and martial bearing, carrying aloft, with
peculiar pride, the national emblem. They were formed into a line of
battle, behind the breastworks, to await the result of the shotted-
salute.

At Dutch Gap, our guns, in commemoration of the victory, opened
with thundering, rumbling, and successive reports. Huge columns of
smoke went up, and dark, threatening clouds came down. Before the
sounds died away, the salute here opened with terrible determination. One hundred guns, belching forth shot and shells, shook, if it
did no more, the nervous part of the tottering Confederacy. These are
merely the forerunners of that terrible cannonading which is to
unearth the very roots of the rebellion.

It seems that the disposition to treat colored persons as if they
were human is hard for even some loyal men to acquire. The wrongs
which they have suffered in this department would, if ventilated,
exhibit a disgraceful depth of depravity, practiced by dishonest men,
in the name of the Government. These poor people are not only
plundered and robbed, but are kicked and cuffed by those who have
robbed them of their hard earnings and then sent them to other parts
of the department, confident that their ignorance would be a guard
against discovery. At Dutch Gap there is an occasional specimen of
inhumanity exhibited towards the freedmen which is worthy of
mention. It appears that Major Ludlow[2] has charge of the grand
operation of cutting the canal through on the James river, where the
working parties are continually exposed to shot and shell. Among the

---

became commander of the Army of the Shenandoah in August, 1864, and he recorded
victories over Jubal Early at Winchester on September 19 and at Fisher's Hill three days
later, for which he was promoted to brigadier general. *DAB*, IX, 79–80; Shelby Foote,
The Civil War: A Narrative. Red River to Appomattox (New York, 1974), 553–58.

2. This is probably William Ludlow (1843–1901), just out of West Point and
appointed chief engineer of the XX Army Corps. *DAB*, VI, 495.

colored troops are many laborers who are employed by the Government, and because they cannot continue their work like their soldier brethren, when shells are falling and exploding among them, this gallant Kentucky major amuses himself by tying up these redeemed freemen. It is generally believed that his success in this great canal enterprise will be a brigadier general's commission of colored troops. This, to be as mild as possible, would be exceedingly unfortunate, and unjust to those who are making so many willing sacrifices for the perpetuation of the Union. Gen. Butler by no means justifies or allows any man, black or white, to be treated in an unwarrantable manner.

For several days past colored recruits have been arriving to fill up depleted regiments. The 45th U. S. C. T.,[3] from Camp Wm. Penn, arrived at City Point yesterday. It looked as if it was made of good material.

Desertions from the enemy in our front have been so numerous that he has put forth the most vigorous and vigilant means to prevent any more. A camp guard patrols their entire picket line, each sentry walking his regular beat, which, for greater security, is very short, rendering it next to impossible for the repentant rebels to desert. To Colonel G. W. Cole,[4] commander of the picket line of the 2d United States Colored Cavalry,[5] more than any one else, is to be attributed the credit of so general a circulation of General Grant's order, which daily thinned the enemy's pickets in our immediate front. The gallant Colonel is now suffering from the effects of a wound which he received some time ago, and as soon as he is able to mount his favorite war charger, it is generally supposed that he will open up a

3. Raised in Pennsylvania in 1864, the 45th USCT was assigned to the 2nd Brigade, 3rd Division, X Corps, under Terry. With Butler's reorganization, it became part of the 2nd Division under Birney in the XXV Corps. Frederick H. Dyer, *Compendium of the War of the Rebellion* (Des Moines, Iowa, 1908), 250; *OR*, Ser. I, Vol. LXII, Pt. 3, pp. 465, 1126.

4. George W. Cole (1828–1875) mustered in as captain of the 12th New York Infantry. Cole transferred to the 3rd Cavalry and was promoted to major in December, 1862. He served in that capacity until February, 1864, when he was promoted to colonel, 2nd United States Colored Cavalry. Frederick Phisterer (comp.), *New York in the War of the Rebellion, 1861 to 1865* (5 vols.; New York, 1912), I, 55, 790, III, 1880, IV, 4170; Mark Mayo Boatner III, *The Civil War Dictionary* (New York, 1959), 166.

5. Organized at Fortress Monroe in December, 1863, the 2nd U.S. Colored Cavalry became part of the 2nd Brigade, 3rd Division, XVIII Corps, in August, 1864, and later the Cavalry Brigade, XXV Corps. Dyer, *Compendium of the War of the Rebellion*, 246; Joseph T. Wilson, *The Black Phalanx: A History of Negro Soldiers of the United States in the Wars of 1775–1812, 1861–65* (Hartford, 1869), 385.

way for all those who are disposed to return to their allegiance. There is no braver soldier in the service, and no one enjoys to a greater degree the respect of his officers or the affection of his men.

CHAPIN'S BLUFF, 5 1/2 MILES FROM RICHMOND, OCTOBER 5, 1864.

Never since the organization of the Army of the James has it exhibited in its various departments so much strength and vitality as at present. Its operations give to the north bank of the James quite an animated appearance. The various branches are all working harmoniously together for the accomplishment of the grand object in view. Having done so well in its onward movement, it is risking nothing to assure the hearts which are pulsating between hope and fear that it will triumphantly accomplish what it is necessary for them to undertake, and fully vindicate the reputation of Gen. Butler as a martial leader. Encouraged by the success which has so lately attended its advance on the rebel capital, it is impatiently chafing under the necessary delay. Another move, inaugurated under auspices equally as favorable, and the rebel capital will submit, with as much good grace as New Orleans, to the masterly but just rule of Gen. Butler.

When the smoke of a battle has partially cleared away, and the thinned ranks of brave men are closed up by the surviving heroes, we can form a fair idea of the bearing of those under fire, and how they acquitted themselves. In the onward to Richmond move of the 29th ult.,[6] the 4th United States Colored Troops, raised in Maryland, and the 6th United States Colored Troops, from Pennsylvania, gained for themselves undying laurels for their steady and unflinching courage displayed in attacking the rebels at great disadvantage. These two regiments were deployed as skirmishers.

It was just light enough to see as they pushed out of a skirt of woods from our breastworks at Deep Bottom; and as soon as emerging from it they were fired upon by the rebel sharpshooters, who fell back before these advancing regiments. They pushed on

6. On the afternoon of September 29, Union forces, which had just captured Fort Harrison, braced themselves for a counterattack by Confederates. The attack was successfully repulsed, with the Confederates suffering two thousand casualties. The 6th USCT also had heavy losses—almost one-third of Company D were killed or wounded. Horace Montgomery, "A Union Officer's Recollections of the Negro as a Soldier," *Pennsylvania History*, XXVIII (1961), 175–80.

across a ravine, where they were exposed to a severe enfilading fire by the enemy's sharpshooters, occupying a house in a skirt of woods on our left. It was under that fire the first men of these regiments were killed, among whom was Captain S. W. Vannuys. The sharpshooters were soon dislodged, and our troops then entered another woods, pushed beyond it, and crossed the Three Mile creek. On account of the marshy state of the ground, slush, timber, undergrowth, and briers, this line became somewhat confused, but soon advancing out of these difficulties they reached the enemy's abattis in front of his breastworks, which they charged with cheering. Two lines of abattis had here to be overcome, which was handsomely accomplished. It was here that many of the colored troops fell while attempting to force a passage over the abattis. There was no flinching by these two regiments in this terrible position, but they manfully received and returned the fire until they were three times ordered to fall back, which they did in good order. An assaulting column was then formed, which, as I informed you in a previous despatch, "jumped the rebels" out of their breast works, who took the nearest road to Richmond.

The officers and men of these two regiments could not have done better. The same must be said of the entire division under General Paine. It has covered itself with glory, and wiped out effectually the imputation against the fighting qualities of the colored troops.

In the attempt of the 4th and the 6th Regiments to pass over the abattis, the 4th lost its entire color guard. Alfred B. Hilton,[7] of the 4th carried the American flag, which was presented to it by the colored ladies of Baltimore, to the very edge of the breastworks, and, lying down, held aloft the national colors. When they were ordered to fall back, this brave man was shot down, but is not dangerously wounded, and his first exclamation was, "Save the flag!" Sergeant Major Fleetwood[8] successfully brought the colors back, riddled with some thirty rents, with no other loss to himself than a shot through his boot leg.

7. Alfred B. Hilton (?–?) was promoted to first sergeant for carrying both the national and the regimental colors until he was wounded. George Washington Williams, *A History of the Negro Troops in the War of the Rebellion, 1861–1865* (New York, 1888), 336.

8. Christian A. Fleetwood (?–?) of the 4th USCT received a special medal for gallant conduct. Williams, *A History of Negro Troops*, 336.

The gallantry of Major Augustus S. Boernstein,[9] commander of the 4th, has been acknowledged by placing him in temporary command of the 3d brigade, while Col. Duncan remains in the hospital, from wounds received in this onward movement.

I neglected to mention in my despatch of yesterday that on the afternoon previous a party of rebels, twenty-four in number, were promised all they could get by their officers if they charged on the extreme picket post on the left of this army. Seventeen of them were gobbled up by the colored troops, five killed and wounded in our hands, and one, an officer, escaped. He would not have gotten away if he had not been mounted, and from the swift manner he sped over the ground when our black troops made for him, it was supposed he had the fastest horse in the Southern States. One of our officers would probably have overtaken him if his horse had not stumbled.

EXTREME FRONT, CHAPIN'S FARM, BEFORE RICHMOND, OCT. 9, 1864.

The excitement attending the attack of the enemy day before yesterday, the retreat of Kautz's cavalry,[10] and the subsequent defeat of the enemy by the right of the 10th Corps (Terry's division), has subsided, and the grand work of preparation is being diligently prosecuted. Though the enemy assaulted and carried our right, they were easily driven from the position by General Birney, who followed them till dark with a view of giving battle, but without success. He fell back within his entrenchments before Richmond, while our right is being extended to meet any emergency.

The loss in Kautz's cavalry was between three and four hundred,

9. Augustus S. Boernstein (?–?) led the 4th USCT, part of the 3rd Brigade, XVIII Corps, in October, 1864. The 3rd was made up of the 4th, 6th, and 10th USCT. *OR*, Ser. I, Vol. XLII, Pt. 3, p. 467.

10. Augustus Valantine Kautz (1828–1895). Born in Germany, Kautz was a graduate of the United States Military Academy. He was captain of the 6th Cavalry at the beginning of the war. He was promoted to brigadier general of volunteers in May, 1864, and commanded a cavalry division in the Army of the James between April, 1864, and March, 1865. The engagement referred to occurred on October 7 at Darbytown as Kautz's forces covered the left flank of the Army of the James. Kautz was later promoted to commander of the 1st Division, XXV Corps. *DAB*, V, 263; Foote, *The Civil War . . . Red River to Appomattox*, 56; Dudley T. Cornish, *The Sable Arm: Negro Troops in the Union Army, 1861–1865* (New York, 1956), 280.

mostly, however, in prisoners; but the success of our infantry in the afternoon more than wiped out the defeat of the morning. The prisoners all say that if the army had marched on, instead of stopping to take forts, there being only twenty-five hundred rebels between them and Richmond, it could easily have captured the rebel capital. The authorities fled out of the city for safety, and the greatest consternation prevailed.

Yesterday morning the two great armies confronting each other in front of Richmond were in a state of fermentation, each expecting an attack from the other. Our army awaited with pride and confidence for the hosts of Lee, but they did not come. The enemy gathered themselves into their fortifications, while their rams and gunboats in the James went higher up than usual, and for fear that our monitors would pass the obstructions, chains were stretched across the river to impede their progress.

There are three rams in the James river, the Virginia, Richmond, and Fredericksburg, and four gunboats, the Drewry, Beaufort, Nansemond, and Raleigh. This is their entire naval force afloat for the defence of Richmond, though other vessels are being constructed, one of which has been launched, but is by no means ready for service. I had a good look at most of these crafts, especially what I thought was the ram Virginia, which was at one time within pistol-shot of the barn behind which I hid. She is a very ugly-looking customer, but by no means a match for our monitors. The rams steam down the river every night as far as Bishop's, and come up in the morning as far as Chapin's Farm. Six deserters came in from this fleet yesterday, disgusted with the rebel services, and disheartened by the prospects of the Confederacy. Desertions from the enemy are of such frequent occurrence that they do not excite any surprise. In conversing with some this morning, they gave as their reason, which is general among them, that the throne of Jeffdom was tottering, and they availed themselves of the first opportunity to stand from under. They all frankly admit that it is generally conceded in the Southern army, and among the people, that Grant has, in the present movement, as on other occasions, outgeneralled Lee. It is this fact which has caused the depletion of the enemy's ranks, and is fast dissipating all hope in the success of the rebel cause.

Last night I slept in the trenches, with a view of witnessing an attack which Longstreet[11] was to make this morning on our left flank. The colored troops who hold this part of General Butler's line were anxiously waiting for the enemy to come. It may be laid down as a rule that the rebels never come when they are expected. There was a deep solemnity in the scene of our troops watching by their camp-fire, silently awaiting the assault.

When or where the next movement will take place is difficult to conjecture, but one thing is certain, that the present position of the Army of the James is by no means a permanent one. If we do not get into Richmond soon we shall be a little disappointed. This army cannot fail.

AIKEN'S LANDING, JAMES RIVER, OCTOBER 9, 1864.

The flag-of-truce boat New York is now at this landing, with six hundred or more officers and soldiers, exchanged and paroled by the rebel authorities, soon to steam for the North, and to enjoy by a reunion with relations and friends, family joys and associations so dear to the patriot and soldier.

In speaking of this party of returned prisoners, there is one feature which deserves especial mention. Onboard of the New York are two officers of colored troops, who were captured while leading on their men—Capt. Wm. H. Sigreaves, Company K, 30th U. S. C. T., and Lieut. Viers,[12] of the 5th U. S. C. T. It would seem from this that the rebel authorities have resolved to exchange the officers of colored

11. James Longstreet (1821–1904) had a checkered career as a Confederate officer. A rising star in the early years of the war, he was later criticized for tardiness, indecisiveness, and a lack of tenacity. Yet he remained an important figure and emerged as Lee's most distinguished officer after Stonewall Jackson's death. He was sent to Georgia after Gettysburg but quickly brought back to Virginia, where he participated in the battles of the Wilderness and around Richmond. Interestingly, Longstreet was commanding officer of the Louisiana State Militia in the 1870s during the time Chester served as brigadier general. *DAB*, VI, 391–92; Jon L. Wakelyn, *Biographical Dictionary of the Confederacy* (Westport, Conn., 1977), 288–89.

12. John B. Viers (?–?) served as an officer in three companies of the 5th USCT. He entered service as a second lieutenant in November, 1863, was wounded at New Market Heights, and was mustered out as a first lieutenant. *Official Roster of the Soldiers of the State of Ohio in the War of the Rebellion, 1861–1865* (12 vols.; Akron, 1893–95), I, 600, 609, 621.

troops. The wisdom of such a course has no doubt been made plain by the determination of Gen. Butler to adhere only to what is right.

The capture and treatment of Captain Legreaves furnishes a story of hellish barbarity which exceeds anything that has yet come from the land of chivalry. The following is his own statement, and the man who can read it without being shocked at the brutality which he suffered will certainly vote for General McClellan: Cap. Legreaves was ordered, with his company, to charge upon the fort after the explosion of the mine in front of Petersburg. While pushing his way on, he found that a body of rebels had flanked him and got in his rear. His gallant company cut a way for him to get through several times with the colors, but he could not succeed on account of a gunshot wound which he had received. While clinging to the old flag, he was bayoneted in both thighs and in the left shoulder, but continued to grasp the colors until he was rendered insensible by a blow upon the head.

Two rebel soldiers now dragged him to the rear to plunder him, as the firing was too severe where he was captured. Previous to this, he had shot four of the enemy, bayoneted one, and wrested a sabre out of the hands of a lad of thirteen, who attempted to run him through. He had the satisfaction of sending a ball through the mouth of the rebel who shot him through the leg. After he had been plundered of all of his valuables of which they could possess themselves, he was left with brutal curses.

In this condition he was found by two Union officers, who were also prisoners. They undertook to carry him to the rear on a shovel, whereupon a rebel colonel took the shovel away, and threw it down an embankment, forbidding its use for any such purpose. The officers then found a stretcher, and were again about to bear the bleeding and almost insensible Captain from the field, when they were halted, and the Captain was thrown off the stretcher and placed where he was exposed to the shells of our army, the rebels saying, "Let us see how he can stand Yankee shells." One of them, striking and exploding within ten feet of him, covering him with dirt, caused him to wince, whereupon the rebs mocked at him with boisterous laughter. Seeing the effect of his shrinking, he remained firm while these missiles were exploding around him, but, fortunately was not injured.

Some rebels, more humane than others, again put him upon a stretcher, carried him some six or eight yards out of the way of danger and left him upon the banks of a ravine. A rebel soldier passing by him remarked that he was too comfortable, and giving the stretcher a kick, knocked it from under him, and he fell into the ditch, where he remained in his helpless condition for over two hours. Some one, not recognized by the sufferer in his exhausted condition, placed him upon the stretcher again, where he laid pleading and begging for water. The rebels passed by him heedless of his en- treaties, until one, more heartless than the rest, actually spat tobacco juice into his wounded side and face, saying that was water enough for him. Others taunted him by pointing to the helpless wounded colored troops by his side, suffering equally with himself, saying, "Ask your niggers to get it for you."

In this state, neglected, insulted, and exhausted by his painful wounds, he became delirious, and he was informed, in coming to his senses, that he had said a great many harsh things against the South and its cause, for which he was to be immediately hung, a rope having already been obtained. Several of them, abusing him in the most violent manner, declared that they ought to hang the "d——d nigger."

The Captain was then carried to the hospital in Petersburg, where more indignities and outrages greeted him. Being the first officer of negro troops ever seen in Petersburg, he was a curiosity, and attracted crowds of visitors. In his almost dying condition they had the courage to abuse and taunt him. At very long intervals some one would come to him with a look of compassion and a word of comfort. Only such would hand him water to drink.

When he was carried to the hospital he was placed between two colored soldiers, who were both wounded in the abdomen, and when they moved, or attempted to raise themselves, the blood would spurt through their wounds over the Captain. Before these suffering negroes died the most unpleasant substances were emitted through their perforated abdomens. After their death the next two worst cases that could be found from among the wounded colored troops were placed each side of him.

Among the many who visited Captain Segreaves was Governor Henry A. Wise,[13] who, as on a former occasion, was not at all

13. Henry Alexander Wise (1806–1876). A former congressman and a former governor of Virginia, Wise is best known for putting John Brown to death. The legion he raised in Virginia served at Roanoke Island. Wise also saw action in South Carolina,

frightened on approaching the bleeding and prostrate body of an old man. The ex-Governor, now General Wise, after looking at the negroes beside him, asked the Captain how he liked his position. He replied that he had no complaints to make. This valiant general, with a view of wounding his feeling, remarked that "you ought to lie in bed with one of them niggers." Such, and many more, were the outrages to which this wounded defender of the Union was obliged to submit while in the hospital at Petersburg, where he remained until September 17th. He was captured on the 20th of July.

The wards in this hospital were built to accommodate fifty-five patients, yet the rebels cram one hundred and fifty into each.

Captain Sergreaves was moved to Libby Prison[14] in Richmond, where he received the same treatment which was accorded to other officers, of which the public has already been fully informed. He comes back on crutches a mere wreck of his former self. The Captain has witnessed the rebels bayoneting wounded colored troops begging piteously to be spared. In the charge before Petersburg, the enemy rushed upon them with the cry of no quarter, and afterwards slaughtered the wounded without mercy. He saw a rebel officer place the muzzle of a pistol to the head of five dying negroes and blow their brains out. He saw a colored soldier across whose eyes a ball had passed, effectually blinding him and coming out of the top of his head, and, in addition to that, had his left arm broken in two places. The Captain asked him if he would fight again should he recover, and his reply was that he would do so much harder the next time. This poor, dying colored soldier was sitting upon the edge of a ditch, begging for water, when a young rebel officer came along and kicked him into the ditch, where he remained for over two hours. He was taken out by our own soldiers, and died soon after.

Richmond, and Petersburg. *DAB,* X, 423–24; Wakelyn, *Biographical Dictionary of the Confederacy,* 443.

14. Formerly a warehouse, Libby became the most notorious Confederate prison after Andersonville. One prisoner wrote of fellow inmates dying from exposure because of a lack of adequate clothing and blankets. They were forced to sleep on bare floors, and the prison's unplastered walls did not protect them from the cold. Another prisoner, F. F. Cavada, recalled meals of half a "loaf of bread twice a day washed down with James River water"; filthy blankets "soiled, worn, and filled with vermin." Patricia L. Faust (ed.), *Historical Times Illustrated Encyclopedia of the Civil War* (New York, 1986), 436–37; William B. Hesseltine, *Civil War Prisons: A Study in War Psychology* (Columbus, Ohio, 1930), 119, 122; F. F. Cavada, *Libby Life: Experiences of a Prisoner of War in Richmond, Va., 1863–64* (1865; rpr. Lanham, Md., 1985), 27.

Such is the brutal treatment which colored soldiers and their officers have received from the enemy, and such they will continue to receive until the Government shall demand for its colored soldiers and their officers the same usage which is accorded to other troops among civilized nations. I am glad to learn that the Captain and a second lieutenant, whose name I have not heard, were demanded from the rebel authorities. If this is so, it will give great cause for rejoicing, that the policy of the Government in this respect has been successful, and our emaciated prisoners, who have been so long incarcerated in Southern dungeons, will soon be set at liberty.

Lieutenant J. B. Viers, of the 5th U. S. C. T., was captured by the enemy in the recent "on to Richmond" movement. His regiment having suffered a temporary repulse, he fell into the enemy's hands badly wounded in the leg. He saw the rebels killing wounded colored soldiers, and from the insolent manner that they cursed and threatened him, he expected to share the fate of his men. With an oath they would ask him if he was not ashamed to command niggers, and he would reply that he was proud to be an officer of such organizations. The Lieutenant was wounded on the 29th ult., but his wound was not dressed until the following day, when some young surgeons were, for the sake of practice, very anxious to amputate his leg. He begged so hard that they yielded, and, hardly half attending to it, they had him chucked into an ambulance, which, over a very rough road, went to Richmond on a gallop.

It is the Lieutenant's impression that he owes his parole to a mistake—the second lieutenant of colored troops, who had been demanded by the Government, was released the day before. It is supposed the rebel authorities forgot the fact, and as Lieut. Viers was the only officer of that grade and kind in the same ward, he was paroled. Let us hope, however, that it was not a mistake, but that the rebels are going to respect all the officers and soldiers in the uniform of the Government.

HEADQUARTERS IN THE FIELD

BEFORE RICHMOND, OCTOBER 14, 1864.

The quiet of the past few days was broken yesterday morning by an advance of the 10th Corps, under General Terry, Major General

Birney being absent on a sick leave. It was a grand reconnaissance in force to develop the enemy's new line of works between the Charles City and New Market roads. Kautz's cavalry moved out in the morning as early as three o'clock, in fine order and excellent spirits, bearing no evidence of the temporary reverse of last Friday, on the extreme right of the line, and advanced in the course of the day within two miles of Richmond. The 1st Brigade, under Colonel Curtis, and the 2d, under Colonel Moore,[15] were stationed in the extreme left of the line joining the works of the 10th Corps, to prevent a flank movement of the enemy.

General Ames,[16] of the 1st Division, commanded the right of the line, while General William Birney marshalled the left. The 7th U. S. Colored Troops was thrown out as skirmishers, and they advanced without faltering, driving the enemy into his entrenchments around Richmond. This regiment remained on duty until about noon, when it was relieved by the 5th U. S. Colored Troops, who fully sustained the good opinion which the 7th had acquired during the earlier part of the day.

After the enemy had been driven into his strongholds about the city, General Ames thought he discovered a weak point in his defences, and advanced against it. This idea proved, however, to be a delusion, and the assaulting party was ordered to fall back, which they did in good order. The enemy, feeling a little disappointed that General Ames was not entrapped, made a sortie, which was handsomely repulsed.

The object of this reconnaissance was to ascertain the strength of the new works which the enemy was constructing. Of course, the firing was very heavy, the musketry quick and sharp, and many good men fell to rise no more. But the object of the advance being accomplished, the troops all, as they had during the entire day, returned in the best of order, without the loss of a man on the way. Rarely has a reconnaissance been so satisfactorily made. The soldiers

15. Although Chester later refers to a Brigadier General C. Curtis, in his lengthy December 26, 1864, dispatch, there is no one by the name of Moore or Curtis in the 1st or 2nd Brigade, X Corps, in October, 1864. *OR*, Ser. I, Vol. XLII, Pt. 3, p. 465.

16. Adelbert Ames (1835–1933). Ames was wounded at First Bull Run and later fought in the Peninsular campaign and at Antietam, Fredericksburg, Chancellorsville, and Gettysburg. He moved to the XVIII Corps as a division commander, then to the 1st Division, X Corps, and finally to the 2nd Division, XXIV Corps, in December, 1864. Boatner, *The Civil War Dictionary*, 11–12.

came up and relieved each other in grand style, while the unbroken fire of the artillery was sufficient evidence of its excellent working order. About twilight, or a little before, the 11th Corps reached the point from which it moved, not pushed back, but returning at will. The enemy feared to leave his works even to follow us on our return.

The information which General Butler has been able to obtain by this movement is deemed invaluable, but, of course, it could not be obtained without some loss, which, in killed and wounded, will not exceed three hundred. We lost none by capture. Among the killed is Capt. A. G. Dickey, 8th U. S. C. T.[17] He belonged to Lewistown, Pa., where he is well known as a gentleman, while here he was highly appreciated as an excellent and brave officer. Major Kemp, 10th Connecticut,[18] was also killed.

> Lieut. Colonel Smith, 62d Ohio, is mortally wounded.
> Capt. Lewis, 8th U. S. C. T., wounded, abdomen.
> Lieut. Lewis, 8th U. S. C. T., flesh wound, hand.
> Lieut. Krilis, 8th U. S. C. T., flesh wound, leg.
> Adjutant Spaulding, 29th U. S. C. T., slightly in the foot.

HEADQUARTERS, CHAPIN'S FARM
5 1/2 MILES FROM RICHMOND, OCT. 17, 1864.

It is a source of complaint, and very justly, too, that the colored troops and their officers have not received their meed of praise from the chroniclers of events in the army, for their splendid advance and gallant bearing on the 29th ult. There is no disguising the fact that the post of honor and danger was assigned to the 3d Division (Colored), 18th Corps, under General Paine, and that in every respect the troops acquitted themselves grandly. With a view of performing an act of

17. Recruited in Pennsylvania, the 8th USCT saw action at the bloody battle of Olustee, Florida, in February, 1864, losing more than half its men, dead and wounded, including Colonel C. W. Fribley, whose body was stripped by Confederates angry at white officers who commanded black troops. The regiment was reorganized as part of Birney's forces and transferred to the Army of the James. Montgomery, "A Union Officer's Recollections," 405–407, 409; Cornish, *The Sable Arm*, 224.

18. Organized in Hartford in October, 1861, the 10th served in North and South Carolina and Florida before joining the X Corps, Army of the James, in April, 1864. There is no mention of a Major Kemp in its records. Dyer, *Compendium of the War of the Rebellion*, 115.

justice to the living, as well as merited tribute to the lamented dead, I now place on record the gallant charge of the 2d Brigade, under Colonel A. G. Draper, which handsomely carried the enemy's works, making a passage to the very gates of the rebel strongholds.

On the memorable 29th ult. the 2d Brigade, composed of the 36th, 38th, and 5th U. S. C. T., was formed in column in the rear of the woods, near the Bennen house. Every man looked like a soldier, while inflexible determination was depicted upon every countenance. The officers, as they went along the line, were impressed with an unwavering confidence by the martial bearing of the troops. The fears which generally precede the preparation for a desperate conflict soon gave place to hope, and, as the eye ran down the line, the unconquerable purpose manifested in the brightened eyes of re-deemed freemen inspired the officers in command with a settled conviction of victory.

The 4th and 6th U. S. C. T. being thrown forward as skirmishers, at the same time ordered to carry the enemy's works if possible, moved out in echelon order over two lines of well constructed abattis, to a palisade within twenty feet of his entrenchments, into which he was driven at a speed to which double quick is no comparison. Here the enemy rallied, and encouraged by reinforcements, subjected these two regiments to the most galling fire, which they stood without flinching. Gen. Paine, comprehending the state of affairs, ordered them to fall back, which they did with great reluctance, as they wished to have the honor of being the first to mount the enemy's breastworks.

Col. Draper was now ordered forward with his brigade, which advanced in line of double column to the left, when he was ordered to the right immediately, to assault the enemy's works. When within about twelve hundred yards of his entrenchments the brigade was shelled severely from a battery on the New Market Heights, when the men were ordered to lie down, in which position they remained half an hour. The line of column was then reformed near where the 4th and 6th had failed to carry the works, and the 22d U. S. C. T. was deployed as skirmishers to the left, though out of sight of the brigade. It now advanced without support, pushing through under-brush and thick woods, which somewhat confused the men, and came out upon about 800 yards of open ground, across which it charged with loud cheering. The firing here was very severe, yet by no means checked our progress, for with confidence the men pushed forward in good order until they came to a swamp, which somewhat delayed the line for about half an hour. The firing here was terrible, and the enemy's sharpshooters with unerring aim picked off many officers and men, their balls passing in almost every instance through the head.

Some new recruits, in the 5th who were in the advance, having loaded their muskets against orders, commenced firing, which unfortunately had the effect of causing the column to discharge their pieces. Notwithstanding this delay, with the advantage greatly in favor of the enemy, it seemed almost impossible to encourage the troops upon the works, and they were equally as stubborn in their resolution not to retreat. They, however, advanced to the very muzzles of the rebels' muskets, when the most galling fire was poured into them.

Colonel Draper now, amid a shower of bullets, rushed up and down the line, inspiring the brigade with every degree of confidence, and leading off in the war yell which precedes a desperate charge, and which was swelled to the liveliest chorus of enthusiasm by the troops, immediately made a grand assault upon the enemy's breastworks. The rebels seeing us coming, one of their officers leaped upon the parapet, crying: "Give it to them, my brave boys," when Private Gardener, Company I, 36th Regiment, rushed in advance of the column, shot him down, and ran his bayonet through him up to the muzzle. Before our troops could get over the breastworks, the rebels had him wrapped in a blanket, and carried off. Over the works the colored troops went after them, driving them out in much confusion.

The rebels made for a woods about three hundred yards to the rear of their works, on Spring Hill. Here they made a stand, but Colonel Draper assaulting them again, drove them out of the woods, and the last seen of them, during that day, they were going to Richmond on an improved doublequick.

To Colonel Draper, the commander of the brigade, Colonel Pratt, 36th, Colonel Clapp, 38th, and Colonel Shurtleff,[19] of the 5th United

---

19. Giles Waldo Shurtleff (b. 1831). A Canadian, Shurtleff joined the 5th USCT as a lieutenant colonel in July, 1863, rising to brigadier general the following March. He led the 5th at New Market Heights, where he was wounded. *Official Roster of the Soldiers of Ohio*, I, 593; Boatner, *The Civil War Dictionary*, 759; Williams, *A History of Negro Troops*, 334–35.

States Colored Troops, belongs all the credit which is usually given to officers who inspire their commands with heroic fortitude to achieve a crowning victory.

In this day's work there were instances of bravery and good conduct which deserve special mention. Colonel Shurtleff, 5th, after he was wounded, insisted on attempting to lead his men to victory. Lieutenant Bancroft,[20] 38th, who was wounded in the head and unable to stand, led his company, of which he was in command, on his hands and knees, frequently waving his sword and marshaling his men onward. Lieutenant Gaskill,[21] 36th, though badly hurt, rushed ahead of his company, and called upon them to follow. Adjutant Andrews,[22] 36th, who had been ten months sick and excused from duty, volunteered to accompany the regiment. He mounted his horse, and when within sixty yards of the enemy's works was shot down, but not seriously hurt. Lieutenant Backup,[23] who had been deemed unfit for service in consequence of lameness, limped on with his company until he fell mortally wounded.

Sergeant Major Henry M. Adkins, 36th, was among the most conspicuous in rallying his regiment, and furnished an exhibition of gallant bearing which would rank with the brightest individual records of that day's glory. Many of the companies went into action commanded and manoeuvered by the first sergeants, who are colored. Their superior officers speak well of them all, for the proficiency which they evinced, the courage which they displayed, and the perfect discipline which they enforced under the most trying circumstances. Among those sergeants who thus distinguished themselves were Jeremiah Gray, Company C; William Davis, Company E;

20. Samuel B. Bancroft (?–?) was commended for bravery. Shot through the hip (Chester says the head), he crawled along through a swamp waving his sword and cheering his men on. *OR*, Ser. I, Vol. XLII, Pt. 3, p. 168.

21. Edwin G. Gaskill (?–?) was promoted to captain after leading his troops at New Market Heights even though he was shot through the arm. Williams, *A History of Negro Troops*, 335; *OR*, Ser. I, Vol. XLII, Pt. 3, p. 168.

22. Richard F. Andrews (?–?) was promoted to captain after New Market Heights. There are some differences of opinion over the length of Andrews' illness; Williams says he had been ill for only two months. Williams, *A History of Negro Troops*, 335; *OR*, Ser. I, Vol. XLII, Pt. 3, p. 168.

23. James B. Backup (d. 1864) was promoted to captain after New Market Heights, where he was seriously injured. Here again, there are some discrepancies. Chester writes that the wound was mortal. Williams, *A History of Negro Troops*, 335; *OR*, Ser. I, Vol. XLII, Pt. 3, p. 168.

Miles Shepard, Company I, and Samuel Gilchrist, Company K, all of whom belong to the 36th, and one from a slave State. There were others in the 38th and 5th who did the same equally as well, performing the duties of commissioned officers. Let us all be thankful that we have colored troops that will fight, and white officers, and colored ones, too, who can successfully command them to deeds of daring, and may their efforts in this war grow still brighter and brighter.

HEADQUARTERS, CHAPIN'S FARM, 3D DIVISION, 18TH ARMY CORPS

BEFORE RICHMOND, OCT. 18TH, 1864.

The front at this moment is void of stirring events but how long this oppressive silence may continue, can only be determined by circumstances. In the mean time the army is not idle. Activity and vigor are manifest everywhere. Our lines are being extended, well fortified, and impregnably manned. The appearances are that we have come here to stay until circumstances suggest that we move onward. Our long line of superiorly constructed works is a manifest evidence of the inflexibility of our purpose, while the unwavering confidence impressed upon every countenance in the ability of this army to accomplish what it has undertaken, gives assurances that the next move will be the crowning glory of the grand Army of the James. One thing is certain, that the colored troops who compose this division, whose bearing on the 29th has convinced the most skeptical that negroes will not only fight, but do it desperately, will be assigned to an important position in the grand assault on the rebel capital, which will afford them a still better opportunity to give additional fame to their martial record. With Col. Holman to command the division, who combines the affability of the gentleman with the devotion of the patriot, there is no doubt that it will cheerfully follow wherever this brave officer may lead. He is well supported by Colonels Kiddoo, Draper, and Duncan.

The flag-of-truce boat leaves Aiken's landing this morning for the North, freighted with about five hundred officers and soldiers—sick, wounded, and convalescent—exchanged for a similar number of rebels, who have already arrived in Richmond. The old stories of brutality are corroborated by these suffering, and, in some instances, dying soldiers, many of whom will pass to the resting place of the brave before the New York can reach Annapolis. Many of the men are barefooted, who affirm that the rebels appropriated their boots, shoes, and other apparel to their own use, which shows that these doomed wretches not only tear the clothing from our dead, but strip the living. Their day of retribution, however, draws nigh. Several of the fair sex came down on the rebel flag-of-truce boat, and were received on board of the New York by the assistant commissioner of exchange. I was within twenty feet of this dirty little craft yesterday afternoon, hardly fit to transport cattle from its appearance, and was somewhat amused at the striking contrast of about a half dozen rebel officers who were dressed in excellent suits of gray, perhaps borrowed for the occasion, with a view to give the impression that the ragamuffins of Jeffdom are comfortably clothed. This dodge will neither change our opinion of the enemy's commissariat, or procrastinate one day longer the judgment that will certainly overtake him.

Day before yesterday Chaplain H. M. Turner,[24] of the 1st U. S. C. T., made a serious complaint against Joseph Weir, steward of the steamer Manhattan, for inhuman treatment while coming up from Fortress Monroe on the 12th inst. The conduct of the steward was outrageous, if one-half that is alleged against him be true. It appears that he locked the entrance through which passengers passed to their dinner, and obliged this officer and two soldiers' wives, who were in his charge, to go down between decks, through intense darkness, to reach the table. Everything was pretty well gotten up, yet the chaplain and his charges attempted to dine off the crumbs, for which the steward demanded one dollar cash. This brought a protest from the officer, which was replied to by the steward in the most brutal and insulting manner, flourishing a knife which he happened to have in his hand, and threatening the most fearful consequences if the chaplain did not immediately leave the dining-saloon. The full price was paid, and the officer, as soon as his

24. Henry McNeal Turner (1834–1915). Author, editor, and bishop of the AME church, Turner was named chaplain of the 1st USCT by Lincoln in 1863. He was also war correspondent of the *Christian Recorder*, organ of the AME church. Rayford W. Logan and Michael R. Winston (eds.), *Dictionary of American Negro Biography* (New York, 1982), 609; *DAB*, X, 65–66; William L. Simmons, *Men of Mark, Eminent, Progressive and Rising* (Cleveland, 1887), 805–19; Edwin S. Redkey, "Black Chaplains in the Union Army," *Civil War History*, XXXIII (1987), 334, 338, 350.

affairs would permit, preferred charges against the steward, and on the arrival of the boat at City Point, evening before last, he was arrested, and is now detained upon the charges as alleged. He will likely be arraigned before Gen. Butler, and should these facts be substantiated, and that just man squint at him under the impression that such conduct is the effervescence of concealed disloyalty, an individual about his proportions will be sent to Dutch Gap to assist with others of corresponding sentiments in cutting through the canal amid the showers of shot and shell from rebel batteries. The Manhattan is in the employ of the Government, and carries the mail between Washington and City Point. These negro-haters do not incur much risk in their ill-treatment of unprotected colored persons; but when they insult, on a Government boat, a chaplain, though he may happen to be a little darker than themselves, they become involved in a difficulty which is rendered worse by the prospect of being summoned before Gen. Butler.

VARINA, JAMES RIVER, OCT. 19, 1864.

The flag-of-truce boat Mary Washington, having on board about one hundred and fifty privateersmen and pirates, including about forty of their chiefs, arrived here yesterday morning to exchange them for the brave sailors who have been for a long time languishing in Southern dungeons.

THE APPEARANCE OF THE PIRATICAL CREW

On going aboard of the steamer, I was surprised to find that this class of men were well and tidily dressed, with clean shirts and apparel suitable for the approaching winter, while their chiefs sported well-fitting suits of gray, elaborately trimmed with gold lace and corresponding shoulder-straps. So far as dress went, the leaders looked like aristocrats, while the buccaneers, at a distance, would have been mistaken for gentlemen. In addition to their respectable appearance, and healthy aspect, many of the chiefs had new trunks, which were, no doubt, well filled with something, though the contents may not be contraband, which they were carrying with them to the South. All of them had valises, and most of the freebooter crew were provided with fashionable leather travelling bags. When one considers that these pirates—not excepting their chiefs—are brought within our lines in the most filthy condition, covered with infamy and vermin, and as destitute of money as they are of principle, the question naturally occurs, Who furnished these splendid outfits? Treating these individuals with humanity is one thing; but the extravagant consideration of which they have been the recipients evinces a degree of humiliation which reflects discreditably upon those who permitted it.

But little delay was required in facilitating matters for the disembarkation of these well-dressed prisoners. Colonel Mulford,[25] under whose auspices the exchanges are conducted, soon settled the preliminaries, after which the chiefs and their crews were landed without any demonstrations of joy whatever. They left the steamer in silence, which strongly assumed the appearance of regret. Each man acted as his own porter, while those who had trunks were assisted by their comrades.

Those prisoners who sported shoulder-straps were furnished with United States ambulances to ride to the rebel flag-of-truce boat, Wm. Allison, distance about one mile off. Their physical appearance by no means justified such consideration. Col. Mulford is a humane man and a courteous gentleman of the highest type, and such attentions from him, to such a class of beings, can only be accounted for on the basis, that he never fails in politeness to a friend, or in kind treatment to an enemy.

OUR NAVAL PRISONERS SEE A WELCOME SIGHT

Everything being now in readiness, the ambulances filled with the chiefs moved off, followed by the crews on foot, slowly wending their way for the rebel flag-of-truce boat. Col. Mulford, as usual, preceded them on his horse, and when he came near enough for our gallant sailors to see him, with his flag-of-truce attached to his boots, these brave but suffering patriots immediately arose to their feet, with feelings of the highest exultation expressed in every countenance,

25. John Elmer Mulford (?–?) mustered in as captain in July, 1861, rising to colonel in April, 1865. Mulford was a pivotal figure in the exchange of prisoners. In 1863 he was in charge of truce boats and was later promoted to assistant to Brigadier General Samuel Meredith, Union commissioner of exchange. Phisterer (comp.), *New York in the War of the Rebellion*, II, 1733; Hesseltine, *Civil War Prisons*, 102.

which brightened up under the prospect of immediate release from rebel authority.

On coming near the little rebel flag-of-truce boat, formerly a tow tug, I found its deck full of men, whose appearances at once impressed me that they were rebels. Upon inquiry I ascertained they were our half-starved and half-clothed sailors, whose external semblance gave evidence of bad treatment and worse fare. It was a sad sight, after witnessing the comfortably-clad freebooters, in all the style of gentlemen, to look upon these heroes, shivering under the cool breeze of the morning, many of them with nothing to wrap themselves up, while others were obliged to keep themselves as comfortable as possible with some very dirty blankets, of an inferior quality, furnished probably by the rebels.

It took but a short time to get things in readiness, under the direction of the assiduous Col. Mulford, when our gallant tars, the officers leading off, marched with inexpressible pleasure upon the soil which acknowledges the conquering sway of the old flag. As soon as they left the rebel craft, they asked how the military situation was in these parts, and on being assured that it never was better, they expressed additional feelings of joy. A large crowd of colored troops, those constituting the defences of this part of the line, with a very few white ones, were there to extend to them a cordial reception, and assure them that they had not suffered in vain. Many of these returned prisoners asked why the old flag was not here, and how far they would have to go before their eyes would again be blessed with the sight. On being informed that a short distance would bring them to a point which would gladden their hearts, they manifested great satisfaction.

How the Buccaneers Were Received by the Rebels

When these fat and comfortably-clad freebooters appeared in sight of their flag-of-truce steamer, the band on board, and a very good one at that, played with melodious softness, "Home, Sweet Home." As they passed by our officers, who were formed in double column a short distance from the enemy's craft, the usual salutes were exchanged, and they filed on board. They went as silently as if they were going to their graves. No demonstrations of joy were manifested.

Our Seamen Start for a Sight of the Old Flag

Everything now being in readiness, the officers, many of them not waiting for ambulances, and the men closely following, took the shortest road for the steamer Mary Washington. It was amusing to see how both threw away the dirty blankets, cooking utensils, corn bread, and many other articles of which they now had no further use. None of them brought, as I saw, any trunks or well-filled valises, as those for whom they were exchanged had done. They are returned in as untidy a condition as possible, with a full supply of graybacks to mix with the Northern breed. When these brave sailors reached the Mary Washington, and many other vessels nearby flying the old flag (what they had long been wanting to see), their exultation knew no bounds.

As soon as they were on board of the flag-of-truce boat the officers and crew crowded the upper deck and paddle-boxes of the gunboat Delaware, and gave them such a cheering reception as awakened memories of the past, and fired up their enthusiasm which had been chilled by long suffering. The returned patriots, nearly all of whom had recently come from Andersonville, Ga.,[26] the prison-house of death, sent back an answering shout, which told the jolly tars of the Delaware that their devotion to the old flag which now floated over them is still as unwavering as ever.

The Sanitary Commission

It is due to this noble institution[27] to state that one of their tugboats, laden with clothing and other good things, came alongside

26. The prison was constructed in late 1863, in southwest Georgia, to relieve Richmond's overcrowded military prisons. Confederate authorities were concerned that the presence of so many prisoners could pose problems if the Union attacked the capital. Andersonville quickly became a charnel house. By July, 1864, there were 32,000 Union prisoners crammed into its stockade. Food and medicine shortages, poor sanitation, and inadequate shelter made conditions intolerable. By war's end, nearly 13,000 Union soldiers had been buried there. Williams, *A History of Negro Troops*, 304–307; Faust (ed.), *Historical Times Illustrated Encyclopedia*, 16.

27. The United States Sanitary Commission was organized in 1861 with the purpose of providing care for sick and wounded soldiers and support of their dependent families. Its wide range of services included field ambulances, hospitals, nursing, temporary shelters, and aid for veterans. Most of its staff were volunteers or worked for very small salaries. Its 7,000 auxiliaries raised and dispensed supplies worth more than $20 million. Faust (ed.), *Historical Times Illustrated Encyclopedia*, 656.

of the Mary Washington to afford such relief as in its power. It shortly after moved off with, no doubt, the assurance from Colonel Mulford that Government, under his direction, would attend to their necessities.

The Rebels Exchanging Colored Seamen

With this number of prisoners came six colored sailors whom the rebels exchanged, and, from an understanding, this class of Union defenders are henceforth to be treated as prisoners of war. The enemy will soon reach General Butler's standard, and then all will be well.

The Suffering of the Union Prisoners

The account which these prisoners bring of the suffering of our soldiers at Andersonville, Ga., is painful to relate, and more than corroborates the inhuman treatment which has been so fully given to the public. The rebels have succeeded in placing the responsibility of their non-exchange upon the shoulders of Mr. Lincoln, against whom many of them are very bitter. Their eyes will soon be opened, however, to the facts by a short residence in a land of civilization.

The flag-of-truce boat, probably the New York, which did not leave yesterday as expected, will carry all of our returned sufferers to Annapolis this morning.

List of Officers and Seamen Exchanged

The following is a list of the naval officers and some of the seamen who have been exchanged and are now on the flag-of-truce boat, soon to steam for the North. They are arranged under the names of the vessels to which they were attached:

Steamer Reliance.

James M. Caulley, second assistant engineer.

Alex. Renshaw, third assistant engineer.

Thomas Brown, master's mate.

These were captured on the Rappahannock, Aug. 23, 1863, and have since been confined in Libby, Danville, Macon, Savannah, and Charleston prisons.

Ceres.

George A. Dean, assistant engineer, who was captured at Plymouth, North Carolina, April 20, 1864, and underwent confinement in Salisbury, N. C., Macon, Ga., Columbia, Charleston, and Libby prisons.

Southfield.

Wm. D. Newman, acting master.

Thomas B. Stokes, acting ensign.

George W. Pratt, acting master's mate.

Wm. F. Goff, acting second assistant engineer.

John A. Struby, acting third assistant engineer.

William C. Williams, pilot.

George W. Brown, paymaster's clerk.

Robert McKermey, seaman.

Benjamin F. Farr, landsman.

William H. Ellingworth, colored seaman.

William A. Johnson, colored seaman.

These were captured at the time and confined in the same place as those of the Ceres.

Housatonic.

Edward F. Brown, lieutenant.

J. H. Harmany, third assistant engineer.

These were captured at the assault on Fort Sumter, September 9, 1863.

Satellite.

Wm. H. Fogg, acting master's mate.

Isaac M. Johnson, second assistant engineer.

John Mee, third assistant engineer.

Christopher McCormick, third assistant engineer.

Edwin Robinson, pilot.

These were captured, August 23, 1863, in Virginia.

Gunboat Stockdale.

John Lowrie, acting ensign.

James Lockwood, third assistant engineer.

These were captured on Lake Pontchartrain, La., May 16, 1864.

Gunboat Wissahickon.

E. G. Drayton, acting ensign, was captured at Fort Sumter, September 9th, 1863.

Brig Perry.

George Anderson, acting ensign.

Wm. B. Horrants, acting ensign.

Geo. W. Burkett, acting assistant

paymaster.

John Reinhart, coxswain.

Peter Kergle, seaman.

These were captured at Murrell's Inlet, December 5th, 1863, and have been confined in Georgetown, Charleston, Columbia, and Libby prisons.

Steamer Shawsheen.

Wm. Cromack, acting master's mate.

Wm. Rushmore, acting master's mate.

Charles Hickey, acting third assistant engineer.

H. C. Marrow, acting third assistant engineer.

E. D. Smith, paymaster's clerk.

These were captured on the 7th May last.

Steamer Columbine.

H. J. Johnson, acting third assistant engineer.

G. C. Whitney, acting third assistant engineer.

W. B. Spencer, master's mate.

J. T. Allison, paymaster's steward.

These were captured in the St. John's river, Florida, May 23d last.

Gunboat Petrel.

Thomas McElroy, acting master, commanding.

Kimball Ware, pilot.

John H. Nibler, quartermaster.

These were captured April 22d last, and confined in the Canton, Cahaba, Macon, Savannah, Charleston, and Richmond prisons.

Steamer Rattler.

W. E. H. Fentress, acting master.

Simon H. Strunk, acting ensign.

These were captured September 13, 1863, and were confined in Richmond, Danville, Macon, Savannah, and Charleston prisons.

Gunboat Underwriter.

E. H. Seers, acting assistant paymaster.

John B. Dick, acting second engineer.

Henry K. Steener, acting third engineer.

Samuel B. Ellis, acting third engineer.

Wm. K. Engell, acting master's mate and executive officer.

Daniel Ward, acting master's mate.

John McCormick, acting master's mate.

Chas. H. Stewart, acting master's mate.

These were captured 2d February last, at New Bern.

Water Witch.

Austin Pendergrast, lieutenant commanding.

C. W. Budd, acting master.

C. H. Billings, acting assistant

paymaster.

A. D. Stever, acting ensign.

C. P. Weston, acting master's mate.

E. D. W. Parsons, acting master's mate.

T. Genther, acting first assistant engineer.

J. P. Cooper, acting third as-sistant engineer.

James Hollingworth, acting third assistant engineer.

Isaac A. Conover, acting third assistant engineer.

SEAMAN.—P. A. Farrel, Hugh Fagan, Thomas Donarow, Harry Turms, Hemlett R. Cook, F. Cambell, W. H. Purden, W. Gloomis, John Williams, Wm. Price, John Parker, John Harris, Henry Hill, Francis Johnson, Chas. A. Barks, Thos. Bowers, Jas. Murray, H. Fenner, Henry Thornton, James Hazleton, Joseph Mason, John Williams, Chas. H. Kimball, Wm. Saage, Chas. Midlick, Cyrus Bissel, Chas. Farmer, John Williams, James Alexander, J. Hedson, and Thos. Gilling.

These were captured at Osolow Sound, Georgia, June 3d last, and, while the men were confined at Andersonville, the officers were shut up in Savannah, Macon, and Richmond prisons. Of the Water Witch's officers who died is Wm. S. Williams, paymaster's clerk, and Henry Wilson, yeoman.

Steamer Picket No. 2, Monitor.

Andrew Stockholm, acting ensign, commanding; Ed. T. Beardsley, third assistant engineer. These, with five seamen who have returned, were captured October 8th.

Lieut. S. N. Preston, of Admiral Dahlgren's staff, was captured in the assault on Fort Sumter, September 8th, 1863, and has since been confined in Charleston and Columbia jails, and in Libby.

Ensign B. H. Porter, of the New Ironsides, was captured in the attack on Sumter, and confined in Columbia, S. C. Acting Ensign Robert M. Clarke was captured at Pensacola, Florida, October 8th, 1863. George H. Pendleton and George M. Smith, third assistant engineers, were captured October 7th. Acting Master Edward L. Haines, of the frigate Powhatan, was captured August 5, 1863, in Charleston harbor. Acting Master Geo. R. Duval, of the U. S. steamer Paul Jones, was captured last July.

CHAPTER 4

The Circle Tightens

HEADQUARTERS 3D DIVISION 18TH ARMY CORPS

BEFORE RICHMOND, OCT. 21, 1864.

Yesterday the Army of the James was thrilled by the good news of another glorious victory in the Shenandoah Valley[1] over the rebel force under Longstreet. It was cause for universal congratulation here, and inspired with additional confidence the exuberant spirits of this grand army. As coming events cast their shadows before, so our successes in the Valley herald the crowning triumph which is soon to be achieved by the forces which threaten the rebel capital. The victory was commemorated by a shotted salute along the whole line of Gen. Butler's army, which, as the good news was not generally known, was supposed to be the opening of the anticipated engagement. As this point is on the left of the line, which is entirely entrusted to the fighting qualities of colored troops, it was particularly gratifying to witness with what good spirits they welcomed what they supposed was an opportunity to meet the enemy.

The spirit displayed is a harbinger of good, and enables one to speak with considerable assurance of the prospects of this army in the approaching conflict. While the forts along the line were honoring the event, the good news was communicated to the soldiers, who made the welkin ring with prolonged cheers of rejoicing. For some time after the roar of artillery had ceased the exultation of an electrified

---

1. A reference to Sheridan's victory at the Battle of Cedar Creek, October 19, following his successes at Winchester, Fisher's Hill, and Tom's Brook days before. The battle was a last desperate attempt by Jubal Early to maintain a foothold in the Shenandoah Valley. The early morning attack in a thick fog surprised Union forces and temporarily put them to flight, but they quickly regrouped to defeat the Confederates. Patricia L. Faust (ed.), *Historical Times Illustrated Encyclopedia of the Civil War* (New York, 1986), 121; Shelby Foote, *The Civil War: A Narrative. Red River to Appomattox* (New York, 1974), 566–72.

army rose higher and higher in an unbroken chorus of joy, until the
echoes rolled along the banks of the James to the disheartened camps
of the enemy. What was surprising to many was the number of forts
which opened along the line, many of them firing for the first time.
Fort Harrison led off in the salute, and the others joined in the
thundering chorus. One of the forts, bearing Little Mac's name,
opened on the rebel rams, but the monsters paid no attention to it
whatever. Some of their mortars threw a few shells, which exploded
wide of their mark.

During the early part of last evening the brass bands, of which
there are any quantity in this army, delighted the various camps with
national airs, which seemed to have an invigorating influence, and
long after they had ceased the cheering of the army was reverberating
along the line.

Yesterday I rode through the camp of the 55th Pennsylvania
Volunteers,[2] and found but a remnant of the fourteen hundred men
who left Camp Curtin just three years ago. The patriotism and
courage of the regiment may be inferred from its re-enlisting, several
months ago, for three years' service. It has passed through such fiery
ordeals as Pocotaligo, S. C., twice before Petersburg, Drury's Bluff,
and Chapin's farm. Its ranks, thinned by many a galling fire, tell of its
struggles on many a hotly-contested field, while its colors, baptised
with the blood of dying patriots, riddled with bullets until but a small
and tattered portion now hangs from its crimsoned staff, attest that
they have been borne proudly and triumphantly on many a bloody
field. Company G, commanded formerly by the lamented Waterbury,[3]
now by Captain Levi Weaver,[4] mustered yesterday but twenty men
for duty. This is about what may be said of the others. Captain J. C.
Shearer[5] now commands the regiment, which would hardly make

2. Organized in Harrisburg in December, 1861, the 55th was stationed at Port Royal,
South Carolina, before joining the X Corps, Army of the James, in April, 1864.
Frederick H. Dyer, *Compendium of the War of the Rebellion* (Des Moines, Iowa, 1908), 221,
1593.

3. Isaac S. Waterbury (d. 1864). Mustered in, August, 1861, Waterbury headed
Company G. He died at Bermuda Hundred in May, 1864. Samuel P. Bates, *History of
Pennsylvania Volunteers, 1861–1865* (5 vols.; Harrisburg, 1869–71), II, 201.

4. Levi A. Weaver (?–?). Mustered in, August, 1861, Weaver was promoted to first
lieutenant in May, 1863, and to captain in July, 1864. Bates, *History of Pennsylvania
Volunteers*, II, 201.

5. John C. Shearer (?–?). Mustered in, October, 1861, Shearer was captain of
Company B. He later commanded the 55th, part of the 1st Brigade, 2nd Division, XVII

three full companies. Without doubt, it will bear its new colors, which it is daily expecting, bravely through the battles to be fought. The sacred old standard is to be forwarded to Governor Curtin.[6]

The rebel prisoners, who were put to work in retaliation for compelling colored troops captured by the enemy to assist in erecting fortifications around Richmond, are still at Dutch Gap, where the experience which they acquired with the pick and shovel in erecting fortifications, within their lines, is of immense utility in progressing this great enterprise. Officers and men, under a guard of Companies E and F, 127th United States Colored Troops,[7] are required to perform a good day's work. The rebels at times furiously shell the workmen from a mortar battery, which renders it exceedingly unpleasant for the Johnnies, who, though they previously refused before they were aware of their destination, are now clamoring to take the oath of allegiance. Their appeals will have no influence with General Butler; but there they will be required to remain, in what will likely prove "the last ditch" to many of them. The prejudice which the rebels have pretended to entertain against negroes seems to be entirely eradicated from these prisoners—for they not only work side by side with the race, but under the superintendence of negro guards, with whose instructions and orders they most cheerfully comply. The rebs have too much good sense to provoke in the least their colored custodians. It was a curious sight to see the proud sons of the F. F. V.'s,[8] who had been accustomed to command negroes wherever they met them, humbly acknowledging the authority of the blackest of the race.

For the satisfaction of those who have been watching the progress of General Butler's canal with much interest, I would state, from personal observation, that it will soon be completed.

Corps. Bates, *History of Pennsylvania Volunteers*, II, 186; *OR*, Ser. I, Vol. XLII, Pt. 3, p. 466.

6. Andrew Gregg Curtin (1815–1894) was elected governor of Pennsylvania in 1861. Curtin initially rejected all efforts to recruit black troops even when Harrisburg was under threat from Lee's forces. He subsequently relented following the Federal government's decision to recruit black troops and under sustained pressure from black Pennsylvanians. *DAB*, 606–607.

7. The last regiment raised in Pennsylvania to reach the James River front, the 127th USCT, part of Birney's division, was one of four black Pennsylvania regiments to occupy Petersburg. Frederick M. Binder, "Pennsylvania Negro Regiments in the Civil War," *Journal of Negro History*, XXXVII (1952), 415; Dyer, *Compendium of the War of the Rebellion*, 253; *OR*, Ser. I, Vol. XLVI, Pt. 1, pp. 1237–39.

8. Fleet-footed Virginians.

HEADQUARTERS 3D DIVISION, 18TH ARMY CORPS

BEFORE RICHMOND, OCTOBER 23, 1864.

The dull and rumbling sound of Union artillery rolled this morning along the banks of the James with serious intent. After an almost unbroken quiet of three weeks, our forts on the left of the line opened fire upon the rebel rams, which did credit to the experience of our gunners. In several instances the shots struck the iron clad ram Virginia, the commodore-ship, and were soon to glance off with a perpendicular tendency. She fired one shot rather wildly, however, and then dropped down the stream a few rods, where the Richmond and the Fredericksburg anchored under a bank, which only exposed a small part of their smoke stacks. From this position they could not fire a shot at our batteries, and they remained there until the forts ceased, when, availing themselves of the cessation, they all steamed towards Richmond.

Of this affair there are all kinds of rumors and impressions afloat, circulated in some instances by those who witnessed it, whose wishes so powerfully quickened their imaginations as to believe that some one of the rebel wooden gunboats received twenty shots, while the smoke stack of the Virginia was perforated by a shell. That one of the rams was struck is certain; but whether any serious injury was inflicted upon her, or any other of the crafts, is, by no means, satisfactorily ascertained. During the shelling I passed under both our own and the rebel fire, and had a fine opportunity of witnessing the perfection of our gunners. The enemy's redoubts on the opposite bank of the James opened very heavy pieces with very bad aim, while our shots, nearly all of them, threw the dust around them high in the air, doing, as it is fair to presume, material damage. The conduct of the rams and gunboats in steaming up the river, frightened off by thirty pound Parrots, is a confession of their weakness, and corroborates the opinion, which I have long entertained, that they are in the James rather as a big scare than a means of defence. That they should quietly remain at anchor within musket range, and permit the lengthening and strengthening of our left, while redoubts during the night would spring up on the most commanding elevations, until they reached the outer picket line, is an evidence that they hesitate to provoke a fire with our batteries. Coupling this with their first crowding under a high bank for protection, and subsequently running up the river from the position where they have been anchoring for the last three weeks, is a very strong case against the impenetrability of these rams, and a frank confession of either their weakness or the cowardice of their officers.

In this connection I will add the information from a deserter of the Virginia, that it is understood on board of the fleet, that should our monitors go up the James river, they, conscious of their inability to engage them, are to run up under the guns of Fort Darling, or such other place of security as will protect them from the fifteen-inch shot which they believe constitutes a part of the armament of our iron-clads. Whether there are such pieces on board or not, is of no importance in this connection, as the rebs believe there are, and that answers every purpose. On this point, the enemy's fleet in the James has had its fears greatly excited, and judgment has long since passed on board of its inability to stop the progress of our navy, should it be disposed to go up the James river, which is not at all unlikely.

It may not be generally known that John J. C. Mitchel,[9] the Irish refugee, is the commodore of the rebel fleet in the James river. So I have been positively assured by a deserter from it. The many desertions from it has put him in a very bad humor, in which he indulges in brutal curses, declaring that there are so many traitors that he found it difficult to trust any one. The four wooden gunboats carry two guns each, while the three iron-clads mount four each, making, in all, twenty guns, which this renegade is attempting to direct against the nation which offered him an asylum of liberty. He will probably be returned to the old country as a vagrant some of these days, where, in undergoing punishment for his crimes, he will have full time to reflect over his treachery to liberty and humanity.

Yesterday and the day before there was a review of the 3d (colored) division, 18th Corps, by brigades. On Friday morning, the 20th instant, the 1st brigade, temporarily under the command of Col. Kiddoo, and in the afternoon the 2d, under Col. A. G. Draper, were reviewed by Col. John Holman, commanding the division. On

9. This could be John C. Mitchel, son of the Irish patriot. The father and three sons enlisted in the Confederate forces. John, Sr., died at Charleston; William, the youngest, was killed at Gettysburg; and James lost an arm. Ella Lonn, *Foreigners in the Confederacy* (Chapel Hill, 1940), 155.

yesterday, the 3d brigade, under Col. Ames, and the 1st[10] and 2d regiments of colored cavalry, dismounted, excepting two companies, were reviewed by the same officer and his dashing staff. The whole affair passed off very creditably to officers and men. There was not much of the ornamental about the brigades, but their usefulness was stamped in unwavering resolution upon every countenance along the lines. The marching was excellent, and, in fact, everything connected with it was highly satisfactory. The commanders of these brigades deserve great credit for bringing their troops to so high a state of efficiency as has been evinced in whatever sphere they have been called upon to act. Many of their colors gave evidences of having passed through the fiery ordeal of battles. The flags of the 6th U. S. C. T. are in mere strips, and form a glorious record of this brave regiment.

In this review, in the 36th Regiment there were but three white officers present, the companies being commanded by the colored sergeants. The same may be said of the 38th. There is no lack of qualification in these sergeants to command their companies; in fact, many of them are superior in drill to some of the officers who are sent here to command them.

Lieut. J. B. McMurdy, who hails from Kentucky, occupying a nondescript position on the staff of the commander of this division, was sent off last night in disgrace to report to General Butler, by Col. Holman, for inwarrantable treatment to a colored sergeant, detailed at these headquarters, and disrespectful conduct to his superiors. The undignified character and swaggering bearing of the lieutenant, with other traits which need not be mentioned, wholly disqualify him to command colored troops or to be brought into association with the gentlemanly officers upon Col. Holman's staff. To the judgment of General Butler I commit him, with the remark that he will give him the full measure of justice.

To the high credit of Colonel Holman, it must be said that no one in this division, so long as he commands it, will be permitted to abuse any man, whether he be white or black. His impartiality is well

10. Organized in Virginia in December, 1863, the 1st US Colored Cavalry served at Fortress Monroe before becoming part of the 1st Brigade, 3rd Division, XVIII Corps, in August, 1864, and later the Cavalry Brigade, XXV Corps. Dyer, *Compendium of the War of the Rebellion*, 246; Joseph T. Wilson, *The Black Phalanx: A History of Negro Soldiers of the United States in the Wars of 1775–1812, 1861–65* (Hartford, 1888), 385.

known and highly appreciated, and has made him the idol of his command.

General Butler's retaliatory measures, in placing rebel prisoners to work upon the canal, which is continually under fire, at Dutch Gap, as an offset to the rebels forcing our colored soldiers to work on their fortifications, have had the desired effect. The colored troops have been relieved from such labor, with the assurance that they are to be treated as prisoners of war, and the rebels have been released from their uncomfortable position at Dutch Gap. While under fire they all wanted to take the oath of allegiance, to which, of course, no attention was paid, and since their release but few have availed themselves of that privilege, the most of them preferring to fight it out a little longer.

The following order was issued by Gen. Butler on the death of the gallant Gen. Birney:

HEADQUARTERS, DEPARTMENT VIRGINIA AND NORTH CAROLINA, ARMY OF THE JAMES

IN THE FIELD, OCT. 21, 1864.

- General Orders, No. 135. -
Soldiers of the Army of the James: With deep grief from the heart, the sad word must be said—Major General David B. Birney is dead.

But yesterday he was with us, leading you to victory. If the choice of the manner of death had been his, it would have been to have died on the field of battle as your cheers rang in his ear. But the All-Wise "determineth all things well."

General Birney died at his home in Philadelphia, on Tuesday last, of disease contracted on the field in the line of his duty.

Surrounded by all that makes life desirable—a happy home—endeared family relations—leaving affluence and ease—as a volunteer at the call of his country—he came into the service in April, 1861. Almost every battle-field whereon the Army of the Potomac has fought has witnessed his valor. Rising rapidly in his profession, no more deserved appointment has been made by the President than Gen. Birney's assignment to the command of the 10th Army Corps. The respect and love of the soldiers of his own corps has been shown by the manner they followed him.

THE PATRIOT—THE HERO—THE SOLDIER. By no death has the country sustained a greater loss.

Although not bred to arms he has shown every soldierly quality and illustrated that profession of his love and choice.

It is not the purpose of this order—nor will the woe of the heart of the officer giving it, nor permit him to write General Birney's Eulogy.

Yet even amid the din of arms—and upon the eve of battle, it is fit that we, his comrades, should pause a moment to draw from the example of his life the lesson it teaches.

To him the word duty—with all its obligations and incentives—was the spur of action. He had no enemies save the enemies of his country—a friend, a brother to us all—it remains to us to see to it, by treading the path of duty as he has done—that the great object for which he has struggled with us and laid down his life—shall not fall and his death be profitless.

SOLDIERS OF THE 10TH ARMY CORPS:

Your particular grief at the loss of your brave commander has the sympathy of every soldier in the army. It will be yours to show your respect to his memory by serving your country in the future as with you Birney has served it in the past.

> By command of Major General Butler:
> ED. W. SMITH, Asst. Adjt. General.

BEFORE RICHMOND, OCTOBER 24, 1864.

Since my despatch of yesterday, informing you of our opening fire upon the rebel navy in the James, and its inglorious retreat up the river, nothing has occurred to disturb the monotony of camp life. The rams came down the river last night, picketing, probably, but steamed up again this morning, having abandoned, it would seem, the anchorage which they have been using for some time.

I have only heard of one casualty in the affair, which occurred to an artillery man who was riding across a farm immediately opposite Cox's Ferry. His horse was killed by a shell, a piece of which severed one of his legs. I regret to say that when Dr. L. Allen, surgeon of the 6th United States Colored Troops, was requested to dress the wounded man's limb, he refused, on the plea that he had his morning sick list to attend to. The most charitable view to take of this officer's conduct, under the circumstances, is probably his innate consciousness of inability to dress such a wound. Charges will be preferred against him, and Butler, the Just, will have an opportunity of passing judgment upon his conduct.

There has been a little excitement around these headquarters for the past few days, growing out of the fact that three sutlers—Henry B. Walker, of the 36th; H. P. Elias, of the 5th; and Frank Stevens, of the 38th U. S. C. T.—have had their establishments closed up by Col. Draper, commander of the 30th Brigade, with three days allowed to remove their effects beyond the brigade limits, and ten to gather themselves out of the department. The immediate cause for expelling these gentlemen was their repeated violation of express orders in practising a system of uniform extortion upon the soldiers. Sutlers in the brigade are permitted to charge fifty per cent over and above the cost of their goods, which Col. Draper deems sufficient profit; but as these went beyond that figure, he dismissed them without ceremony. Elias acted in the capacity of purveyor for these headquarters, but as he only had one establishment, he, after making a desperate effort to remain, by going to the higher authorities was obliged to share the fate of his comrades in misdemeanor. This act of Col. Draper to protect the soldiers of his command from the avariciousness of adventurers is another evidence of his untiring zeal in every thing that pertains to their welfare. By such acts the men are satisfied that, so far as he is concerned, every consideration due to them by the regulations shall be faithfully adhered to.

Lieutenant Colonel B. F. Pratt, commanding the 36th U. S. C. T., is now confined in the hospital at Point of Rocks, with strong indications of having a serious attack of camp fever. The illness of this brave officer does not cause him half as much regret as being absent from his command at the present crisis. The regiment is now commanded by Major W. M. Hart, recently promoted from a captaincy for meritorious conduct. Both of these gentlemen are good officers, and are eminently popular with the men.

Captain Rich, 1st U. S. C. T., has been promoted to the lieutenant colonelcy of his regiment for gallant conduct in front of Petersburg. The opinion of the "1st," on this promotion, was best expressed in the purchase of a sword and riding equipments to be presented to him. Whatever may be said of colored troops, one thing is certain, that they never forget kindness, nor let a favorable opportunity pass without expressing in some degree their grateful recollections of considerate treatment.

HEADQUARTERS 3D DIVISION, 18TH CORPS
IN THE FIELD, OCTOBER 28, 1864.

One corps, the 18th, was put in motion yesterday morning, and marched to the very gates of Richmond, by flanking the enemy's works. Having accomplished the purpose of the expedition, we leisurely returned this evening to our position on the James river, to await what next the authorities may wish to have undertaken. If the grand plan of the commander-in-chief has been successful, then we have gained a substantial victory, and if not somebody will be held to a fearful responsibility. Without stopping to moralize at this time on the expedition or its results, I present the accompanying facts for the attention of your readers, with the assurance that when the Army of the James goes out to challenge the enemy for a general battle the loyal people need not fear for the result. But here is an account of the demonstration of yesterday, in which we had three cannons out of four disabled, but as we silenced the rebel battery it is fair to suppose we did it material injury.

At eight o'clock, Colonel S. P. Spear,[11] commanding 2d Brigade in Kautz's cavalry, moved out from White's Tavern, on the Charles City road, to White Oak Swamp road, following which he came into the Williamsburg road. At the junction of the White Oak Swamp and Williamsburg roads the first pickets of the enemy were seen, and were charged upon by Captain E. P. Ring,[12] 11th Pennsylvania Cavalry,[13] but being some distance in the advance, and well

11. Samuel Perkins Spear (1815–1875). Spear entered the war as a private in a Massachusetts regiment. He rose to colonel in August, 1862, and was brevetted brigadier general for gallantry at Darbytown. Mark Mayo Boatner III, *The Civil War Dictionary* (New York, 1959), 781.

12. Euphronous P. Ring (?–?). A member of Company A, Ring mustered in, September, 1861, and rose through the ranks to captain and to brevet major for "gallant and meritorious conduct" at the end of the war. Bates, *History of Pennsylvania Volunteers,* III, 912; *OR*, Ser. I, Vol. XLVI, Pt. 1, p. 1247.

13. Organized in Philadelphia in 1861, the 11th served in Washington, D.C., and Virginia, where it was attached to the 2nd Brigade, Cavalry Division. Dyer, *Compendium of the War of the Rebellion,* 215.

mounted, they made good their escape. At McClellan's outer line of entrenchments, Capt. Ring came upon a company of the enemy's cavalry, much larger than his own, protected by this line of works, whom he sent to Richmond at a frightful speed, following them some distance along the Williamsburg road.

The infantry, under Brevet Major General Weitzel,[14] coming up at this juncture, Captain Tripp,[15] 11th Pennsylvania Cavalry, with one squadron, moved out from its right upon a body of the enemy's cavalry, formed in the ridge of a thin skirt of woods, and drove them into their fortifications. A squadron of cavalry was kept on the right and left of the infantry during the remainder of the day to observe the movements of the enemy. Sergeant John Peterson,[16] Co. A, 11th Pennsylvania Cavalry, supposed to be captured, was the only loss, excepting a few horses of Col. Spear's cavalry.

The 18th Corps, under General Weitzel, left camp on the morning of the 27th about six o'clock, one hour later than was announced for the march. The soldiers, in good style, moved along the Kingsland road. By a circuitous route we reached the Darbytown road, which we followed up until we came to White's Tavern. A wheel to the right brought us into the Charles City road, and from here we took the route which had been pursued by the cavalry. As the soldiers passed beyond the Seven Pines and the extreme fortifications which Mc-Clellan had erected, they manifested evident satisfaction, while many of them who had figured in that disastrous campaign pointed out places of interest unknown to others. When the column came out upon the Williamsburg road and formed in line of battle, the sight was cheering to behold. From the repeated reports of musketry,

14. Godfrey Weitzel (1835–1884). An engineer, Weitzel was named chief engineer of Butler's forces operating against New Orleans and remained in Louisiana until December, 1863. He was put in command of the XVIII Corps in May, 1864, and later assumed a similar post in the XXV Corps. Initially, Weitzel was strongly opposed to arming slaves, but later came to accept its legitimacy and seems to have had good relations with the black troops in his command. *DAB*, X, 616; Dudley T. Cornish, *The Sable Arm: Negro Troops in the Union Army, 1861–1865* (New York, 1956), xii.

15. Stephen Tripp (?–?). A member of Company K, Tripp mustered in, August, 1861, as a sergeant and rose to captain in November, 1864. He was wounded at New Market Heights. Bates, *History of Pennsylvania Volunteers*, III, 908, 942; *OR*, Ser. I, Vol. XLII, Pt. 1, pp. 838–39.

16. There is no one by this name with the rank of sergeant. There is, however, a Private John Paterson who mustered in, September, 1861, and deserted in November, 1864. Bates, *History of Pennsylvania Volunteers*, III, 914.

which greeted our ears here, it was evident that the cavalry was diverting the attention of the enemy.

But little time was spent in delay, and in the neighborhood of twelve o'clock two brigades of infantry, under Colonels Fairchild[17] and Cullem, commanding respectively the 3d brigade, 2d division, 18th Corps, and the 1st brigade, 3d division, 18th Corps, were ordered to demonstrate in line of battle against the enemy's works, which were about three miles and a half from Richmond. Colonel A. G. Draper, with his gallant colored brigade, which so successfully carried the enemy's works on the 29th ult., formed a line of battle, with some other troops in the rear, in an almost impassable jungle. It was difficult to see any distance from where this line was formed, lying down under cover of the dense undergrowth. The enemy's works at this point, in front of Fair Oaks, were not only strongly built, but were well fortified. This fact having been ascertained, it was necessary to make such a demonstration as would seriously threaten the enemy's line, and prevent the reinforcement of his forces on his right, which we had good reason to believe was being attacked by General Meade.[18]

A skirmish line had previously been thrown out, which drew a portion of the enemy's fire; but when the two brigades, for which he reserved a volley, came up on a charge, a concentrated discharge of musketry was poured into them. Many of the 89th New York, 8th Maine, 118th New York, 5th Maryland, 148th New York, 96th New York, 9th Vermont, and 19th Wisconsin were killed and wounded. An effort was made to continue the charge and demonstrate more fiercely against the enemy's line, but when within twenty rods in front of it our line of battle wavered, and those who remained fell to the ground, where they remained till night shaded the scene. The colored brigade was chafing with impatience to be let loose upon the rebels,

17. Edward E. Fairchild (b. 1841). Mustered in as a sergeant, Company D, 126th New York, in August, 1862, he surrendered at Harpers Ferry three weeks later. Fairchild later joined the 9th USCT and was promoted to first lieutenant after New Market. Frederick Phisterer (comp.), *New York in the War of the Rebellion, 1861 to 1865* (5 vols.; New York, 1912), V, 4176; George Washington Williams, *A History of the Negro Troops in the War of the Rebellion, 1861–1865* (New York, 1888), 338.

18. George Gordon Meade (1815–1872). A veteran of the Mexican War, Meade participated in many of the major battles in the first two years of the war and was severely wounded at Glendale. He was made commander of the Army of the Potomac, a position he held between Gettysburg and Appomattox. *DAB*, VI, 474–76.

but as it was not a part of the plan to capture the works, to a great extent disappointed.

Gen. Weitzel having performed the part allotted to him for the day, began, about 8 o'clock, to withdraw his force from the enemy's front. This was found to be exceedingly difficult, as the dense mass of brush and thickets, coupled with intense darkness, made extremely disagreeable by a heavy rain, which began at noon and continued until midnight, rendered it almost impossible to communicate with our entire line. As it was, the 38th U. S. C. T. and four companies of the 36th U. S. C. T. were not aware of the movement, and were left in their position until the following morning, when, to their astonishment, they discovered that the column had retired. This little incident, more than anything else, manifests how securely we were stationed there, and with what alarm we filled the rebels. When morning broke, and these troops saw that only they were holding the entire rebel force in his entrenchments, they very wisely retired before the enemy discovered the fact. They picked their way through the dense jungle as best they could, and, coming out upon the Williamsburg road, were informed by the cavalry that the infantry was encamped at the White House Tavern, several miles to the rear.

As it was, many of our wounded fell into the enemy's picket lines, and were pressingly requested to remain. Others, having been this way before, under McClellan, knew the route, and piloted themselves and their comrades by the most direct course to the rear. The loss in the two brigades will not exceed 400 in killed and wounded.

Such is a plain account of the part assigned to Gen. Weitzel in the great drama of that day, and if other have performed their part as successfully we shall be greeted, as soon as we return to the rear, with the news of a grand victory.

Col. Holman commanded the 3d Division, 18th Corps, but as one brigade had been left in the entrenchments in front of Richmond, another had been assigned for the day to the division under General Heckman,[19] and the remaining one he headed in person. This force constituted the reserve, and was posted on the Williamsburg road,

19. Charles Adams Heckman (1822–1896) spent the early years of the war in the Union's occupying forces in the Carolinas before he was transferred to the Army of the James. Heckman was captured at Drewry's Bluff in May, 1864, and exchanged in September when he assumed command of the 2nd Division, XVIII Corps. He also commanded the XXV Corps in January and February, 1865, during Weitzel's absence. Faust (ed.), *Historical Times Illustrated Encyclopedia*, 356.

about a mile from White Oak Swamp road. Late in the afternoon
Colonel Holman was ordered to threaten the enemy's left flank with a
severe demonstration. He wheeled out of the Williamsburg road,
crossed the York River Railroad, which, we understand, is out of use,
and cut the telegraph, much, no doubt, to the confusion of rebel
curiosity. As soon as this part of the division, being the brigade under
Colonel Kiddoo, came in sight, the rebels shelled them fearfully.
Colonel Holman knew his men, and as he had tried them before, he
had no fear that they would fail him on this occasion. Major
Weinmann,[20] with a company of excellent colored sharpshooters,
were thrown out as skirmishers, and soon drove the enemy's pickets
into his lines. A squadron of cavalry, of Hampton's Legion,[21] drew up
in the field in line of battle, when five officers of Col. Holman's staff
and three orderlies charged down upon them with drawn sabres and
fierce yelling, and as soon as the rebs discharged their pieces, they
turned and fled in great disorder. Without doubt, this was deemed
quite a gallant affair, especially so, as the surgeon of the division, a
non-combatant, and without weapons, formed one of the party.
When we came close to the enemy, we discovered that he had strong
works in a road under cover of a dense wood. Col. Holman, quickly
perceiving the state of things, immediately deployed the 1st and 22d
U. S. C. T. in line of battle, under cover of the woods, and formed the
37th U. S. C. T. on the right of the enemy's cavalry, which was
threatening an attack. Having waited for the enemy to assault our line
a reasonable length of time, and as night was rapidly approaching,
the Colonel ordered the 1st Regiment, which was supported on the
left by the 22d, to charge the enemy's works. The 1st rushed upon the
rebs with fixed bayonets, and were received by a terrible fire of
artillery, showering spherical case shot, which made great gaps in the
line, which, however, were immediately filled up in handsome style
by the men of the fighting 1st. They continued to go on until they

20. Philip Weinmann (d. 1866) mustered in, October, 1863, and later commanded a
division of sharpshooters. He was promoted to major, 37th USCT, after New Market
Heights. Bates, *History of Pennsylvania Volunteers*, V, 961; Williams, *A History of Negro
Troops*, 335.
21. The Legion was named for Wade Hampton (1818–1902), who recruited a group
of South Carolinians in 1861. It had undergone considerable change when, in the
spring of 1864, it became a cavalry brigade in Pickett's division and participated in the
defense of Richmond and Petersburg. Faust (ed.), *Historical Times Illustrated Encyclopedia*, 335.

reached the fort, capturing a battery of two guns, with the drivers, who were just ready to run them off, and during which the enemy treated them to an abundant supply of canister. Under this fire Col. Holman, at the head of his command, was wounded in the thigh, but not seriously. Colonel Kiddoo took command, and pushed immediately forward, when the brave Kiddoo fell, badly wounded in the back with a piece of shell. To the credit of this excellent regiment it must be said that, notwithstanding they saw their officers carried off the field, and with no one to command them, they still rushed forward until they had captured the enemy's fort and works, the only victory of the kind gained by our forces during the day. Just as our colored troops had captured the rebel lines they received orders to fall back and strengthen the right flank, as there was a large gap between this line of battle and the main body of the column. The 37th was deployed as skirmishers to protect this retrograde movement. The loss in the colored troops is not heavy, occasioned mostly by shells.

Such is the record of the colored troops under Colonels Holman and Kiddoo, who were sent only to demonstrate against the enemy's line, but would not be satisfied until it was captured at the point of the bayonet.

HEADQUARTERS 3D DIVISION, 18TH ARMY CORPS
BEFORE RICHMOND, OCTOBER 31, 1864.

On Wednesday morning, the 26th inst., the 18th Corps, being a part of the Army of the James, left the trenches and camped in their vicinity, to make such preparation for the demonstration against Richmond the following day as is usual under such circumstances. The necessary amount of ammunition and provision for three days were distributed among the soldiers, which at once impressed them with the conviction that a battle somewhere was imminent, in which they were to take a part. Having in a previous despatch informed you generally, I now propose to speak of some things in detail.

Wednesday night was a lively one, particularly among the colored troops under Col. Holman. The early part was spent in singing, with animating effect, the "John Brown" song, "Rally Around the Flag," the "Colored Volunteer," and others of similar import. Never was an army in better spirits, or more confident of a victory.

This assault was intended to be a surprise, but the enemy, it appears, was aware of our movement, and we found, instead of a few hundred cavalry, Hoke's[22] and Fields'[23] divisions, a Texas brigade, and a heavy force of Hampton Legion, and probably others. This of course changed the plan of operation, and, instead of attacking, our plan was reduced to demonstrating against the enemy's works.

Col. Collum's brigade, at another point, charged the enemy's works with no different result to the command under Col. Fairchild. Too much praise can not be given to these two brigades, and their commanding officers, for the heroic manner in which they faced that terrible fire, and the excellent discipline which was maintained under such extraordinary circumstances.

The 1st Colored Brigade, under Colonel John H. Holman, commanding the 3d Division of colored troops, was drawn up as reserves, in column by division closed in mass, to the right of the Williamsburg road, about a half mile from the rear line of battle. It remained in this position for about an hour after the charge of the two brigades, when it was discovered that the enemy was moving troops to the right, for the purpose of flanking us. This brigade of negroes then moved by the right flank, the 22d U. S. C. T. being in the advance, followed by the 1st United States Colored Troops, with the 37th U. S. C. T. for reserves. Having crossed the York River Railroad, the 22d wheeled to the left, and advanced about a mile, in column, and then deployed in line of battle, between the York River Railroad and what I suppose to be the York river pike, a road running parallel with the railroad at this point, with its left resting upon the railroad, and its right upon the pike. Captain, now Major Weinmann, with his well organized company of sharpshooters, was thrown out in front without encountering any serious opposition, driving the enemy's pickets within their entrenchments. The line of battle being

22. Robert Frederick Hoke (1837–1912). By 1862, Hoke was considered one of Lee's most talented young officers in North Carolina. He saw further action at Antietam, Fredericksburg, and Chancellorsville, where he was seriously wounded. In late 1864 he served in the Petersburg and Richmond campaigns. Jon L. Wakelyn, *Biographical Dictionary of the Confederacy* (Westport, Conn., 1977), 233–34; Faust (ed.), *Historical Times Illustrated Encyclopedia*, 365.

23. Charles William Field (1828–1892). A general, Field was injured at Second Manassas and retired from active duty for a year. In February, 1864, he was given command of Hood's old Texas division and successfully staved off Grant's flank movement during the Battle of the Wilderness in May. *DAB*, III, 356–57; Wakelyn, *Biographical Dictionary of the Confederacy*, 185–86.

formed, the 22d marched rapidly towards the enemy's works, which were nearly a mile distant, and when within five hundred yards the rebels opened a galling fire which the 22d encountered with commendable courage. Here a charge was ordered, to which the regiment replied by an immediate advance, but unfortunately a dense woods through which it was obliged to pass, seriously deranged the line, and the troops came out in such a state of confusion as to be in no condition for an assault. Nevertheless their daring colonel, Kiddoo, placed himself at their head and shouted "Forward!" From this point the enemy's works were about one hundred and fifty yards distant, toward which the hastily formed line dashed with much gallantry, until its right had advanced within about ten yards of the rebel flags on the breastworks, when a severe fire caused the line to waver. Even this would not have happened if a number of new recruits, who unfortunately had been sent to this regiment without drill, went into this, their first engagement, had not given way in much confusion. The regiment fell back about three hundred yards and reformed the line, preparatory to charging the works again, when Major Weinmann reported a heavy body of rebels massing in the right of the 22d, which was deemed sufficient to countermand the order for another assault. The officers and men, mortified at the conduct of the new recruits, and regretting the absence of supports, fell back in good order, bringing off their wounded with them.

The enemy's works at this point formed an angle opposite to the centre of the advancing line, and enabled him to pour an enfilading fire upon both flanks. Such is the record of the 22d United States Colored Troops on the 27th, in the demonstration against Richmond; and had it been intended that they should capture the works the rebels would have been jumped out of them on a double quick.

The 1st United States Colored Troops deployed the column, in line of battle, in the rear of the 22d United States Colored Troops, and entered a skirt of woods in the rear of that regiment, by the right flank, filing to the left. It passed into this woods a short distance, then facing about, emerged from it by the left flank, when a two-gun battery opened upon their left. The regiment immediately filed to the left, and was ordered by Col. Holman to capture this battery. The troops immediately rushed over an uneven ground for about half a mile; then passing over two unfinished lines of the enemy's works, and when within a few yards of his entrenchments, not liking to meet colored troops on anything like equal terms, he fled from the works, leaving two guns in our possession. Being inside of the enemy's entrenchments, this gallant regiment was preparing to charge down the interior of his line, when it discovered that it was being rapidly flanked by a large force, which obliged it to retreat, after having spiked the guns and brought off some prisoners. All of their wounded, with the exception of thirty, were carried from the field as the movement was made to the rear.

The colored troops are the only ones that entered the enemy's works and made any captures on that day, and if it had been intended that they should have done more than make a demonstration they would have been sufficiently supported to have enabled them to hold them. The 1st U. S. C. T. is a fighting regiment, and when Col. Holman urges them forward they have never been known to fail or falter.

On Thursday morning we began our march about six o'clock. In one part of our circuitous march, which was at least twelve miles long, I came across several muskets and accoutrements, which were heaped together, and no one near to claim them. Such is the course pursued when a soldier wishes to desert, and it is my impression that the owners of the articles were rebel spies in our army, who availed themselves of the first opportunity to escape, with such information of our advance and force as their opportunities afforded them to learn. By means of the telegraph, such information was, no doubt, communicated, which prepared the enemy for our attack.

We passed but few houses along our route, where I found only women, who freely gave satisfactory answers to my inquiries as to distances, and the names of the roads. One or two decrepit men were seen, whose courtesy was astonishing. In one or two instances the column happened to rest before well-supplied barns, where we subsisted our horses. In some cases the females pretended to be good Union folks, but the dodge would not serve to cover their hypocrisy.

It was about half-past two when Col. Fairchild, commanding the 3d Brigade, 2d Division, after a fatiguing march from 6 o'clock in the morning, drew up in line-of-battle and charged the enemy's works with seven hundred men. A terrible fire was poured into them as they marched up, in good order, but it was impossible for this small force to stand their ground. After wavering for a time the line was readily re-formed, and rushed upon the works of the enemy a second time, but with no better result. In this charge, the enemy, besides pouring an artillery-fire into this little band, had the advantage of a flank-fire upon its right and left.

Here the advancing line, unable to accomplish the task assigned, covered itself as much as possible from the raking fire of the enemy. The men, by twos and threes, fell back to a by-road, which they held for a couple of hours, bringing off as many of our wounded as possible. A little before dusk the enemy threw a skirmish line in front of his works, and picked up such of our wounded as we could not reach, and others who would have been shot had they moved from their cover. Colonel Fairchild, observing the state of affairs, passed the word along for the line to fall back, which was done in good order.

In this demonstration I regret to say that Capt. Paul L. Higgins,[24] inspector general, and Captain Puhlmann,[25] acting assistant adjutant general, both on the staff of Colonel Fairchild, were killed.

The 148th New York[26] had the misfortune to have its entire color-guard killed under the breastworks, and, of course, lost its national flag. By very great bravery and under much exposure the State flag was brought off in safety. Three men volunteered to bring the national emblem from the field, but they were all shot by sharp-shooters in their patriotic effort. The 19th Wisconsin[27] lost their colors, all of its color-guard having been killed in bearing onward the old flag. Sergt. Ed. W. Smith's[28] conduct is deserving of especial mention, as this is the third time he has brought the colors of his regiment from the field, after the color guard had all been killed. This time he was severely pressed and gave up all hopes of succeeding,

24. Paul L. Higgins (?–?). The report from Colonel Fairchild observed that both Higgins and Puhlmann were "slightly wounded and did not leave the field." *OR*, Ser. I, Vol. XLII, Pt. 1, pp. 812–13.

25. Otto Puhlmann (?–?). See note 24.

26. Organized in Geneva, New York, and mustered in September, 1862, the 148th saw action at Norfolk and Yorktown before joining the Army of the James, first as part of the XVIII Corps and then as a regiment in the XIV Corps. Dyer, *Compendium of the War of the Rebellion*, 197.

27. Recruited in Madison in April, 1862, the 19th served in Norfolk, Portsmouth, Yorktown (Virginia) and New Bern (North Carolina), later becoming part of the XVIII Corps. It was later transferred to the XXIV Corps. Dyer, *Compendium of the War of the Rebellion*, 239.

28. There is no one by this name in the 19th Wisconsin, and the only person with this name in a New York regiment is a lieutenant.

and immediately began to scratch a hole in the ground to bury them. He, however, seeing a favorable opportunity to retreat, did so, bringing the colors with him. The loss of the brigade in killed, wounded, and missing is three hundred and ninety-seven.

Three brigades were formed in line of battle, neither one in sight of the other, and attacked the enemy's works. Each one went in on its own account, and did the best it could under the circumstances. It would be more strictly in accordance with facts to say that the colored troops went in by regiments, which from a blunder supposed to rest upon some of the officers of the 22d U. S. C. T., were so far separated as to be unable to render that support to the 1st which might have materially changed the whole face of affairs. This misfortune is not chargeable to a want of a gallantry or military knowledge, but is the result of complicated circumstances which relieve the officers from any reflection. The regiment has ever been known to be a good one, and will soon sustain its past laurels.

The line of battle, with several large gaps between, was commanded by Col. Holman on the right, Gen. Heckman in the centre, and Gen. Marston[29] on the left. With the exception of incidents, which I may forward at another time, I submit for the considerate judgment of an impartial public the account of the 18th Corps' demonstration within three and a half miles from Richmond. We retired in good order, without being followed by the enemy.

CASUALTIES IN 1ST U. S. C. T., OCT. 27, 1864.

Austin Sutton, A. killed	Hy Gallway, A. wounded
Wm H. Ball, A. killed	Henry Gibson, A. wounded
Frank Warner, A. wounded	J Williams, E. wounded
John Bladoy, A. wounded	Capt W Parlin, E. wounded
Wm Wilson, A. wounded	Fred Payne, E. wounded
Thos Ennis, A. wounded	John Lucas, E. wounded
Jos Wolson, A. wounded	Geo Johnson, E. wounded
Geo. Curtis, A. wounded	Thos Cravens, E. wounded
Nath'l Smith, A. wounded	Geo. Cain, E. wounded

29. Gilman Marston (1811–1890). A lawyer and former congressman, Marston saw action at First Bull Run, in the Peninsular campaign, and at Fredericksburg. During 1864 and 1865 he commanded brigades in the XVIII and XVII Corps. Faust (ed.), *Historical Times Illustrated Encyclopedia*, 476–77.

Jan Peters, E. wounded
Wm Hegeman, E. wounded
Wm Bank, E. wounded
Daniel Lane, E. wounded
Jas Peak, E. wounded
Corp S Carter, E. wounded
Wm Warner, E. missing
G Hangerford, B. wounded
M Thomas, B. wounded
Alfred Sheppard, B. missing
An Washington, B. missing
Corp M Johnson, C. wound
Corp G F Johnson, C. wound
Corp T Green, C. wounded
Wm Boos., C. wounded
Richard Cook, C. wounded
Wm Gordon, C. wounded
Nelson Newton, C. wounded
Jas Smith, C. wounded
Wm Sippio, C. wounded
Robt Scott, C. wounded
John Robins, G. wounded
H Williams, G. wounded
Wm Massey, G. wounded
Wm Cooper, G. missing
Edmond Davis, G. missing
Moses Smith, G. missing
R Sedgwick, G. missing
Geo Thompson, H. killed
Sgt Lewis Lincoln H. w'd
Corp J Lacas, H. wounded
Chas Green, H. wounded
Geo W Scott, H. wounded
George Odum, H. wounded
Thos Edwards, H. wounded
Jackson Howard, I. wound
Allen Jackson, I. wounded
John Shuman, I. wounded
Sergt Thos Pauls, I. missing

John Cistis, I. missing
Capt J. E. Rice, K. wounded
Wm Allen, K. wounded
Geo W Carter, K. wounded
Jacob Siles, A. wounded
Wm Jackson, A. wounded
Robt Diggs, B. killed
Cern J. Jackson, B. wounded
Corp C. T. Brown, B. wounded
J Smallwood, B. wounded
Geo. D. King, B. wounded
Benj Butler, B. wounded
J Braxton, B. wounded
Henry Baluey, B. wounded
Thos Beit, D. wounded
Wm Young, F. killed
Geo. Carroll, F. wounded
Abram Palton, F. wounded
J Venville, F. wounded
Moses Warner, F. wounded
H Webster, F. wounded
Fred Gatlin, F. missing
D Thompson, F. missing
John Williams, F. missing
Franklin Macy, F. missing
Willis Jackson, G. killed
Robt Johnson, G. killed
Sergt F Turner, G. wounded
W Washington, B. wounded
Charles Lasco, C. wounded
Wm Lalson, C. wounded
Jos Williams, C. wounded
Nelson Davis, C. wounded
– Sammons, C. wounded
Capt Hen Ward, D. missing
Sgt Theo Ray, D. wounded
Sgt Hen Button, D. wound
Sgt D E Brooks, D. wound
Sgt Alex Brown, D. wound

Sgt Jas Brown, D. wounded
Sgt H Washington, D. w'd
Sgt F Washington, D. w'd
Geo. Allen, G. wounded
Dennis Brown, H. wounded
John Offer, H. wounded
James Ried, H. wounded
Jos Whitfield, H. missing
Saml Smith, H. missing
Wm Fields, I. killed
Henry Jones, I. killed
Frank Cook, I. wounded
Frank Walker, I. wounded

John Scott, I. wounded
Sgt Jno Gordon, I. wounded
Corp S Keelen, I. wounded
Edward N Day, I. wounded
Wash Day, I. wounded
Geo Flamer, K. wounded
Isaac Payne, K. wounded
Hugh Walter, K. wounded
Henry Thomas, K. wounded
Beverly Danerfeld, K. m'g
Wm Dean, K. missing
Philip Young, K. killed

CASUALTIES IN THE 22D U. S. C. T., OCT. 27, 1864.

Col J B Kiddoo, wounded
Capt W B Clark, K. left on field
Capt Levi Graybill, E.
Capt A P Morrey, F. arm
Corpl N. Stanton, E. wounded
Wm H Hassey, wounded
Geo W Connor, wounded
Stephen James, wounded
John Jackson, wounded
John Brown, wounded
Sergt C Hillstock, H. wou'd
Israel Stevenson, wounded
George Watson, wounded
Luther Scott, wounded
Wm Pry, am not
Geo Burgin, K. wounded
P H Burtin, K. wounded
John Parker, K. wounded
John H Peary, K. wounded
John Wright, F. wounded
Moses Cokely, F. wounded
Chas Adams, G. wounded
Wm Jones, G. wounded
Corpl G Eayres, G. wounded

Sergeant Jacob Wright, D.
    wounded, left on field
G W Thornton, D. wounded
Frank Smith, D. wounded
Wm Bachus, wounded
Corpl I Spokly, B. wounded
Albert Sane, B. wounded
C H Hartsurn, B. wounded
Sergt H Kimmel, missing
Ferdinand Halzer, missing
Sergt J Loveday, wounded
Corpl H Johnson, wounded
Jerry Brown, wounded
Peter Bell, wounded
Milfin Curdley, wounded
Elias Harris, wounded
Nehemiah Hanlow, woun'd
John Medley, wounded
Edward Spencer, wounded
Lewis Yates, wounded
Corpt C Evans, C. wounded
Thos Morris, wounded
James Jenkins, wounded

HEADQUARTERS 3D DIVISION, 18TH CORPS
BEFORE RICHMOND, NOV. 8, 1864.

After a movement has been made, a battle fought, a defeat sustained, or a victory won, it is an easy, but not always a pleasant task, to sit in judgment upon the martial bearing of those who were entrusted with important responsibilities. This duty becomes painful when officers known to be brave and generally efficient, fail, from complicated causes which they could not control, to accomplish what is committed to the undertaking of their commands. When the gallant conduct of soldiers, rising above the terrible exigency of the occasion, which can neither be paralyzed by the galling fire of an entrenched foe or the threatening consequences of barbarous chieftains, fails from a lack of concentration, or a misunderstanding of orders—however much circumstances might excuse a man from a citizen's stand-point, military law holds an officer to a fearful responsibility for all the deficiencies in his command. A failure is aggravated in proportion to the position lost or the victory that might have been gained.

One week ago to-day, had the officers under command of Col. Holman, who led the 1st Colored Brigade, 3d Division, 18th Corps, against the enemy's works and occupied them, obeyed his commands, we should have won a victory that would have thrilled every loyal heart. That it may be fully understood how a great advantage was lost, and in what direction the responsibility rests, I subjoin an account of the manoeuvering of the brigade, which consisted of the 1st, 22d, and 37th U. S. Colored Troops, the last-named being drawn up in close column by division as reserves. The 22d was formed in line of battle, with the 1st on its right, when what appeared to be about fifteen hundred rebel cavalry appeared in sight. The 37th was deployed to divert their attention. Immediately, the 1st and 22d marched through a woods which were near by the left flank at a double quick, with the intention of assaulting a rebel battery which was shelling General Weitzel's line with some effect. The enemy now opened two guns upon Col. Holman's right, which caused him to march the regiments back again by the right flank at a double quick. He then gave the order to move by the right flank, which was parallel with the enemy's works, and when he was ready to assault he marched by the left flank. This order not being fully understood by the company commanders of the 22d, the regiment was thrown into confusion at a critical moment. The first, and about half of the second company, moved off correctly by the left flank, while the others marched by the right of companies to the front, which destroyed the line. Instead of halting to rectify this misunderstanding, the charge was made, the first regiment striking the enemy's works at one point, while the 22d rushed at another, each one at too great a distance to lend any support to the other. The 22d did not quite reach the works, and, after a stubborn resistance of the veterans of that regiment, it was obliged to fall back, though not defeated, and far from being demoralized. The 1st was far more successful. It stormed and captured the enemy's works, a battery, and some few prisoners, and was preparing to charge down the interior of his line, when a heavy cavalry force was thrown against it, driving it back. Had it not been for the mistake of the 22d, we would not only have been met, but would have been roughly handled, and sent back in confusion.

The recommendation of General Butler to appoint Colonel Alonzo G. Draper a brevet brigadier general, for gallantly carrying his colored brigade across the enemy's works at Spring Hill, with fixed bayonets, on the 29th of September, has been approved by the President, and that title has been conferred.

Col. E. Wright, the excellent commander of the 10th United States Colored Troops, has been assigned to the command of the 2d Brigade, 3d Division, 10th Corps. This campaign is not ended yet.

HEADQUARTERS 3D DIVISION, 18TH CORPS
BEFORE RICHMOND, NOV. 6, 1864.

In the Army of the James, for the last day or two, there has not transpired an item of interest. The air has been laden with rumors of a favorable character, which are probably the harbinger of some undeveloped result. The rebel chiefs seem to be in a fever of ferment, which will hourly increase until after the election, should their fears not be realized before that event. They have an idea that General Grant feels it to be his duty to electrify the North with a grand victory, to place the hopes of the Union party beyond dispute. This idea has excited a good deal of nervous sensibility in Richmond, and has quickened the perceptive faculties of rebel scouts and lookouts to imagine movements, and carry back to the doomed capital information which has its origin nowhere but in their apprehensive brains.

The military situation never was in a more satisfactory state than it is to-day, and it is daily brightening with accumulating prospects. The army has not gone into winter quarters yet, though the weather would suggest such accommodations; nor do I believe that we will be in our present position when that order is passed along the line of the Army of the James. We have several weeks of weather ahead that will be by no means unfavorable to our movements, and of which it is probable we will take advantage. Gen. Grant will not only fight it out on this line, but, from present indications, is sure to win the prize of which he is in such close pursuit.

I am strongly impressed with the belief that the rebels will attempt something, if there is the least idea of success, with a view of aiding McClellan at the polls. They are laboring incessantly to defend their capital, and, at the same time, are endeavoring to mature plans for the surprise and defeat of General Butler's army. How well they will succeed in attempting to take this army unawares will be shown in the result, which will be in nowise unfavorable to our arms. One thing is certain, the rebels will not attack us openly, but if they can mature any plan which will effect a surprise and a catastrophe at the same time, there is little doubt that they will avail themselves of all the advantage which they can hope to gain by such means. Our officers are ever on the alert, and would like nothing better from the enemy than an effort on their part to catch them napping.

The work on the Dutch Gap canal is being pushed rapidly to a successful completion. The sight is really inspiring. A personal observation of the success which has attended this great enterprise is more suggestive of a victorious termination of this campaign than anything which I have noticed.

Brig. Gen. Paine, commanding the 3d (colored) Division, who has been North on sick leave, returned to these headquarters night before last, and yesterday assumed command. Brevet Brig. Gen. Draper, who has been in temporary command, is again at the head of his famous brigade.

HEADQUARTERS IN THE FIELD

BEFORE RICHMOND, NOV. 9, 1864.

In a word, there is nothing in the way of military operations to communicate. The martial spirit has been slumbering for the past few days, if we except the spasmodic shelling at Dutch Gap. When and where the next line of battle will be formed are matters which legitimately belong to the future. That it will come there can be no doubt, and the preparation and organization to correspond with the occasion give confidence of a crowning success.

Yesterday some of the soldiers in this army expressed, by their suffrages, who should guide the helm for the next four years. The election, so far as I saw and was able to learn, passed off in a very orderly manner. There was no excitement, or any stimulus in the vicinity of the polls to get up an unnecessary pressure. Any one not aware that it was election-day might have passed the polls without seeing anything that would have impressed him with the act. The voting of the 5th United States Colored Troops, who came from Ohio, was a little amusing, and attracted much attention from the McClellan men on the other side of the line. The supporters of Little Mac were gathered together in quite a crowd opposite the place of election of the 5th; and it is more than probable they would have come over and given expression to their choice had it not been for the precaution of the supporters of Mr. Lincoln in stationing an extensive line of armed men to prevent their indulging in any such luxury. The colored men in front of the 5th were particularly vigilant lest those who had been so intently watching them from early morn should claim their "constitutional privilege" and avail themselves of the opportunity to express their admiration for McClellan. This class of men here are called Johnnies, but in the North they are known as Copperheads—a distinction without any difference. That no votes were cast at the polls of the 5th for the little general cannot be attributed to the absence of his supporters, but rather to the armed resistance which threatened such fearful consequences should they attempt to vote their convictions. Should there be vitality enough left in the Copperhead concern, after the drubbing which it now appears it received yesterday, there is no doubt but that it will hiss its venom, with all of its concentrated bitterness, at the Government for permitting colored loyal men to vote in its support, to the exclusion of their "Southern brethren".

As there has been much straggling in our advances which could not be accounted for, it is probable that they are the friends of the defeated McClellan, who, like him, are not going to hurt the rebels if they can help it.

The vote in the regiments in this army is small compared to the men on duty. The New York troops have sent their votes home, which, of course, cannot be ascertained here at present, while a very large class are minors and of foreign birth, who are not naturalized. There are—well, it does not make much difference how many persons of African descent, but enough to be equal to any great emergency.

The telegraph has already flashed sufficient intelligence to place Mr. Lincoln's election beyond doubt, which is quite cheering to the army. If they all could not vote, they all rejoice over the result, whose shouts will do as much to paralyze the enemy as if he had met with a disaster.

With the view that the vote of the armies operating against Richmond may be as complete as possible, I herewith subjoin the vote in the Army of the James:

1ST DIVISION, 18TH CORPS.

	Lincoln.	McClellan.
2d New Hampshire	65	4
10th New Hampshire	14	46
13th New Hampshire	86	40
5th Maryland	250	50
58th Pennsylvania	77	52
188th Pennsylvania	214	174
	706	366

2D DIVISION.

	Lincoln.	McClellan.
55th Pennsylvania	116	117
Detachment 9th Vermont	20	2
8th Maine	179	15
2d Penn'a Heavy Artillery	452	297
19th Wisconsin	66	73
Battery A, 1st Pennsylvania	53	23
	886	527

3D DIVISION.

	Lincoln.	McClellan.
5th U. S. Colored Troops	194	0

1ST DIVISION, 10TH CORPS.

	Lincoln.	McClellan.
199th Pennsylvania	337	203
67th Ohio	223	90
206th Pennsylvania	276	147

2D DIVISION.

	Lincoln.	McClellan.
97th Pennsylvania	108	112
76th Pennsylvania	152	76
203d Pennsylvania	419	206
9th Maine	136	4
4th New Hampshire	84	21

3D DIVISION (COLORED).

	Lincoln.	McClellan.
Officers	34	4

OTHER TROOPS, WHOSE LOCATION IS IMMATERIAL.

	Lincoln.	McClellan.
Detachment 9th Vermont	10	0
Detachment 13th N. H.	18	1
12th New Hampshire	86	39
200 Pennsylvania	381	225
207th Pennsylvania	441	202
208th Pennsylvania	401	279
209th Pennsylvania	311	254
211th Pennsylvania	430	141
Company A, 3d Pa. Art.	20	15
Three companies 3d Pa. Art.	94	68
1st Maryland Cavalry	91	82
5th Pennsylvania Cavalry	171	201
Base Hospital of 10th Corps.	44	0

The forty-four votes cast in this hospital for Mr. Lincoln are all from Maine soldiers. All the others were permitted to go home to enjoy their suffrage.

Such is the vote in the Army of the James, and from it you will see that McClellan runs much better, as I informed you in a previous despatch was likely, than many supposed.

HEADQUARTERS 3D DIV., 18TH CORPS

BEFORE RICHMOND, NOV. 8.

Yesterday morning and night before last, there was considerable firing at Dutch Gap, to interfere with the workmen on the great canal.

The men are so accustomed to the showers of exploding shells that they continue on laboring whenever the enemy choose to favor them with a supply. The workmen are the colored defenders of the Union. In whatever position this class of persons has been placed, whether in digging trenches, besieging cities, storming works, or meeting the enemy in an open field, they have fully illustrated what a powerful element they are in aiding to suppress the rebellion. When the canal is finished, General Butler will no doubt handsomely congratulate the living and do justice to the memory of the dead.

Our videttes were driven in yesterday morning on our right, by a reconnoitering force of infantry. That such a move threatens an attack is highly probable. The rebels, thinking that we will be busily engaged in the election, may expect to surprise us; or, confident that Mr. Lincoln will have a majority in the army, may engage us with a view to prevent the soldiers voting. An attack this morning will take no one by surprise. We were on the alert last night, and, as day breaks this morning, we may hear the rebel yell. Should they attempt to charge this time, many of them will find their "last ditch."

HEADQUARTERS 2D BRIG., 3D DIV., 18TH CORPS

BEFORE RICHMOND, NOV. 21, 1864.

The protracted season of rain, by no means unusual during the present month in this State, has rendered army movements imprac-ticable, and seriously impaired the roads for land transportation. A few days of fair weather will, from the nature of the soil, considerably improve the roads and leave them in a much more desirable state. While such weather not only prevents martial movements on a grand scale, it also tends to the discomfort of the brave men who, for the cause of an unbroken Union, are periling their lives in a way which may be slow, but none the less sure, death.

The stake for which the Commander-in-Chief has been playing seems now to be so near his grasp that our soldiers very cheerfully suffer a little longer for the good of the country.

For the past week scarcely an item of interest has transpired for record, excepting the gobbling of our picket line on the Bermuda Hundred front, on the night of the 17th inst., and the successive efforts on the following evenings to retake it. I have not yet heard that our forces have been able to re-establish the line where it was, though the rapid and sharp report of musketry every evening bears evidence of our determination to succeed. In the rebel assault upon our lines we lost about one hundred and fifty men, and a colonel, who happened to be out inspecting the picket line at the time that it was assaulted.

The return of General Butler to the army has occasioned very general congratulations, as it began to be generally understood that he would be assigned to the Secretaryship of the War Department, which, it is supposed will soon be made vacant. The admirers of this gallant officer, although they would be pleased with any good fortune that would likely overshadow him, are by no means jubilant over the prospect that is to take him from the field, though it places him in a higher position so eminently suited to his distinguished abilities.

A night or two ago two soldiers deserted to the enemy, under circumstances which have justified the arrest of two officers that were along the picket line. A strict observance of orders on their part would have defeated any such nefarious efforts on the part of bounty-jumpers and others who are tired of the war. I suppress the names of the officers, as an investigation will soon take place, which will determine how far they are culpable. If innocent, the insertion of their names would do them injustice; and if guilty, they will not escape their full measure of reproach.

The rebels on the James river are determined that no serious, or at least unexpected, danger shall happen to their iron-clad fleet. Every precaution, of which we are fully acquainted, is taken every night to prevent surprise. The wooden boats picket the river below the iron-clad fleet of three vessels, to observe what may take place, and give the alarm when they may see any advance on our part for their capture or destruction.

We have a little firing along the lines every day and night, which, however, is attended with no serious results. We have become so accustomed to the reports of cannon that nothing but the successive reports of musketry occasions any inquiry. The picket-firing last night on the Bermuda Hundred front, supposed to be another effort to re-establish our lines, was not as protracted as on the evening previous, and hardly sufficient to accomplish the result desired.

HEADQUARTERS 2D BRIG., 3D DIV., 18TH CORPS
BEFORE RICHMOND, NOV. 24, 1864.

The mail at the front closes so early in the morning that it precludes the recording of any matters on the day of date, excepting those which transpire very early. To-day being Thanksgiving in this army, as well as in the loyal North, there is little doubt but that the brave soldiers will enjoy the good things which they have learned are in store for them. Every one of them, for the past day or so, has had his mouth set turkey-fashion, and his teeth in a position to masticate mince pies. Having already been officially informed that the good people of the North have sent a Thanksgiving dinner to them, they will partake of it with grateful recollections. Such tangible re-membrances serve to cheer the spirits and nerve the hearts of the nation's defenders in enduring the hardships incidental to military campaigning. Our colored troops have not been forgotten in the general preparations for a feast to-day. They will receive their share in that spirit of gratefulness which the race ever manifest, in the knowledge that they are not forgotten. Both colored and white soldiers will to-day receive a new impulse, when they fully realize, in the good things which will soon be set before them, that their sufferings have been commended, their endurance honored, and their fortitude ennobled.

There has been no change in the military situation along the entire line of the James, and from the Richmond journals of yesterday you will observe that the quiet of the last few days remains unbroken. Of course the rebs continue to shell Dutch Gap, but it is strange that so little damage is sustained. It is rarely ever that any one is in the smallest degree harmed. The men seem to care less for the enemy's messengers of death every day, and prosecute their grand enterprise with fortitude and industry. If the machinery necessary to its construction can be kept in running order for a week, which past experience would suggest is extremely doubtful, there is no doubt but what the North would be electrified with the gratifying intelligence that the gunboats and monitors had passed through Butler's canal, and saluted our Southern brethren in a manner more emphatic than polite. With the completion of this enterprise there is no doubt but what Gen. Butler will have Richmond at his mercy.

An explosion was heard yesterday morning on our extreme right; which occurred in the enemy's lines. It was probably one of his torpedoes, which he was placing somewhere for the obstruction of this army, which was exploded through ignorance or carelessness. It has not been long since a rebel officer found his "last ditch" in setting torpedoes to obstruct our fleet on the James. He accidentally stumbled against one, which had the effect of landing him on the other side of Jordan. It is probable that one or more went yesterday to bear him company, and to communicate the latest unpleasant intelligence from rebeldom.

Capt. Levi Weaver, Co. G, 55th Pennsylvania Regiment, has received an order to be mustered out of the service at his own request. He has served three years with credit to himself and his country. The captain will probably leave for the North on the 27th inst. The 55th is increasing in numbers lately from the convalescents who have recently returned to the regiment, who give to its ranks quite a creditable appearance. It has done honorable service both in South Carolina and Virginia, and will probably distinguish itself in engagements yet to be enacted. The boys complain that they are not allowed to erect winter quarters and make themselves more comfortable, which is a misfortune to them, but is probably deemed a military necessity by the authorities.

HEADQUARTERS 2D BRIG., 3D DIV., 18TH CORPS
BEFORE RICHMOND, NOV. 25, 1864.

Yesterday being Thanksgiving day in the loyal States, the good people of the North, in their abundance, did not forget the brave men in the field. The turkeys and other good things—which were

forwarded, received, and distributed among the soldiers, and of
which they partook heartily—had the tendency of recalling many
cherished recollections, and suggested thoughts of home and kindred, when each and all were gathered around the family hearth to
partake of the Thanksgiving dinner in times of peace. After the
copious showers of rain with which we have been favored for the
past five or six days, it was exceedingly gratifying to welcome the
genial rays of the sun, and experience the refreshing influences of an
unclouded day. The dull routine of martial affairs was diversified by
the unusually exuberant spirits which were everywhere manifested
throughout the various camps. From early dawn until late in the
evening, cheerful voices, songs, and bands of music playing national
airs, were invigorating the monotony of martial existence, and giving
evidence that the "old folks at home," in their kind remembrance on
Thanksgiving day, had struck a chord in the hearts of the defenders
of the Union which vibrated to the highest note of general exultation.
As the brass bands, with more than ordinary melody, played "Rally
round the Flag," the soft cadences of which floated far in the
distance, the brave defenders, who caught the inspiring strains,
joined in the chorus with animation, until the united harmony was
wafted into the camps of our enemy. As if to remind us that one still
dwells amid the stern realities of war, the dull heavy roar of the
enemy's mortar batteries belched forth their terrible missiles of
destruction for the benefit of those laboring in the Dutch Gap Canal.
Otherwise the day passed off with uninterrupted quiet. Could the
good people of the North have seen the radiant faces of the soldiers,
as they were seated around the camp-fires cooking their turkeys, and
witnessed with what peculiar gratification they discussed their
qualities, they would, on other occasions of national significance,
cheer them with bountiful supplies of eatables out of their
abundance.

Last night was spent in singing patriotic songs and sentimental
melodies. A string band was improvised from the 5th U. S. C. T., and
under the inspiration of some of the officers about these headquarters, discoursed very good music.

The officers of the 36th U. S. C. T., now commanded by Major
Hart, enjoyed together a Thanksgiving dinner, which was distinguished by the presence of Brigadier General Wild.[30] Chaplain

30. Edward Augustus Wild (1825–1891) attended medical schools at Harvard and
Paris. He aided Governor Andrew's efforts to raise black troops and commanded

Stevens,[31] a gentleman of color, was also present, from which I would infer that the guests were not at all afraid of his color rubbing off by association. Other dinners were given by regimental and staff officers, which were enjoyed with peculiar feelings of gratification. As they gathered around the tables they thought of the loved ones at home, for whose remembrance of them they cherished the most endearing recollections for affording them a cause for genuine thanksgiving.

The explosion to which I referred in my despatch of yesterday was, as I inferred, the result of carelessness. The Richmond papers of yesterday say that "while some hands were unloading a wagon load of shells, at the testing-ground, above the Tredegar works,[32] one of the shells exploded, setting off the balance". Three negroes and a white foreman, Nicholas Ingleson, were killed, while several others were wounded.

"African brigades" in North Carolina during 1863 and 1864 before moving to the XVIII Corps. In the last year of the war he commanded the 3rd Division and then the 1st Division, XXV Corps. Boatner, *The Civil War Dictionary*, 919.

31. David Stevens (b. 1803). A resident of Harrisburg who claimed to be a drummer boy in the War of 1812, Stevens was chaplain of the 36th USCT. Redkey, "Black Chaplains in the Union Army," 338, 350.

32. The South's only major ironworks before the war, Tredegar produced nearly 50 percent of the cannon used by Confederate forces. By 1863, the foundry employed 2,500 workers, a large percentage of whom were slaves. Faust (ed.), *Historical Times Illustrated Encyclopedia*, 761–62.

CHAPTER 5

The Winter Lull

HEADQUARTERS IN THE FIELD

BEFORE RICHMOND, NOV. 27, 1864.

With propriety I may say that all is quiet along the lines, except the usual cannonading in the vicinity of Dutch Gap. Occasionally, in this quarter, we are apt to experience a spasmodic manifestation of surcharged venom. Day before yesterday the programme was a little varied from the customary routine. Instead of the enemy beginning, our batteries near the Howlett House took the initiative, giving to him a specimen of our artillery practice. In a short time a shell, containing Greek fire, was thrown into a house which the enemy used as a picket post, which, exploding, immediately wrapt the building in flames. This seemed to exasperate the rebels. For almost immediately his batteries in the vicinity of the "grave yard" opened upon a picket post, which was at this place, with crushing and fatal effect. Three shells passed through the house, doing it fearful damage, and killing John Richmond, Co. F, 6th U. S. C. T., and Andrew Newbern, Co. G, 36th U. S. C. T., and wounding Silas Hollis, 38th U. S. C. T., severely in the left hand. The bodies of Richmond and Newbern were torn to pieces and scattered in every direction for sixty yards around. Quivering pieces of flesh indicated the locality of the frightful scene, while fragments of the hearts and intestines were hanging upon the branches of the neighboring trees. These men died at their post, and their bodies, or as much of them as could be collected together, received Christian burial on the spot where they fell in defence of the Union.

About the same hour another scene was being enacted in the 10th Corps. William Thompson, Co. E, 3d United States Light Artillery, suffered the extreme penalty of military law in the presence of his own company, and the 3d Brigade, 3d Division, for endeavoring to encourage desertion to the enemy from the 9th Maine, from which regiment the firing party was selected. The evidence against the accused was strong in every particular, and left no doubt as to his guilt. He died protesting his innocence, and with a degree of fortitude which excited special admiration and regret that so brave a man should meet such an ignominious fate. He took his stand by his coffin, and when a look convinced him that he would likely fall against it, he, with much composure, stepped a little aside, buttoned his blouse, and, as an indication for the firing, struck his hand against his left breast. At his own request his hands were left free and his eyes were unbandaged. Nine shots struck the condemned man, eight of which were mortal, and three of which passed through his heart. Major J. L. Stevens, provost marshal of the 10th Corps, conducted the execution.

On Thanksgiving day a number of recruits came to the 6th, 7th, and 10th Connecticut Regiments, in the 10th Corps, and on the same evening it was discovered that a number of them were missing from camp. General Terry immediately sent out in pursuit, and overtook some nine of them pressing on to the right of our line, where the videttes are far apart, and the opportunities for escaping into the lines of the enemy are most favorable. These bounty-jumpers will probably be tried on Monday, and shot on Tuesday. The summary manner in which General Butler will deal with this class of persons will materially diminish the number of bounty-jumpers, should they attempt to practice their profession in the Army of the James. One thing is evident, that the manner in which these persons struck for the rebel lines shows a familiarity with the country and the position of the two armies, which favors the impression that they had gone the same way before. Enlisting under the auspices of large bounties, coming to the army, and deserting to the enemy, by whom they are sent back to the North to repeat the iniquity, have become quite a business, and one in which it is to be feared too many have succeeded. General Butler has determined that this practice shall cease, and you may rely upon it that he will make short work of all who may happen to fall into his power.

The untiring industry of the enemy to defend Richmond on the north side of the river, in front of the Army of the James, is manifest in the construction of every conceivable means of defence. What they lack in men they more than make up in admirably built works. In front of Fort Burnham, formerly Harrison, they have three lines of palisade works, one of torpedoes, and then a well constructed line of breastworks. The torpedoes are placed in the ground, about four feet apart, with a very little dirt thrown over them, that they may readily explode, should an advance take place in that direction, of which the enemy is in daily fear.

Bushrod Johnson[1] and Lee's brigades are in front of Burnham. For some days past I have learned that Early's[2] troops from the Valley were in front of the 10th Corps, but hesitated to mention it until I could do so beyond all possibility of a doubt. It is now certain that Kershaw's[3] division is here, and it is fair to suppose that the information which reports more of the rebels from the Valley in our front is correct. Early has not yet left that scene of operations, but may be expected here daily.

The custom of saying fine things about officers has degenerated into such ludicrousness that it is almost a compliment to pass over in silence the merit of a good officer. But when a soldier like Captain Charles N. Cadwalader,[4] of the 2d Pennsylvania Heavy Artillery,[5]

1. Bushrod Rust Johnson (1817–1880). A West Point graduate, Johnson entered the Confederate army as a colonel of engineers, rising to brigadier general in January, 1862. He fought at Shiloh and Chickamauga and opposed Butler's advance against the Richmond railroad in May, 1864. He was commander of South Carolina troops during the Battle of the Crater. DAB, V, 91–92; Jon L. Wakelyn, Biographical Dictionary of the Confederacy (Westport, Conn., 1977), 254.

2. Jubal Anderson Early (1816–1894) distinguished himself as a capable commander at Gettysburg, the Wilderness, and Spotsylvania, where he defeated Burnside. He was promoted to lieutenant general in May, 1864, and subsequently led the daring raid on Washington, D.C. Early was relieved of his command by Lee because of growing discontent with his failures. DAB, III, 598–99; Wakelyn, Biographical Dictionary of the Confederacy, 175–76.

3. Joseph Brevard Kershaw (1822–1894). A South Carolina state legislator, Kershaw entered the Confederate army as a colonel in April, 1861, and participated in the attack on Fort Sumter. Following his promotion to brigadier general, Kershaw's contingent, part of the Army of Northern Virginia under Longstreet, was known as Kershaw's Brigade. Promoted to major general in May, 1864, he participated in the Battle of the Wilderness and the defense of Petersburg, among others. DAB, V, 359; Wakelyn, Biographical Dictionary of the Confederacy, 272–73.

4. Charles N. Cadwalader (?–?). Mustered in, Battery G, November, 1861, Cadwalader rose to lieutenant colonel before his discharge in November, 1864. Samuel P. Bates, History of Pennsylvania Volunteers, 1861–1865 (5 vols.; Harrisburg, 1869–71), III, 1101.

5. Organized in Philadelphia in 1862, the 2nd served in Washington, D.C., before joining the Army of the James. Frederick H. Dyer, Compendium of the War of the Rebellion (Des Moines, Iowa, 1908), 216.

does his country such eminent service, it would seem like ingratitude to fail to acknowledge his merits. Three years ago he personally recruited some two thousand men in his monster regiment, and, with the discipline of a soldier and the chivalry of a gentleman, he has followed the fortunes of his regiment through the trying ordeal of the summer's campaign down to the recent reconnaissance on the 27th of October. His health having become impaired by the hardships of a life in the field, he has been mustered out of service, and leaves to-day for the North, amid the regrets of a large circle of friends belonging to his own and other regiments.

STEAMER DANIEL WEBSTER

JAMES RIVER, NOV. 27, 1864.

We have just been the witness of one of those river conflagrations which are so generally destructive in their results. The Grayhound, Gen. Butler's fast-sailing and splendidly fitted-up steamer, took fire to-day, about 1 o'clock, under the following circumstances, and was burnt to the water's edge.

Gen. Butler and staff, with several of his personal friends, and Admiral Porter,[6] were on board at the time, all of whom were saved by the timely assistance rendered by the steamer Pioneer and tugboat Columbia, which happened to be near the scene of disaster. About 1 o'clock, while those on board were at dinner, the Grayhound was being driven with a little more pressure of steam than she could bear, when the furnace doors were burst open, and the fire scattered about in such profusion as to render it impossible to extinguish it. The wood being dry, the flames spread rapidly. As the pennant of Gen. Butler was flying above the flames, it was evident that that officer was on board, for whose safety no little apprehension was experienced.

As soon as Captain Deering saw the fire he drove the Webster on

6. David Dixon Porter (1813–1891). One of the Union's premier admirals, Porter was intimately involved in planning the expedition against New Orleans in 1862. He also saw action at Vicksburg and the Red River. He was subsequently put in command of the North Atlantic Blockading Squadron and organized the fleet sent against Fort Fisher in December, 1864. He held a similar position in the second expedition against Fort Fisher the following month. *DAB*, VIII, 85–88.

to render whatever assistance might be in his power. His boats were all manned, and his hose gotten ready, but by the time he reached the point opposite Hog Island, where the Grayhound was burning, the general and all on board had been placed on the Pioneer. It was fortunate that the steamer and the tug-boat Columbia were at hand to render such timely assistance. As we passed the Pioneer, General Butler called out to Captain Deering to take him on board, but when the captain sent a boat for him, he declined coming, preferring to reach Fortress Monroe in the tug-boat Columbia, in which he and the rescued passengers and crew had taken passage.

Some jolly tars safely lowered the stars and stripes while the Grayhound was nearly enveloped in roaring flames, and after everything else was brought off, they ventured on board and secured the broad pennant of General Butler.

It may be well to state that the Grayhound, when not used for the General's transportation, ran between City Point and Varina Landing as a despatch-boat. She left that landing as usual this morning with the mail, and being some what behind time, did not reach City Point until after the Webster had left. The Grayhound having overtaken us, the mails and passengers were put on board this boat. She soon passed us with her distinguished company for Fortress Monroe.

The scene of conflagration was about half-way between City Point and Fortress Monroe. One thing is certain, namely, that the party on board had a very narrow escape.

HEADQ'TERS 1ST BRIGADE, 3D DIV., 25TH CORPS
BEFORE RICHMOND, DEC. 6, 1864.

The last day or two has been a little more active than the customary routine of camp life. The long projected scheme of organizing all the negro troops into a separate corps has at length been put into practical operation. It is now under full head way, successfully working in all its details, with every promise of equalling the expectations of those who have so long cherished this their favorite project.

General Weitzel commands the Corps d'Afrique, while the 1st, 2d, and 3d Divisions are marshaled by Generals Paine, Birney, and

Heckman. It was generally expected that Brigadier General Wild would have had a command in this corps, but it seems that it has been decided otherwise.

The most remarkable fact about this organization is that the rebels seemed to know just when it went into effect. Day before yesterday the necessary movements towards carrying out the project began, and early yesterday morning the enemy's pickets wanted to know when the "smoked Yankees" were to confront them. It was generally supposed that the Johnnies might be disposed to fire upon these "smoked Yankees," but it is now understood that they will be sufficiently agreeable to bear their presence. This determination was no doubt quickened by the reflection that our colored troops are similarly supplied with weapons, and because the enemy has never known them to hesitate to meet him on any terms which he might feel disposed to offer.

There was considerable firing along the Bermuda Hundred front yesterday evening. Dutch Gap was also remembered with a copious shower of fragments from exploded shells, but with no serious results. This cannonading has become such a customary affair that when a day passes without hearing it, the silence becomes op-pressive, and furnishes a cause for speculation.

Considerable complaint, and very justly, too, is being made by the surgeons at the field hospital, that colored soldiers are continued with their regiments too long after it is evident that they are threatened with a protracted illness. Patients are frequently sent to the hospital in a dying condition, when, if they had been forwarded earlier, they might have been benefited. The complaint most prevalent is the lung fever, which has proved fatal in many cases.

The difficulty of colored troops being discharged from the service is illustrated in the cases of about a dozen men in the 4th U. S. C. T., whom the surgeon has declared unfit for duty, and sent to the base hospital for examination to that effect. These persons are all incapaci-tated by honorable wounds received, and are manifestly disabled from military duty, yet the surgeons at the hospital have refused to examine them, and returned them to their regiment with the consola-tion that they will be sent back as often as the surgeon forwards them to the hospital. Should there be an attack, these helpless persons would only tend to create a panic, as in their inability to defend themselves they would have to seek safety as best they could in flight.

The military situation remains unchanged, with every indication of favorable results when active operations begin. The Army of the James never was so thoroughly organized as at this period, and never exhibited such fine promise of success.

BEFORE WILMINGTON, DEC. 26, 1864.

You have already been placed in possession of all the main facts concerning the character and strength of the expedition of Porter and Butler against Wilmington, and of the preparations the rebels have been making through all the long years of the war to resist any attempt of ours to take away from them one of their finest seaports—one of incalculable value to them. Wilmington is guarded by Nature, and by Nature's anger on the broad sea—howling winds, terrific storms, gigantic ocean waves. Situated thirty-five miles up the Cape Fear river, nearly forty miles from the ocean, it has been, since the closing of the ports of Savannah and Charleston, the principal if not the only port of entry to the Confederacy. Your readers have often read of the immense amount of trade carried on between island rebel-sympathizing England. Millions on millions of dollars' worth of all the material required in war, and all the articles that go to make up domestic comfort and happiness, have come into that river in ship after ship, defying our best efforts to prevent them. We have made many captures, to be sure. Our vigilant blockading fleet, that has cruised around in the very waters where blue dreariness surges, and stretches out before me as I write, made many captures, and brought the dreams of many a rebel financier and speculator to grief. But though vessel after vessel lowered its stars and bars before our stars and stripes, and went North a prize, still they bore but a small proportion to the numbers that stole in when skies were overclouded and stars were dim, and brought more life-blood to swell out the withered arteries of the Confederacy. The Government has always been well aware of the value of this port to the rebels. But the immense drain of the war, the thousand and one duties it had to perform on the long frontier of the rebellion facing the loyal States, have prevented any marked attention being paid the grim Cerberi who frown fiercely over there on those low sand-banks which skirt the heaving waters, and are black with close-growing pine trees. This expedition was at last organized to attack, and, if possible, crumble the proud rebel city.

But I do not wish to anticipate. What the expedition has done, and with what success, I present to you in the account which follows. And although you have received and published details of the "Landlay" here, a brief recapitulation is necessary to make that account perfectly plain and intelligible. There are three bars obstruct-ing the entrance to the river—New Inlet, Main, and Western; but since the fleet attempted entrance at New Inlet only, which is, indeed, the only one we could have attempted with any show of success, I will confine my remarks entirely to that entrance. A narrow strip of land juts out from the coast into the sea. One side is washed by the waters of the Atlantic, and the other forms part of the east bank of the Cape Fear river. The strip is called Federal Point, and on it are situated all the principal works which form the main defence of Wilmington. It is one of the, if not the, largest casemated earthworks in the Confederacy, mounts forty heavy rifled guns, which proved themselves during the action just closed to be of great range and accuracy, and stands about 200 yards from the shore. Along the ocean shore stretch a series of batteries about twelve or fifteen hundred yards in length, culminating in an immense mound, about forty feet high, mounted with immense guns, which are distinctly visible above the parapets. Here a lighthouse stands, which directs the blockaders in their course into the inlet. This battery is called by three names— the Half Moon, the Lamb, and the Mound Battery—and commands the only channel for an attacking fleet—the main one. Every shot fired from it would, of course, be a plunging one, and might test rather severely the strength and endurance of our iron-clads, if they should ever be brought under its fire. It would be a very difficult battery to attack, as our guns would have to be fired with a dangerous, and, in the case of the iron-clads, with an almost impossible elevation. There are other batteries, which have been previously described, and need not be here, since our expedition attacked Fisher only, I am sorry to say, without the success which I expected, and for which every one in the great North hoped and prayed. And now to the

DEPARTURE OF THE EXPEDITION FROM FORTRESS MONROE.

On the evening of the 7th, the 1st Division of the 25th Corps (colored), under Brigadier General Paine, and a division of the 24th Corps, commanded by General Ames, Major General Weitzel commanding the whole, broke camp in front of Richmond, and after considerable marching, camped for the night in the vicinity of Point of Rocks. On the following day they all embarked at Bermuda Hundred, and on the succeeding day the transports, about fifty in number, rendezvoused at Fortress Monroe, where they remained until Tuesday morning, the 13th.

Nothing could have exceeded our surprise when we found ourselves going up the Chesapeake Bay, whither the transports were ordered. On our arrival off Matthias' Point the sealed instructions were to be opened. I was on board the fast steamship Montauk, which was among the first to arrive at the point designated, when we learned that we must put about, and proceed to Cape Henry. No one could see the exact force of this marching up the hill and then down again, but upon the intimation that it might be strategy, all seemed to be satisfied. The fleet was about sixty miles from Washington when we put about to return, passing Fortress Monroe in the night, and anchoring to the westward off Cape Charles. Here we remained until the evening of the 14th, when the steamship Ben Deford, bearing the department flag of General Butler, and having on board, besides that distinguished officer and staff, General Weitzel and his aides, came down the bay and stood out to sea. The transports followed, and as they passed Cape Henry the sealed orders which were to be read at that point were opened, which indicated that Wilmington was our destination.

THE ARRIVAL OFF THE SCENE OF OPERATIONS.

On the evening of the 15th the transports arrived off Masonborough Inlet, far out at sea, where we remained, enduring a demoralizing monotony with commendable impatience, until the morning of the 19th. when the Montauk steamed away to Morehead City, N. C., for coal. Excepting the important fact that more cotton is raised now around this place and the neighboring town of Beaufort than previous to the rebellion, no item of interest could be obtained.

A Storm at Sea.

On the morning of the 20th we came out from the harbor and sailed for the rendezvous of the fleet. A stiff breeze from the north sprang up, and increased in fury until a young gale was howling over the ocean, continuing through the nights of the 21st and 22d. The usual indications of sea-sickness were manifested by most of those on board the transport, and the 4th Regiment Colored Troops, which has earned a high reputation for discipline and courage, has never wavered from fear before the fiercest batteries of the enemy, trembled with natural terror during the last and most violent night of the storm, when the winds and waves buffeted our ship about as if it were an egg-shell. The sea was in a perfect tumult of foam and high-reaching billows. The transports and war vessels around us danced from crest to crest, now nestling away down in the foam depths, now tossed high up to descend again with lightning velocity into the valleys that lay between the great ever-shifting water mountains. Of course the fleet became separated, driven hither and thither, till one was lost to the sight of the other—disappearing in the carnival of seething, dashing spray. But in the midst of this elemental discord and before the violence of the tempest had scattered the fleet, it was a pleasing sight to see how bravely the little monitors behaved. Let it be a noteworthy fact that, if the monitors have failed on some occasions to weather a severe gale, *they did not on this occasion.* They rode over the waves with a seeming consciousness of their power and endurance against the assaults both of man's ingenuity and the force of the elements. Their sea-going staunchness excited general admiration. Sometimes they would seem to be buried beneath the water, but they would soon again rise to the surface and shake off the foam like a sturdy Newfoundland coming up from his dive. I think that hereafter there will be more confidence placed in them, not only as efficient war vessels, but also as safe and staunch sailers. The storm did not, of course, pass us by without inflicting some damage. One of the horses tied on the deck of the Baltic was thrown overboard by the violent rolling and pitching of the vessel, and about thirty-six others, most of which were on the steamer Salvo, were by the same means badly injured. At each lurch they were knocked about till the stalls in which they were placed were broken down. They were then dashed from one side of the ship to the other, until some of them were killed outright and others had their legs broken. The sufferers were in pity thrown overboard. On the morning of the 23d our ship's provisions were at an end, but having a line quartermaster on board, in the person of A. P. Barnes, we were all supplied with Government rations, which consisted of coffee, bacon, and hard-tack three times a day, slightly diversified. The prompt manner in which he provided for the necessities of the occasion induces one to the belief that he is fully competent to keep hotel.

A GIGANTIC TORPEDO-BOAT.

About four o'clock on the morning of the 24th we were somewhat startled by an explosion, which shook the very vessel under us. It took place about ten miles distant, in front of Federal Point. I have since learned that the explosion was heard even as far as Newbern, where the people had been expecting this crash. They had been informed by talkative persons connected with the fleet that a great boat was to be blown up to shake down the rebel fortifications, and they must have been waiting for it day and night. This vessel was an iron propeller of about 250 tons, built at Wilmington, and originally owned by a firm (S. & J. T. Flanagan) of your city, and was for some time engaged in the Southern coasting trade from New Orleans to Port Lavacca, Texas. At the outbreak of the war she was taken from her peaceful avocations, and made a gunboat to patrol the Chesapeake and the mouth of the James. She was with Burnside[7] in his attack on the Roanoke Island works, and was somewhat injured in these fights. She went afterwards into the Neuse, and aided Gen. Foster[8] considerably when he was cooped up in Washington, N. C. She remained in those waters until the Ordnance Department selected and manipulated her into a monster torpedo. The explosions of the last decade at Rouen, the effect of the great explosion in England, a short time ago, and even the comparatively small explosions in

7. Ambrose Everett Burnside (1824–1881). His forces had captured Roanoke Island, North Carolina, in February, 1862, taking 2,600 prisoners. The island had been fortified by the Confederates to defend Albemarle Sound. *DAB*, II, 310.
    8. John Gray Foster (1823–1874) was also involved in the capture of Roanoke Island and was placed in command of the Department of North Carolina. He was assigned to command the Department of the South in 1864 and participated in Sherman's moves against Savannah and Charleston. *DAB*, III, 49–50.

Connecticut, and at Dupont's, in Delaware, were carefully considered, and their effects marked. It was concluded that if houses could be shaken down by pigmy gunpowder explosions, solid masonry could be toppled over by the concussion of a thunder rivalling Jove's. This vessel was therefore taken to Norfolk, and fitted up to receive an immense charge of gunpowder. Her masts were unshipped, her whole hull hollowed out, so to speak, by the removal of all partitions, etc., and made impervious to water. Two funnels were placed in her, and other alterations made so that she would have the precise appearance of a blockade runner. This was done so that when the attack on the rebel forts was about beginning she could rush in as if attempting to escape us, our vessels were to make believe to pursue, and she was to beach immediately under the guns of Fort Fisher. Powder was placed in a bulkhead occupying all the berth-deck, except that near the boilers. A little further forward, and nearer the boilers, a section of the deck and part of the hold were filled. The rest of [the] hold remained empty, to prevent the force of the explosion from going downward instead of upward and sideways. A house on the spar-deck was covered over closely with tarpaulin, extending to the bow from the boilers, and piled up. The powder was laid in tiers— the first in barrels with the heads taken out, and the rest in bags. The arrangements for firing this tremendous charge were very complete. There was a fuse in each gang way, and one forward near the boilers, and from those a Gomez fuse extended all around the vessel, and terminated at one end in the berth-deck and at the other in the hold. The fuses were those known to military men as "three-clock" fuses. There were also fuses that led from each of the clocks to the points of ending of the other fuses. Each stretch of fuses intersected one another at different points, and were plaited together at the intersection. When the expedition left Fortress Monroe hence, this powder-ship was towed all the way to Beaufort by the Sassacus. On her arrival here she was put under steam and run ashore. Two hundred and fifty tons of powder were aboard her, and, as I have told you, we were suddenly startled by the terrific thunder of her explosion. Little boats could be seen approaching us, and about half way from the ship—five miles—rowing as if for life. They contained the commander of the magazine, Captain Rhind, of the steamer Agawam, Lieut. Proston, Engineer Mullen, and Ensign Cassell—devoted men, who had risked their lives to give this novel engine of war-fare its proper success. The explosion was awfully grand to those who were not stunned with surprise at the reverberating roar. Sheets of fire, like the projecting leaves from a pine-apple (pardon the homely simile) shot up like winged flames, bearing in dark, tangled chaos black smoke and *debris* of the vessel. The concussion seemed to come over the water like a hurricane. The sea broke into great majestic swells, heavy even at our distance, considering that they were the outer circles rolling out from a centre ten miles away. The vessel was a great shell. Her iron hull was disrupted as if it was made of tissue paper, and the broken fragments, small almost to diminutiveness, went whistling through the air with the speed of the lightning, and a million of tapering columns shot up from the water far and wide, falling back gently and in graceful curves when the power that reared them into sight had ceased to exist. Up went the black column, like a great magic funnel, widening as it rose, until it covered the whole sky, and was carried away and dissipated on the air currents that wafted it towards Wilmington. It was to that city the baptism of sulphur fumes that heralds what will come, sooner or later—the baptism of fire. Although the vessel was close—not more than two hundred and fifty yards away—it is to be questioned whether, after all, the explosion had the effect that was expected. The fort, by subsequent developments, seems to have been but little injured. The intention was, however, to load the vessel with five hundred tons of powder, but as she would hold but two hundred and fifty, that quantity was, of course, all that was used.

COMMENCEMENT OF THE ATTACK.

About eight o'clock it was evident that active measures would soon begin. I looked hurriedly around for the transports, freighted with Union defenders, but only three were present—the Baltic, the Montauk, and the Victor—the last one having no troops on board. There were fifty-eight vessels-of-war and six iron-clads in the grand fleet of Admiral Porter, and some twenty-one transports—the largest force ever concentrated against any point upon the continent. The vessels-of-war got under way about 8 A. M., and stood in for Federal Point, on the right bank of Cape Fear river. It is hardly possible to conceive of a much grander sight than the advance of this fleet in the three lines of battle which you have no doubt already described, as the description was forwarded. The stars and stripes waved proudly from each peak, as each ship gradually neared the land. When a short distance from Federal Point the Ironsides and monitors steamed ahead, and bore down upon the enemy, while the wooden vessels followed close after without having taken the precaution of sending down their spars, customary before going into action.

THE FIRST SHOT FROM THE IRON-CLADS.

About one o'clock, a shot from one of our iron-clads at Fort Fisher is the signal for the beginning of the action, and at intervals, which under the circumstances seem protracted, another and another follows—each succeeding its predecessor in more rapid succession—until one of the grandest naval conflicts of American history is opened. About half of the fleet was soon engaged, and the terrible roar of artillery seemed to be beyond endurance; but when they all participated, the thundering from the fleet intermingled with that from the heavy guns of the enemy, immense columns of white smoke brooded over the water, fringed and colored with bright yellow flame. Now and then the flame seemed to come forth in bright sheets, and cover the water as if with a fiery pall. Reader, imagine all this, so grand, so confusing, so blinding to the eye, presented to you at the same time that the ear was tingled and tortured, not exactly with that thunder which
> "Leaped from peak to peak
> The rattling crags among,"
but that which came out sharp and terrible from the yawning throats of a thousand of those terrible engines of modern war. Then, amid all this splendid panorama of death and this crashing thunder, could be heard the screaming of the great shells as they leaped through the air back and forward from fort to ships and ships to fort. The rebel fire was one of much precision, and some of their immense shells exploded over our vessels with great accuracy. The united concert of belching artillery seemed almost unbroken for hours. The fleet continued to pour into the forts, Fisher and Caswell, showers of shot and shell, until it seemed that they would be buried beneath the fragments of these missiles.

About half-past two o'clock the Montauk stood in close enough to afford a distinct view of the rebel colors, amid the clouds of almost unbroken smoke, upon Fisher, which is nearly as strong as Fortress

Monroe. The soldiers pointed them out to me enthusiastically, with a wish that they might soon be sent to lower them. At a quarter of four o'clock a dark smoke arose from the enemy's works. Fifteen minutes later an immense conflagration was distinctly seen, which indicated that the barracks in Fort Fisher were on fire.

THE ENTHUSIASM OF THE SOLDIERY.

At this sight it was difficult to restrain the enthusiasm of the troops on board, and prevent them from lustily cheering. If they had, our transport would probably have drawn the fire of the enemy. Such expressions as "get out, Johnny," "isn't it too hot for you," and others of similar import were freely indulged in. No words could adequately express the terrible bombardment at this juncture, or give an impression commensurate with the scene. As night lowered, rendering more distinct the meteoric flash of flying shells, the cannonading gradually ceased, until every gun was quiet.

THE INJURIES TO THE FLEET.

About a half an hour before the action ended, there was but one of the gunboats that hauled off, or gave evidence of being injured. It had burst one of its guns, killing and wounding several of the crew. Shortly after, another was towed away, but not until after the engagement was over. Thus ended the first assault on Wilmington.

Neither Generals Butler or Weitzel were present during the action, but were detained in the harbor of Beaufort, with the rest of the transports, by the severe storm, excepting those that had put to sea for safety. Late in the afternoon, General Butler's boat hove in sight, and in the course of the night all the fleet withdrew about ten miles to the sea.

Such was our Christmas Eve. We retired to rest thinking of the probable injuries sustained by the fleet, and the condition of the forts. We thought, too, of the loved ones at home, wondering whether their Christmas would be as happy as ours promised to be glorious.

THE EVENTS OF CHRISTMAS DAY.

On the ever-memorable 25th we were gratified by the arrival of all the transports, and soon a despatch-boat passed by the Montauk, shouting the following order to the commanding officer on board: "Follow the Ben Deford; take your position on her left; have your men ready to land, with one day's rations and canteen of water, at a moment's notice." Immediately the various transports gave evidence of that kind of activity which precedes landing. The troops were thrilled at this juncture with the gratifying intelligence that General Sherman had captured Savannah,[9] and that General Thomas[10] had thrashed Hood.[11] The effect of this news was to strengthen their good resolution and inspire additional confidence.

THE BOMBARDMENT RENEWED.

In the midst of these preparations, and in fact from early dawn, the fleet was pouring a storm of shot and shell into the forts, while for a distance of eight miles along the beach several of the gunboats shelled the clustering forest, in which the enemy were supposed to be in ambush, with excellent effect. All previous cannonading in the history of this rebellion, though in many instances frightfully grand, pales before this Christmas bombardment of Federal Point. If great Jove had sent forth the heaviest thundering of his artillery, surcharged with vindictiveness, it is hardly possible to conceive that it could have surpassed that of the combined artillery of the rebel forts and the "Yankee" fleet.

THE LANDING OF THE TROOPS.

About five miles to the northward of Federal Point, and about six across the country to Wilmington, the transports neared into the

9. One of the South's major ports, Savannah had 10,000 defenders against a massive force of 62,000 under Sherman, who was reluctant to attack the well-fortified city. He chose instead to try to seal it off. Concerned to protect his army, General William J. Hardee escaped over a pontoon bridge across the Savannah River on December 20, 1864. Patricia L. Faust (ed.), *Historical Times Illustrated Encyclopedia of the Civil War* (New York, 1986), 658–59.

10. George Henry Thomas (1816–1870). A Virginian who fought for the Union, Thomas saw action at Corinth, Shiloh, Stones River, and Chickamauga, among other important battles. He was second-in-command in Sherman's Atlanta campaign, and in the march through Georgia his forces defeated Hood at Peach Tree Creek (July, 1864). Faust (ed.), *Historical Times Illustrated Encyclopedia*, 754.

11. John B. Hood (1831–1879). A career officer in the army before the war, Hood resigned his commission to join the Confederate army as a captain in April, 1861. He saw action at Seven Days and Second Manassas, after which he was promoted to major general. Hood lost an arm at Gettysburg and a leg at Chickamauga. He fought later at Atlanta and Nashville. Wakelyn, *Biographical Dictionary of the Confederacy*, 238–39.

shore to land the troops, and, when nearly ready, some suspicious symptoms caused them to haul out a little, until the gunboats made it so warm for the Johnnies that they were obliged to betray their presence in batteries which were supposed to be deserted.

REBEL BATTERIES ON THE BEACH.

At this point the rebels had thrown up several small batteries on the beach, but had covered them over with sand, so as to pretend that they were mounds reared up by the force of the breakers. There were two or three houses, which had probably been used as a barracks. From their location they could hardly have served any other purpose so near the forts. Upon one of them a white flag was conspicuously displayed, prompted, no doubt, by the irresistible gunboat argument. The batteries on shore opened fire upon our fleet, but as they only seemed to have field pieces, with which they hoped to prevent a landing of our forces, they were without the least effect. General Butler's flag-ship was most of the time within range of the enemy's shots, and remained much nearer to the shore than many of the transports.

ONE LANDING FRUSTRATED—ANOTHER SUCCESSFUL.

The programme of landing being a little changed by the discovery of an ambushed foe, skirted by batteries, the transports dropped down about one mile and a half to the southward. When all things were in readiness, at a given signal, a swarm of surf-boats and launches, filled with soldiers, and the naval brigade glided away from the sides of the transports and the vessels of war, and presented a scene of almost magic beauty. They slowly headed away for the shore, with a couple of howitzers in the bows of the launches to remove any rebel objections. What a spectacle was here presented! The decks and rigging of the transports and naval fleet were crowded with anxious spectators. Hope and fear seemed to be the conflicting emotions depicted in every countenance, as they intently, with bated breath, gazed upon the animating scene. On, on, and still onward, our soldiers sail toward the foaming surf, while, with nerves strung to their utmost tension, we momentarily expect that, from the near forest, a sheet of deadly fire will flash from the almost impervious pines. Excitement could scarcely have reached a higher climax. We were relieved by a most thrilling succession of shell explosions from the broadside of a frigate whose fragmentary showers scattered the concealed foe and afforded safety to the landing force. Conscious of the advantage gained by this brilliant firing of the frigate, the boats swiftly glide into the breakers, pass safely through them, and amid the most intense solicitude on board of the whole fleet, clustered on the spars, even at the mast heads, covering all the decks, now the gallant tars and soldiers, each one striving to be the first, leap from the boats upon the desecrated soil of North Carolina. Of the first five hundred that landed, Brevet Brigadier General C. Curtis, with the stars and stripes, jumped into the surf before his boat reached the beach, by which he gained the distinction of being the first to land. Never did the national emblem look so glorious as at this memorable moment. Major General Weitzel, commander of the expedition, and General Graham[12] had the honor of springing upon the soil from the second launch. To the 142d New York was entrusted the glory of rallying around the flag upon this hostile shore, and the inspiring manner in which they followed their leaders was an evidence of their patriotic devotion.

A BATTERY CAPTURED.

At this grand incident a murmur of approbation and suppressed cheers passed from vessel to vessel with electric effect, but when the standard-bearer rushed up to one of the enemy's batteries, and placed upon it the old flag, the very welkin rang with the patriotic shouts of thrilled sailors and soldiers. Tears of joy gushed down the cheeks of some, who say that the spectacle was one of the grandest they ever witnessed. Hardly had the cheering died away, when from one of the batteries, whose defenders were probably flanked by the gunboats and those landed, the white flag went up in a hurry, which caused another outburst of exultation from the fleet.

AN ADVANCE ON THE FORT COMMENCED.

Skirmishers were immediately thrown to the right, left, and in front, when a line of battle was formed, with the old flag in the

12. Charles Kinnaird Graham (1824–1889) saw action at Chancellorsville and Gettysburg, where he was captured. Imprisoned in Richmond, he was not exchanged until

centre, which marched down the beach to assault Fort Fisher. About seventy rebels in the battery surrendered themselves as prisoners as soon as the skirmishers came upon them. Upon the latter the flag of loyalty soon was hoisted in triumph. In almost the briefest possible time the beach was swarming with Union soldiers. It seemed as if they came up out of the ground by magic, or the very grains of sand had become occupied, and transformed into fully equipped lines of battle, following each other at short intervals in grand assault upon Fisher.

A Sudden Rebel Assault.

The skirmish line, which had been thrown out in front to guard against any surprise from the woods, seeing no evidence of an enemy being present, advanced toward the timber, when they were greeted with a volley of musketry. Some four of our soldiers were each wounded in the leg, and one in the hand. The line immediately dropped down behind natural defences, formed by the washing up of the sand, and opened a sharp skirmish fire. The gunboats, observing the state of affairs, sprinkled a few shells in that vicinity, which had the effect of sobering the Johnnies down to a dignified, though probably an unwilling silence. All this time the bombardment of these strongholds had by no means ceased during the disembarkation, but had become fearfully terrific.

A Conflagration in the Fort.

About twilight the musketry was engaged, and soon a huge mass of smoke, and an immense conflagration burst out in the midst of the enemy's works. Cheer after cheer again resound throughout the fleet, as we behold the defences of Wilmington tottering before our eyes. In the very midst of this flame shell after shell is hurried with fearful accuracy, whose explosions prevented the extinguishment of the fire, which continued for several hours. Night closed upon the scene, but the cannonading from our gunboats and monitors knows no cessation. Guided by the burning fort, they could continue their shower of fire upon this stronghold of rebellion.

September. He joined the Army of the James two months later as commander of a naval brigade. *DAB*, IV, 471.

An Advance on the Fort, Which is Found to be Too Strong.

The infantry under Gen. Weitzel advanced down the beach to within one hundred yards of Fort Fisher, and upon a careful inspection of it, it was discovered to be too well fortified with armament and men to carry by an assault. Having made no consultation for a siege, no implements were brought for that purpose, and as the fort was impregnable to the force at command the gallant band was ordered to return to the transports about 10 o'clock in the evening. A heavy wind from the eastward during the night rolled in from sea those combining billows which so furiously dash along the Atlantic coast. In the energetic efforts of the marines to re-embark the troops, several boats and launches were lost, and the attempt was given up. Gen. Curtis and about two hundred soldiers were left on the beach with one day's rations, which they carried with them. They had to wait until the breakers were sufficiently calmed down to admit of a passage through them with safety. The gunboats will afford them sufficient protection against the enemy until an opportunity will permit of their re-embarkation. The storm suggests the only cause of solicitude, which, if it continues, may cause them to suffer for water and provisions, but even these can be thrown into the breakers, which would wash them safely to the gallant band.

The Losses, Captures, etc.

The infantry captured about three hundred prisoners, a rebel color, and two pieces of artillery. The flag was captured by Lieutenant Wallen,[13] of the 142d New York, from the outer bulwarks of Fort Fisher. I have not heard of any one being killed, though several were wounded, more, however, by the shells from our gunboats than the shots from the enemy. As the troops marched up the beach it was under the cover of the navy, which effectually checkmated Kirkland's[14] brigade of rebel troops, which was concealed in the woods.

13. There is no one by this name in the records of the 142nd New York. There is a Captain William H. Walling (?–?) who won a medal of honor for gallantry during the assault on Fort Fisher and who was brevetted lieutenant colonel in March, 1865. Phisterer writes that during the bombardment of the fort, Walling "captured and brought off the flag of the fort." Frederick Phisterer (comp.), *New York in the War of the Rebellion, 1861 to 1865* (5 vols.; New York, 1912), I, 448.

14. William W. Kirkland (?–?). A colonel in the 11th North Carolina, Kirkland fought

Who Caused the Failure of the Expedition.

There will probably be much speculation in reference to the failure of this expedition, attributing it to a want of military foresight on the part of Gen. Weitzel, in not providing the expedition with the necessary implements for a siege. Two other causes are, however, responsible for the result, the first being the publicity which naval officers in Norfolk, previous to sailing, gave their impressions as to the destination of the fleet, and, secondly, the delay caused after the arrival of the fleet off Masonborough Inlet. We experienced, previous to the storm, four days of splendid weather. There could not have been better weather for the attack.

Lee Reinforces Wilmington with His Veterans.

On Tuesday, the 20th, the day upon which the storm began, the chiefs at Richmond sent Kirkland's brigade, of Hoke's division, from the defences of Richmond, and other troops, who, from the round-about way in which they were obliged to travel, did not reach Fort Fisher until after the first day's bombardment. But two companies of local troops constituted its defence. But for this unfortunate result of delay, that feathered nest of treason would have been garrisoned by loyal troops. Yesterday Gen. Butler expected to present to the nation, as a Christmas gift, the redeemed city of Wilmington, but all his plans were frustrated, and like an enraged tiger, wounded in spirit, he is obliged to withdraw from the scene.

Abandonment of the Attack.

At about 8 o'clock A. M. the transports with troops were ordered to return to Fortress Monroe, but the navy still continues its furious bombardment. Gens. Butler and Weitzel have already started for the Chesapeake bay. So far as the military is concerned, the attack upon Wilmington is for the present abandoned.

at First Bull Run, Winchester, where he was injured, Gettysburg, and Murfreesboro. He was promoted to brigadier general in August, 1863, and saw duty in the Wilderness campaign with Longstreet. Mark Mayo Boatner III, *The Civil War Dictionary* (New York, 1959), 465.

THE HOSPITAL-BOAT WESTERN METROPOLIS.

Accompanying the expedition was the magnificent steamer Western Metropolis, fitted up in every respect as a hospital-boat. To speak of all of the details of her interior arrangements calculated to promote the comfort and convenience of sick and wounded soldiers would consume more space than you could possibly spare. Let it suffice to say that substantial berths were erected—clean, comfortable clothing was provided. There was an excellent arrangement of machinery, by which prostrated patients were gently lowered from the deck to the different wards below, where, if necessary, the use of stretchers obviated their rough handling. Here were too the attentions of the accommodating stewards to all their wants; the attendance of medical gentlemen whose appearance excited respect, and doubtless of eminent fitness. There were the ministrations of ladies, whose inspiring influence never fails to restore happiness, if not always health; together with all of the necessarily constructed apartments for a variety of purposes. All these were exemplified in a conspicuous degree, and all working in harmony for the relief of our sick and wounded soldiers. The Metropolis is under the superintendence of Surgeon J. C. McKee,[15] a gentleman whose mild and persuasive manner will equal his restoratives in assisting Nature, and is aided by Drs. Lain, Pennington, Wright, and Defontaine, who seem to be well fitted for the responsibility. A corps of sixty nurses usually constitutes the number required on board, but in the present instance about one hundred had been detached for that purpose. It must be confessed that the hospital-boat is quite an institution, and is well calculated to promote the comfort of those for whose use it is intended.

BERMUDA HUNDRED, JAN. 10, 1865.

GENERAL BUTLER.

The event of the past week was the removal of General Butler, day before yesterday, from the command of the Department of Virginia and North Carolina. As soon as the fact became known, it caused a

15. J. Cooper McKee (?–?) was assistant surgeon in July, 1862, and served at Lincoln Hospital, Washington, D.C., in December, 1864. *The Medical and Surgical History of the War of the Rebellion* (3 vols., 6 pts.; Washington, D.C., 1888), Vol. I, Pt. 3, pp. 60, 960.

general feeling of depression among that class of persons who believe that the most vigorous means should be applied for the suppression of the rebellion. Those of doubtful loyalty are scarcely able to conceal the satisfaction which the news gave them. There is much speculation as to what field of labor he will next enter, his admirers generally indulging in the belief that he will be sent to Kentucky, while the opposite class seem unanimous in the opinion that Lowell, Mass., will be his destination in the future. One thing is certain, that the poor soldier and the humble contraband have lost a faithful friend, and the cause of the Union an uncompromising champion of loyalty. Gen. Ord[16] succeeds Gen. Butler, but whether he will be able to continue the efficient government of the Department of Virginia and North Carolina is a subject which should be left to the future, rather than to speculation. Gen. Butler left his headquarters with bag and baggage on Sunday afternoon, took passage on his splendid boat River Queen at Varina, stopped at City Point, where he paid his respects to General Grant, remaining several hours, and then sailed for Fortress Monroe and Washington.

THE UNDERGROUND RAILROAD.

The underground railroad, from Richmond, seems to be thoroughly repaired, and is not only in running condition, but is doing an increasing business. The former officers of this company were obliged, under a press of appealing circumstances, to grant many free passes, which prevented the institution from being a paying concern, but under a more systematic management it has become regular and profitable. Previous to the war, the road was only used by negroes; but now both colors, upon terms of singular equality, patronize it with much satisfaction. Formerly the conveniences of the road only accommodated passengers, but now transportation is furnished to personal effects and a small amount of freight. For some time past we have had an arrival from Richmond every day, and not unfrequently two or three times in the twenty four hours. Notwithstanding this road is considered contraband by the rebel authorities, its officers thus far have been able to

16. Edward Otho Crepas Ord (1818–1883) saw action in Virginia and Mississippi before he was named commander of the XIII Corps in the Army of Tennessee. In July, 1864, he was made commander of the VIII Corps and later commander of the XVIII Corps facing Confederates at Richmond. *DAB*, VII, 48–49.

baffle the vigilance of their detectives, and fulfil the obligations which they have made to the public. Men, women, and children, of all colors, with their household effects, are daily coming into our lines and report at this place. Mr. Robert Frances, a colored barber, who lived on Main street, nearly opposite the old market, between Seventeenth and Eighteenth streets, brought his family, his bedding, a considerable luggage, and nine hundred and twenty pounds of excellent tobacco. Joe Griffin, the Ethiopian performer, better known as Tim Morris; Mr. Wm. Munday and lady; Joseph G. Hill, lady, and child; Solomon Parker and lady, with his child, mother, and sister, and a number of others, are among the recent arrivals from the rebel capital. It is hardly necessary to inform our Southern brethren that what they consider as chattels, but what we regard as men, may be found industriously engaged about the quartermaster's department, or under the inspiration of martial airs keeping step to the music of the Union.

AFFAIRS IN RICHMOND.

The hard times in Richmond, which are now severely felt by all classes in that doomed city, are having a wonderful effect towards quickening the return to loyalty of some of the most violent traitors.

While it is generally admitted that the markets are well supplied with the necessaries of life, yet the prices are so extravagant that they are not within the reach of the poorer classes of persons.

The fear of starvation is now driving many away, and they have good cause to congratulate themselves that the underground railroad can be made available for their escape.

One thing is particularly noticeable among the colored persons who are leaving Richmond. All of them have announced their determination to return as soon as the Union forces occupy it. This class rarely go farther away than Norfolk, that they may be ready to return to their homes without any protracted delay.

THE WEATHER.

For the past six hours we have been visited with a heavy shower of rain, which, with what has already fallen, will leave the roads in a condition altogether unfavorable for military movements, and in some places impassable for wagons. The storm still continues, but with every indication of its soon ceasing. The weather otherwise is exceedingly pleasant, and feels more like the beginning of spring than the middle of the winter.

GUERILLAS.

The rebels, between here and Fort Monroe, are disposed to be annoying. They have cut the telegraph, which necessitates General Grant to send his boat to the fort with despatches, before he can use the wires in communicating with Washington. It is not known at what point the telegraph has been severed, but it is supposed to be in the vicinity of Fort Powhatan. This is probably the work of some of Jeff's peaceable inhabitants, a character which they assume when their interests can be subserved by it, but at other times they are the most villainous cut-throat guerillas in the land of rebeldom. Their speedy suppression would save much annoyance and prevent many of our soldiers from being surreptitiously spirited away to Libby. By giving them the benefit of the doubt, many a Union volunteer is overtaken with misfortune.

ASSUMPTION OF COMMAND BY GEN. ORD.

WASHINGTON, JAN. 11

—A letter from the Army of the James, dated January 9, says: "The weather is mild, and clear. All is quiet to-day. Major General Ord has taken command of this department, succeeding Major General Butler."

INCIDENTS OF THE DEPARTURE OF BUTLER FROM HIS ARMY.

The correspondent of the *Herald*,[17] at the headquarters of the Army of the James, says that the order for Butler's removal reached there at 11 1/2 A. M., on the morning of the 8th. The only person present who did not appear to be at all surprised was the General himself. He was not at all disturbed. Immediately on its reception his orders were

17. The New York *Herald*'s correspondent at the headquarters of the Army of the Potomac, Sylvanus Cadwallader, scooped other correspondents by first announcing Butler's recall. J. Cutler Andrews, *The North Reports the Civil War* (Pittsburgh, 1955), 616–17.

issued clearly and decisively, and before three o'clock he was ready to vacate his command at the front. Adopting the theory that Gen. Butler was removed on account of the Wilmington expedition not meeting with the expected success, only one question remained to puzzle curious military men. They could not imagine why the General had not been removed some days ago. This question, however, received a final solution when General Ord was assigned to the command. The hero of Fort Harrison was away on leave of absence, and the authorities only waited for his return to remove Gen. Butler.

Immediately on the promulgation of the order relieving General Butler and replacing him by General Ord, the staff of the Army of the James assembled around the quarters of their late commander, reinforced by numerous other officers of the command; but any expressions of sorrow were cut short by the rapidity of the General's arrangements. He had received his orders to report at Lowell at the earliest moment, and before 3 P. M. he announced that he was ready to leave. The orders directing this change instructed General Butler to proceed to Lowell, Mass., and report from thence to the Adjutant General of the army. Before three P. M. the General started for the North. He was accompanied by General Ord, General Devins,[18] General Turner,[19] General Ludlow,[20] Captain Bruce, Captain Clark, Captain DeKay,[21] Lieutenant Merrill, Medical Director Suckley,[22] Major Davis, and Captain Wheaton. All of the above-named officers

18. This could be Thomas Casimer Devin (1822–1878), whose brigade fought at Gettysburg and in the Wilderness campaign. He also fought under Sheridan in the Shenandoah Valley and was promoted to brigadier general in late 1864. *DAB*, III, 263.

19. John Wesley Turner (1833–1899). A graduate of the Military Academy, Turner first served in the commissary department under Hunter in Kansas and later under Butler in New Orleans. He was promoted to brigadier general of volunteers and in 1864 commanded a division in the Army of the James, serving as chief of staff between November, 1864, and January, 1865. *DAB*, X, 67.

20. Possibly William Hardy Ludlow (d. 1890). An agent for prisoner exchange and an aide to Major General John A. Dix in 1862, Ludlow was mustered in as a second lieutenant in the 73rd New York. He was later brevetted brigadier general for war services. Boatner, *The Civil War Dictionary*, 496; *OR*, Ser. I, Vol. XVIII, p. 518.

21. Sidney B. DeKay (?–?) was Butler's aide. *OR*, Ser. I, Vol. XLII, Pt. 1, p. 970.

22. George Suckley (1830–1869). A graduate of the College of Physicians and Surgeons in New York, Suckley had served in the Pacific before the war. He entered the war as a staff surgeon to Union volunteers and was promoted to colonel in 1865. Howard A. Kelly and Walter L. Burrage (eds.), *American Medical Biographies* (Baltimore, 1920), 1116.

accompanied the General to Aiken's Landing, where he went on board his flagboat, the River Queen. Gen. Butler was accompanied by two captains of his personal staff, while the remaining officers turned homeward.

BERMUDA HUNDRED, JAN. 10, 1865.

This is the base of the grand Army of the James. Here is where activity and industry may be daily seen. Schooners, tugboats, steamboats, and seagoing craft are constantly going and coming to the newly and somewhat substantially constructed wharves. Army wagons and ambulances are momentarily passing between here and the front, while fast horses, with faster riders, are continually dashing along at charging speed. Here may be seen all classes and conditions of adventurers, who follow in the wake of the army. Sutlers' establishments, wholesale and retail, loom up with grasping significance; barbers are ready to shave you for fifteen, and cut your hair for thirty-five cents; ambrotypists are here to place your beautiful countenances in a town, while the embalmers, with solemn countenances, will undertake to forward to the North the honored dead, and at the same time use the top of the coffin as a means for advertisement, by consuming more space, and using larger letters in announcing their business than those with which they indicate the name and rank of the dead. Life here may not be very gay, but it is very active, and at times quite stirring. The different quartermasters have as much as they can perform, from the supercilious Dodge[23] to the accommodating Walbridge.[24] The laborers in the quartermasters' department are nearly all persons of color, who, from their industry and application, continue in situations which they find to be profitable.

The arrivals from Richmond, on the underground railroad, still continue. An individual of the "contraband 'suasion" came in last evening, and tells of the sure threatening distress which is likely to overtake the people of that city. He gave twenty dollars in gold, and

23. George S. Dodge (?–?) held quartermaster appointments throughout the war. He was brevetted brigadier general in January, 1865, following the capture of Fort Fisher. Boatner, *The Civil War Dictionary*, 242; *OR*, Ser. III, Vol. V, p. 344.

24. C. E. Walbridge (?–?). A captain, Walbridge was brevetted major for "faithful and meritorious services." *OR*, Ser. III, Vol. V, pp. 349, 351.

twenty in Confederate shinplasters, for his passage to this place. He reports that Jeff Davis has been quite ill, but is now recovering, and is supposed to be out of danger. As the arch-traitor was born to be hung, there need be no fear of his passing out in the natural way.

Capt. Isaac Phillips, of the mail-boat Thomas Colyer,[25] has been recently attracting more than his legitimate share of attention. Last evening it arrived at this port, with the captain under arrest for unbecoming conduct while in a state of intoxication. He drew his revolver upon the pilot, and otherwise acted in a manner which made it necessary to restrain him of his liberty.

Everything is what we regard as quiet at the front, though one who is not a "vet" might think differently. Dutch Gap Canal was shelled yesterday with the customary venom, though without any serious effect. But few persons are engaged in laboring there.

Yesterday afternoon the rebels opened a vigorous fire upon Fort Burnham, in which they were allowed to indulge until it became annoying, when the fort belched forth a shower of shot and shell which had the desired effect of quieting the Johnnies.

Last night a skirmish line of rebels, in front of the 24th Corps, attempted to drive in our videttes and capture our picket line, but were driven back in confusion. These demonstrations against our picket line are dictated by the necessities of the enemy, more with the view of capturing our warm blankets than for any other consideration. A few of those who are shivering with cold are selected for what they regard as a daring enterprise, under the impression that the prospects of comforts will quicken their determination to accomplish what may be undertaken.

About noon yesterday we were all astonished, in the midst of a heavy rain, to see the lightning and hear the thunder in the good old way, as if it was the breaking up of winter and the dawning of spring. This morning the weather is quite cool, but the sun has made its appearance under circumstances which will not only give us a fine day, but will do much towards improving the bad condition of the roads.

25. There is no mention of Isaac Phillips, but the *Thomas Colyer*, a Confederate steamer, was captured in May, 1861, at Alexandria, Virginia, and became part of the Union fleet. United States Naval History Division, *Civil War Naval Chronology, 1861–1865* (6 vols.; Washington, D.C., 1971), I, 15.

BEFORE RICHMOND, JAN. 13, 1865.

The severe rain storm, of which I spoke in a former despatch, has done much for the Dutch Gap Canal. The explosion, on the 1st instant, which it was hoped would be sufficient to open the cut to successful navigation, as you know, failed to realize general expectation. Two explosions since, in which torpedoes were used, have been exceedingly gratifying in their results. The dirt was not only blown high in the air, but far upon the opposite bank of the James. Then came the protracted rain of the past few days, which raised the water in the James several feet, and in front of Dutch Gap, swamping the low lands for miles around. The current is going down the stream at the rate of four miles an hour, and is rushing through the canal at the rapid speed of at least ten miles, which has swept away the bulkhead which was left by the failure of the explosions. The fall in the river, from the upper to the lower end of this cut, is about five or six feet, which, with the comparatively narrow channel through which the river must flow, satisfactorily explains the rapid passage of the water, which sweeps through the entire width with great velocity. It is believed that, with this aid of the elements, the canal is sure to be a success. Indeed, there is no doubt now entertained, as the rapid force of the water is supposed to be sufficient to accomplish what weeks of dredging, under perilous circumstances, could only have effected.

Deserters are daily coming into our lines, whose loyalty is no doubt quickened by the chilling weather we are now experiencing. Last night seven came from Battery Simes, immediately in front of these headquarters, who were obliged to come through a considerable depth of water, fired upon all the time by the Johnnies. They expressed great joy at the success which attended their escape, and asserted that thousands in the rebel army would desert if they were not afraid to make the attempt. These deserters report that the chiefs at Richmond, believing that another attack is to be made upon Wilmington, have sent to its defence large reinforcements. The enemy is sending troops to South Carolina, to impede, if possible, the operations of Gen. Sherman. Upon the best authority, I have learned that Pickett's[26] division has refused to leave Virginia to reinforce the

26. George Edward Pickett (1825–1875). A Mexican War veteran, Pickett gained a reputation for being dashing and brave. He was named commander of the Department

rebel army in the South. This division is composed mainly of troops from this State. It is generally believed in military circles that Richmond will be evacuated before spring. Indeed, intelligence of a trustworthy character has already been received, which gives strong coloring of truth to the report.

The 1st Brigade of the 1st Division of the 20th Corps, commanded by General A. G. Draper, has received large accessions of strength. The following gentlemen are on the staff of Gen. Draper:

R. W. Simpson,[27] First Lieutenant 22d U. S. C. T., Acting Assistant Adjutant General.

Wm. D. Milliken,[28] First Lieutenant 22d U. S. C. T., Acting Assistant Inspector General.

O. M. Clemens, Captain and C. S. Vols., Commissary of Subsistence.

G. C. Prichard, First Lieutenant and R. Q. M., 38th U. S. C. T., A. A. Q. M.

S. C. Hawkes,[29] First Lieutenant 38th U. S. C. T., A. A. D. C.

D. L. Way,[30] First Lieutenant 5th U. S. C. T., A. A. D. C.

E. F. Hynes, First Lieutenant 118th U. S. C. T.,[31] Assistant Provost Marshal.

Wm. H. Rock, Second Lieutenant 36th U. S. C. T., A. A. D. C.

---

of Virginia and North Carolina following Gettysburg, where his forces suffered heavy losses when he launched an attack against entrenched Union positions. His troops took the brunt of the final Union push against Richmond. *DAB*, VII, 570; Wakelyn, *Biographical Dictionary of the Confederacy*, 347.

27. Robert W. Simpson (?–?) mustered in, January, 1864, as a first lieutenant, Company E, 22nd USCT. Bates, *History of Pennsylvania Volunteers*, V, 999.

28. William D. Milliken (b. 1837) mustered in as a private, 4th New York Artillery, in August, 1862. He was promoted to second lieutenant, 22nd USCT, in December, 1863, and to first lieutenant the following August. Bates, *History of Pennsylvania Volunteers*, V, 998; Phisterer (comp.), *New York in the War of the Rebellion*, V, 4197.

29. Seymour C. Hawkes (b. 1841) mustered in as a private, 148th New York, in August, 1862. He resigned to join the 38th USCT in March, 1864, finally mustering out as a first lieutenant. Phisterer (comp.), *New York in the War of the Rebellion*, V, 4185.

30. David L. Way (b. 1838) mustered in as a private, Company F, 79th Ohio Voluntary Infantry, in November, 1863. He was promoted to second lieutenant in the 79th before leaving to become a first lieutenant in the 5th USCT. *Official Roster of the Soldiers of the State of Ohio in the War of the Rebellion, 1861–1865* (12 vols.; Akron, 1893–95), I, 603, 606.

31. Organized in Baltimore in October, 1864, the 118th USCT was attached first to the XVIII Corps and then, with reorganization, to the XXV Corps. Dyer, *Compendium of the War of the Rebellion*, 253.

BERMUDA HUNDRED, VA., JAN. 17, 1865.

The good news from Federal Point has had a very cheering influence upon the troops in the Army of the James, as evinced by the usual demonstrations which follow every signal triumph of the Union army. The result is what every one expected, though, as usual, the chiefs at Richmond were informed of the expedition under Gen. Terry, and had despatched troops to the defences of Wilmington.[32] In a previous despatch I assured you that both North and South Carolina were being reinforced by the enemy from the works in front of his capital. The rebels did not arrive in time or in sufficient numbers to successfully resist the combined attack of probably one of the best, planned expeditions ever undertaken upon this continent. Under the inspiration of this victory the forces in front of Richmond never were in better condition or spirits to attack the enemy, and could be relied upon to fully realize public expectations.

Whether the Army of the James will or will not move soon, are questions which depend upon contingencies. At present, however, that army serves a good purpose. It keeps Lee around Richmond with all the forces he can raise, while Gen. Grant, with his anaconda system, is gradually environing him with inevitable destruction.

The intelligence which we have daily received from refugees, that the evacuation of Richmond is not only determined upon, but is actually commenced, is very generally credited here in military circles. The cause which leads to this demoralizing result upon the part of the enemy is the unpleasant realization that the rebel army can no longer be fed in its present position. The war has long since suspended every branch of industry in Virginia, while General Grant has severed enough of the enemy's communications to prevent the transportation of adequate and regular army supplies. The closing of the port of Wilmington may tend to hasten the event already decided upon, but where Jeff will set up his establishment next is a question which the future must answer.

Military operations may be summed up in a few words—all quiet on the James.

32. In the weeks following Butler's failure to take Fort Fisher, Grant assigned the task to Terry, whose forces took the fort on January 15, 1865, following heavy bombardment by Porter's fleet. Shelby Foote, *The Civil War: A Narrative. Red River to Appomattox* (New York, 1974), 740–47.

BERMUDA HUNDRED, VA., JAN. 20, 1865.

Since circumstances have suspended any movement of magnitude, until the weather and operations elsewhere will admit, it has been determined upon to turn the present inactivity to the benefit of the colored soldiers. It is gratifying to observe that orders have been issued that school houses be built in each of the regimental camps of negro troops, where they are to be instructed by the chaplains. Commissioned officers are invited to aid in this good work when their engagements will permit. The prosecution of this missionary spirit, among this class of soldiers, has already done much towards acquainting them with the elementary studies and fitting them for the positions which they hold in the service. As an illustration, I may mention the 36th U. S. C. T., recruited in North Carolina from the depths of ignorance, has, through tutorship of self-sacrificing spirits, been improved by hundreds since they have been in the field. Through this means, men have been instructed sufficiently to serve as non-commissioned officers. The efforts of the instructors are sure to be appreciated by that patient and persevering industry which has ever marked the character of the race when difficulties were to be overcome.

Persons must not always suppose that the utmost feeling of bitterness constantly prevails between the two armies now confronting each other. Whenever picket firing is indulged in, the most venomous feeling is apt to pervade both sides, and if one is imprudent enough to exhibit his head to the other, he is most certain to get a bullet through it. In front of Richmond, very unlike Petersburg, there is no firing. The pickets not unfrequently, and in different ways, manifest the most cordial feelings for each other. The colored soldiers are by no means an exception in advancing or reciprocating this harmonious intercourse. A few days ago this cordiality was thrillingly illustrated in the vicinity of what is known as "The Graveyard," not far from Dutch Gap. Between the two lines there is a considerable quantity of corn, which the rebs in their haste were obliged to leave ungathered. For some time the rebs were rather indisposed to allow our men to pluck the excellent ears, and not unfrequently fired upon them, and claimed the undisturbed privilege of reaping this entire harvest. By mutual consent, however, foraging parties of both armies were permitted to gather corn without fear of molestation, and more recently they have been meeting in the field for the same object. On one of these occasions a hog suddenly appeared, from somewhere, to the intense gratification of all parties. Both Yanks and rebs joined in the chase with much animation, and upon the best of terms. The anxiety of the Johnnies to catch the squealer induced one of them to try a shot, the report of which, especially the whizzing of the ball by the head of one of our men, brought the bluecoats to a defensive attitude, who shouted "Halloo, Johnny! what do you mean?" "I am not shooting at you," replied grayback, "but at that other hog." The explanation was satisfactory, and the Johnnies being the hungriest, captured porky.

I see no reason to change my opinion in reference to the evacuation of Richmond. Corroborating testimony is daily arriving from the rebel stronghold. The machinery is being removed to Danville. The bankers have already sent their deposits to that place, and it is generally believed by the people that the rebel chiefs will soon pack up their traps and start South. Danville is distant about one hundred miles from Richmond.

The greatest dissatisfaction now exists in the rebel army. The feeling is very intense against the administration of Jeff Davis, and if General Grant does not soon capture him, it is asserted the rebels will be certain to hang him. It is further asserted that even now he dare not walk the streets of Richmond without a strong guard, from fear of assassination by some fellow-rebels, who charge upon him the disasters to their God-forsaken cause.

If you have not been informed, I would mention a very unpleasant state of affairs in the rebel camps in our front. The Georgia troops refused to remain any longer in Virginia. Virginia and North Carolina soldiers were drawn up to bring them to terms, but without effect. The mutiny for a time threatened terrible consequences, and the way in which the rebel authorities deemed best to suppress it was to allow the Georgia troops to return to their State. It is more than likely that this feeling has been stimulated by a realization of the inevitable defeat of their entire armies. These soldiers will return not only to their homes, but to their allegiance.

Deserters who came in yesterday report that they had not learned that Fort Fisher had fallen. The tottering state of the Confederacy will not bear the shock of such disastrous news.

HEADQUARTERS 25TH CORPS

BEFORE RICHMOND, JAN. 22, 1865.

The weather during the past twenty-four hours has been exceedingly disagreeable. Yesterday morning we were chilled by one of those uncomfortable rains, whose glaciations tended to increase the unpleasantness of service in the field during a winter campaign. Soldiers gathered around their fires, in their quarters, communing with absent loved ones, while the ever watchful and faithful sentries upon their beats, covered over with ice, were the only persons stirring about the camp. The pickets, standing at their post, looked like men who had been glaciated. After the rain ceased, last evening, the wind sprang up several degrees cooler, which forcibly reminded one that winter was upon us, with all of its misfortunes.

This kind of weather has a very convicting effect upon the rebs towards stimulating them to a return to their allegiance, especially as their commissariat is well nigh exhausted. The stories which have heretofore been published about the starvation in the rebel army have been premature, but there can be no doubt, not only of their truth at this time, but of the demoralization of the enemy on account of his scarcity of provisions. One-third of a pound of meat and a little mite of corn meal is all that the rebel soldier receives for his allowance. This state of affairs has produced a wonderful revolution of feeling in the army of the enemy in our front, which has tended to quicken desertions. During the last week we have had as high as forty Johnnies in one day, along the line of the Army of the James, coming voluntarily into our lines, and expressing themselves as satisfied that the Confederacy was about used up. Scarcely a day passes but what a dozen or more of these penitent brethren come over and ask to be received upon probation. Officers are not unfrequently among the number.

During the past few days, previous to the rain, the roads were getting into excellent condition, which seemed to give the enemy considerable alarm. He has been apprehensive of an attack, and has been most vigilant in guarding against surprise.

With the troops that the enemy has sent South, and what have deserted, there is but a small force in our immediate front. With his numerous torpedoes and line of batteries he has good reason for feeling secure for the present. In an advance his artillery could have an enfilading fire upon our storming column, while his infernal machines might be expected to do fearful execution. At the proper time these obstructions will all be overcome by Gen. Grant. Since the rebels themselves have but little doubt of the fact, it only tends to confirm the opinion which I have long entertained, that the Commander-in-chief is able to reduce Richmond whenever he seriously undertakes it.

From deserters yesterday I learn that the rebel iron-clad Columbia, stationed at Charleston, was recently sunk in that harbor by running against a snag. The Columbia has been regarded as the best of the enemy's vessels of war afloat of its kind, and its loss, like all other disasters to the Confederacy, will be of no importance!

Fort Fisher, the scene of Gen. Terry's and Admiral Porter's brilliant operations, is to be included in Gen. Foster's department.

Major Gen. Gibbon,[33] of the Army of the Potomac, has been placed in command of the 24th Corps, and has entered upon that duty.

Col. John Holman, who so eminently distinguished himself on the 27th of October, and was badly wounded, has returned to the field, though unable to walk without the aid of a cane, to report for duty. Col. H. is deservedly popular with his command.

HEADQUARTERS 25TH CORPS

JAN. 25, 1865.

A couple of hours after I had forwarded my despatch of yesterday, I was astonished to learn that on the evening previous, while general attention was attracted by the spirited shelling from the enemy's batteries upon the opposite side of the James, two rebel rams (the Virginia and Nansemond) and the gunboat Drewry quietly came down the river, floated by Fort Brady, and then, as if no longer caring to conceal their movements, steamed down the stream. They passed the end of Dutch Gap Canal, which was blown out, the obstructions which we had sunk, and about daylight were nearing the other end

33. John Gibbon (1827–1896). A West Point graduate, Gibbon is best known as the commander of the "Iron Brigade," which saw action at South Mountain. He also led divisions at Fredericksburg and Gettysburg, where he was wounded. He returned to participate in the battles around Petersburg and in January, 1865, was in command of the XXIV Corps. Faust (ed.), *Historical Times Illustrated Encyclopedia*, 309.

of the canal, where one of our double-turreted monitors—supposed to be the Onondaga—was anchored. If we may credit the report about headquarters, and it is somewhat credited, this Onondaga strategically backed out of the way. Previous to the rebel vessels-of-war making their appearance, the monitor was reported to be in a disabled condition. This might excuse the vessel, but what the Commodore was doing at such an important post, unfit for service, is a question of serious import. The rams and gunboat, however, returned again, when our experienced cannoniers in Fort Brady opened upon them with much effect. They were struck several times. A well directed shell from the fort passed into the magazine of the gunboat Drewry and ended her career in smoke. The destruction of this craft is said, by deserters from the rams, to have seriously affected them, as she was very close to them at the time of her explosion. Many were killed, others wounded, and a few, availing themselves of the opportunity afforded, came into our lines.

Although it is not definitely ascertained, yet it is generally believed here that Semmes,[34] the rebel pirate, is in command of this daring enterprise, and is at present on board of one of the vessels. It is now understood that it was the intention of these piratical crafts to reach Bermuda Hundred and City Point, and possibly Fort Monroe, where the chief hoped to destroy the immense number of ships in their vicinity, and do such other damage as occasion presented.

The conflagration of our shipping at our base of supplies would have tended to revive the drooping spirits of the enemy, and at the same time furnish sufficient illumination in the rebel capital to commemorate the event.

Another view of this affair is worthy of consideration. For some time we have had intimations that Lee intended to astonish the world and in some way it leaked through the lines that it was his purpose to gobble the entire Army of the James. Taking this view of it, it is probable that the rams came down the James to destroy our pontoons, and being unable to receive reinforcements from the Army of the Potomac, or the other side of the river, hoped to overwhelm us

34. Raphael Semmes (1809–1877). Considered a pirate in the North, Semmes was almost a legend in the South. Throughout 1861, his cruiser *Sumter* played havoc with Union shipping, destroying seventeen Union merchant ships. He continued his depredations as captain of the CSS *Alabama* between 1862 and 1864. Semmes took command of the small James River Squadron in February, 1865. Faust (ed.), *Historical Times Illustrated Encyclopedia*, 666–67.

with superior numbers, and, our retreat being cut off, finally capture us. I do not know whether the world or Gen. Lee would be most astonished at the result.

The rebel rams are still below the upper end of the Dutch Gap Canal, under the guns of the Howlett House battery, where, during yesterday, they gave every indication of being crippled by the accurate fire from Fort Brady. It can be made impossible for these vessels to return to Richmond if the authorities here are disposed to put obstructions in the river and otherwise impede their progress. A move of this kind has undoubtedly a daring and considerable purpose. They are probably intended to co-operate with some plan of the enemy's forces which is yet undeveloped. A few days may solve the mystery. We feel so firmly entrenched in our position that no fears whatever are entertained of experiencing a reverse upon this line. The destruction of the rebel gunboat by our cannoniers had a very galling effect upon the enemy, as evinced by the thundering of his artillery from his batteries for several hours after. Several shells exploded over Fort Burnham, which immediately returned its ac-knowledgments in a manner that was, no doubt, deemed abundantly satisfactory. During the firing at Fort Brady one of the 100 pounders was dismounted, and three men were killed—John Jewell, of the 118th U. S. C. T., a man named Simmons, and another, name unknown, who belonged to the 1st New York. These persons, strange to say, were all killed at the same time, and by the last shell of the enemy fired at the fort. Lt. Filbrooke, 118th U. S. C. T., was wounded in the face and eyes. It was supposed that the rebels had ceased firing, and the men were ordered out of the bomb-proofs, when the fatal shot killed the three first that had just come from their protection. They were blown to pieces.

There is no disguising the fact that the rebel artillery displayed wonderful precision in firing. At Brady they put three shots, one after the other, into the same place, the last one passing entirely through the parapet. The enemy's batteries are about a mile off, and their excellent gunnery yesterday has given the impression that it would be an easy matter for them to knock a man off of our breastworks.

Such reflections are by no means the most agreeable to your correspondent, who, in the darkness of night before last, came near losing the top of his quarters by a Brooks shell, which went into the ground but a few feet beyond. In going into the earth it put out its fuse, and the nervous system of "Yours truly" did not receive a serious shock.

After midnight the artillery along the rebel lines opened again, and is still throwing shells into our camps and at our batteries. Fort Brady, as usual, replied. About 4 o'clock this morning there was considerable firing of musketry on the Bermuda Hundred front.

HEADQUARTERS 25TH CORPS

JAN. 26, 1865.

My despatch of yesterday was closed under rather nervous circumstances. I delayed it until the last moment to learn the nature of the terrible firing I then heard, and, while writing, was constantly reminded by the impatient messenger that it was already time for him to be on the way; and while inditing the last sentence a rebel shell came in such close proximity as to leave the impression, until I glanced around, that some part of my quarters was carried away, and the aforesaid messenger injured, for he did some ludicrous feats of ground and lofty tumbling. This practice was indulged in yesterday and the day before. Our cannoniers have hesitated to retaliate from motives highly creditable. A shower of iron retribution over their camps along the banks of the James, within easy range of our batteries, would have the effect of checking their malignity.

RETURN OF THE REBEL FLEET UP THE RIVER.

To the disgrace of somebody, the rebel fleet on the James, which ought to have been captured or sunk, or at least prevented from returning to Richmond, quietly steamed up the river this morning, about four o'clock. This was the occasion of the firing to which I alluded in my despatch of yesterday. When one reflects that the fleet boldly passed, in going and returning, some two or three miles of the river exclusively in our possession, and so close to Fort Brady that a stone could be pitched upon the vessels, and when he remembers, in addition to this humiliation, that the strategetical manoeuvre of our iron-clad monitor, the Onondaga, is subject to grave suspicions, it should not be surprising if, in our mortification, monstrous was applied to somebody's neglect.

THE NUMBER OF THE REBEL FLEET—ITS DISPOSITION—INCIDENTS OF ITS RETURN.

It now appears that, instead of three rebel crafts coming down the river, as reported, there were six, three of which were lashed to the others to disguise the number, or probably the wooden boats were placed outside of the rams as a means of protection. It was known some few weeks ago that the enemy had three iron-clads, the Virginia, Richmond, and Fredericksburg, and four gunboats, the Drewry, Nansemond, and two others, whose names I do not remember. It was reported, about the same time, that two new rams were in course of construction in Richmond, ready to be launched, but as deserters from the fleet have not said anything about them lately, it is fair to presume that they are not afloat. The fact that the fleet came down in pairs favors the impression that but three of them were iron-clad, while the destruction of the rebel gunboat Drewry, by our battery at the Crows' Nest, and not by Brady, as at first reported, leaves no doubt that the enemy was desperate enough to run by our guns in his wooden crafts.

Just before the fleet passed by Fort Brady, in returning up the river, our troops poured volley after volley into all the vessels to prevent them from opening their ports. Both above and below the fort our cannoniers fired rapidly at them, and are confident of striking every one of them, as each vessel went by disconnected with the other. The fact that more of them were sunk, after being subjected separately to such a severe fire, has fixed the impression in Brady that the five returning crafts were all iron-clads. One thing may be relied upon, that one of the rams came to a stand still in front of the fort, where it is supposed that it was badly crippled, and remained, receiving a concentrated fire of thirty-pounders, until another vessel went alongside of it, and they both passed up together. It is more than probable that the latter vessel towed the former one up the river.

THE ALLEGED COWARDICE OF THE ONONDAGA.

When the rebel fleet came down the James, it is now beyond all question that the monitor Onondaga did retire from Dutch Gap to below the pontoon bridge at Aiken's landing, a little over a mile, and leave two of our wooden gunboats, the Massasoit and Hunchback, to engage the enemy. The reason now assigned for this manoeuvre, which at the time seemed inexplicable, was that, above the bridge the channel was sufficiently wide to enable some of the enemy's crafts to run by easily as our gunboats engaged others; while, just below, the channel was so narrow that but one at a time could pass through. A good substantial draw bridge is nearly completed below the pontoon, which necessarily contracts the channel. The move would have been a good one for a gunboat, but for the only monitor within signaling distance to fall back as a reserve and leave two wooden vessels to engage five rebel crafts of war, three of them known to be iron-clads, is sufficient to suggest the most unfavorable comments. The captain of the Onondaga has been relieved from his command, from which you may infer the light in which his manoeuvering is viewed by the Navy Department upon the representations of General Grant.

An Engagement With the Fleet.

After the enemy's fleet retired under cover of the batteries of the Howlett House, about noon the Onondaga steamed up the river, with the Massasoit and Hunchback, where for two hours they engaged the enemy's fleet and batteries. The officers and their crews all behaved handsomely; but as the Massasoit was the only boat that was injured, a better opportunity was afforded for her commander and his men to manifest those higher qualities of unwavering firmness at the post of duty and danger than the others. It was the first time that the men or the vessel had ever been in an engagement. The sailors were cool and unflinching; the officers brave and cheerful; while Lieutenant Sumner[35] (quite a young man, who happened to be in command), endeared himself to all on board by his gallant bearing and the ability with which he handled the guns and manoeuvered the ship.

The Injuries to the Massasoit.

The Massasoit was struck some seven or eight times. One of the shots cut off the rim of the wheel, passed through a casting plate some two inches thick, and buried itself into the fresh water

35. There is no record of a Lieutenant Sumner. In January, 1865, the *Massasoit*, a ten-gun vessel, was under the command of R. T. Renshaw. *Civil War Naval Chronology,* V, 113.

condenser, which may be regarded as out of order. Her boats were riddled, some plating on the bow torn off, to make a passage for a persevering messenger from the enemy, and otherwise disfigured, though by no means seriously injured. The following are the casualties on board the Massasoit in this engagement:

LIST OF WOUNDED JANUARY 24.

> Wm. Mosher, captain after guard, head and back, serious.
> Wm. G. Hudson, right breast, serious.
> Thos. Fogerty, shoulder, slight.
> Horace Randall, boy, leg, slight.
> Jas. S. H. Black, in face, slight.
> Jas. Frazer, boy, in leg, slight.

THE OBJECT OF THE EXPEDITION.

It is now known that the enemy started for our base, whose crews were cheered to undertake this hazardous enterprise by the prospect of plunder. They solemnly pledged themselves to reach City Point or be sunk in the attempt, but the blowing up of the Drewry, giving them some idea of such an alternative, inspired them to rescind their entire resolution, and be more than satisfied if they could only return to Richmond. Availing themselves of the darkness of the night, they retired beyond the range of our guns, where they will probably remain until spring, when they, like the Drewry, will end their career in smoke. Why no obstructions were put in the James to prevent the enemy's fleet from returning to Richmond is a source of profound wonder. There is still, however, much cause for congratulation that the enemy has been driven back. City Point and Bermuda Hundred, whose tempting attractions of supplies are daily being augmented, still give evidence of future prosperity, based upon the honest and compensated industry of freemen.

Nothing can exceed the quiet that has prevailed along the lines during the last twenty-four hours.

CHAPTER 6

The Objective Is in Sight

ARMY OF THE JAMES

BEFORE RICHMOND, JAN. 27, 1865.

THE DETAILS OF THE "ASTONISHING MOVE."

As time speeds along the more fully we become possessed of the enemy's intention in advancing his flotilla down the James. It was the move by which Lee hoped to astonish the world, as the public has been frequently apprised. The rebel rams were provided with torpedoes to blow up our monitors, after which they were to destroy our pontoons, which would cut off this army from its base and all hope of immediate reinforcement from the Army of the Potomac, and then proceed to Bermuda Hundred and City Point to capture the immense storehouses of supplies which are located at those places. As soon as the flotilla, consisting of three iron-clad rams and three gunboats, were through our obstructions, and, as they sanguinely expected had destroyed the only monitor which happened then to be in the river, and proceeded on their way rejoicing, our line was to be attacked at several points, while Longstreet, with thirty thousand men, was to assault Fort Burnham. The recapture of this work would necessitate a retreat of several miles, and, under ordinary circumstances, would occasion a mortifying humiliation, but, had it fallen by the plans of the enemy, the disaster might have been overwhelming. Rising above these speculations, there is not now, nor has there ever been, the least fear that the enemy would ever recapture this work. The day after we captured this important position not even the inspiration of Lee's presence could rally the rebels to a successful charge. The recollection of what a bloody day that was to the rebels will never be forgotten, and had they attempted it on last Tuesday, as now seems was their intent, their slaughter would have been fearful.

SUPPLIES TO BE OBTAINED FROM OUR WELL-STORED "BASE."

The people of Richmond had been assured for the purpose of appeasing their hunger and allaying their discontent, that as Lee had on former occasions obtained immense supplies from McClellan, he only had to make a desperate effort to reach General Grant's base, from which he was to obtain sufficient food and clothing for his army and the destitute around Richmond and Petersburg.

DISAPPOINTMENT AND CHAGRIN.

Instead of returning with the good news of success the flotilla has the mortification to report that but one vessel passed our obstructions, the Fredericksburg, while the Richmond and Virginia, two other rams, got aground. In this dilemma our batteries opened on them, doing great damage to the Virginia, killing some and severely wounding five of her crew and some of her officers. The unerring fire of our forts, coupled with the manifest determination of our land and water forces to dispute the passage of the river, brought the flotilla to a consultation, the conclusion of which was hastened by our cannoniers sending a shell into the magazine of the Drewry. The flotilla then ran under the guns of the Howlett House battery, where it remained until near four o'clock on Wednesday morning, when it endeavored to quietly pass up the river. It then received the attention of Fort Brady and the Crow's Nest.

THE CO-OPERATIVE MOVEMENT OF THE LAND FORCES.

Gen. Pickett, whose forces oppose ours on the Bermuda Hundred front, more sanguine of success than Longstreet and other rebel chiefs, actually made a demonstration against our works, which, though it amounted to nothing, may have gained for him some credit in being prompt and ready to do his share of the battle. It is evident that somebody must shoulder the responsibility of this failure, and it is not unlikely that it may be put to the account of Pickett, for what the rebels may now term rashness, in disclosing an attack before the proper moment arrived.

A DAY OF FASTING AND PRAYER.

The rebel President is out in another proclamation, in yesterday's Richmond papers, appointing a day of prayer, fasting, humiliation, and all that kind of "bosh." These posters of Jeff have come to be such an annoyance, from their frequent occurrence and their hypocritical nature, that they scarcely deserve a passing notice. In fact, I do not see the necessity of this proclamation to advise fasting and humiliation, since necessity has long since imposed these Christian virtues upon his wicked people. The desperate effort of the enemy to reach City Point would leave one to infer that the rebels had ceased praying, assumed their pride, and resolved to eat as soon as supplies could be obtained.

SUPPLIES FOR REBEL PRISONERS.

The rebel flag-of-truce boat Wm. Allison came down the James yesterday morning, with such articles as the friends and relatives of prisoners of war in our possession could send them, consisting chiefly of tobacco. Some cotton also was brought down, with which, no doubt, our authorities will purchase blankets and clothing for the Johnnies. Wagon loads of good things were forwarded to our soldiers in Southern prisons, which will cheer them in their gloom, and serve to keep fresh in their recollections how dear they are to the loved ones at home.

EXTRACTS FROM THE LOG-BOOK OF THE DREWRY.

The blowing up of the Drewry has placed in our possession a good portion of its log-book, containing the reports of its commander and the general orders to the squadron. For the satisfaction of the public and information of the Navy Department, I annex such as I deem of sufficient interest for perusal. The following report of the part which the Drewry took on the memorable 29th of September, when Fort Harrison was captured, is worth reading, as affording an inside view of the rebellion:

C. S. STEAMER DREWRY

JAMES RIVER SQUADRON, SEPT. 29, 1864.

SIR: I have the honor of submitting to you the following report of the part borne by this vessel in shelling the enemy at Fort Harrison and the outer works of "Chaffin's Bluff." At 9 A. M. I was ordered by

Commander Thomas R. Rootes[1] to proceed from my anchorage off
"Grave-yard," James river, to Chaffin's Bluff and render any assistance
in my power to the defence of the bluff. I immediately steamed up
the river and reported to the commanding officer. Colonel Maury,[2]
however, being absent and supposed to be in the enemy's hands, the
officer in command could give me no instructions. Learning, however, the position of the enemy (the occupation of Fort Harrison), I
steamed down below the bluff and took position and opened fire on
the fort at 10:45 A. M., with an elevation of from 1,800 to 2,100 yards.
After firing one or two shots I ascertained from those on shore that I
had the range, and that my shells were destructive. At one o'clock
you came down by me and gave me orders to continue firing, which
was kept up until five o'clock, when my supply of ammunition being
nearly exhausted, I ceased firing. The amount of ammunition expended during the day sums up as follows: Thirteen 5-inch shell,
fifteen 10-inch shell, five 15-inch shell, nineteen percussion shell, two
10-inch charges, forty-eight 8-inch charges. During the early part of
the day a piece of shell struck me on the rib tier about two feet from
water line, without doing any damage. I take pleasure in testifying to
the uniform good conduct of all under my command. No casualties,
either accidental or from the enemy, occurred.

> I am, sir, very respectfully, your obedient serv't,
> Wm. H. Wall,[3]
> Lieutenant Commanding.
> To Flag-officer John K. Mitchell,[4] Commanding
> James River Squadron.

1. Thomas R. Rootes (?–?) was commander of the *Fredericksburg*, one of the
Confederate James River Squadron's ironclads. In August, 1864, the squadron consisted
of several ships under Flag Officer John K. Mitchell. The squadron constantly harassed
the black soldiers digging the canal at Dutch Gap. The *Fredericksburg* was blown up by
retreating Confederates in April, 1865. United States Naval History Division, *Civil War
Naval Chronology, 1861–1865* (6 vols.; Washington, D.C., 1971), IV, 104, VI, 229.

2. John S. Maury (?–?) commanded the 166-ton wooden gunboat *Hampton* in the
James River Squadron that shelled the soldiers at Dutch Gap. He subsequently took
command of the *Richmond*. *Civil War Naval Chronology*, IV, 82, 105, VI, 246–47.

3. William H. Wall (?–?). A lieutenant, Wall commanded the *Drewry*, one of the
wooden gunboats in the James River Squadron, which was damaged by Union batteries
in October, 1864. Wall's ship was destroyed in January, 1865, by an explosion after a
mortar shell penetrated the magazine. *Civil War Naval Chronology*, IV, 82, V, 26.

4. John K. Mitchell (?–?) was flag officer when the Union navy under Farragut
attacked New Orleans in April, 1862. He later assumed command of the James River

ORDER AGAINST DESERTION.

The following general order is also a corroboration of the statements which I have so frequently made, as to the depletion of the enemy's ranks by desertion:

OFFICE OF ORDERS AND DETAIL, C. S. NAVY DEPARTMENT
RICHMOND, VA., OCT. 18, 1864.

Commanding officers of stations and vessels will at once adopt the most stringent measures to stop desertions from the navy. Two officers will be sent in charge of boats, and the most reliable men selected for all duty affording opportunity to desert.

Deserters from the Yankees will be carefully excluded from duty of this character; such as shore duty, picket, etc.

By command of the Secretary of Navy.
S. S. LEE,[5]
Captain in Charge.

INSTRUCTIONS TO THE REBEL SQUADRON ON THE JAMES.

The following instructions to the enemy's squadron may be of general interest, especially to naval officers, as they disclose some of the matured plans of the enemy's movements on the James river.

GENERAL INSTRUCTIONS FOR PATROL SERVICE.

FLAG-SHIP VIRGINIA
JAMES RIVER SQUADRON, DEC. 12, 1864.

First. Vessels on patrol service will patrol the river from the booms above Kingsland creek to the river, just below Battery Semmes, at Bishop's.

Squadron. Both navies carried on a relatively ineffective set of engagements in 1864 and 1865. In August, 1864, Mitchell complained that high levels of sickness among his crews were limiting his effectiveness. But the Confederate navy was clearly inferior, and Mitchell could do little more than lay obstructions in the river in an effort to impede the enemy. *Civil War Naval Chronology*, II, 50, IV, 103, V, 6.

5. Sidney Smith Lee (1805–1869) is the brother of Robert E. Lee. He joined the navy at fourteen and later fought in the Mexican War. In the 1850s he held commands at the

Second. Vessels having the patrol duty and relief patrol will drop below the booms at early dusk and remain below till it is fairly daylight, when they will come above them, but they will not anchor until sunrise.

Third. The patrol vessels are required to keep under weigh from early dusk until sunrise, and not to anchor unless rendered absolutely necessary on account of thick weather, or other sufficient cause.

Fourth. They will keep their torpedo traps set whenever they pass below the booms; with a little care the yard will be found very serviceable in making short turns in the river.

Fifth. On the first trips down, and their first trips up, the patrol vessels will drag with a grapnel for wires of any electric torpedoes which the enemy may place in the river, keeping, for this purpose, as close in to the north shores as they can go without danger of grounding. Should any wires be brought up, leading to the north bank, they are to be cut at once, and the wires hauled in as much as possible, and again cut, and the place carefully noted on the chart.

Sixth. Whenever the current is so strong as to interfere with dragging on their first trips down, it may be done on their first trips up.

Seventh. The patrol gunboats will keep the edge of the channel, close aboard on their starboard hand, whenever there is danger from thick weather, or their running into each other.

Eighth. Their torpedoes are to be kept shipped, loaded, fused, and ready in all respects for immediate service, but they will be well triced up until preparing to receive or make an action; and on returning from patrol duty will have the safety caps placed over the sensitive tubes. The utmost care is enjoined at all times to take every precaution to prevent accidents from collision with each other, and when employed on any service where they may be exposed to such danger, and are beyond the reach of the enemy, the torpedoes should be unshipped.

Ninth. They will keep in constant readiness to return any fire the enemy may open upon them from the banks of the river, with field-

Philadelphia Navy Yard and at Annapolis and was chief of the Bureau of Coast Survey. He resigned his commission at the beginning of the war to serve the Confederacy as a captain, as an examiner of the Confederate Naval Academy, and as chief of the Bureau of Orders and Details. Stewart Sifakis, *Who Was Who in the Civil War* (New York, 1988), 382.

pieces or small arms, and will promptly take up an enfilading position, if practicable, to rake the banks with shell, grape, or canister, as circumstances may call for. They will move promptly to the assistance of each other, or the picket boats if attacked, and oppose any attempt they may discover of the enemy to cross the river to interfere with our torpedoes, or any other offensive movement.

Tenth. One half of the crew is to be always on watch-on-deck with their side arms and small arms, and prepared for instant action, to man the batteries, to board, or repel boarders.

Eleventh. Two sentinels are to be kept on the upper deck armed with muskets, who, with the quartermaster, and all other petty officers of the watch, are to be provided with hand grenades and caps, to be used against boarding parties.

Twelfth. The patrol gunboat will commence its trips from the booms at 5:30 P. M.; the second will leave at six; and thereafter, when two are on duty, at intervals of half an hour, so that each boat will leave every two hours in the one case, or every hour and a half in the other case.

Fourteenth. The gunboats will perform patrol duty in succession in the following order, viz: The Hampton, Nansemond, Drewry, Beaufort, and Roanoke.

Fifteenth. The boat having the last, or leaving the last in order at night, will be off duty the following night, when the two preceding her on the list will have the patrol duty, and the boat preceding them will have the relief patrol, and those preceding her will be off duty for the following night and so on successively.

Sixteenth. With a proper understanding of this rule, each boat will know its duties for every night, and perform them without further orders.

Seventeenth. They will be prepared at all times to repeat any signals that may be agreed upon, either with guns, rockets, lanterns, or any other way.

Eighteenth. Any information obtained respecting the movements of the enemy will be communicated by signal or boat, or by both if of sufficient importance to be immediately known to the commanding officer of the squadron.

Nineteenth. Commanding officers of the patrol vessel will apply to the commanding officer of the guard vessel for orders for the night, should none be furnished by sunset.

Twentieth. The commanding officer of each patrol boat will forward to the commanding officers of the squadron, every morning, an account of his service during the preceding night, giving time of departure from and arrival at each end of their boat or route, the time, place, and cause of anchoring whenever it may be rendered necessary, and such other occurrences or information he may obtain as may be proper for the flag-officer to know, which account must also be entered in the log book, except such as may be secret.

Twenty first. When more than four boats are available for patrol services, three will be on duty every night; when less than five only two will be on patrol every night.

> JNO. K. MITCHELL,
> Flag-Officer James-River Squadron.
> LIEUT. WM. H. WALL,
> Commanding C. S. Gunboat Drewry.

BERMUDA HUNDRED, JANUARY 31, 1865.

The great topic here for the past few days has been the severity of the cold weather. The "Sunny South" is a very nice expression, and may be applicable here during the season of flowers, but will by no means give the reader an intelligent idea of this climate, unless perchance I have been dwelling upon the shady side. The interruptions in the arrivals of the mails from the North are supposed to be occasioned by the accumulation of ice in the rivers leading from Baltimore to Washington. Had the weather continued as cold as it was during the past few days, the James river would also have been blockaded with ice. There is plenty of ice in the James, but not of sufficient thickness to interfere with navigation.

By the arrival of the train on the underground railroad it was my good fortune yesterday to meet passengers who are just from Richmond, whose opportunities for being acquainted with the state of public feeling are the very best. They assure me that the Richmond daily papers in no wise represent either the feelings of the people or those of the editors themselves, but are conducted wholly with a view of keeping up the spirits of the rebels in arms, among whom they are gratuitously circulated. The poorer class has long since given up all hope of succeeding, and now the F. F. V.'s are conscious of, and in their drawing rooms admit the impossibility of, Southern independence. The capture of Fort Fisher, which the rebels regard as the greatest disaster of the war, has quickened the mortifying conclusions of many who were previously very sanguine.

The authorities cannot get supplies for their troops, and are now bringing starvation nearer to the doors of the rich by seizing the provisions which they had stored up for such emergencies, and turning them over to the quartermasters' and commissary departments. One baker recently had the misfortune to lose one hundred and ten barrels of flour. Others have been obliged to give up what they had stored away for hard times, but just as they are coming upon them the rebel chiefs are appropriating their private stores for the support of their half-starved soldiers.

This state of affairs has produced a profound sensation in Richmond, and now in the mansions of the F. F. V.'s may be heard the prayers of the wives of rebel chiefs that the Yankees may soon come to their deliverance. This is no speculation, but a fact just communicated by a reliable eye-witness. The arrival of Mr. F. P. Blair, Sr.,[6] in Richmond was hailed as the dawn of peace. The rebel authorities would have refused him permission to visit their capital had it not been for the overwhelming peace feeling frankly manifested in that doomed city.

The conviction is now firmly rooted in the South that there is no hope for Southern independence, and that the further continuance of this unhappy strife will be a sacrifice of blood and treasure without the ghost of a probability of success.

It is now frankly confessed by the rebel authorities that they cannot hold Richmond and Charleston, and sooner than allow the latter to fall they will evacuate the former. Of course, the prospect of starvation must have some credit for bringing them to such a conclusion.

6. Francis Preston Blair (1791–1876). A journalist and politician, Blair worked actively for reconciliation during the war. His hope for peace led him to Richmond in December, 1864, on an unofficial mission to consult with Davis. He proposed joint military operations against Emperor Maximilian in Mexico on the assumption that a decision to cooperate on this venture could form the basis for further discussions. The meetings with Davis and reports to Lincoln paved the way for the Hampton Roads Conference two months later. *DAB*, I, 330–32; Patricia L. Faust (ed.), *Historical Times Illustrated Encyclopedia of the Civil War* (New York, 1986), 65.

The arrival of Alexander H. Stephens[7] at City Point, and his probable departure for Washington in the mailboat Dictator this morning, may be regarded as suggestive, and tending to confirm the feeling in Richmond which I have mentioned.

BEFORE RICHMOND, FEB. 3, 1865.

THE ARMING OF THE SLAVES.

From what I can learn from deserters and refugees, of both colors, who may be relied upon, there is no subject which is engrossing so much attention in Richmond as the proposition to arm a corps of negroes.[8] General Lee, Jeff Davis, and many of the rebel chiefs are known to be in favor of the measure. The F. F. V.'s, who, through favoritism, are detailed to stay at home, see, in this movement, a crushing of all their fondest hopes. This class, of course, oppose the measure as impracticable, and beneath the dignity of Southern gentlemen. The officers in the rebel army, who lose everything dear to man when the authority of the Union shall be maintained, seem to be free of the scruples.

THE FEELING OF THE SOLDIERS ON THE SUBJECT.

The rank and file, most of whom have been thrust into the army against their inclination, and all of whom are retained therein by a remorseless despotism, are only praying that the rebel chiefs may put black troops into their service, as it would serve as the cause, and be

7. Alexander Hamilton Stephens (1812–1883). The Confederate vice-president was on the way not to Washington, but to Fortress Monroe for the Hampton Roads Conference, which Stephens hoped would lead to peace and the independence of the South. The conference quickly collapsed over the issue of independence, which Lincoln flatly refused to entertain. *DAB*, IX, 569–75; Jon L. Wakelyn, *Biographical Dictionary of the Confederacy* (Westport, Conn., 1977), 398–99; Faust (ed.), *Historical Times Illustrated Encyclopedia*, 716–17.

8. Enlisting black soldiers was heatedly contested in the South. Davis favored it but met stiff resistance from those who opposed the idea on the grounds that it violated all the Confederacy stood for. Six weeks after the Hampton Roads Conference, the Confederate Congress passed an act permitting enlistment of blacks, but it came too late to help the South. George Washington Williams, *A History of the Negro Troops in the War of the Rebellion, 1861–1865* (New York, 1888), 292; Shelby Foote, *The Civil War: A Narrative. Red River to Appomattox* (New York, 1974), 859–61.

made the occasion, for their laying down their arms and returning home in disgust. Such an opportunity for indignation among the chivalry would be hailed with suppressed feelings of exultation. The rebel authorities are by no means ignorant of this feeling, but ascribe it to the disinclination of their soldiers to fight alongside of the negro, which they believe can be overcome by the rigor of discipline. There is another class of persons who are more honest in their opposition to the measure than all other classes. They are the negroes themselves.

THOUGHTS OF THE SLAVE—THE REASON PLAIN TO HIM.

When this question was first broached to the public, it was as evident to the most ignorant slave of the South as to Davis himself that it was dictated by rebel necessity. The idea was so repulsive to these poor, humble people that they immediately began to devise ways and means to escape to our lines, or, in their own vernacular, "to flank de pickets." The more thoughtful of the negroes in Richmond rather liked the idea, and, hoping that it would be put into execution, began to prepare the minds of their people for an important chapter in this struggle, in which they were praying to be permitted to take a part.

A GREAT SECRET ASSOCIATION OF "LIBERTY."

Secret associations were at once organized in Richmond, which rapidly spread throughout Virginia, where the venerable patriarchs of this oppressed people prayerfully assembled together to deliberate upon the proposition of taking up arms in defence of the South. There was but one opinion as to the rebellion and its object; but the question which puzzled them most was, How were they to act the part about to be assigned to them in this martial drama? After a cordial interchange of opinions it was decided with great unanimity, and finally ratified by all the auxiliary associations everywhere, that black men should promptly respond to the call of the rebel chiefs, whenever it should be made, for them to take up arms.

HOW SLAVES WERE TO FIGHT FOR REBELLION.

A question arose as to what position they would likely occupy in an engagement, which occasioned no little solicitude, from which all minds were relieved by agreeing that if they were placed in front as soon as the battle began the negroes were to raise a shout for Abraham Lincoln and the Union, and, satisfied there would be plenty of support from the Federal force, they were to turn like uncaged tigers upon the rebel hordes. Should they be placed in the rear, it was also understood that as soon as firing began they were to charge furiously upon the chivalry, which would place them between two fires, which would disastrously defeat the army of Lee, if not accomplish its entire annihilation.

The Proof of Authenticity of the Plan.

Such is the plan which I learned from the vice president of the combined movement, who delayed his exit from Richmond some six weeks, under the impression and the hope that negroes would be armed in the rebel service. Being satisfied that it would not be attempted, he took passage upon the underground railroad and arrived safely within our lines. Although my informant is of the opinion that negroes will not be armed, yet, from later intelligence which I have received, I am assured that the rebel authorities, who place much reliance upon what might be accomplished with this element of strength, under drill and discipline, are using every means which necessity can suggest or artifice devise to make the measure popular. With the view of making it palatable to that class of rebels who do not realize the necessity of sacrificing the system to secure their independence, it is to be manoeuvered upon such a treacherous basis as will enable the rebel chiefs to keep their word of promise to the negro's ear, but break it to their hopes.

The Slaves Not All Union-Loving.

It must not be supposed that the blacks to a man are loyal to the old flag. The hesitating policy of the Government at the outbreak of the war, coupled with the terrible recollection that fugitive slaves were returned by Union officers, and were made to pass through the severest ordeal of Southern torture, and the impression which this engendered, that the Yankees would sell them to Cuba, and other stories which worked equally upon their fears, have induced many to cling to the cause of the South under protest, and suffer the evils they have than fly to others they know not of. These, however, are the exception, while the millions, whose faith has never wavered, are still praying that the old flag may ever be victorious.

ROMANCES OF SLAVE-REFUGEES.

There are abundant instances of unfaltering devotion to the Union among this class, and the perils through which both bond and free have passed, to escape from the dominion of Southern chiefs, would make the basis for many thrilling romances. Justenia Gerad, a quadroon of rather prepossessing appearance, sooner than marry in Richmond, where the laws refused to recognize the sacredness of the compact, fled with her betrothed to our lines, where they arrived after having concealed themselves many days, travelled many nights, and waded through cold streams of water up to their necks. A short time before leaving rebeldom, she, with a number of others of the F. F. V. colored people, was arrested and confined in prison for three days for attending the wedding of a friend in the country, and only escaped the disgrace of stripes at the public whipping post through the earnest aid of counsel, pleading that they were assembled upon a white man's plantation. Others, no less eventful and equally thrilling, are occurring almost daily, and to the novelist I commend these interesting incidents in their experience.

THE SLAVES WELL FED AND CLAD.

Most of the slaves that come into our lines have a respectable and well-dressed appearance, and have cheerful countenances. When one considers that negroes dare not smoke cigars in the streets of Richmond; that a half-dozen males or females are not permitted to assemble, by accident or invitation at the house of a friend; that they are excluded from riding inside of coaches, except at funerals when only four are allowed, however urgent may be the necessity, or the inability of this number to accommodate all the family; that it is forbidden them to have carriages at their weddings; that black ministers are not allowed to preach to their own people, in churches built out of their own money, from the pulpits, but on the floor; that even now it is being agitated that colored people shall not be permitted to dress as fine as they have been indulging in, and innumerable other measures calculated to humble their pride and brutalize their manhood, involving, as any infraction of these prohibitions certainly will, a public disgrace at the whipping-post, it is no wonder that the negro's head is clear and his heart right upon the question of sustaining the Union.

ARMY OF THE JAMES

BEFORE RICHMOND, FEB. 2, 1865.[9]

The chilling breath of winter has again been warmed by the glow of a more genial sun. In our jubilant feelings over the pleasant weather of the past few days we are quickened to the conclusion that the "sunny south" may not all be poetry, but a kind of romantic reality. Were it not that the severest month of the year has just commenced, we would congratulate ourselves that the Rubicon was passed, and that warm weather and warmer work would occupy the attention of this army for some time to come. The condition of the roads never was more favorable for offensive operations.

Desertion from the enemy still continue without exciting any surprise here, knowing as we do the untold sufferings and privations which the rebels have entailed upon themselves by this secession plot. They all come in dispirited, humble, and penitent, assuring us that their future deportment will in part atone for their past offenses. Some days ago, in the cornfield upon the Boulware estate, there were about thirty rebels gathering the ears to appease their hunger. Some of them conversed with our pickets, and begged that they would come upon them with a few men, as they would cheerfully surrender, but they wished to avoid the appearance of desertion. Such a move being expressly forbidden, the officer of the picket lines was assured that this evening quite a number would come in, as they would be able to collect their friends together, and bid adieu to Jeff and his doomed crew.

Quite an amount of straw on the Boulware estate has been heaped up in stacks, presenting a temptation to Gen. Draper for some time, as it was immediately in front of his lines. On one or two occasions he organized foraging parties to gather in the harvest, but the vigilance of the rebel rams, coupled with other unfavorable circum-

9. This was published after Chester's February 3 dispatch.

stances, prevented the execution of his purpose. On last night and the night previous, the General circumvented the Johnnies, and taking due precaution to prevent a surprise, or repel an attack, he seized the straw and brought it off in safety, from within hearing of the camp chat of the enemy. The success of this foraging party gave to many of us warmer and softer couches than we have heretofore enjoyed.

One Benjamin of the contraband "suasion," like his namesake of Biblical chronology, had the misfortune yesterday to be arrested for having property in his possession which did not belong to him, or to which other parties had strong claims. Benjamin's chronic complaint is severe cramps in his fingers when brought into contact with "green-backs," for which no adequate remedy has yet been applied. General Draper, about whose headquarters he has had recently a remarkably convulsive attack of his unfortunate disease, caused him to bundle up his traps, and, with a card labeled "thief" upon his back, to the tune of the Rogue's March, to be dishonorably escorted beyond his brigade limits, a remedy which, it is to be hoped, may produce a successful cure.

About 8 o'clock last evening the rebel vessels-of-war, as is their custom, came down the river, and were fired upon by the pickets of the 1st brigade, 1st division, 25th Corps. The crafts beat a hasty retreat up stream, shelling our pickets as they steamed toward Richmond.

Nothing could possibly be more quiet than the condition of the two armies now confronting each other.

BEFORE RICHMOND, FEB. 6, 1865.

THE PEACE FEELING IN RICHMOND.

My facilities for becoming acquainted with the state of public feeling in Richmond on the peace question are numerous, and for some time I have been observing the state of affairs as exhibited behind the curtain, abstracts of which I have occasionally forwarded. There need be no question as to the honest conviction of the people of Richmond and the Confederacy in reference to peace. They are not only tired of the war, but are willing to return to the Union. The rebel papers as a part of the plan, may endeavor to keep up appearances and some show of spirit, with the view only of inducing better terms for themselves. They think, by manifesting a disposition to continue the struggle, that our Government will yield them more satisfactory conditions in a peaceable adjustment. This continued harping on the ability of the rebellion to attain its ends has also for its object the inspiration of the rebels in the field.

THE FEELING IN THE REBEL ARMY.

If the army of Lee, dispirited to some extent, as the numerous desertions daily testify, were as much demoralized and as hopeless as the citizens of Richmond, whose opportunities for knowing the extent of the resources of the rebellion are unlimited, the poor conscripted specimens of shivering humanity would at once retire from the field. But it is generally the pangs of a craving appetite that are proving powerful incentives towards quickening these desertions. Many of these vipers, impelled by suffering and destitution, sur- render themselves, cold and shivering, to our pickets to avail themselves of the favor of General Grant's order and the bounty of the Government, with the purpose of using their fangs, after they may be warmed and clothed, against constituted authority.

DEFIANCE OF SOME OF THE DESERTERS.

Two of this class came into our lines a day or two ago, and, after declaring that they were obliged to desert on account of general destitution, they remarked, with some confidence, that the rebel army was unwavering in its determination to remain in Virginia.

NEEDY LEADERS MADE PRISONERS.

Yesterday two rebel soldiers, driven by necessity, came up to our picket line in front of the 25th (colored) Corps to exchange tobacco for such eatables and clothing as our colored sentinels were willing to trade. In the midst of their negotiations a corporal, more mindful of orders than the pickets, presented arms to the Johnnies and invited them into our lines. They protested; but on being informed that it was against orders for our pickets to hold any communication with the enemy, and for the present must bid farewell to "Dixie," they endeavored to resign themselves to their fate.

UNWAVERING REBELS.

The cornfield on the Boulware plantation still attracts the hungry Confederates to gather what they can to appease their appetites. It is the easiest thing possible to capture these foraging parties, but as coming there for subsistence furnishes splendid opportunities to desert, the Johnnies are permitted to use their discretion. Many of them come into our lines, while others return to their camps. Day before yesterday, while the division officer of the day, Major Wm. H. Hart, was visiting his picket line, he saw three rebs in the cornfield, which is between the lines of both armies. He rode up to them, and extended a pressing invitation for them to advance to our picket line. This they at first declined, alleging that they feared the colored sentinels would shoot them—an opinion very generally entertained, since the Fort Pillow massacre, among the rebel soldiers whenever they come in contact with colored troops. Major Hart, naturally very persuasive, assured them that they should not be injured, and they accompanied him to the picket reserves, where he gave them the opportunity of electing for themselves whether they would come into our lines or return to their own. They acknowledged that the Southern army was unanimous in its desire for peace, and that it would hail the day with great rejoicing when they should return to the Union. They, themselves, were anxious to come back, but did not wish to desert, but would cheerfully give in their adhesion when the Southern people yielded. While these half clothed "gray-backs" were shivering over the picket fire, eating the hard corn from the ears, the comfortably-clad negro reserves were partaking of fresh beef and soft wheat bread, with a nonchalance that indicated plenty and content- ment. They were then permitted, on their own choice, to return to their rebellious camps, where the magnanimity of Major Hart, the rations to our soldiers, and the disposition of our colored troops to receive them on deserting, were, no doubt, duly discussed.

DISAFFECTION AMONG DAVIS' FOLLOWERS.

An absolute want of faith in the Davis concern is manifest in many of the stores in Richmond closing up rather than dispose of their goods for rebel scrip; in bankers refusing to part with their gold at any price in Confederate currency; if they even were corruptible, are no longer so. Both white and colored refugees have solicited their aid for a consideration, in reaching our lines, which has been cheerfully rendered. Ladies in Richmond, of wealth and known secesh proclivities, have, in ways which it would be impolitic to reveal, aided many colored persons to reach our lines in safety. Many persons, high in position, who are detained by circumstances, have not hesitated to assist others from the inevitable crash which all have realized is only a question of time. Moral, political, and constructive treason are daily weakening the rebel Government and impairing its efficiency in the field.

ARMY OF THE JAMES

BEFORE RICHMOND, FEB. 9, 1865.

The changeable weather which we have been experiencing for the past few days is both unpleasant and inconvenient. Sometimes it is quite cool, but does not continue so more than twenty-four hours, when the warming influence of the sun materially improves the climate. At present, in consequence of the unfavorable weather, all military operations upon any grand scale may be regarded as suspended. Days pass into nights, and nights into mornings, with nothing more exciting than the unvarying monotony of military routine. Not even the dull rumbling of distant artillery is heard to quicken the martial circulation of patriotic enthusiasm. But all is as quiet as if the angel of peace had paralyzed the confronting armies. This very stillness is not only oppressive, but is the calm which precedes the storm. Further more the deponent sayeth not.

The spring campaign, soon to be commenced upon a scale of terrible magnitude, will fully meet public expectation. What part the Army of the James will take will be announced after the drama shall have been enacted. One thing, however, may be assumed, that though there was much regret occasioned by the removal of General Butler, the manifest fitness of General Ord to command this army, uniting as he does the polish of the gentleman with the discipline of the soldier, is already inspiring it with renewed assurances of confidence in his ability to govern it in camp or handle it in the field. Fears were at first entertained that the colored troops, whose good conduct and discipline upon all occasions were very much stimulated by their admiration for General Butler, would to a certain extent be depressed. The friends of these organizations need entertain no fears in this respect. In the opinion of General Ord they are not inferior in discipline or martial bearing to any other soldiers, and all that can be done to increase their comfort and effectiveness is in rapid progression. He has personally visited their camps, entered their quarters, and observed for himself what improvements were necessary for their convenience and the good of the service. His modest bearing, coupled with almost the entire absence of military trappings, when wrapped in his surtout, would leave the impression that he was a visitor in the field rather than the commander of this department. His venerable appearance, with a countenance of stern resolve not unmingled with gentleness and other eminent characteristics, presents a type of American nobility born to command.

It must not be inferred that General Ord is any more solicitous about the welfare of his colored troops than his white soldiers. He is a soldier of the regular army, and, recognizing both elements as essential to the overthrow of the rebellion and the preservation of the Union, he has risen above all prejudices and partiality, and acts with reference to what is right and just. Under such a general the Army of the James will not fail to make brighter its record in the campaign so soon to be opened.

The report, which for some time has been in circulation, that this army is to be united with the Army of the Potomac, is received by officers and men of this command with the greatest disfavor. None are more severe in their condemnation of this proposed union than those who have served in the Army of the Potomac. The officers all say that, having left it, they never want to return to it again. As the rumor goes, General Meade is to be relieved and General Sheridan is to command the united armies, all of which the readers of *The Press* may take for what they are worth, themselves estimating their value.

While the negotiations for peace were transpiring at Fortress Monroe, the rebel soldiers were so much elated with the prospects of a favorable and satisfactory adjustment of the pending difficulties that desertions ceased. Since, however, it is understood that the peace mission ended in smoke, the poor, half-starved, penitent "graybacks" are again wending their way into our lines, full of assurances for their future good conduct. A day or two ago a rebel soldier requested permission to go into the corn field on the Boulware plantation, of which I have frequently spoken in former despatches, to gather the scattering ears. A guard of two men were sent to accompany him, when, upon a very little consultation, all three of them delivered themselves to our colored pickets as deserters, including the arms of the guard. Such and similar occurrences are witnessed daily upon different parts of our line.

ARMY OF THE JAMES

BEFORE RICHMOND, FEB. 10, 1865.

The weather has reached an uncomfortably cool degree, but will not continue so for many hours. The roads are frozen, but the ground is not frosted to any extent beneath the surface.

Deserters continue to come into our lines. Fourteen arrived yesterday—a lieutenant, sergeant, and corporal were of the number.

All is quiet on the James.

The following is the organization of the enemy's force between the rebel Fort Gilmor and the James river:

The 18th Georgia Battalion, Major Bossenger commanding—Company A, Captain Sevioven; B, Captain Stiles and Lieutenant Smith; C, Captain Rice. In this battalion there are about one hundred and twenty men for duty, the number of which is daily lessened by desertions. The 18th is stationed in front of Fort Burnham.

The 1st Virginia or Arsenal Battalion, Major Ayres commanding— Company A, First Lieutenant Clarke; B, Captain Forsythe; C, First Lieutenants Green and Horner; D, Captain Tucker; G, Captain Munden. The 1st is posted on the right of the 5th Battalion, which is nearly opposite Fort Burnham, whose ranks are being much depleted by desertions. First Lieutenant Green came into our lines on the 1st of January, thoroughly disgusted with the fortunes and prospects of the Confederacy.

The 5th Virginia or Arsenal Battalion, Lieutenant Colonel P. J. Eunie—Company A, Captain Locke; B, Captain R. Boyce; C, Captain R. Allen; D, Captain Sherry; E, Captain Brown; F, Captain Sherry; G, Captain Hoots; H, Lieutenant Ramure. The 5th is a very small organization, having only about thirty men for duty, the remainder being on detached service in Richmond. Companies D and F have been consolidated. It is stationed in front of Fort Burnham, to the left of the 1st Battalion.

The 2d Virginia, or Shoemaker Battalion, Col. Scruggs commanding—Company A, Capt. Sinton; B, Capt. Vaughn; H, Capt. Mayo; K, Capt. Bowley. The 2d is stationed on the left of the 5th. The remaining six companies of this regiment are on duty in Richmond.

The 18th Virginia Battalion, Major Harding commanding—Company A, Capt. Griffin; B, Capt. Hendrew; C, Capt. Orgain; D, Capt. Norton; E. Capt. Smoot. There are only one hundred and sixty men in the 18th for duty. It is stationed to the left of Fort Shields.

The 25th Virginia, or City Battalion, Lieut. Col. Ellet commanding—Company A, Capt. Graynor; B, Capt. Fisher; C, Capt. Anderson; D, Captain Potts; E, Capt. Beykin; F, Lieut. Wells; G, Capt. Bairs; H, Capt. Allison. The 25th is stationed between Fort Burnham and Fort Fields.

The 4th Virginia Battalion, Major Curling commanding—Company B, Capt. Brown; C, Captain Pettel; D, Capt. Bushwell; E, Capt. Thomas.

The 4th is stationed to the right of Fort Burnham and the left of Walker's brigade.

The 9th Virginia Battalion, Major Laden commanding—Co. A, Lieut. Lofton; B, Captain Guess; C, Captain Willihan; D, Lieuts. Brown and Lovelace; E, Captain Wiley.

The 9th is manning guns at different points along the entire line.

The 1st Virginia Light Artillery—Captain Jones, Captain Richardson, Captain Talley, Captain Allen, and Captain Young.

The 1st is doing garrison duty along the lines at different points. Lieut. L. T. Davis, of this artillery, deserted to our lines on the 20th of January.

The 22d Virginia Battalion, Lieut. Col. E. P. Taylor—Co. A, Captain Tompkins; B, Captain Winn; C, Captain Winn; D, Lieut. Hatcher; E, Lieut. Ward; G, Lieut. Sheppard; H, Lieut. Coates.

The 47th Virginia Infantry, Col. Mayo commanding—Co. A, Captain Brooks; C, Lieut. Davis; F, Lieut. Motley; G, Lieut. Motley; H, Lieut. Flipper; K, Capt. Tollins.

The 4th and 55th Virginia Infantry, united with the 22d and the 7th, compose Gen. Walker's brigade of Major General Heath's division. Brigadier General Barton, recently commanding the line of works from Fort Gilmor to the river, was assigned to the command of this brigade about the 15th of last month. It was stationed near the river, but moved on the 30th ult.

The mortar battery in front of Fort Burnham comprises twenty-two guns in two sections, distant from each other about fifteen yards—one of ten guns and the other of twelve. The mortars in each section are distant one from another about six or eight feet, and each gun covered by a high mound of earth, distinct from the one adjoining. The guns all bear upon Fort Burnham, and are under the direction of Captain Lambkin, who has Lieuts. Stanfield and Massey for each section. In front of the right section, and to the right, is a four-gun battery—six-pounders and smooth-bore—and covering the left section is a two-gun battery of the same sized guns. These batteries are manned by the 9th Georgia Battalion.

The following four brigades compose Major General Pickett's division. The New York *Herald* of the 30th ult. purports to give the roster of this command, which may have been correct at some period of the war, but by no means agrees with its present organization:

1st Brigade, Brigadier General Cose commanding.—15th Virginia Infantry, Lieut. Col. Morrison; 29th Virginia Infantry; 30th Virginia Infantry; 32d Virginia Infantry, Colonel Burkley.

2d Brigade, Brig. Gen. Hunton commanding.—19th Virginia Infantry, Col. Gaunt; 8th Virginia Infantry; 28th Virginia Infantry; 50th Virginia Infantry.

3d Brigade, Brig. Gen. Terry commanding.—1st Virginia Infantry; 7th Virginia Infantry; 11th Virginia Infantry, Col. Mayo; 24th Virginia Infantry.

4th Brigade, Brig. Gen. Stewart commanding.—9th Virginia Infantry; 14th Virginia Infantry, Col. White; 38th Virginia Infantry; 53d Virginia Infantry, Col. Eilet; 57th Virginia Infantry, Col. Fountain.

Pickett's division will not number three thousand men for duty. It is stationed at different points in front of the Army of the James.

Rebel Navy in the James River, John K. Mitchell Commanding.

Virginia, iron-clad, 4 guns; Richmond, iron-clad, 4 guns, Lieut. Warton; Fredericksburg, iron-clad, 4 guns, Capt. Rootes; Nansemond, wooden gunboat, 2 guns; Hampton, wooden gunboat, 2 guns; Beaufort, wooden gunboat, 1 gun; Raleigh, wooden gunboat, 1 gun.

ARMY OF THE JAMES

BEFORE RICHMOND, FEB. 14, 1865.

It is very evident that the resolutions of the ruling classes, recently passed in Richmond at the several meetings to urge a more vigorous prosecution of the war, are not regarded by the rebel rank and file as being binding upon them. This very action has tended to increase desertions from the enemy. The rebel soldiers seem to have come to the conclusion, that as all prospects of success are now at an end, their interests in the welfare of a Southern Republic cease, and have no compunctions in forsaking a color which is certain to entail upon its supporters a dishonorable death. Such resolutions from the chiefs at Richmond tend to foreshadow the fate of their duped soldiers, though it seems that many of them are becoming conscious of the necessity of looking after their own interests, and are leaving those who have come to the unalterable conclusion to continue the war until their independence is achieved, or fall in the struggle, to fight it out on their line of resolutions.

Where the picket lines of the confronting armies are close together there are some amusing incidents daily occurring. The destitute condition of the rebel soldiers serves to make them particularly polite to even our colored troops. In front of the 25th Corps (colored) our pickets have been in the habit of trading clothing for money and tobacco. The Johnnies would pay in gold or greenbacks for such articles as our boys would be willing to dispose of. A few days ago a very needy rebel approached our line, and selected certain things for which he was desirous of trading. Our colored pickets agreed to part with them, and handed them over. The Johnny paid in return such articles as he had on hand, and promised to make up the deficiency on the following day. The soldiers coolly informed him that they would receive what he brought, and, in order to make the trade satisfactory, he must throw himself in the bargain, which last condition was resignedly assented to under the persuasive influence of a couple of bayonets.

In front of Brig. Gen. Birney's lines this unfortunate practice of trading, by which means information, not unfrequently of a highly-prized character, is unintentionally communicated to the enemy, was too often indulged in. Stringent orders have been issued against it, much to the disgust of the rebels, who no doubt regard it as the most recent act of Lincoln despotism. Previous to these orders, and while bargains were being exchanged between the pickets, nothing could exceed the respectful bearing of the Johnnies towards our colored troops. They invariably addressed the white soldiers as "Yankees," but in approaching the colored ones, they always saluted each as "Uncle"—a word which is used by Southerners as a term of respect towards negroes. After orders had been promulgated against any and all intercourse with the enemy, by which his supply of necessary comforts were interdicted, the rebs forgot their former respect, and found consolation in calling our pickets "smoked Yankees," when they refused all communication with them.

Brig. Gen. Shepley,[10] who for some time has been the military governor of Norfolk, is to be Major Gen. Weitzel's chief of staff, vice Brig. Gen. Heckman, who has been disabled by a fall from a horse, and has gone home on a leave of absence. There is no reason why this acquisition to the 25th Corps should not give very general satisfaction.

ARMY OF THE JAMES

BEFORE RICHMOND, FEB. 15, 1865.

Yesterday was a fine day, indicating that spring was already upon us, and it was taken advantage of. Commands went through their manoeuvres more cheerfully, and the officers, without the haste occasioned by the cold weather, gave more attention to the troops and their evolutions. The most interesting of these ceremonies was the drill of General Draper's famous brigade of colored troops—a command that has distinguished itself on several occasions, and not unfrequently received especial mention from the general command-ing. The brigade is composed of the 22d U. S. C. T., who, under Colonel Kiddoo, achieved a name and a fame in front of Petersburg on the 15th of June, and at Newmarket Heights on the 29th of September. This regiment, regarded as among the best in the service,

10. George Foster Shepley (1819–1878) was a colonel, 12th Maine, during the campaign against New Orleans. He became military governor of Louisiana in June, 1862. Two years later, he was assigned to the District of Eastern Virginia. Shepley was promoted to chief of staff, XXV Corps, under Weitzel and was appointed military governor of Richmond following the Confederates' evacuation. *DAB*, IX, 78–79.

was recruited in Philadelphia, and the people of Pennsylvania may justly feel proud of its record. The 36th U. S. C. T., under Major Wm. H. Hart, and the 38th U. S. C. T., under Colonel Hall,[11] two North Carolina regiments, which have never in any instance wavered or faltered, and the 118th U. S. C. T., from Kentucky, constitute one of the best fighting brigades in the service.

It was this brigade, commanded by Brevet Brigadier General A. G. Draper, that was on drill yesterday, in a large field in the vicinity of Fort Brady. The regiments, with the exception of the 118th, have been in the service for some time and may be justly regarded as veterans. When the brigade was drawn up in line-of-battle it presented a fine martial appearance. The drill, in nearly every manoeuvre, was well executed, and the few slight mistakes which did occur were due, perhaps, to the misapprehension of commands rather than any other cause. The various intricate evolutions of the brigade drill were executed in a manner which was highly gratifying to both officers and men.

The rebel flag-of-truce boat William Allison came down to Cox's Landing yesterday afternoon, and received from Colonel Mulford, our commissioner of exchange, about seven hundred rebels, recently prisoners of war. They were mostly well clothed, and in good fighting condition. Some of our colored troops who were near by amused themselves by assuring them that, if they ever fell into their hands during an engagement, the Government would not be annoyed with complicated questions of exchange, so far as they were concerned. They reminded the Johnnies that they had not forgotten Fort Pillow, which was still their battle-shout. As the rebs approached their boat, they raised that yell of theirs, when our colored troops suggested to them they had better keep their breath, as they would want it soon when they got after them.

Some three or four hundred more rebel prisoners are at Varina, to go to Richmond to-day, and in a few hours we shall have the pleasure of welcoming one thousand of our returned heroes from Southern dungeons. The steamer New York, freighted with our brave but suffering soldiers, fresh from the charnel-house of southern torture, will start in a day or two for Annapolis, where these brave fellows

11. Robert M. Hall (d. 1874). A Scots, Hall mustered in as a sergeant and was brevetted brigadier general after Darbytown Road. Mark Mayo Boatner III, *The Civil War Dictionary* (New York, 1959), 366–67.

will no doubt receive a reception due to their merits and the services which they have rendered to their country.

In this connection it is but just to add that my letter of the 7th inst.,[12] which animadverted upon the consideration extended to Moseby, the horse thief, by certain officers, was, in no manner whatever, intended to reflect upon Colonel Mulford. During the exchange of prisoners, the Colonel is too much engrossed to attend to anything or any body but his official duties, and, besides, no one acquainted with him would suppose him to be capable of volunteering courtesies to a fellow after the pattern of Moseby. This statement is made in justice to Colonel Mulford, as some have thought that, as he was commissioner of exchange, the inference was that he either entertained the scape gallows or it was done with his consent and approval. In this matter Colonel Mulford is free from all complicity or suspicion.

Major General Weitzel has returned to the command of the 25th Corps. His headquarters have been besieged by officers anxious to pay their respects to him.

ARMY OF THE JAMES

BEFORE RICHMOND, FEB. 21, 1865.

Some time ago I informed you of the attention which the arming of negroes was receiving in the rebel capital, previous to the protracted discussion which the subject has since received in the Richmond papers and Confederate Congress. The public sentiment of rebeldom is not yet ripe for the measure, but it is being gradually prepared in such a manner as to commend it to general favor. From information which I deem reliable, I now inform you that at no very distant day the rebels will put negro troops in the field. It is only a question of time. The policy is not yet determined upon, but the influences at work will certainly be able to make the measure successful.

The impressions which I gave you of the feelings of the negroes, in reference to this use of themselves, may be relied upon as being the consolidated sentiment of the best informed bondmen and freemen. Discipline may influence some, and enlist their sympathies in the

12. I have been unable to find any dispatch dated February 7, nor is it clear who Moseby "the horse thief" is.

rebel cause, but the great majority may be regarded as so many allies in the enemy's camps. The organization of this element of supposed strength in the Confederate cause will from time to time furnish many interesting incidents to interest your readers.

This army still continues in its present position, rendering a more effective service to the cause of the Union than if it were to capture Richmond. The military combinations, in which the Army of the James is playing a quiet but important part, are gradually encircling the doomed Confederacy with inevitable destruction. The present aspect of military affairs will soon necessitate Lee to assume the offensive. One thing may be relied upon, that the situation never was more encouraging, nor has any campaign opened with more assurances of success than that which the respective armies, under the special direction of the Lieutenant General, are now entering upon. You will soon hear of a succession of brilliant movements which will carry grief to the enemy and joy to the hearts loyal to the Union.

The exchange of prisoners, which has been progressing at Varina Landing for the past week, has returned some two or three thousand of our suffering soldiers to homes of comfort and hearts of affection. Since one of the rebel flag-of-truce boats was blown up by one of their own torpedoes, the river is so obstructed with the wreck that the exchange of prisoners takes place at Boulware Landing, a point which may be regarded within the enemy's line. Some time this morning quite a number of our returned heroes are expected down from Richmond in return for an instalment of animated treason which was forwarded yesterday.

Brigadier General Wild, commanding the 1st Division of Colored Troops, 25th Corps, has gone North on a short leave of absence. General A. G. Draper is in temporary command of the division during his absence.

Mr. E. J. Courtney, who for some time acted as quartermaster's sergeant in the 36th United States Colored Troops, was, for meritorious discharge of his duties, promoted to second lieutenant, and recently to first lieutenant and regimental quartermaster in the 36th.

ARMY OF THE JAMES

BEFORE RICHMOND, FEB. 22, 1865.

Yesterday was a day of deliverance to one hundred and fifty officers and eleven hundred and eighty enlisted men from the prisons of the

South, and the terrible sufferings which depraved ingenuity could accomplish. The hardships and privations which they have been forced to endure have partially produced the effect which was intended. Disease was manifest in their countenances—idiocy was evident in their vacant and haggard staring, and death was written upon many in characters of unmistakable significance. With exultation those whose strength had been sufficient to pass through the ordeal were landed at the Boulware wharf, and walked about two miles to Varina, where they were received on our flag-of-truce boat by Lieut. Col. Mulford. These all bore evidence of having experienced the very greatest hardships, and looked as if considerable time would be necessary, under the best sanitary regulations, to restore them to a healthful and vigorous aspect. Some were hatless, shoeless, and almost clothesless, gathering their threaded garments around them as perfectly as possible to protect them from the frosted influence of the morning. They were all about half starved, and rushed for hard tack wherever our soldiers had the forethought to remember their destitution.

These prisoners came through that part of the lines held by the 25th (colored) Corps, and were received and welcomed with loud and prolonged cheering from the long line of troops, who crowded upon the breastworks and other convenient posts to testify their gratification at the return of these heroes.

One canal boat was towed down to Cox's Landing by an insignificant steamer, about teapot power, with our sick and wounded prisoners, from which they were conveyed to Varina, about a mile distant, in ambulances. Most of these suffering soldiers presented a spectacle of mingled misery, destitution, starvation, and horrible treatment. Officers and soldiers gathered around them, and in their honest indignation asserted that the rebels were not entitled to any consideration, nor should they receive, after such inhumanity, the treatment due to civilized nations. Some of the returned prisoners remarked that they would much love to have charge of rebels who have been captured, that they might return to them in kind the bitter usage to which they had been subjected. One said, "I used to treat them like Christians, but now I should not have any scruples, if I had them under my authority." The same one was interrogated, previous to leaving Danville, by a Johnny, as to what he would do with him should the "grayback" fall into his hands. His reply was, "I would rob you, kick you to the rear, and treat you afterwards with the corresponding indignities and sufferings to which I have been subjected." Among these returned prisoners is Major E. L. Brown, the paymaster, who was captured on the Baltimore and Ohio Railroad last summer, with sixty thousand dollars in greenbacks in his possession. The Major has formerly lived in Harrisburg, but at present has his residence in Lancaster, where his family hearth will soon be cheered by his presence.

From these prisoners I learned some melancholy facts. Our colored troops at Danville have not only been forced to erect breastworks for the cowardly rebels to skulk behind, but in several cases they have been severely whipped, when it pleased the Johnnies to administer such disgraceful castigation. Out of eighty-three colored soldiers who were captured last July and confined at Danville, only five survived the barbarous treatment which has been perpetrated upon them. In the same length of time, four out of twenty-six only have survived out of the 9th New Hampshire, and thirty-five out of one hundred and six in the 9th New York Heavy Artillery. From seven to nine bodies would be carried into the dead-house daily.

It was the custom to keep our men in the prisons until they were so near dead that frequently, on bringing them to the hospitals, they would not survive twenty-four hours after. As a sanitary regulation of these rebel institutions, it is obligatory upon patients to send out their clothing to be washed, which, if it is the comfortable uniform of our army, is never returned, but a suit of ragged gray is substituted instead. The hospital attendants, like all the other inhabitants of rebeldom, have no compunctions in boldly robbing all the soldiers of the Union, when powerless to defend themselves. Shortly after the assortment of blankets and clothing, which was recently forwarded to our prisoners, was distributed to those in Danville, many of whom were still left unsupplied, the hospital attendants were heard plotting among themselves how to get some of those from the prisons, who had been favored with these comforts, into the hospital, where, under the regulation of sending all clothing out to be cleansed, they could appropriate these articles to their own use.

One of the returned prisoners assures me that two of our colored soldiers, who were captured about last July, were taken into the woods by rebel officers, and placed as targets, where with their pistols they fired for their amusement and to improve their aim. This terrible affair was told in the presence of some of Brigadier General

Birney's fighting colored troops, who reaffirmed their resolution to avenge Fort Pillow and all other rebel atrocities. The accounts which these prisoners bring of their suffering and the treatment which they received fully confirm all previous information of rebel barbarity. The only food they received was corn bread and water, which may have been a little slower in the progress than arsenic, but equally as sure in its results. The men affirm that they have not tasted meat for four months.

The news of the evacuation of Charleston and the occupation of Columbia[13] was commemorated in this army yesterday by firing a salute of one hundred guns, and by protracted cheering along the entire lines.

To-day being Washington's Birthday, it will be observed by an abstenance from all duties but those which may be deemed necessary.

13. Threatened by Sherman's forces on the march from Georgia, and anxious to prevent the loss of the garrison, Confederate forces evacuated the city on February 17. They had evacuated Columbia the day before, setting fires that destroyed half the town. Foote, *The Civil War . . . Red River to Appomattox*, 792–93, 797, 800.

CHAPTER 7

Preparations for the Spring Offensive

ARMY OF THE JAMES

BEFORE RICHMOND, FEB. 23, 1865.

The weather is gradually moderating to a summer climate. The ground is sufficiently frosted during the night to enable persons to walk over it early in the morning without encountering any mud, but as soon as the sun comes forth we have the misfortune to experience several inches of disagreeable mire. The warming influences of advancing spring will soon evaporate the muculent roads, and leave them in a condition to favor the movements of any military operations. The more genial atmosphere is having a very pleasant effect upon the various commands in this army.

Yesterday being Washington's Birthday, and all unnecessary labor being suspended in the Army of the James, it was celebrated by a grand review of the 1st Division, 25th (colored) Corps, under Brevet Brigadier General A. G. Draper, by Major General Godfrey Weitzel, the commander of the corps. The hour for the ceremony was 11 o'clock, but some fifteen minutes before the time every regiment was in place, awaiting the reviewing general. The division was manoeuvered into three sides of a square, as none of the large fields in this vicinity were sufficient to enable it to form a line of battle. The lengthened lines presented quite a martial appearance, not unmingled with animation. The blackened shoes, though softed by the miry state of the ground; the shining bayonets, the glittering crosses, the cleansed clothing, the splendid banners of new regiments, without a blemish or a rent, and the perforated colors of veteran commands which have received their baptism of fire, presented a spectacle of discipline and military grandeur which very justly excited the admiration of all officers, and kindled conscious pride along the entire line.

The preparations incident to the ceremonies were all made by Gen. Draper, in that confident but easy manner which at once evinced his capacity for manoeuvering a division. He was well sustained by Col. Geo. M. Hale,[1] who commanded the 1st brigade, and Brevet Brig. Gen. Chas. S. Russell,[2] who headed the 2d brigade. Brig. Gen. Henry G. Thomas,[3] who marshaled the 3d brigade, did not get through without blundering. The respective staffs of these officers were out in all the paraphernalia of military display, and, being mounted upon pouncing steeds, presented quite an imposing appearance.

At the exact hour General Weitzel appeared on the ground upon his gray war charger, followed by a large retinue of officers and orderlies. The necessary formalities incident to the reception of the commanding general were conducted by the blasts from a bugle, sounded by General Draper in person, who, in fact, dispensing with the services of the fugleman, handsomely manoeuvered the division throughout the review by the sound of that instrument. As General Weitzel reviewed the respective brigades, the bands of each played "Hail to the Chief". While the division passed in review the marching was excellent, even the new regiment doing as well as could be expected. While this was being done a halt was caused on the right of the line, which necessitated a marking of time by one of the regiments in front of the reviewing officer, which was well done—a movement which, simple as it may seem, is scarcely ever well executed under similar circumstances.

All the regiments did well on the occasion, if some misapprehensions in the 118th U. S. C. T. may be overlooked. No particular one

1. There is no one by this name in the records. Draper commanded the 1st Brigade in February. There is a Colonel Robert M. Hall, commander of the 38th USCT, part of the 1st Brigade, to whom Chester refers in his February 15 dispatch. *OR*, Ser. I, Vol. XLVI, Pt. 2, p. 750.

2. Charles Sawyer Russell (d. 1866) mustered in as a sergeant and served as a captain in the 2nd Brigade, 2nd Division, V Corps, which fought at Fredericksburg in December, 1862. As a lieutenant colonel, he commanded six companies of the 28th USCT in Ferrero's division, which participated in the abortive Crater encounter. Mark Mayo Boatner III, *The Civil War Dictionary* (New York, 1959), 713; *OR*, Ser. I, Vol. XXI, p. 56, Ser. I, Vol. XL, Pt. 1, pp. 106–107.

3. Henry Goddard Thomas (1837–1897). A lawyer, Thomas mustered in as a captain, 5th Maine, and saw action at First Bull Run. He was rumored to be the first regular officer to accept a colonelcy of black troops, that of the 19th USCT. He was promoted to command the 2nd Brigade under Ferrero in May, 1864, and fought at the Crater and in the campaign against Richmond. Boatner, *The Civil War Dictionary*, 836–37; *OR*, Ser. I, Vol. XXXIII, p. 1046, Ser. I, Vol. XXXVI, Pt. 1, p. 114, Ser. I, Vol. XL, Pt. 1, p. 598.

can claim any superior credit, either in bearing or evolutions, but it must be confessed that the 43d U. S. C. T.,[4] recruited in Pennsylvania, attired in cleansed white leggings, attracted a good deal of attention. The object of reviews on a large scale is to demonstrate whether there is sufficient discipline in the respective commands to induce the commanding general to rely upon their obedience to all orders, and a prompt execution of all plans. That fact was clearly manifest in the punctuality and address of the entire division. A ready and cheerful compliance with all orders is one of the chief characteristics of the colored soldiers, whether in camp or in the field.

Gen. Weitzel's headquarters were illuminated last night, in honor of the many victories which have recently blessed the cause of the Union.

There was considerable cannonading in front of Petersburg yesterday morning, but I have not learned that it was anything more than the general spirit of the complimentary exchange of civilities which have so long been in practice before that city.

ARMY OF THE JAMES

BEFORE RICHMOND, FEB. 26, 1865.

The military situation in Virginia, and particularly at this point, promises to furnish soon some interesting developments. The combinations of the commander-in-chief of the armies of the United States are gradually encircling Lee and his forces, whom he has driven into trenches around Petersburg and Richmond, with a cordon of moveable columns which will soon change the aspect of affairs. One important thing seems now settled, that Lee will soon be obliged to assume the offensive or leave his best fortified position without fighting. The complications which threaten the Confederacy are so numerous that but little doubt is entertained as to the advantage which has already been gained by strategy, and brilliant prospects now loom up in advance of the spring campaign. Officers begin to see

4. Organized in Pennsylvania in June, 1864, the 43rd USCT joined the 4th Division, IX Corps, and fought in the Battle of the Crater. It was then transferred to the XXV Corps. Frederick H. Dyer, *Compendium of the War of the Rebellion* (Des Moines, Iowa, 1908), 250; Frederick M. Binder, "Pennsylvania Negro Regiments in the Civil War," *Journal of Negro History,* XXXVII (1952), 412–13.

the end of the war, and to speculate that military campaigning upon any large scale will not be necessary after the next four months. From this standpoint the end seems in view. The weather is not at all favorable for military operations, but the enemy, being so sorely pressed on all sides, may be driven to attack our fortified positions, or to evacuate his strongholds. News of a battle or an evacuation may reach you any day.

Day before yesterday, one thousand more of our brave prisoners of war, from North and South Carolina, were exchanged at Cox's Landing. They look as destitute and have suffered as much as any previous company of victims of the barbarism of the South.

There was some firing last evening in the direction of Petersburg. A report was in circulation yesterday that that city was being evacuated, from which you may judge of the cheering confidence which animates the armies here. There is smoke, it is true, but the fire will soon be seen.

ARMY OF THE JAMES

BEFORE RICHMOND, FEBRUARY 28, 1865.

It has been customary to announce that in consequence of the unfavorable weather military operations for the time would be necessarily suspended. The roads now are in a horrible condition, and it is not probable that the weather for some weeks to come will improve them. Notwithstanding these symptoms, from which one would naturally infer a period of inactivity, there is a probability that strategy may attempt to neutralize the present inconvenience; and bring on one of the most terrible battles of the war. Fortunately for the cause of the Union arms, the enemy will be obliged to assume the offensive. He must attempt something soon, or lose the last opportunity of even problematical success. In a case where the existence of the best army of the rebellion, with its chief, is involved, it is not likely that weather or bad roads will delay the enemy, for he is aware that by waiting for them he seals his own destruction.

The rebel papers for the past day or so pretend that Gen. Grant is massing a large force to make an attack near Hatcher's Run, and at the same time they assure their readers that proper dispositions have been made to receive him. This may be set down as an effort to throw our forces there off their guard. The dodge will not work, for either of the Union armies in this vicinity is prepared to repel any assault which the rebels, from the necessity of their circumstances, must make at no very distant day. Gen. Grant is master of the situation.

ARMY OF THE JAMES

BEFORE RICHMOND, MARCH 2, 1865.

Yesterday was the first day of spring, and if it did not quite equal our expectation in the genial influences of the climate, it changed the monotony of camp life by an incident which gave rise to considerable speculation about the various headquarters. Our sluggish blood ran quicker, and our eyes opened wider, when, almost before the least intimation, Mrs. Lieut. Gen. Anderson, Mrs. Murdock, Miss Murdock and servant, G. Taylor Jenkins, and two little girls, on their way to reside with their grandmother, and said to be the nieces of Senator Chandler, drove into our lines in rebel ambulances. With the exception of the two children, they were all possessed with the necessary passes from the authorities at Washington. Mr. Jenkins was permitted to go beyond our lines, and is just returning.

The reticence of the entire party gives coloring to the impression that, though driven by inexorable circumstances to seek a residence in the North, like other kindred spirits, they may not lose any opportunity to manifest, while enjoying the bounty and favor of the Government, their partiality for the traitor Davis and his subordinates. The females looked seedy and much in want of apparel to correspond with their pretensions. The effect of blockaded ports was evident in their appearance, but in Philadelphia or New York, when robed in fashion and extravagance, and partaking of the honest bread of loyalty, they may be in a good condition to espouse most violently, like all other rebels in the North, the cause of Davis and his crew. This rebel lieutenant general's wife claims that she has a nephew on the staff of General Grant.

The party spent some time at General Draper's headquarters, after which they were forwarded to General Ord, under the escort of Lieut. Seymour C. Hawkes, who, probably selected for his pleasing exterior, performed that duty with a delicacy that sustained General Draper's choice.

All military operations may be regarded as suspended, so far as this army is concerned, until the weather shall improve the roads to a passable condition.

From refugees I learn that the rebels have already begun to drill the negroes in Richmond, in squads, preparatory to the part which every one is confident the rebel Congress will authorize them to play in the spring campaign.

ARMY OF THE JAMES
BEFORE RICHMOND, MARCH 3, 1865.

About a week ago we had a prospect of active operations, but the daily rains and almost impassable condition of the roads make it next to impossible for an army to advance. Fortunately for our cause, the indications are that the rebels will be obliged to assault our strongly entrenched positions. We are expecting it, and have been disappointed more through the influence of unfavorable weather than the disposition of the enemy. When the muddy swamps—for the roads can be likened unto nothing better—shall be dried up and admit of active operations, the strong probability is that the shock of arms will be heard all over the land.

Recruits are beginning to arrive in cheering numbers. Many of the depleted regiments will soon be up to their maximum number. This is very cheering to the bronzed heroes of many battles, and gives them that practical assurance of sympathy which never fails to have a good effect.

Among the recruits sent here we unfortunately find specimens of that vile class called "bounty-jumpers", who, when placed on picket, desert with their arms and equipments, which they hope to sell to the rebel authorities. These renegades are announced in the Richmond papers as deserters from the Yankee army to strengthen the wavering minds, to stimulate the drooping spirits, and stiffen the weak knees which the tottering state of the Confederate concern has everywhere engendered. This class of recruits is not wanted here, and it would be better to furnish them with opportunities to desert before they reach the front and carry arms over to the enemy with which to shoot Union soldiers.

Wonders never will cease. Mr. Brady,[5] the correspondent of the

5. John A. Brady.

New York *Herald*, and not unfrequently spoken of as the best one from that establishment in the Army of the James, has already signified his willingness to lay aside the quill, buckle on the sword, and accept, from preference, a captaincy in some colored organization. We may well exclaim that the world moves, when an attache of the *Herald*, who so long underrated the character and qualifications of the negro, consents to occupy such a relation with him. How long Mr. Brady may have been in arriving at this conclusion I am not prepared to say, but even at this late day he is to be congratulated for a choice which some of America's best soldiers have long since made. Such a conversion is well worth a special despatch, but concurrent items have deprived Mr. Brady of that distinction.

Some time ago I intimated that the resolutions, which have so frequently appeared in the Richmond papers, purporting to express the sentiments of the rebel conscripts, were not genuine exponents of their feelings. I have now the authority for speaking more definitely. At the meetings held in the various regiments, in which there was a free interchange of opinions, and a fair and satisfactory vote as to whether the soldiers would return to the Union and enjoy peace upon the basis of the propositions submitted by President Lincoln at Fortress Monroe, a considerable desire to return to the old Government was shown. In the 1st, 2d, 5th, and 6th South Carolina Regiments, and the 16th and 17th North Carolina troops, the greater portion were in favor of peace and Union. The propositions of Mr. Lincoln were submitted to the armies of the enemy around Richmond and Petersburg for their expression of opinion, and, strange to say, there was a large majority in favor of returning to their allegiance. The Texas brigade, Gary's cavalry,[6] and some other organizations voted in the negative, but the result was, as stated, against the rebellion. The officers, however, instead of publishing the expressed and known opinion of the men, drew up resolutions pledging the rank and file to an unwavering and protracted prosecution of the war until rebel independence should be achieved. This action surprised no

    6. "Gary's cavalry" was led by Brigadier General Martin Witherspoon Gary (1831–1881), Harvard graduate and a lawyer. He had fought at both Bull Run battles, the Peninsula campaign, Antietam, and Chickamauga, among other significant battles of the war. He commanded the remnants of the 7th South Carolina ("Hampton's Legion"), the 24th Virginia, and a portion of the 7th Georgia at war's end. A. A. Hoehling and Mary Hoehling, *The Day Richmond Died* (San Diego, 1981), 148–49; Boatner, *The Civil War Dictionary*, 326.

one so much as it did the majority of the regiments who voted just the reverse.

When the Richmond papers came to camp with the false resolutions, there was the greatest indignation manifested by the men against the officers. The most violent utterances were made against those who had perpetrated such a gross wrong upon them. If the aristocratic traitors at the rear were deceived by these resolutions, the subsequent and more expressive action of the Johnnies, wherever opportunity has offered, may serve to awaken them from their delusion. I refer to the large number who daily come into our lines; and the larger numbers who, disgusted with the rebel authorities for continuing a struggle in which no one has the slightest prospect of success, are returning to their homes in defiance of the entreaties of Lee or the penalties of Davis. So great is the demoralization in the rebel camps in our front, that as soon as information reaches them that Sherman has captured any important point, the men, in presence of their officers, cheer for Sherman, not even excepting South Carolina regiments. The more rapid and successful his marches, the more confident are they of the speedy termination of the rebellion.

It is proper here to state that the impression is very general among the rebel troops that the war is continued merely to save those most guilty from the impending penalties. Not the ghost of a belief lingers even in the fruitful imagination of the most credulous rebel of anything approaching towards the realization of dreams of independence. The men believe that even now the officers are planning means of escape to Texas, where they can easily cross to Mexico, and leave their deluded followers to their fate. This matter is openly discussed among the rebel troops in their camps, and this may account for the daily depletion of the enemy's ranks. The men are determined to get the start of their officers in the race for life by availing themselves of the inducements which General Grant holds out to deserters.

Poor Jeff Davis does not seem to have any friends on either side of the line. The repentant rebels are very severe against him, and nothing would please them better than to witness the just retribution which his crimes have merited. They all think, however, that he will make good his escape from the country before he shall be entirely surrounded. Jeff is very unpopular with the enemy, many of whom would cheerfully shoot him, if a favorable opportunity occurred.

It is also the general belief in the enemy's camp that Richmond is being evacuated, or that preparations having that end in view are in progress, so that at the necessary time but little delay may be required. For some time it has been death to any rebel soldier to go any distance to the rear from his camp. This stringent order is supposed to conceal what may be transpiring within the inner lines. Vendors of pies and cakes from Richmond inform their soldiers that all the heavy guns are being removed, and such other dispositions are being made as to leave no doubt that preparations are actively on foot for the evacuation of this citadel of the rebellion. It is generally admitted that Lynchburg will be the next place in which the army of Lee will endeavor to fortify itself, should it fall back from its present position. All this is highly probable, and would not surprise any one here, if it should take place at any time after the roads shall have been improved to a passable condition.

I have been informed, by persons whose intelligence and candor give weight to their statements, and whose opportunities for becoming acquainted with the facts have been most favorable, that it is the settled conclusion of thousands of the enemy's troops to remain where they are, and be captured when Richmond is evacuated. This resolution having become so general, and so well known by both officers and men, that a general order has been issued, and read at dress parade, that any person found in the rear of his regiment without a surgeon's certificate of disability is to be immediately shot. This order has also stimulated many to come into our lines.

ARMY OF THE JAMES

BEFORE RICHMOND, MARCH 21, 1865.

Yesterday about noon this army was thrilled with the gratifying intelligence that General Sheridan and forces had arrived safely into these lines, in the vicinity of Deep Bottom. The horses looked a little jaded, the men somewhat bronzed by exposure, but bearing themselves like conquerors and evincing the most confident assurances of their ability to repeat the thrashing exercises upon Lee with which Early is so familiar. They marched like true soldiers, under the inspiration of their commander, with an apparent faith in his ability to bring them out of every conflict with honor. General Sheridan came mounted upon a black horse, equipped in an overcoat which, in the absence of the usual insignia, concealed his rank. His unostentatious manner, and the amiable deportment which he evinced towards the members of his staff, are some of the influences which endear him to his command. The General planted his headquarters' flag at Jones' Landing, on the James river, where he was joined by a number of officers of his army who had been North, absent on a leave, and remained there no matter how long. Due notice will be given of his operations in the future, which must satisfy public curiosity until something more tangible is forwarded for their consideration.

Another event of yesterday which attracted considerable attention in this army was the arrival of President Lincoln, and his reviewing parts of the 24th and 25th Corps. Both white and colored troops looked well, and, if possible, marched better than on former occasions. It was a grand sight, and must have been a source of considerable satisfaction to his Excellency, Mrs. Lincoln, Miss Wells, and other ladies who accompanied the President to the front and witnessed the martial ceremonies. A host of generals also swelled the suite of the Commander-in-chief to proportions beyond the primitive ideas of republican simplicity.

Everything is quiet along the lines this morning. The sun in unbroken splendor is just emerging from behind the trees, which betokens one of those pleasant and refreshing days of spring that give renewed vigor to humanity. Affairs here are progressing as rapidly as can be expected or could be desired.

BERMUDA HUNDRED, MARCH 22, 1865.

The apprehended but not dreaded realities which will soon cloud the air with smoke, and crimson the soil of Virginia with the mingled blood of patriots and traitors, is momentarily approximating to a crisis. It can no longer be regarded as contraband to assure the loyal and anxious minds of the country that the past winter has been spent in the most thorough preparation for a vigorous spring campaign; that the soldiers are cheerfully conscious of the hope which solicitude cherishes; that movable columns are ready to attack, or lend support, should our lines be assaulted, at a moment's notice; and that among all the troops the most perfect confidence exists as to the speedy termination of the rebellion, through the terrible combinations which will shortly manifest themselves in the maturity of their development. The scenes which will soon be enacted here would, if it were not for our civilization, which shudders at misery and sickens at the necessary sacrifices upon the country's altar, be regarded, in the martial array of concentration; in the full equipments and appliances which science has developed in the art of war; in the measured tramp of armies; in the clash of steel, and in the victorious shouts of a triumphant army, as attaining a standard of sublimity unequalled in resources and power. Not even the groans of the dying can altogether shade the glory of the living, though it has been achieved through fields of blood and carnage. A spectacle will soon be presented to the nation which, in the grandeur of its success, will lift the loyal hearts and eyes from the graves and hospitals to the fullest admiration of Lieut. Gen. Grant and his victorious army. Let these assurances suffice until the country is electrified with the official announcement of what is here foreshadowed.

Furloughed officers and soldiers are now returning in great numbers daily to their regiments. They come back cheered and reinvigorated by the influences of home, and especially with the blessings of the valiant home guard. Their own pleasant countenances, smiling with cherished recollections, united with the tokens of affection and friendship from loved ones at home to those who have been obliged to remain with their commands, have changed their countenances, which had been elongated by disappointment, to a degree of liveliness which could only have been effected by such substantial assurances. Soldiers are generally solicitous to visit their homes, but they are equally as anxious to return to their regiments. There is a charm about the service, with all of its dangers, which allures the patriot to embrace it regardless of its consequences. In a spirit of renewed devotion, and sacrifice, if necessary, these light-hearted heroes are stepping into their places with alacrity, to be ready for the long-looked for word which shall thrill the grand Army of the James—Forward!

I have just seen some Indian refugees of the Rommonkey tribe, a small remnant of whom reside upon an island in King William county, surrounded by the river Rommonkey, which, with another stream, forms the York river, who left the White House Landing day before yesterday morning, where they left Gen. Sheridan and a very large force. It is now some nine days since Sheridan's army camped in the vicinity of the White House, where it is well supported by gunboats and supplied with subsistence. No rebels are, or have been, between him and Richmond, excepting scouts. The daily communications of the Indians with Richmond afforded them abundant opportunity of becoming acquainted with the position of the enemy's forces. Sheridan was then, if not nearer now, within thirty-five miles of Richmond, and with no fortifications on that line extending beyond three miles from the city. It is no wonder that the camps along this line are enlivened by that animating song, "Babylon is Falling".

The weather here for several days past has been most excellent. Yesterday we experienced just rain enough to settle the dust, which came in such frequent showers as to quicken our apprehensions for the condition of the roads. They could not be better at present. During the night the equinoctial gale raged with considerable fury. The artillery, which could not be heard in consequence of the storm, but the flash of which could be seen in the vicinity of Dutch Gap, justified the impression that our forces are marshaling for a combined assult upon the rebel strongholds. Had it not been for the rain of yesterday, which threatens to be protracted, and render the roads impassable, and the storm of last night, the readers of *The Press* would have been electrified with the details of active operations at some point along our extended lines, instead of the despatch which is herewith submitted.

This morning has dawned beautifully, and the sun shines brightly, with no impediment in the roads, or weather to prevent an advance.

ARMY OF THE JAMES

BEFORE RICHMOND, MARCH 24, 1865.

Reviews and drills are the constant occupation of this army, which is attaining a degree of excellence highly satisfactory. The men have faith in their ability to accomplish what may be committed to their valor, and the commanding generals have the fullest confidence in the efficiency of their soldiers.

Deserters from the enemy continue to come into our lines as

rapidly as circumstances will permit. Many of these ragged specimens of repentant humanity are obliged to run the gauntlet of death to reach our lines; still, they come with the same old stories of exhaustion and inability of the South to continue the struggle much longer. With the daily depletion of the rebel ranks and the arrival of recruits to ours, it is no longer a doubt as to the fate of the rebellion. Confidence and courage will soon explode the whole affair.

The following general order foreshadows light marching orders and active operations. It is by such straws, in the absence of more definite intelligence, we are tolerable well assured of what is to follow:

HEADQUARTERS DEPARTMENT OF VIRGINIA. ARMY OF THE JAMES

BEFORE RICHMOND, VA., MARCH 20, 1865.

GENERAL ORDERS No. 33—Corps commanders and officers commanding independent divisions or brigades will see that the baggage of their commands is reduced to the lowest possible limits.

The surplus baggage of all officers and enlisted men can be sent to Capt. Blunt, A. Q. M., at Norfolk, for storage. To avoid loss, all the baggage of a regiment must be sent off at a time, and each package or box must be indelibly marked with the name of the owner, his regiment, brigade, and division, and also numbered. The regimental quartermaster will prepare an abstract containing the names of all those sending baggage, with the numbers marked on it, set opposite their names, and will give each person a check numbered correspondingly to that on the baggage and abstract. These abstracts will be made in duplicate, the regimental quartermaster retaining one copy for reference, and sending one copy to the corps quartermaster, who will forward it to Capt. Blunt, A. Q. M., at Norfolk. Capt. Blunt will assign some suitable person to the charge of these abstracts, and will have the baggage stowed in such manner as to be readily found by reference to the abstract of the regiment when the check of any officer or enlisted man wanting his baggage is sent him. The baggage will be carefully guarded and safely kept.

The allowance of personal property to each officer in the field will be a small valise and a blanket roll for bedding. All cumbersome or useless articles, such as benches, bedsteads, cook-stoves, and unnecessary mess arrangements, will be dispensed with. No hospital tents will be carried, except those of the medical department, save one to each corps headquarters, for an office; all papers, desks, and material not absolutely necessary, must be stored; uniform coats of enlisted men, and overcoats, and all save a change of clothing, should be sent away; the blouse will be worn instead of the uniform coats.

This order will be carried into effect at once, and no request to send baggage to the rear after that of regiments has been once sent, will be regarded.

Suitable guards will be allowed—of convalescent men—to go in charge of baggage, and store it at Norfolk.

Corps commanders and commanders of independent divisions and brigades will be responsible for the execution of this order, and will give instructions in regard to the details necessary to carry it into effect.

By command of Major General Ord;

THEODORE READ,
Assistant Adjutant General.

ARMY OF THE JAMES

BEFORE RICHMOND, MARCH 26, 1865.

Another week is ended, and another Sabbath has dawned. The daily routine of affairs scarcely differs from any other day, with the exception that no fatigue parties but what are deemed imperatively necessary are required to labor on the Sabbath. The soldiers generally give their clothes an extra brush, patronise the sutlers for a paper collar, and those from whom the early impressions of piety are not entirely erased attend the rudely-constructed chapels, where the Gospel is preached unto them. We are within six miles of Richmond this morning, but where will we be next Sunday!

One of those nice little ceremonies which illustrate the cordiality, respect, and confidence which exist between officers and their superior occurred an evening or two ago at the headquarters of Brevet Brig. Gen. Alonzo G. Draper. The members of his staff, after his amiable adjutant general, Lieut. W. H. Rock, had enticed him from his quarters, passed in unobserved and pleasantly seated themselves. The moment the General entered the door, and before he had time to recover from the surprise which the scene occasioned, Lieut. G. C. Prichard began to address him in a very impressive manner—to assure him of the respect which members of the staff possessed for him as a gentleman, and the confidence which they reposed in him as a soldier—that such expressions were not the adulations of a flatterer, but the sentiments of the gentlemen by whom he was surrounded, whose opportunities were unlimited for acquainting themselves with the attributes of his character. After many other good things well spoken by the Lieutenant, he presented to the general, in the name of the staff, a splendid sword, elaborately gotten up, a magnificent sash, and superb belt. The whole affair being a perfect surprise, General Draper, being unprepared for such a mark of respect and affection, found considerable difficulty in recovering his usual composure. He appropriately thanked the staff for their assurances, and accepted the articles in the same spirit in which they were given. His reply had the ring of a man who had done his duty with an approving conscience.

This was not one of those presentations so frequently gotten up in the Army of the Potomac, where some general, anxious for a little distinction, agrees to defray all the expenses of the gifts, and furnish what frequently follows such scenes, if a few officers will only make him the hero of the occasion.

A great many mysterious manoeuvres are being made along these lines, which, if they puzzle the rebels as much as they do us, will make the strategy of General Grant complete. Everything continues in a state of fermentation; still, all is quiet, which resembles the calm that precedes the storm. There are certain forebodings, which no one can mistake, that indicate that the word "Forward" will soon be heard along these lines.

The very best spirits pervade the troops in this army. They are weary of their life of inactivity and long to grapple with the Johnnies. They will give a good account of themselves.

The enemy is doing a rushing business in recruiting their depleted armies with negro troops. Some twenty thousand are already as-sembled at Camp Lee in the vicinity of Richmond, and the number is rapidly increasing. Twenty-two regiments are in progress of forma-tion, which is having a very exhilarating effect upon the spirits of the quaking rebels. The officers of colored troops in this army, knowing the merits of the race as soldiers, are a little anxious to learn whether the negroes can be induced to fight for the South. They will, no doubt, inflict terrible results upon our forces, with a view to disarm the suspicions of the rebels, and also to improve their opportunities to escape to that freedom which the Union promises, but which is denied in Jeffdom. The negroes thoroughly understand this war, and no fears need be entertained for them, as they will, without doubt, turn right side up with care at the earliest practicable moment.

The weather this morning is just cool enough to be refreshing, with a fair prospect of warming up to an uncomfortable degree before the day is over. It is such Sabbaths as this that cause soldiers to think of home, and the old church where, with their families, they have so frequently worshipped.

Senator Lane, of Kansas,[7] and suite, who have been on a visit to the front for several days past, receiving considerations from Gens. Grant, Ord, and Meade, were the guests of Captain Dearing, of the mail boat Dictator, last night, upon which they will take passage for Washington this morning.

ARMY OF THE JAMES

BEFORE RICHMOND, MARCH 28, 1865.

"Now, by St. Paul the work goes bravely on". At last there is something tangible to allay our conjectures, and give an insight into movements which are in motion to open the spring campaign. Commands have put the war paint on, and are now upon the war path, and before this reaches you you may learn more thrilling information through official sources. Operations in this department may be regarded as commenced, the nature of which I deem prudent to withhold for the present. The rebels are hardly prepared for the strategy which is at this moment effectually checkmating them, though their manifest uneasiness indicate that they have some forebodings of the approaching retribution. Upon the eve of a great battle there has generally been some anxiety as to the result, but in

7. James Henry Lane (1814–1866). A Mexican War veteran, Lane is best known as a leading free-soil advocate in the bloody battles in Kansas during the 1850s. He was elected a Republican senator and, when Kansas was admitted to the Union in 1861, represented the state in Washington. He raised a number of regiments during the war and throughout was an ardent supporter of Lincoln. DAB, V, 576–77.

this case there is an unswerving confidence in the ability of the movable columns, the thunders of whose artillery will be heard before many hours have passed, to accomplish all that General Grant has undertaken.

The evacuation of Richmond for some weeks has frequently been announced in *The Press* as being actually in progress. It is now credited in the best military circles to such an extent as to make a disposition of the forces to meet such a contingency. The authorities obtain their information from scouts and reliable persons, which is to the effect that all cumbersome munitions of war and contraband property are being removed from the city. Lee must either assault our works, and what is more difficult, defeat our armies, or vacate his stronghold, if he would save his hordes from immediate capture. It is more than probable that he will give up Richmond with accumulated regrets, and fall back to some point where he can best defend himself and receive supplies for his army. His decision upon this matter will, no doubt, depend considerably upon the combined movements of Lieutenant General Grant, who has, no doubt, caused the said Lee the most unpleasant anxiety of his unnatural life.

The weather, that necessary concomitant to all martial movements, is in a most excellent condition, with not even a cloud to dampen our spirits or delay the operations.

The protracted stay of Sheridan and his forces at the White House gave his men abundant time to rest, and on their junction with the united armies confronting Richmond and Petersburg they were ready to undertake, in co-operation with Meade and Ord, such plans as the commander-in-chief wished executed.

ARMY OF THE JAMES

BEFORE RICHMOND, MARCH 30, 1865.

THE GREAT WORK COMMENCED.

Yesterday was a day of anxiety to those who were aware that General Grant proposed to move upon the enemy's works, not so much from fear of the result, as the fact that all seemed quiet along the lines. About ten o'clock last night the flash of artillery, with its rumbling report, indicated that the ball was open.

A VITAL POINT STRUCK ON THE 29TH.

It can no longer be regarded as contraband to announce, if you have not already been informed, that a grand movable column was put in motion on the 27th instant. Never did soldiers strike their tents with more pleasant spirits of assurance or greater confidence. The long-looked for advance came, but found them cheerfully ready. A vital point was probably assaulted last night; if not carried by them, will most likely be this morning, which, without doubt, will be the beginning of successive victories in Virginia. As there has been no firing heard since daybreak, let us suppose the victory is gained, rather than delayed by the rain which commenced about three o'clock this morning, and has continued in showers for the past five hours.

STORY OF A "UNION MAN".

Since so many influential persons, who, in the early days of the rebellion, were its most violent supporters, and most venomous against the Union, are, like rats whose instincts lead them to avoid danger, deserting the Confederacy, it is nothing more than proper that the acts of such should be placed upon record, that the authorities may judge whether they acted under constraint, or willingly espoused the cause of treason. In this vicinity there is an individual named Albert Aiken,[8] who has had the good fortune to reside in the finest dwelling along the banks of the James; whose cultivated farms were extensive, soil rich, and negroes plenty. When the war broke out Mr. Aiken, who, in all probability, belonged to the F. F. V.'s—it would be a curiosity in this State to find an individual who does not urge his claims to that distinction—was one of the most rabid rebels in Virginia. He distinguished himself above others for his unmerciful persecution of free colored persons for their loyalty to the old flag. At Deep Bottom, about one mile and a half below Aiken's Landing, on the left bank of the James river, resided quite a number of industrious persons of color, previous to the war, who supported themselves by fishing and farming in their respective seasons. The timid policy of the Government with reference to negroes was well

8. Albert M. Aiken (?–?). Near the home of this major landowner, in 1862, prisoners of war were exchanged. Francis Trevelyan Miller (ed.), *The Photographic History of the Civil War* (10 vols.; New York, 1957), VII, 109, 111, 113, 115.

understood by these people when McClellan was in command of the armies. They purposely abstained from having any communication with our fleet when it first ascended the James. When the rebels began to put torpedoes into the river no one labored harder in the execution of this nefarious undertaking than Mr. Aiken. In company with his brother James, who was then in the rebel service, and a Captain Davis, he not only submerged these infernal machines, but made their existence the plea for continued persecution upon the loyal people at Deep Bottom. After a great many pretexts, he had men, women, and children seized by a squadron of cavalry and carried to Richmond upon a gunboat, upon charge of giving information to our navy on the occasion of its first visit up the river. The soldiers of course plundered the houses, and left them all without an inmate to look after their furniture. Mr. Aiken, in his zeal for the rebel cause, upon his oath, charged Robert Fagan, Wm. Scott, and Edward Bowman with having communicated with our fleet and giving the officers information. There is abundant testimony in the vicinity to convict Mr. Aiken of perjury. After an imprisonment of a few weeks the men, women, and children were discharged, but his insatiable desire to harass these loyal people did not cease. Through his influence he procured an order which prohibited them from returning within two miles of their homes, which they had accumulated by honest industry. These deserted houses, by which Mr. Aiken passed daily to personally superintend the putting of torpedoes into the river, had no influence upon his stony heart, though their inmates were, through his instrumentality, made wanderers. In the course of time General Butler, with his forces, incorporated Mr. Aiken's house within his lines. Instead of being consistent and following his retreating comrades in crime into Richmond, he remains and proclaims himself a Union man. Even under such circumstances, while wearing the loyal mask, he could not control his venomous disposition against the negroes for what he proclaimed, in the Court House at Richmond, to be their disloyalty to the South. As incredible as it may seem, Mr. Aiken, after being the ringleader in placing torpedoes in the river to blow up our gunboats—after having, by a military order, driven all the colored families from their homes for fear they would point out the infernal machines to our naval officers, and after having had some of them severely punished for returning for some of their property—this specimen of Southern chivalry actually points out to the naval fleet the deserted houses as those of the persons who submerged the torpedoes, and who ran away, on the approach of the fleet, for fear of punishment. The sailors immediately applied the torch to the humble homes of the loyal blacks, and they were all consumed. Gen. Butler, whom rebels never cheated, only took one look at this individual, which was sufficient to consign him to one of the cells in the Rip Raps,[9] where he remained until General Ord assumed command of this department. Mr. Aiken, of course, announces himself as a Union man. There are plenty more like him in Richmond, who will soon be fugitives and outcasts from their native land.

Mr. Aiken did the cause of the Union all the harm he could while it was in his power, and wronged the loyal people of this part of Virginia to the extent of his malignant disposition. These persons should not be made to suffer without some restitution, and the most becoming under the circumstances would be the sequestering of sufficient amount of his lands for those whose homes were reduced to ashes upon his false representations. In this connection it may be appropriate to state that Mr. Aiken with his own hands inflicted a frightful gash with a shovel upon the head of Wm. Scott, an old man some 55 years of age, for declining to work upon Drewry's Bluff fortifications in consequence of the infirmities accompanying his age. It is expected that many great rebels will escape the punishment due their offences, but it is to be hoped that Mr. Albert Aiken will receive a proportion commensurate with his guilty record.

Kautz in a New Command.

Brevet Major General A. V. Kautz, of cavalry fame, has assumed command of the 1st Division, in the 25th Corps, vice Brigadier General Ed. A. Wild, who is assigned to the command of the 2d Brigade. The fact that regular army officers accept such important trusts among colored troops is an evidence of the high opinion which this element of strength is regarded in this army.

9. A fortification one mile south of Fortress Monroe near Norfolk. Richard Wheeler, *Sword Over Richmond: An Eyewitness History of McClellan's Peninsula Campaign* (New York, 1986), 174–75.

CHAPTER 8

The Fall of Richmond

HALL OF CONGRESS

RICHMOND, APRIL 4, 1865.

Seated in the Speaker's chair, so long dedicated to treason, but in the future to be consecrated to loyalty, I hasten to give a rapid sketch of the incidents which have occurred since my last despatch.

To Major General Godfrey Weitzel was assigned the duty of capturing Richmond. Last evening he had determined upon storming the rebel works in front of Fort Burnham. The proper dispositions were all made, and the knowing ones retired with dim visions of this stronghold of treason floating before them. Nothing occurred in the first part of the evening to awaken suspicion, though for the past few days it has been known to the authorities that the rebels, as I informed you, were evacuating the city. After midnight explosions began to occur so frequently as to confirm the evidence already in possession of the General-in-chief, that the last acts of an out-generalled army were in course of progress. The immense flames curling up throughout the rebel camps indicated that they were destroying all that could not be taken away.

The soldiers along the line gathered upon the breastworks to witness the scene and exchange congratulations. While thus silently gazing upon the columns of fire one of the monster rams was exploded, which made the very earth tremble. If there was any doubt about the evacuation of Richmond that report banished them all. In a very few moments, though still dark, the Army of the James, or rather that part of it under General Weitzel, was put in motion.

It did not require much time to get the men in light-marching order. Every regiment tried to be first. All cheerfully moved off with accelerated speed. The pickets which were on the line during the night were in the advance.

Brevet Brigadier General Draper's brigade of colored troops, Brevet Major General Kautz's division, were the first infantry to enter Richmond. The gallant 36th U. S. Colored Troops, under Lieutenant Colonel B. F. Pratt, has the honor of being the first regiment. Captain Bicnnef's company has the pride of leading the advance.

The column having passed through Fort Burnham, over the rebel works, where they were moving heavy and light pieces of artillery, which the enemy in his haste was obliged to leave behind, moved into the Osborn road, which leads directly into the city.

In passing over the rebel works, we moved very cautiously in single file, for fear of exploding the innumerable torpedoes which were planted in front. So far as I can learn none has been exploded, and no one has been injured by those infernal machines. The soldiers were soon, under engineers, carefully digging them up and making the passage way beyond the fear of casualties.

Along the road which the troops marched, or rather double quicked, batches of negroes were gathered together testifying by unmistakable signs their delight at our coming. Rebel soldiers who had hid themselves when their army moved came out of the bushes, and gave themselves up as disgusted with the service. The haste of the rebels was evident in guns, camp equipage, telegraph wires, and other army property which they did not have time to burn.

When the column was about two miles from Richmond General Weitzel and staff passed by at a rapid speed, and was hailed by loud cheering. He soon reached the city, which was surrendered to him informally at the State House by Mr. Joseph Mayo,[1] the mayor. The General and staff rode up Main street amid the hearty congratulations of a very large crowd of colored persons and poor whites, who were gathered together upon the sidewalks manifesting every demonstration of joy.

There were many persons in the better-class houses who were peeping out of the windows, and whose movements indicated that they would need watching in the future. There was no mistaking the curl of their lips and the flash of their eyes. The new military Governor of Richmond will, no doubt, prove equal to such emergencies.

1. Joseph Mayo (?–?) had served as mayor of Richmond since 1853. Emory M. Thomas, *The Confederate State of Richmond: A Biography of the Capital* (Austin, 1971), 19.

When General Draper's brigade entered the outskirts of the city it was halted, and a brigade of Devin's division, 24th Corps, passed in to constitute the provost guard. A scene was here witnessed which was not only grand, but sublime. Officers rushed into each other's arms, congratulating them upon the peaceful occupation of this citadel. Tears of joy ran down the faces of the more aged. The soldiers cheered lustily, which were mingled with every kind of expression of delight. The citizens stood gaping in wonder at the splendidly-equipped army marching along under the graceful folds of the old flag. Some waved their hats and women their hands in token of gladness. The pious old negroes, male and female, indulged in such expressions: "You've come at last"; "We've been looking for you these many days"; "Jesus has opened the way"; "God bless you"; "I've not seen that old flag for four years"; "It does my eyes good"; "Have you come to stay?"; "Thank God", and similar expressions of exultation. The soldiers, black and white, received these assurances of loyalty as evidences of the latent patriotism of an oppressed people, which a military despotism has not been able to crush.

Riding up to a group of fine looking men, whose appearance indicated that they would hardly have influence enough to keep them out of the army, I inquired how it was they were not taken away with the force of Lee. They replied that they had hid themselves when the rebel army had evacuated the city, and that many more had done likewise, who would soon appear when assured that there was no longer any danger of falling into the power of the traitorous army.

These scenes all occurred at the terminus of Osborn road, which connects with the streets of the city, and is within the municipal limits. There General Draper's brigade, with the gallant 36th U.S.C.T.'s drum corps, played "Yankee Doodle" and "Shouting the Battle Cry of Freedom," amid the cheers of the boys and the white soldiers who filed by them. It ought to be stated that the officers of the white troops were anxious to be the first to enter the city with their organizations, and so far succeeded as to procure an order when about three miles, distant, that General Draper's brigade should take the left of the road, in order to allow those of the 24th Corps, under General Devin, to pass by. General Draper obeyed the order, and took the left of the road in order to let the troops of Devin go by, but at the same time ordered his brigade on a double-quick, well knowing that his men would not likely be over taken on the road by any soldiers in the army. For marching or fighting Draper's 1st Brigade, 1st Division, 25th Corps, is not to be surpassed in the service, and the General honors it with a pride and a consciousness which inspire him to undertake cheerfully whatever may be committed to his execution. It was his brigade that nipped the flower of the Southern army, the Texas Brigade, under Gary, which never before last September knew defeat. There may be others who may claim the distinction of being the first to enter the city, but as I was ahead of every part of the force but the cavalry, which of necessity must lead the advance, I know whereof I affirm when I announce that General Draper's brigade was the first organization to enter the city limits. According to custom, it should constitute the provost guard of Richmond.

Kautz's division, consisting of Draper's and Wild's brigades, with troops of the 24th Corps, were placed in the trenches around the city, and Thomas' brigade was assigned to garrison Manchester. Proper dispositions have been made of the force to give security, and, soldier-like, placed the defences of the city beyond the possibility of a surprise.

As we entered all the Government buildings were in flames, having been fired by order of the rebel General Ewell. The flames soon communicated themselves to the business part of the city; and continued to rage furiously throughout the day. All efforts to arrest this destructive element seemed for the best part of the day of no avail. The fire department of Richmond rendered every aid, and to them and the co-operate labors of our soldiers belongs the credit of having saved Richmond from the devastating flames. As it is, all that part of the city lying between Ninth and Fourteenth streets, between Main street and the river inclusive, is in ruins. Among the most prominent buildings destroyed are the rebel War Department, Quartermaster General's Department, all the buildings with commissary stores, Shockoe's and Dibbrel's warehouses, well stored with tobacco, *Dispatch* and *Enquirer* newspaper buildings, the court house, (Guy) House, Farmers' Bank, Bank of Virginia, Exchange Bank, Tracers' Bank, American and Columbia hotels, and the Mayo bridge which unites Richmond with Manchester. The buildings of the largest merchants are among those which have been reduced to ashes.

The flames, in spreading, soon communicated to poor and rich houses alike. All classes were soon rushing, into the streets with their goods, to save them. They hardly laid them down before they were picked up by those who openly were plundering everyplace where anything of value was to be obtained. It was retributive justice upon the aiders and abettors of treason to see their property fired by the rebel chiefs and plundered by the people whom they meant to forever enslave. As soon as the torch was applied to the rebel storehouses, the negroes and poor whites began to appropriate all property, without respect to locks or bolts. About the time our advance entered the city the tide of this inadmissible confiscation was at its highest ebb. Men would rush to the principal stores, break open the doors, and carry off the contents by the armful.

The leader of this system of public plundering was a colored man who carried upon his shoulder an iron crow-bar, and as a mark of distinguishment had a red piece of goods around his waist which reached down to his knees. The mob, for it could not with propriety be called anything else, followed him as their leader; moved on when he advanced, and rushed into every passage which was made by the leader with his crow-bar. Goods of every description were seized under these circumstances and personally appropriated by the supporters of an equal distribution of property. Cotton goods in abundance, tobacco in untold quantities, shoes, rebel military clothing, and goods and furniture generally were carried away by the people as long as any thing of value was to be obtained. As soon as Gen. Ripley[2] was assigned to provost duty, all plundering immediately ceased, the flames were arrested, and an appearance of recognized authority fully sustained. Order once more reigns in Richmond. The streets were as quiet last night as they possibly could be. An effective patrolling and provost guard keeps everything as quiet as can be expected.

The F. F. V.'s have not ventured out of their houses yet, except in a few cases, to apply for a guard to protect their property. In some cases negroes have been sent to protect the interest of these would-be man sellers. It is pleasant to witness the measured pace of some dark sentinel before the houses of persons who, without doubt, were outspoken rebels until the Union army entered the city, owing the security which they feel to the vigilance of the negro guard.

When the army occupied the city there were innumerable inquiries

2. Edward Hastings Ripley (1839–1915) spent most of the war in Virginia, first in the XVIII Corps in front of Richmond, then as commander of the 1st Brigade, 3rd Division, XXIV Corps. Ripley's brigade was one of the first to enter Richmond. *DAB*, VIII, 619–20.

for Jeff Davis, but to all of which the answer was made that he went off in great haste night before last, with all the bag and baggage which he could carry. The future capital of the Confederacy will probably be in a wagon for the facilities which it affords to travel. Jeff's mansion, where he lived in state, is now the headquarters of Gen. Weitzel.

Brigadier General Shepley has been appointed Governor of Richmond, and has entered upon the arduous duties of the office. A better selection could not have been made.

It is due to Major Stevens, of the 4th Massachusetts Cavalry, provost marshal, on the staff of Gen. Weitzel, to give him credit for raising the first colors over the State House. He hoisted a couple of guidons, in the absence of a flag, which excited prolonged cheering. Soon after General Shepley's A. D. C. raised the first storm flag over the Capitol. It is the acme standard which General Shepley laid a wager would wave over the St. Charles Hotel in the beginning of the rebellion, and he also laid another that it would be hoisted over Richmond, both of which he has had the satisfaction of winning.

During the early part of the day a number of rebel officers were captured at the Spottswood House, where they were drinking freely. They belonged to the navy, the last of which disappeared in smoke, excepting a few straggling officers and men. These fellows, when arrested, did not wish to walk through the street under a guard, but solicited the favor of being permitted to go to the provost marshal in a carriage. Their impudence was received as it deserved, with suppressed contempt.

On Sunday evening, strange to say, the jails in this place were thrown open, and all runaway negroes, those for sale and those for safe keeping were told to hop out and enjoy their freedom. You may rely upon it that they did not need a second invitation. Many of these persons will have no difficulty in convincing themselves that they were always on the side of the Union and the freedom of the slave. Great events have a wonderful influence upon the minds of guilty, trembling wretches.

When the rebels blew up the magazine in the vicinity of French Garden Hill, the people were not informed of the fact. Some of them knew it, but the great body of those in the vicinity were ignorant of what was taking place. The result was that quite a number were killed. Nearly if not quite all the paupers in the poor house—the numbers not being large—which was very near the magazine, were instantly killed also.

The fire is still burning, but not to much damage.

HALL OF CONGRESS

The exultation of the loyal people of this city, who, amid the infamy by which they have been surrounded, and the foul misrepresentations to allure them from their allegiance, have remained true to the old flag, is still being expressed by the most extravagant demonstrations of joy. The Union element in this city consists of negroes and poor whites, including all that have deserted from the army, or have survived the terrible exigencies which brought starvation to so many homes. As to the negroes, one thing is certain, that amid every disaster to our arms, amid the wrongs which they daily suffered for their known love for the Union, and amid the scourging which they received for trying to reach our army and enlist under our flag, they have ever prayed for the right cause, and testified their devotion to it in ten thousand instances, and especially in aiding our escaped prisoners to find our lines when to do so placed their own lives in peril.

The great event after the capture of the city was the arrival of President Lincoln in it. He came up to Rocket's wharf in one of Admiral Porter's vessels of war, and, with a file of sailors for a guard of honor, he walked up to Jeff Davis' house, the headquarters of General Weitzel. As soon as he landed the news sped, as if upon the wings of lightning, that "Old Abe," for it was treason in this city to give him a more respectful address, had come. Some of the negroes, feeling themselves free to act like men, shouted that the President had arrived. This name having always been applied to Jeff, the inhabitants, coupling it with the prevailing rumor that he had been captured, reported that the arch-traitor was being brought into the city. As the people pressed near they cried "Hang him!" "Hang him!" "Show him no quarter!" and other similar expressions, which indicated their sentiments as to what should be his fate. But when they learned that it was President Lincoln their joy knew no bounds. By the time he reached General Weitzel's headquarters, thousands of

persons had followed him to catch a sight of the Chief Magistrate of
the United States. When he ascended the steps he faced the crowd
and bowed his thanks for the prolonged exultation which was going
up from that great concourse. The people seemed inspired by this
acknowledgment, and with renewed vigor shouted louder and
louder, until it seemed as if the echoes would reach the abode of
those patriot spirits who had died without witnessing the sight.

General Weitzel received the President upon the pavement, and
conducted him up the steps. General Shepley, after a good deal of
trouble, got the crowd quiet and introduced Admiral Porter, who
bowed his acknowledgments for the cheering with which his name
was greeted. The President and party entered the mansion, where
they remained for half an hour, the crowd still accumulating around
it, when a headquarters' carriage was brought in front, drawn by four
horses, and Mr. Lincoln, with his youngest son, Admiral Porter,
General Kautz, and General Devin entered. The carriage drove
through the principal streets, followed by General Weitzel and staff
on horseback, and a cavalry guard. There is no describing the scene
along the route. The colored population was wild with enthusiasm.
Old men thanked God in a very boisterous manner, and old women
shouted upon the pavement as high as they had ever done at a
religious revival. But when the President passed through the Capitol
yard it was filled with people. Washington's monument and the
Capitol steps were one mass of humanity to catch a glimpse of him.

It should be recorded that the Malvern, Admiral Porter's flag-ship,
upon which the President came; the Bat, Monticello, Frolic, and the
Symbol, the torpedo-boat which led the advance and exploded these
infernal machines, were the first vessels to arrive in Richmond.

Nothing can exceed the courtesy and politeness which the whites
everywhere manifest to the negroes. Not even the familiarity peculiar
to Americans is indulged in, calling the blacks by their first or
Christian names, but even masters are addressing their slaves as "Mr.
Johnson," "Mrs. Brown," and "Miss Smith." A cordial shake of the
hand and a gentle inclination of the body, approaching to respectful
consideration, are evident in the greetings which now take place
between the oppressed and the oppressor.

Masters are looking through the camps of our colored troops to
find some of their former slaves to give them a good character. The
first night our troops quartered in the city this scene was enacted in

Gen. Draper's brigade limits, his being the first organization to enter the city. His troops now hold the inner lines of works. The rapid occupation of the city cut off the retreat of many rebels, who are daily being picked up by the provost guard.

Every one declares that Richmond never before presented such a spectacle of jubilee. It must be confessed that those who participated in this informal reception of the President were mainly negroes. There were many whites in the crowd, but they were lost in the great concourse of American citizens of African descent. Those who lived in the finest houses either stood motionless upon their steps or merely peeped through the window-blinds, with a very few exceptions. The Secesh-inhabitants still have some hope for their tumbling cause.

The scenes at the Capitol during the day are of a very exciting character. The offices of General Shepley, the Military Governor, and Colonel Morning, the Provost Marshal General, are besieged by crowds, mostly poor people, with a small sprinkling of respectability, upon every kind of pretext. They want protection papers, a guard over their property, to assure the authorities of their allegiance, to take the oath, to announce that they are paroled prisoners and never have been exchanged, and don't desire to be, and innumerable other circumstances to insure the protection of the military authorities.

The people of Richmond, white and black, had been led to believe that when the Yankee army came its mission was one of plunder. But the orderly manner in which the soldiers have acted has undeceived them. The excitement is great, but nothing could be more orderly and decorous than the united crowds of soldiers and citizens.

The Capitol building all day yesterday from the moment we took possession was surrounded by a crowd of hungry men and women clamoring for something to eat. The earnestness of their entreaties and looks showed that they were in a destitute condition. It was deemed necessary to station a special guard at the bottom of the steps to keep them from filling the building. These suffering people will probably be attended to in a day or so in that bountiful manner which has marked the advance of the Union armies.

I visited yesterday (Tuesday) several of the slave jails, where men, women, and children were confined, or herded, for the examination of purchasers. The jailors were in all cases slaves, and had been left in undisputed possession of the buildings. The owners, as soon as they were aware that we were coming, opened wide the doors and told the confined inmates they were free. The poor souls could not realize it until they saw the Union army. Even then they thought it must be a pleasant dream, but when they saw Abraham Lincoln they were satisfied that their freedom was perpetual. One enthusiastic old negro woman exclaimed: "I know that I am free, for I have seen Father Abraham and felt him."

When the President returned to the flag-ship of Admiral Porter, in the evening, he was taken from the wharf in a cutter. Just as he pushed off, amid the cheering of the crowd, another good old colored female shouted out, "Don't drown, Massa Abe, for God's sake!"

The fire, which was nearly extinguished when I closed my last despatch, is entirely so now. Thousands of persons are gazing hourly with indignation upon the ruins. Gen. Lee ordered the evacuation of the city at an hour known to the remaining leaders of the rebellion, when Gens. Ewell and Breckinridge,[3] and others, absconded, leaving orders with menials, robbers, and plunderers, kept together during the war by the "cohesive power of public plunder," to apply the torch to the different tobacco warehouses, public buildings, arsenals, stores, flour mills, powder magazines, and every important place of deposit. A south wind prevailed, and the flames spread with devastating effect. The offices of the newspapers, whose columns have been charged with the foulest vituperation against our Government, were on fire; two of them have been reduced to ashes, another one injured beyond repair, while the remaining two are not much damaged. Every bank which had emitted the spurious notes of the rebels was consumed to ruins. Churches no longer gave audience to empty prayers, but burst forth in furious flames. Magazines exploded, killing the poor inhabitants. In short, Secession was burnt out, and the city purified as far as fire could accomplish it.

As I informed you in a previous despatch, the Union soldiers

3. John Cabell Breckinridge (1821–1875). Presidential candidate for the southern faction of the Democratic party in 1860, he was, in 1861, declared a traitor by the U.S. Senate for joining the Confederacy when he was still theoretically a member of the Senate. Breckinridge led Confederate forces in Louisiana, Mississippi, Tennessee, and the Shenandoah Valley. He was made secretary of war by Davis in February, 1865. *DAB*, II, 7–10; Jon L. Wakelyn, *Biographical Dictionary of the Confederacy* (Westport, Conn., 1977), 108.

united with the citizens to stay the progress of the fire, and at last succeeded, but not until all the business part of the town was destroyed.

About three o'clock on Monday morning the political prisoners who were confined in Castle Thunder,[4] and the Union prisoners who were in Libby, were marched out and driven off. Some of our officers escaped and were kindly cared for by the good Union folks of this city. The rebels also gathered together as many colored persons as possible, and were forcing them ahead with drawn sabres, but before they were out of the city Spear's cavalry came down upon them, rescued the negroes, and captured seventeen of the Johnnies, with their horses.

Yesterday afternoon I strolled through Castle Thunder, where so many Union men have suffered every species of meanness and tyranny which the rebels could invent. The only thing that attracted especial attention was the large number of manacles which were for the benefit of the prisoners. This place has been so often described, that it would be unnecessary to weary the reader again. The Castle is empty at present, and is in charge of Capt. Mattison,[5] 81st New York Volunteers, who, by the way, is a very accommodating officer. The Hotel de Libby is now doing a rushing business in the way of accommodating a class of persons who have not heretofore patronized that establishment. It is being rapidly filled with rebel soldiers, detectives, spies, robbers, and every grade of infamy in the calendar of crime. The stars and stripes now wave gracefully over it, and traitors look through the same bars behind which loyal men were so long confined.

Quite a large number of rebels were brought into the city last night. I did not for a certainty learn whether they were captured, or deserted from a bad cause—most probably the latter.

4. There were two Confederate prisons known by this name, one in Richmond, the other in Petersburg. Political prisoners were housed in Richmond—among them, those who had helped blacks escape to Union lines. The prison had such a reputation for harshness that the Confederate House of Representatives investigated it in 1863. Patricia L. Faust (ed.), *Historical Times Illustrated Encyclopedia of the Civil War* (New York, 1986), 120.

5. Lucius V. S. Mattison (b. 1840). Mustered in as a private, 81st New York, in September, 1861, he was promoted to sergeant three months later. Mattison rose through the ranks and left the army as a lieutenant colonel. Frederick Phisterer (comp.), *New York in the War of the Rebellion, 1861 to 1865* (5 vols.; New York, 1912), IV, 2877, 2891.

Lieut. Gen. Grant will arrive in this city tomorrow, and will doubtless receive an ovation equal to President Lincoln's.

BUSINESS RECOMMENCING—A JUBILEE AT THE AFRICAN CHURCH.

RICHMOND, APRIL 9, 1865.

The excitement attending the occupation of this city by the Union army is gradually subsiding, and places of business are beginning to be opened.

The provost marshal's office is still thronged by crowds of persons to avail themselves of the protection of the authorities and various purposes of business. It requires the utmost efforts of the guards to keep a passage open that officers may pass in and out of the State House.

General Shepley, Military Governor of Richmond, is almost exhausted by receiving and attending to the business of the hundreds and thousands who daily are pressing to see him.

Day before yesterday there was a grand jubilee meeting in the African Church, the largest building in the city, where Jeff Davis has frequently convened the conspirators to plot and execute treason. The colored people turned out in full force; every seat was taken up and all standing room was occupied; the windows were thronged, and hundreds were outside unable to get within hearing or seeing distance.

The meeting was called to order by T. Morris Chester, who congratulated the people upon the triumph of liberty in Richmond, and urged them, as redeemed freemen, to assume the duties and responsibilities belonging to the change. The remarks were enthusiastically received. Chaplain David Stevens, 36th U. S. C. T., followed in an able speech. Mr. John Henry Butler, of Baltimore, also made an interesting address.

It should be remembered that no colored man had ever in that church, though belonging to that oppressed people, dared to speak to the people from the pulpit. Chaplain Stevens was the first to ascend. Negro ministers were permitted to speak from the altar, but no higher.

Hundreds of rebels, deserters and prisoners, are being brought into the city daily, and give most woeful accounts of Lee's army, and the terrible disaster which it suffered from the Union forces. Their only solicitude is whether they will be permitted to take the oath of allegiance. The Secesh gather around them to learn if there is any further hope for Lee, but find that their worst fears are realized.

RICHMOND, APRIL 10, 1865.

SALUTE FOR VICTORY.

Quite early this morning the loyal hearts of Richmond pulsated with fear, in consequence of the heavy firing of artillery which was thundering around the city. They supposed that Lee, in accordance with the wishes of the rebels here, was making an effort to recapture this citadel of treason. The cannonading arose from a far different purpose. It was salute after salute over the good news that *Lee had surrendered*, with the remnant of his badly whipped and demoralized forces. It was the funeral service over a God-forsaken Confederacy, with the artillery of the Union army and Porter's fleet, to chaunt the requiem. The denizens of the city are not yet stirring, and are ignorant of the cause of so much thundering, but they will soon learn that the rebellion is virtually at an end, and that freedom and the Union will henceforth maintain their supremacy over every inch of desecrated soil. This intelligence that Lee had surrendered was received last evening by General Weitzel, and caused great rejoicing at his headquarters, the mansion from which Jeff Davis skeedaddled just seven days ago. The General communicated the good news to Admiral Porter, who, with a part of his fleet, is still in this city. The jolly tars testified their joy by cheers, and a grand salute from the different ships of war in the harbor.

CLEARING THE JAMES.

I have not heard that any of the monitors have reached here, but they are all down the James, clearing out the obstructions and the torpedoes from the river. They are admirably fitted-up for such purpose, with the necessary netting to remove these terrible instruments of death from the channel. If the river is not entirely clear of them it will soon be.

BUSINESS FACILITIES.

Uninterrupted navigation is now going on between Richmond and Washington, and the army mails run through daily each way. In a few days it is expected that the post office will be opened in this city for the accommodation of the public. Next door to the Spottswood Hotel Adams' Express has opened for business. The facilities afforded by this institution are highly appreciated in the army. Messrs. J. B. Carroll and O. F. Webster are the obliging messengers to whom *The Press* is indebted for repeated favors.

SERVICES IN THE CHURCHES.

Yesterday being Sunday, many of the people went to their churches, not with a view of religious worship, but to hear such consolation as the hypocrites who have so long disgraced the pulpits of the South might have the nerve to offer for their treasonable cause. Of course, they had the good sense to abstain from any direct outrage of sentiment, but covertly administered such comfort as was possible under the circumstances. They prayed for the Powers that be, but it was evident that they meant Jeff. The tenor even implied a hope that if the people were faithful they might still enjoy the blessings of a Southern Confederacy. This is the kind of doctrine that was enunciated at St. Paul's church, and may be recorded as a fair sample of the loyalty of the Richmondites who belong to the better class of society.

FEELING OF THE "CONFEDERATES."

Since the occupation of this city the F. F. V.'s, and particularly the women, have been disposed to remain in their houses, curling up their noses, probably, behind their window blinds. The news of this morning will probably straighten the faces of the women, and bring the wondering minds of the men to a loyal conclusion. Many officers who were in the rebel army remarked this morning, in my hearing, that, as Lee has surrendered, they are willing to take the oath of allegiance. Since these traitors have defied the powers of the Government to the extent of their endurance, a little discrimination ought to be exercised to ascertain who are worthy to be readmitted to the privileges of American citizens. Those who have forfeited that claim should be brought to a speedy and just punishment. They refused, with scorn, to heed the mercy of the Government; now let them experience its justice as a warning to treason in the future. Quite a number of deserters, refugees, contrabands, and prisoners of war are hourly arriving here, all of whom confirm the opinion already entertained, that the rebellion is virtually at an end. It is amusing to see the faith which the rebels have in Lee, even after they have deserted his standard. Many of them refuse to believe that he has surrendered, or in the ability of the Union army to capture him. Their eyes will shortly be opened to the fact, when, at the same time, they will also realize the extent of their own folly.

A CLERGYMAN REBEL TO THE LAST.

The colored churches yesterday were densely crowded with delighted audiences. The African church, the largest one in Richmond, was densely packed, and to the astonishment of a redeemed people Mr. Byland,[6] the white pastor, preached a rebel sermon, so marked in its sentiments that the colored soldiers many of whom happened to be present, abruptly left the building. The speaker emphatically discouraged enlistments in the Union army. When the services were over the colored soldiers met Mr. Byland at the door as he came out, and arrested him. Strange as it may seem, notwithstanding the madness of this canting hypocrite, and his desire to continue the perpetration of the wrongs of oppression upon the negroes, the members of his church begged and entreated that he might be spared the indignity of an arrest, out of respect to his age. He was then required to report to the provost marshal, to answer the charge of using improper language. I have not learned the result.

ARRIVAL OF A COLORED DETACHMENT.

Last night the division of colored troops, the 2d, 25th Corps, under command of Brigadier General William Birney, arrived here, after participating in the battles which gave Richmond, Petersburg, and Lee's forces as trophies to the Union army. The division is composed

6. Chester may be referring to Robert Ryland (1805–1899), white pastor of the First African Baptist Church in the 1850s and 1860s. My thanks to Peter Rachleff for the information on Ryland.

of good material, and, if a faithful record has been published of its acts, they will not be inferior to any of the former deeds of valor performed under their beloved and accomplished leader.

Who First Entered Richmond?

In this connection it is not inappropriate to do justice to the 1st Division of colored troops, under General Kautz, to which belongs the honor of being the first to enter Richmond. Quite an effort is being made to give that credit to Gen. Devin's division, but, whatever may be the merits of his troops, they cannot justly lay any claims to that distinction. The white soldiers, when orders for advancing were passed along the line, were posted nearer Richmond than the negroes. But, with that prompt obedience to orders that has ever made the discipline of the blacks the pride of their officers, they soon passed over their own and the rebel works, and took the Osborne road directly for the city. When within a few miles of the city I heard Gen. Kautz give the order to Gen. Draper to take the left-hand side of the road, that Devin's division might pass by. Gen. Draper obeyed the order implicitly, and, in order that he might not be in the way with his brigade, put it upon a double-quick, and never stopped until it entered the limits of the city. *The colored troops had orders not to pass through the city,* but to go around it and man the inner fortifications. When Devin's division came within the outskirts of the city, and marched by General Draper's brigade, who had stacked their arms, and whose drum corps was playing national airs, they were loudly cheered by the colored troops, and they failed to respond, either from exhaustion or a want of courtesy. To Gen. Draper belongs the credit of having the first organization enter the city, and none are better acquainted with this fact than the officers of the division who are claiming the undeserved honor. Gen. Draper's brigade is composed of the 22d, 36th, 38th, and 118th U. S. colored troops, the 36th being the first to enter Richmond.

Rejoicings Among The Emancipated.

Nothing can exceed the rejoicings of the negroes since the occupation of this city. They declare that they cannot realize the change; though they have long prayed for it, yet it seems impossible that it has come. Old men and women weep and shout for joy, and praise God for their deliverance through means of the Union army. The stories of horror which, many of them relate, through which they have passed would be hard to credit, were it not that there are so many corroborating circumstances to remove all doubts. The highest degree of happiness attainable upon earth is now being enjoyed by the colored people of this city. They all declare that they are abundantly able to take care of themselves. Nothing can be more amusing than the efforts of some of the most violent rebels, who in other days never let an opportunity pass to show their love for Jeff Davis, or manifest their vindictive feelings against the negroes in every conceivable manner, to cultivate the friendship of the colored people, with the hope that the forgiving nature of the race may induce them to forget the wrongs of the past and befriend them in these times of sore tribulation. Persons who were instituting all manner of complaints against the respectable colored persons who happened to live in their neighborhood have suddenly realized that they were very desirable companions, and possessing social qualities worthy of cultivating. What a wonderful change has come over the spirit of Southern dreams.

INCIDENTS.

Among the amusing sayings that have occurred since we have been here, one was occasioned by several hundred rebels being marched towards Libby yesterday, when some one remarked, "They ain't got any arms." "No," answered a colored soldier, "but they've what they can use better—their legs."

A female of strong Secesh proclivities, but whose love of romance rises above political considerations, had occasion to visit the provost marshal's office, and returned so favorably impressed with the courtesy of that functionary as to exclaim in the presence of her better half, among other complimentary things: "Oh, what a beautiful man the provost marshal is!" This was too much for the husband, who, rising up in the majesty of his authority, thundered out: "By G——! you're not to go to that provost marshal's office any more." Of course the solicitude of the husband arose from fear that his partner might be allured from the political faith in which he had indoctrinated her. A large squad of rebels, being escorted through the streets yesterday by colored guards, came to a halt in front of Libby, when one of them observed his former slave pacing up and down the line with genuine martial bearing. Stepping a little out of ranks he said: "Hallo, Jack, is that you!" The negro guard looked at him with blank astonishment, not unmingled with disdain, for the familiarity of the address. The rebel captive, determined upon being recognized, said, entreatingly, "Why, Jack, don't you know me!" "Yes, I know you very well," was the sullen reply, "and if you don't fall back into that line I will give you this bayonet," at the same time bringing his musket to the position of a charge. This, of course, terminated all attempts at familiarity.

WHERE IS JEFF DAVIS!

Among the conflicting rumors concerning Jeff Davis, the only one of any reliability is that he succeeded in reaching Danville in safety, from which he has, no doubt, taken his departure to some sequestered spot, where, free from the cares and perplexities of government, he may console himself with having escaped the penalty due to his treason. It is a little singular that while the rebel soldiers are very solicitous for consideration to be extended to Lee, they seem unanimous in their conclusions that Jeff should have no leniency shown to him. The fugitive chieftain has, no doubt, realized that republics are ungrateful.

VISITORS TO RICHMOND.

The city is being visited by a large number of distinguished persons from the North. Mr. Arthur Leary, of New York, the owner of the mail-boat George Leary, came around in her from the Empire City, with a number of ladies and gentlemen, among whom is Prince John Van Buren. They have visited here and Petersburg, and will return in the Leary this morning for Washington, making her first trip as a mail steamer.

CONDITION OF THE CITY.

It is hardly necessary to say that the influence of the war has impeded the progress of every public enterprise in this city not absolutely necessary to prosper military operations. Improvements which had begun to beautify Richmond and increase the facilities of her citizens have been delayed, or altogether suspended. Persons who were disposed to erect houses upon their lots feared to do so in the unsettled state of the country. The wharves present a deserted appearance. The few dirty canal boats and one or two steamers which the rebels had not time to destroy looked as if they had long since been abandoned as unworthy of repairs. A large amount of timber is piled up along the dock in the vicinity of Rocketts, where it has been left, from its appearance, to crumble to dust. The railroads could hardly be in a worse condition. The engines look as if they could be much improved, and the destruction of the numerous rickety cars, as was the intention of the rebels, would have occasioned no regrets if no other damage had been sustained. The two or three draw-bridges below the city seem to have long since become unserviceable. And, as if these evidences, with innumerable others, were not sufficient to induce the Richmondites to cease their efforts to resist the national authority, they now have the mortification of seeing the whole of the business part of the city reduced to ashes, and many of them are experiencing that humility which never fails to attend poverty.

INJUSTICE TO REBEL SOLDIERS.

It is hardly fair that Libby should be filled with rebel soldiers, while the officers, who are much to blame for the continuance of the struggle, should be allowed to walk by without molestation, merely glancing at those who have been the dupes of their unholy ambition. This, to a certain extent, may not be avoided, but they can be divested of the treasonable uniform so offensive to loyal tastes, in which they have causelessly murdered the defenders of the Union. They sport their best suits of gray with a degree of arrogance which should not be tolerated—more with the bearing of conquerors than routed vandals, as they are.

HOW COLORED CHILDREN LEARNED.

The colored Sunday schools in Richmond were amusing institutions. The children were not allowed any books or to learn their alphabet. They were taught the days of the week, months, and year, and how to count their fingers and toes. When a chapter was read in the Bible, the little ones were required to repeat it after the superintendent. Some of the children can repeat Psalms with great rapidity. This, with singing, constitutes their instruction in the Sunday school. There have always been secret schools in this city for the instruction of colored children, but they were conducted with a great deal of privacy. The little boys and girls were obliged to carry their books hid under their clothes, and when school closed they had to pass out singly to keep from attracting attention. The little ones all seem to realize that there is no longer any necessity to learn in secret, and have asked, in many instances, their parents whether they could not go to school publicly and carry their books openly.

LAW AND ORDER IN RICHMOND.

Richmond may be said to be perfectly quiet, and as orderly a city as is in the Union. There are large crowds on the streets and around the offices of the military governor and provost marshal, but nothing could exceed the propriety which seems general throughout the city. Many of the places of business have opened, and numerous adventurers are endeavoring to obtain establishments to commence their various pursuits. There are not many greenbacks among the people, but nearly all of them have reserved a little gold or silver in anticipation of the present event. The sutlers who have been fortunate enough to get their establishments in running order are literally reaping a golden harvest.

RICHMOND, APRIL 16, 1865.

THE CHANGES IN THE CITY.

It is just two weeks since our forces occupied this city, and the changes which have been wrought are not without their influence upon the minds of the principal secessionists. The suffering and destitution which the poorer classes experienced, and in many instances those who left homes of comfort in Washington, are being relieved by the charities of the Sanitary and Christian Commissions,[7]

7. The United States Christian Commission, organized in 1861 by the Young Men's Christian Association, worked closely with the Sanitary Commission. Not only did it

and the magnanimity of the Government. The markets are being well supplied with vegetables, and the finest beef that has adorned the stall since the war began is daily exposed for purchasers. Several enterprising spirits have opened places of business.

VEHEMENT REBELS.

While prosperity and future happiness are producing a change among many of the former adherents of the rebellion, there are innumerable others who continue their bitterness and venom. One of the female aristocrats on Leigh street, whose property is guarded by a Federal soldier, said yesterday, with considerable vehemence, that "I will die and go to hell before I would take the oath." Another, upon hearing that Lee had surrendered, assumed a tragical attitude and declared that she "would rather see him in hell than marched through the streets of Richmond." These females are well known in the best society of this city, and are among the wealthiest of the State.

ARRIVAL OF LEE AND STAFF—HIS RECEPTION.

The excitement of yesterday was the arrival here of General Lee and his staff, about three o'clock P. M. The chieftain looked fatigued, and rode along at a jaded gait. The general with affable dignity received the marks of respect which were manifested by those who happened along the pavement. Several efforts were made to cheer him, which failed, until within a short distance of his residence, previous to which his admirers satisfied themselves with quietly waving their hats and their hands, when they were more successful. At his mansion, on Franklin street, where he alighted from his horse, he immediately uncovered his head, thinly covered with silver hairs, as he had done in acknowledgment of the veneration of the people along the streets. There was a general rush of the small crowd to shake hands with him.

During these manifestations not a word was spoken, and when the ceremony was through, the General bowed and ascended his steps.

-----

provide free lunches and coffee and special diets for the sick and wounded, it also opened, where possible, reading rooms filled with Bibles, newspapers, magazines and with free writing paper and stamps to encourage soldiers to write home. It spent over $6 million during the war. Faust (ed.), *Historical Times Illustrated Encyclopedia*, 140.

The silence was then broken by a few voices calling for a speech, to which he paid no attention. The General then passed into his house, and the crowd dispersed. The military authorities here will extend every consideration to Lee. Orders will soon be promulgated affording him and his staff such protection and accommodation as their circumstances may require.

Other Arrivals.

General Pickett and staff, I understand, also came into the city yesterday. Quite a number of rebel generals and soldiers are daily arriving. The effect upon the population is not very pleasant. The rebels continue to strut in their uniform, and in many cases make remarks which are offensive to Union soldiers. The influx of rebel soldiers here tends to strengthen their nerves in the utterance of disloyalty.

Schools for the Freedmen.

Many encouraging efforts are being made to establish schools for colored children. Professor Woodburry,[8] in connection with the Freedmen's Aid Society,[9] is prosecuting this enterprise, in connection with others equally as indefatigable, with considerable success. The colored children were called together yesterday, graded, and the necessary books sent for to instruct them.

Personal.

Colonel John W. Forney[10] and friends, among whom are Gen. Geo. M. Lanman; Col. Wein Forney, of the Harrisburg *Telegraph;* D. P.

8. William H. Woodburry (?–?), the American Missionary Association's superintendent in Norfolk, started schools in Richmond, attended daily by fifteen hundred students, seventeen days after the occupation of the city. Joe M. Richardson, *Christian Reconstruction: The American Missionary Association and Southern Blacks, 1861–1890* (Athens, Ga., 1986), 33, 71.
9. Possibly the New England Freedmen's Aid Society, successor to the Boston Educational and Relief Society organized in February, 1862. James M. McPherson, *The Struggle for Equality: Abolitionists and the Negro in the Civil War and Reconstruction* (Princeton, 1964), 169–70.
10. John Wien Forney (1829–1890). Journalist, editor, and newspaper proprietor, Forney was publisher of a number of newspapers including the *Press* and the Washington *Chronicle*. DAB, III, 526–27; Philip S. Klein and Ari Hoogenboom, *A History of Pennsylvania* (University Park, Pa., 1980), 390.

Forney, Esq., of the Washington *Chronicle;* Hon. Samuel Randall[11] and Robert Randall, Esq., of Philadelphia, and several others, arrived here night before last, and put up at the Spottswood House. The Colonel and party will leave tomorrow for Washington, having satisfied themselves with the various points of interest to be seen in this city, and with such relics of barbarity as they could collect.

A COLORED BISHOP.

Right Rev. John D. Brooks,[12] one of the colored Methodist Bishops, is here looking after the spiritual welfare of his brethren. His reception has been quite flattering, and the good which he will likely accomplish will be a great blessing to the people. The reverend gentleman has certainly moved in time, and in the right direction.

GOOD FRIDAY SERVICES.

We have been experiencing showers for a day or two, but this morning has dawned with every appearance of an excellent day. Religious services will be held in the different churches today upon no other condition than that nothing shall be said of a disloyal character. Where prayers were heretofore offered for Jeff Davis, the pastors are ordered, in the absence, and especially in consequence of the unworthiness of that individual, to substitute President Lincoln.

RICHMOND, APRIL 17, 1865.

The dreadful intelligence from Washington was received in this city yesterday about noon. The first report came that he was dead, which smote the hearts of the loyal people with deep sadness, but they resolved not to credit it. But soon the official confirmation removed all doubts, and the people were overwhelmed with profound grief. The

11. Samuel J. Randall (1829–1890). A force in Pennsylvania politics, Randall was Democratic state chairman during and after the Civil War. A congressman, he later became Speaker of the House of Representatives. *DAB,* VIII, 350–51; Klein and Hoogenboom, *A History of Pennsylvania,* 369–70.

12. John D. Brooks (?–?) was a prominent figure in Philadelphia during the war and a bishop in the AME Zion church. See Vol. I of David Henry Bradly, Sr., *A History of the AME Zion Church* (2 vols.; Nashville, 1956, 1970), for references to Brooks.

effect of this sad news has filled the heart of loyalty with mourning, and caused the rebels to quake with apprehension when they heard that the consideration heretofore extended to them had been returned in a spirit of such fiendish barbarity, by assassinating the Chief Magistrate to whom they are indebted for the conciliatory measures which have marked the triumphs of the Union army. Persons who were prominently connected with the rebellion have signified their intention, and will soon move in public meetings, to denounce the act in fitting language, and adopt such expressions of condolence as the circumstances require. This may serve a purpose, and may for a time pass for genuine sincerity, but to every reflecting mind there can be but one conclusion—that the death of the President of the United States is another one of the infamous crimes which logically followed the efforts of treason to dismember the Union. It was, no doubt, committed at the instigation of traitors, with the object of affording them the consolation of making good their boast that Abraham Lincoln should never be acknowledged as their President. This class of persons need a little looking after, or we shall soon learn that some other idol of the loyal North has been murdered by those whose opportunities for slaying Union patriots in the field have so greatly diminished, but who do not hesitate to avail themselves of the services of the assassin.

Though Lincoln, the great, the good, and the honest patriot, has fallen, let us all trust that his successor may be imbued with the same spirit that has not only made the late President immortal in the estimation of his own countrymen, but which has gradually endeared him to the hearts of all lovers of freedom in foreign lands, until he has become the idol of the progressive spirit of mankind.

The *Whig* of to-day says, editorially:

"The people of Petersburg had this afflicting news yesterday, before it was made public here. Judge W. T. Joynes, Roger A. Pryor, John Lyon, and other prominent citizens, united in a call for a public meeting to express, if words could do so, their grief for so sad an event, their abhorrence of the deed, and their sympathy for the bereaved. We know that the citizens of Richmond will take similar action."

The flags of the shipping, both navy and merchantmen, were displayed at half-mast yesterday, and still continue so. Other marks of respect will no doubt be shown to the venerated dead.

This city at no period of the war was ever as quiet as it is at present. The soldiers have all been removed beyond the limits in order to avoid the difficulties which would likely occur between them and the people. Business is beginning to be prosecuted, and the various channels of industry will soon be in successful operation. Everything indicates that at no very distant day Richmond will be one among the most prosperous cities in the Union. At present the restraints which the military authorities deem necessary to prosecute operations in this State may prevent or confine the business in certain directions; but as soon as individual enterprise shall be permitted to operate, the burnt districts will soon be rebuilt, and such improvements in the city completed as were suspended by the rebellion.

The good work of organizing schools for the benefit of the colored children of this city is rapidly progressing, and soon they will be in successful operation. Quite a number of ladies and gentlemen are here as teachers, under the auspices of the Freedmen's Association,[13] and are anxious to begin the work, from which they are confident that the same gratifying results will attend their efforts as have marked those of their institution in other parts of the country.

The churches yesterday were very generally opened, and the people attended divine service more fully than they did last Sunday.

By every mail boat from Washington visitors and adventurers continue to reach this city, notwithstanding the stringent orders to the contrary. Many Union refugees are now returning to look after their property and other interests which they were obliged to leave to the mercy of the rebels.

PETERSBURG, APRIL 19, 1865.

JUBILANT TRAITORS.

It matters not where I may go, whether stopping in towns or cities, or passing through the country, the unfeigned grief of an afflicted people, caused by the assassination of President Lincoln, is everywhere manifested by loyal hearts. There is no disguising the fact that the paroled rebel officers and soldiers, strutting about in their red sashes, swords, and pistols, evince the most jubilant manifestations

13. Possibly the National Freedmen's Relief Association of New York, organized in 1862. McPherson, *The Struggle for Equality,* 160.

of satisfaction. Such exhibitions were always offensive to the soldiers of the Union, but since the murder of the fountain head of loyalty, by the conspiracy of treason, they have become an outrage upon the feelings of our patriot troops. Every consideration of right, as well as justice to the memory of the venerated dead and respect for the feelings of living heroes, demands that these arrogant rebels, who are hourly declaring that, as soon as they are exchanged, they are resolved to enter the field in behalf of Jeff Davis, should be stripped of the villainous gray in which they delighted to murder soldiers of the Union, and the color stamped with infamy.

THE COLORED TROOPS.

I would state that, as a historical fact worthy of special mention, the colored troops of Brigadier General Wm. Birney's division were the first to enter Petersburg. The 7th United States Colored Troops, recruited in Maryland, and the 8th United States Colored Troops, recruited in Philadelphia, were the advance forces to occupy this city. It must be a source of great gratification to the friends of this element of Union strength to be assured that the first organizations to enter these strongholds of the rebellion, Richmond and Petersburg, were colored troops.

Gen. Birney was relieved of his command on the field, and has been assigned instead to command a small garrison at Harrison's Landing. Brevet Brig. Gen. Jackson[14] who was inspector general on the staff of Gen. Weitzel, succeeds him. This division, which is the 2d in the 25th Corps, returned to this vicinity yesterday afternoon, having participated in the vigorous campaign which has crowned the Army of the Potomac with immortal glory. The division was temporarily attached to it with Turner's division, under the command of Gen. Ord.

THE FIRE IN PETERSBURG.

The fire here was not as destructive as in Richmond. The rebels satisfied themselves with burning the Central Warehouse, West Hill

14. Richard Henry Jackson (1830–1892). A strict disciplinarian, Jackson met with considerable criticism for his abrasiveness. He had fought in Florida and South Carolina, before being transferred to the Army of the James in early 1864. Faust (ed.), *Historical Times Illustrated Encyclopedia*, 390–91.

Warehouse, Norfolk depot, Rowlet's lumber house, Pocahontas bridge, a pontoon bridge, a bridge leading from the Southside yard over to finishing shops of the Southside Railroad, and Cammel's bridge. The combined efforts of the firemen and the soldiers soon extinguished the flames and saved a beautiful city from destruction.

VISIT OF THE LATE PRESIDENT.

The visit of President Lincoln and Gen. Grant to this city on the first day of its occupation by our forces was no doubt intended as an exemplification of that leniency which characterized the policy of the late Chief Magistrate. They were both enthusiastically received, and stopped at the residence of Thomas Wallace, who was suddenly transformed into a Union man by the magic influence of triumphant bayonets.

THE COLORED PEOPLE.

The colored people being aware that the city would be evacuated on the evening of the 2d of April, and fearing that the rebels would drive them before them, passed the night in the negro churches, where they remained until they saw the colored soldiers arresting rebel soldiers found in the city. Notwithstanding this city has been purified by a new order of things, there are some guerillas in this and other counties adjacent, who are prowling about plundering the people and tearing up the railroads.

During the period of rebel rule, it was a common occurrence for these God-overlooked wretches to knock down citizens and rob them, or promise to conduct negroes through the lines, and meeting them at an appointed place, they having changed all their Confederated money and property into greenbacks or gold and silver, would not only plunder them of everything, but actually hand them over to the rebel authorities for attempting to run the blockade.

ROBBING THE DEAD.

The vandals have even in this city, gone to the vaults of the dead and stripped them of their clothing and such jewelry as they were buried in. Nothing can exceed the depravity and infamy of this class, either in their treatment to their own people or their barbarism to ours.

POLICE REGULATIONS.

Since the occupation by the Union forces Petersburg has never been so quiet or orderly as is now being experienced. The regulations of the authorities are such as to insure the safety and property of citizens. The difference between law and order, which the citizens are now enjoying, and the bold robbery which was openly enacted under the Davis rule, cannot help but make a favorable impression upon the minds of all reasonable persons.

It was hardly possible to conceive of the extent of corruption pervading all classes of rebels from privates to generals. They could be bought to run either colored or white persons through the lines. So rotten has been the whole concern, that it is generally believed that even Jeff Davis could be induced to aid the escape of persons through the lines for a respectable consideration.

EFFECTS OF WAR.

As an evidence of how much the war has affected many persons here, I know a slaveholder, who, at the beginning of the rebellion, purchased a beautiful residence on Long Market street at a cost of twenty thousand dollars, paying five thousand dollars down, with the privilege of paying the balance after the war. When we captured Richmond this man was there, and was obliged to borrow money from the husband of a woman whom he owns to pay his fare from Richmond to Petersburg. Oh! how have the mighty fallen!

FEEDING THE HUNGRY.

The military authorities, with that mingled magnanimity and charity which have marked the advance of the Union army, and its treatment of its enemies, are issuing rations to those upon whom the misfortunes of war have brought so much suffering and destitution. Many who, no doubt, were blatant rebels three weeks ago, are eating the bread of loyalty with a relish of satisfaction, if not with thanks. The crowd around the commissary is a graphic illustration of the madness in which these people have been indulging for the last four years. The white men who apply for subsistence are mostly paroled prisoners, but the stream of women seems continuous. If one were to judge by their dress, very few of them would be regarded as objects of charity. Many of them come in silks, and are otherwise respectably attired, and in some instances bring a few flowers for the obliging clerks behind the counter. In such cases it would not be surprising if the scales went down a little heavier than generally marks the routine of issuing rations. The commissary is located on Old street, where the charity of the Government, like the mercy of Heaven, is being distributed alike to the just and the unjust.

How Loyalty is Certified to.

It is a source of great regret that the former members of the Common Council of this city, who were always the enemy of the loyal blacks, and the friends of the rebel whites, have been designated to determine those who are destitute, and are in need of subsistence. Of course, all those who were the most bitter against the Government have no difficulty in getting the necessary papers or endorsements from those extemporized Union men. Colored persons, whose loyalty was never doubted, and whom the rebels hated because it was known they never invested any faith in their cause, have in very many instances been refused, or obtained the necessary signatures under a great deal of difficulty. And when they did present their papers, properly authenticated, they only received pork and corn meal, while rebels in uniform and persons of known treasonable sentiments were drawing pork, meal, flour, beans, coffee, and sugar. I immediately conferred with Brevet Major Gen. Ferrero,[15] commanding the city, and Captain Asa Gregory, his commissary of subsistence. To Gen. Hartsuff's[16] credit it must be recorded, that in three hours

15. Edward Ferrero (1831–1899). A well-known New York dance instructor, Ferrero fought at Roanoke, Chantilly, Antietam, and Knoxville, among other battles, before he was transferred to command the 3rd Division, IX Corps, which was involved in the Battle of the Crater. *DAB*, III, 338–89; Dudley T. Cornish, *The Sable Arm: Negro Troops in the Union Army, 1861–1865* (New York, 1956), 281.

16. George Lucas Hartsuff (1830–1874). A graduate of the Military Academy, Hartsuff was severely wounded at Antietam. He commanded the XXIII Corps, which fought in Kentucky and Tennessee during 1864. He participated in action against Richmond and Petersburg and was in command at City Point and Petersburg. *DAB*, IV, 369–70.

from the moment that it was first intimated to him, the distinction was promptly suppressed, and the loyal blacks were receiving an equality of rations. The major general commanding was entirely ignorant of this injustice, until it was brought to his notice, but the prompt manner in which he remedied it evinces that impartial spirit which should be the animating sentiment of all in authority.

It must be confessed that the individual who gives to the whites the pieces of paper upon which the exact amounts to be drawn are written, which, of course, he inscribes, is dressed in rebel uniform, and only a day or two ago was in one of the Richmond batteries in arms against the Government, the amount of whose rations he now has the satisfaction of designating to his disloyal brethren. This may be regarded a rapid restoration to favor, and, should the same spirit increase in all other respects in similar proportion, how long would it be before Jeff Davis is President?

Gens. Hartsuff and Ferrero will, so far as inequalities come to their notice, without regard to color, deal justly with all classes of persons. Subordinates will not be tolerated in the exercise of their negro-hating prejudices as one of the means of working off the ebullitions of their effervescent spirit of disloyalty.

It is but just to General Weitzel to say that while he was in command at Richmond his administration was marked with that impartiality which an honest heart never fails to approve. In a former despatch the words, *the colored troops are not allowed to pass through the city*" (Richmond), need a little ventilation. No soldiers were permitted to enter the city except those designated to do provost-guard duty. I now learn from reliable authority that such a source was proposed to allay excitement—to save the troops from a long march, and in order to enable them to move at once to their places without passing through the city. The reason that rebel officers and soldiers were not divested of their uniforms under the governorship of General Shepley was not because this gallant officer did not recognize the propriety of such a course, but rather tolerated them in order that he might the more readily capture certain chieftains who had forfeited their right to be at liberty.

It is also due to General Weitzel to acknowledge that he is not aware that Mrs. General Lee ever had a guard over her property, and that, if a white one was substituted for a colored one, he is entirely ignorant of the fact. General Weitzel is the pride of the 25th Corps, both among the officers and men, who believe him incapable of doing wrong to the former or injustice to the latter. With his honest nature ever manifesting itself through the simplicity of his character and the modesty of his greatness, he will ever receive the admiration of those who are capable of appreciating manly virtues and valor.

PETERSBURG, APRIL 19, 1865.

THE DEATH OF THE PRESIDENT.

The murder of President Lincoln continues to be the all-absorbing topic. All other matters, whether news or otherwise, sink into insignificance when mentioned in the present state of national affliction. There continues to be one undisguised feeling of horror. Yesterday all business was suspended here and at City Point, in accordance with the recommendation from the Acting Secretary of State. The people seemed to take little notice of the catastrophe. Two bells out of six upon the places for public worship made out to toll, while the others remained silent. Still the Government is feeding thousands of these broken-down rebels, who are cursing it with the same breath which its charity has infused into them.

THE CONDITION OF THE CITY.

Under the energetic influence of Yankee enterprise this city begins to wear quite a business appearance. Stores are being opened by the sutlers, and many of the citizens, with the aid of the market, cater to the wants of the people. It will not be long before the houses which have been damaged by the shelling of our batteries before the occupation will be put in perfect repair. Bolingbrook street received more injuries than any other; but still those meteoric but unwelcome visitors perforated many of the finest places of business and resi-dences in the city. Old and dilapidated ones are being rebuilt, while the number of vessels in the Appomattox give quite a prosperous aspect to affairs of business. The gas in this city has not been interfered with, except by the poverty of circumstances, which somewhat dimmed its lustre. The streets are not lighted up, except where sentinels are posted to guard the city. For a long time before our occupation, gas was only used in the houses under the immediate command of General Ferrero. The city enjoys a more cleanly appearance than at any period since the war. Sweeping the streets and carrying away the filth presented so novel an attraction to the natives, as to bring from them a grudging degree of admiration for the authorities in this respect. The markets are being bountifully supplied with the various good things of life, which disappear, if not mysteriously, certainly effectually, under the magic influence of the legal tender.

Quasi Unionism.

The Petersburg *Express,* than which no paper could have been more treasonable, nor indulged in fouler vituperation against the spotless character of the late President, is now being issued by the same man as a Union journal. This is carrying indulgence beyond the degree of propriety. If any class of men deserve any punishment for their great crime of treason, it is the cultivated rebels, who prostituted themselves to deceive the masses, through the medium of their papers, and continued their malignant spirit until the flag of the Union vindicated its authority. Mercy to this class is a weakness.

Arrival of Troops.

The Second division (colored) 25th Corps, formerly commanded by Brig. Gen. Wm. Birney, arrived within four miles of the city day before yesterday. During the recent campaign the division has seen hard service, principally in marching. Some of the men were wounded, but very few killed. The first troops to enter this city were companies A and H, 8th U. S. C. T., and B and G, 127th U. S. C. T. The regiments all came in about the same time. The 127th is the last colored regiment which left Philadelphia for the front, and though it had the good fortune to lose none of its men, its marching and promptness were of the most gratifying character. The 8th is a veteran regiment, and has done good service upon many a bloody field.

CHAPTER 9

The Occupation

RICHMOND, APRIL 24, 1865.

The moral power of the rebellion is not evinced in any public demonstration, but is manifested privately, or under such circumstances as will not incur the displeasure of the authorities.

Some females were walking up Franklin street, a day or two ago, where, in the vicinity of the Exchange Hotel, there was a large American flag. With a degree of malignity, which conciliation rather strengthens than suppresses, one of them avowed that she would not walk under the Union colors, at the same time crossing to the opposite side of the street, followed by the others. This is but one of the little meannesses in which these rebels indulge, by which they comfort the spirits of treason. One thing is evident, that it matters not how much enmity these people bear against the Government, even those who were known to shout when they heard that President Lincoln was assassinated, they do not hesitate to draw rations from the commissary. What a spectacle of mingled destitution and ingratitude is presented in the field officers of the rebel service receiving rations, and families in this city, who were no less mischievous in their influence to destroy the Union, whom necessity obliges to accept the charity of the Government. Humanity demands, regardless of their infamy of the past, their wickedness of the present, and their obvious disposition for evil in the future, that they should to a certain extent be supplied with food by the authorities.

Rebel officers still continue to strut about in the uniform in which they delighted to murder Union soldiers, in a spirit which is almost beyond the degree of loyal forbearance. If it should be alleged that they are unable to purchase others, the Government could furnish them out of the abundance of uniforms now on hand, and for which there is not likely to be any immediate use. As they did not hesitate to strip our wounded and dead, and not infrequently obliged our prisoners to divest themselves of their clothing, which they would put on with a good deal of pride, they could have no more objection to wearing Government clothes than eating Government rations.

Union officers and soldiers are occasionally recognizing those individuals who treated our troops so brutally while they were prisoners of war in this city and vicinity. They at once introduce themselves, informally recur to past and unpleasant experience, and conclude the scene by administering a well deserved chastisement to those brutes in human form.

Some rebel officers are to be seen with crape upon their left arm, which indicates sorrow and respect for the departed; but whether this is feigned regret for the assassination of the late President or sincere sorrow for the death of the Southern Confederacy, may justly be regarded as an open question.

Col. Lamar,[1] whether of the yacht Wanderer notoriety, or the one who outraged the sense of the British public by lecturing them upon the blessing of human slavery, is a matter of very little difference, was in the city last week.

The authorities are now endeavoring to collect all the goods which were taken away by the poor people on the day of our occupation and during the fire. The wisdom of such a course may be judged by circumstances. If this class of persons had not carried the goods away they would have been consumed. The Jews, who have instigated this proceeding, were the most violent rebels in the South, and justly deserve to forfeit their ill-gotten wealth in the same manner that they reaped it. This would be regarded righteous retribution.

Just after closing my last despatch, I was present at a military execution, on the 20th inst., in the vicinity of City Point, where many soldiers have paid the penalty for violating law. The culprit was Samuel Mays,[2] of the 10th U. S. C. T. His offence was disobedience of orders,

---

1. Lucius Quintus Cincinnatus Lamar (1825–1893). A Mississippi congressman, Lamar is best known for his appointment as a commissioner to Russia, France, and England by Davis. Although the Confederate Senate refused to confirm his appointment, Lamar did negotiate some agreements while in London. *DAB*, V, 551–52; Jon L. Wakelyn, *Biographical Dictionary of the Confederacy*, 274–75.

2. This is an error. The person executed was Samuel Mapp. *List of U.S. Soldiers Executed By United States Military Authorities During the Last War* (N.p., n.d.), 10. My thanks to Gwen Crenshaw for bringing this to my attention.

inciting to mutiny, and threatening the life of his superior officer. What was left at that point of the 10th, and the 28th U. S. C. T.,[3] recruited in Indiana, with a squad of white troops, to keep the crowd back, formed the military present. The execution was performed under the official direction of Lieut. Col. Powell, 10th U. S. C. T., recruited mostly in Maryland. The funeral cortege arrived on the ground about twelve o'clock, in the following order: Band of the 16th New York; first firing party consisting of twelve men from the prisoner's regiment; the coffin carried by four soldiers; the condemned, leaning on the arm of Chaplain White[4] (colored), of the 28th U. S. C. T., and closing up with the second firing party of twelve. The ceremonies at the grave were brief. A prayer from the chaplain, a good-by from the prisoner, a well-fired volley, and the spirit of an unfortunate man appeared before the God who gave it. The body and head of Mays was completely riddled. It seemed as if almost every ball perforated him. Thomas Moran, assistant surgeon, and Samuel Morrow, acting assistant surgeon, were present, and examined the body, having no difficulty in arriving at the conclusion that death was instantaneous.

The colored Methodists in this city who, by force of circumstances, were obliged to remain with the M. E. Church South, decided yesterday, by a unanimous vote of the male members, to dissolve their connection with that branch of Methodists. Bishop Brooks' visit here to his brethren has been eminently successful, and the prompt but cordial manner in which the members dissolved their connection from the slaveholders' organization is due to his presence, and the powerful influence which he has been able to exert.

The military authorities have put some three hundred of the rebels,

3. Organized in Indianapolis in March, 1864, the 28th USCT served at White House, Virginia, and with the Army of the Potomac before it was transferred to the XXV Corps in December, 1864. Frederick H. Dyer, *Compendium of the War of the Rebellion* (Des Moines, Iowa, 1908), 249; *Report of the Adjutant General (W. H. H. Terrell) of the State of Indiana* (8 vols.; Indianapolis, 1866), III, 379–83; "Muster Rolls of the 28th Regiment, U.S. Colored Troops," Indiana State Archives, Indianapolis.

4. Garland H. White (b. 1829). Born in Hanover, Virginia, White was a slave in Georgia and then escaped to Canada. There he became a minister. He claimed to have recruited nearly one-half of the 28th USCT. He was appointed a chaplain in October, 1864. Ira Berlin, Joseph P. Reidy, and Leslie S. Rowland (eds.), *Freedom: A Documentary History of Emancipation 1861–1867*. Series II, *The Black Military Experience* (New York, 1982), 82–83, 141, 348–49; *Report of the Adjutant General of Indiana*, III, 379; Indianapolis *Daily Journal*, January 9, 1865; Edwin S. Redkey, "Black Chaplains in the Union Army," *Civil War History*, XXXIII (1987), 330, 350.

who are confined in Libby, to work in clearing up the rubbish, throwing the bricks off the pavement, and otherwise making the streets passable, which have been blockaded by the recent attempt of the vandals to destroy the city. This is a most excellent use of this mixture of ignominy and infamy. This policy will teach this class to work, which has always been done by the negroes, and should they even be discharged from custody, they will be able for the first time to earn their bread by honest industry.

The weather, which was quite cool yesterday, seems more moderate this morning.

The headquarters of the 2d Corps is to be located in this city, from which would be inferred that the troops will be camped in this vicinity.

RICHMOND, APRIL 26, 1865.

THE RECEPTION OF LEE.

In justice to Union officers and soldiers in this city, candor demands that the impression made by the despatch in the New York *Herald*, from this place, announcing the arrival of Lee, which asserted that they uncovered their heads in token of respect for him, be removed. Though present at the entry of this notorious rebel, I saw none of the evidences of respect spoken of by the *Herald*.

APPOINTMENT OF GENERAL HALLECK.

The appointment of General Halleck[5] to the command of this department has given rise to much speculation. It will give, probably, great satisfaction to the rebels, if he has not changed since his notorious order No. 3, in the West.

5. Henry Wagner Halleck (1815–1872). Probably best known for his Order No. 3 issued in 1861, while he commanded the Department of Missouri, which banned fugitive slaves from entering his lines, Halleck was named military advisor to the president in 1862. Two years later, he was named chief of staff of the army and in April, 1865, was assigned to command the Military Division of the James. *DAB*, IV, 150–52; Dudley T. Cornish, *The Sable Arm: Negro Troops in the Union Army, 1861–1865* (New York, 1956), 25.

The Negroes, and Rebels in Authority.

There have been certain indications here which have truly startled the negroes. It is an unpleasant sight to see men who were villainous in their sentiments in behalf of treason occupying positions under the Government, to whom the blacks must go who are in need of rations. In several instances the white traitor has turned away the black patriot with brutal remarks, secretly glad of the opportunity to inflict upon the friends of the Union so grievous a wrong; while those of similar infamy have been cheerfully supplied with every facility to receive the charity of the Government. It has been intimated that these rebels, through their friends who occupy certain positions, have imposed upon the magnanimity of the authorities, and received assistance when not entitled to it. This state of affairs, coupled with the arrival of General Halleck, has caused a good deal of nervousness among those who are not satisfied that his feelings have undergone a radical change in reference to the loyal blacks.

Jeff Davis.

Jeff Davis begins to realize that the way of the transgressor is hard. His departure from this city, though suddenly, and to some extent unexpectedly undertaken, had been previously provided for in a manner which evinces the consideration which he entertains for himself. From a gentleman who left the city with Davis, to follow his fallen fortunes, it is now ascertained that this arch traitor is with Johnston's army. Upon leaving here he carried with him large sums of gold belonging to individuals, and all the specie of the rebel Government. Previous to the hasty exit of Jeff, he had gathered here all the bullion of the Confederacy, to enter into competition with the speculators, and advance the value of the currency. The people had been threatened, in case of refusal, with heavy taxes, to loan their gold to the rebel authorities, with the aid of which they were foolish enough to believe that they could reduce the price of gold. Without entering into the financial failures of the Confederacy, it is only necessary to state that this large amount of gold was carried away by Davis in his retreat from this city.

My informant says that Davis and his immediate followers were hanging around the camps of the army in a very undignified manner. Spirits were drunk freely to revive their drooping courage, and drunkenness was so general among the party as to be disgusting. The gold carried off is producing the most inharmonious results. They are all appropriating or stealing as much of this rebel plunder as they can get within their reach, and each one is embittered against the other for fear he is getting most of the specie. Each one was watching the other, and all were trying to steal as much as possible. Wretchedness was depicted in every countenance, and utter demoralization was manifested by the chieftain and his dishonest followers to such an extent as to disgust my informant, who left them, and arrived here day before yesterday. He says that Jeff is in danger of being captured any day, and that he is sensible of the perils which environ him. It is more than probable that he manoeuvered the negotiations between Sherman and Johnston, which the Government rejected, with a view of securing terms for himself. My informant is positive in stating that Davis is with the army, and that all other reports are with a view of misleading the authorities.

HEADQUARTERS OF BREVET GENERAL MULFORD.

Brevet Brigadier General Mulford, Commissioner of Exchange, has his headquarters on Tenth street, in the Female Seminary. Since the rebel Government has become a mysterious and an indefinite machine, of a somewhat transmigratory character, with Judge Ould[6] and Captain Hatch,[7] the rebel Commissioners of Exchange, as prisoners in our possession, General Mulford is unable to find any one to treat or negotiate with. Hatch was in the general's quarters yesterday, but whether he will even exchange this scion of demoralized aristocracy, under the cartel, is exceedingly doubtful. He comes within President Johnson's classification of intelligent and influential disloyalists, upon whom is to be visited the penalty commensurate with his offence.

A great many of the packages sent from the North to fathers, brothers, and sons, languishing in Southern jails, were detained here,

6. Robert Ould (1820–1882) was appointed assistant secretary of war by Davis in March, 1862, and four months later became Confederate agent of exchange. He headed the Confederate Secret Service and also served as judge advocate. Wakelyn, *Biographical Dictionary of the Confederacy,* 336; Cornish, *The Sable Arm,* 171; William Best Hesseltine, *Civil War Prisons: A Study in War Psychology* (Columbus, Ohio, 1930), 69.

7. W. H. Hatch (?–?) was Ould's assistant. Both were imprisoned in Libby by Halleck on suspicion of diverting funds sent for the relief of Union prisoners. Ould was released soon after, but there is no word of Hatch's fate. Hesseltine, *Civil War Prisons,* 235–36.

and were found upon our occupation of the city. Judge Ould has
turned them over to Gen. Mulford, who is reshipping those whose
contents will admit of it, to those who forwarded them, while others
are being turned over to the Christian and Sanitary Commissions.

THE THIRD DIVISION.

The 3d Division, 24th Corps, which was temporarily attached to
the Army of the Potomac, deserves its share of the laurels for
capturing Lee and his army, arrived in the city yesterday, and camped
upon the outskirts. The dusty and bronzed appearance of the soldiers
gave evidence of having passed through a severe campaign. They
came from Burkesville, and have been several days on the way. Major
General Gibbons, commander of the 24th Corps, accompanied them.

RICHMOND, APRIL 28, 1865.

The intelligence which reached this city yesterday morning, that
Booth[8] had been hunted down and killed, afforded considerable
satisfaction to the authorities, and the few who had been informed of
the fact, insomuch as it was gratifying that he had not escaped to
chuckle over his crime. There was some regret that he did not meet a
more ignominious fate, with abundant opportunities for reflection in
solitary confinement, under such influences as would have obliged
him to disclose all the particulars, and the names of his confederates.
One thing we may congratulate ourselves upon—that the world is rid
of a monster whose soul, blackened with infamy, passed into the
presence of the God who gave it. He has eluded the punishment of
man, but the retribution of Heaven he cannot escape.

THE COLORED PEOPLE AND THE CHURCHES.

During the past few days the colored population of the city has
manifested in two ways the respect which they have for colored
institutions and the confidence with which they regard them. The
Methodists, after having dissolved the connection of their Church

8. John Wilkes Booth (1838–1865). An actor, Booth shot Lincoln at Ford's Theatre in
Washington, D.C. He was later tracked down and killed by Union soldiers in the early
hours of April 26. *DAB*, I, 448–52.

with the South, placed it under the African Methodist Episcopal Zion
Conference. Rt. Rev. John D. Brooks, being here, received this society,
started it under the constitution of his profession, and, in accordance
with the wishes of some of the influential members, and in deference
to the expressed desire of Rev. Mr. Nolley, the pastor, continued him
in his position until the end of his conference year, which expires in
November.

Twenty-seven dollars in greenbacks, eight dollars in gold, and fifty
cents in silver, were given by an African church of this city, a few
days ago, for the support of the *Anglo-African*,[9] a colored journal
published at the North.

PASSES TO RICHMOND.

I have not seen the order, but was informed at headquarters
yesterday, upon application for a pass for an acquaintance to visit
Richmond, that all military restrictions were removed, and that
whosoever will may come to this partially destroyed city. In a day or
two we may expect to see Richmond crowded by all colors, attracted
here by various impulses. There is no difficulty in coming, but those
going away will be obliged to obtain passes from the provost marshal,
which will be readily given. This restriction is necessary, and is
intended to prevent disloyal persons from going North without the
knowledge of the authorities.

THE NEGROES DO NOT DESIRE TO GO NORTH.

There is no disposition manifested on the part of the negroes to
migrate to the North, but those who are there have already commenced to return with their families, and we may expect to see them
coming back in much larger numbers. The fears entertained that the
North will be over run by freedmen will not be realized. This climate
is most congenial to them, and a little constraint by the military
authorities upon those who are disposed to continue their oppression
would make Virginia the happy home of thousands of redeemed
freedmen. An impartial administration of justice in the Southern

9. Published in New York, the *Anglo-African* (1859–65) was first edited by James
McCune Smith. It was later taken over by Robert Hamilton. Jane H. Pease and William
H. Pease, *They Who Would Be Free: Blacks' Search for Freedom, 1830–1861* (New York,
1974), 119.

States will lay the basis for an enduring peace, prosperity, and good will to all men.

THE PEOPLE.

The rebels in this city, and more particularly the females, refuse, to a very great extent, to make their appearance in the streets, as they are unwilling to walk under the old flag. This class does not hesitate to indulge in the most venomous expressions of disloyalty under what they deem favorable circumstances. How long they may be permitted to continue their enmity to the Government while eating its rations will depend upon the backbone of the authorities. Abundant evidence could be obtained to justify their being placed in confinement. Many of the people in this city are disposed to recognize the logic of events and act accordingly. While some manifest the greatest hatred towards the freedmen, whom they called "Lincoln's niggers," and, in some instances, declared that they would rather see their houses burnt to ashes than rent them to this class; others have adapted themselves to the new state of things, hired their former slaves, and now have the satisfaction of seeing their domestic affairs working along harmoniously.

RICHMOND, APRIL 30, 1865.

Another week of loyal administration has ended, and Sunday, with all of its revered impressions, has dawned upon a redeemed city.

At a meeting of the colored people of Richmond, assembled in the Third-street M. E. church, Thursday, April 18, 1865, to rejoice over our deliverance from bondage, and the triumph of freedom in our land, Mr. Fields Cook[10] was called to the chair, and Mr. Peter Woolfolke[11] was appointed secretary.

10. Fields Cook (?–?). A minister in Richmond and Alexandria, Cook played a prominent role in Reconstruction politics in Virginia. Alrutheus Taylor, *The Negro in the Reconstruction of Virginia* (1926; rpr. New York, 1969), 188, 254, 258; Peter J. Rachleff, *Black Labor in the South: Richmond, Virginia, 1865–1890* (Philadelphia, 1984), 41.

11. Peter H. Woolfolke (?–?) was named president of the Virginia Home Building Fund and Loan Association, a black organization formed in 1868 to finance land acquisition. In 1880 he was one of the incorporators of the Mount Alto Mining and Land Co., which dealt in real estate. Taylor, *The Negro in the Reconstruction of Virginia*, 131, 136.

The meeting was opened with appropriate religious exercises by Bishop Brooks, of Philadelphia.

Mr. George L. Ruffin,[12] of Boston, one of the speakers for the occasion, then addressed the meeting. He thought that, in view of the great calamity which had befallen the nation in the death of President Lincoln, he knew he expressed the feelings of the audience when he said the character of the meeting should be changed to one of condolence and sympathy. Abraham Lincoln's name, no matter what might be said by excited partisans, would go down to posterity as one of the wisest rulers and most sagacious statesmen that this or any other age had produced. Mr. Ruffin thought it peculiarly fortunate that he (the late President) had been selected to carry this country through this ordeal of fire and blood; and now, as peace is about dawning on our torn and distracted country, the Chief Magistrate of the United States, the great Emancipator, is stricken down by the hand of an assassin—Brothers, mourn! sisters, weep! for our best friend has passed away.

A committee was appointed to prepare suitable resolutions. They retired, and, returning, presented the following:

Resolved, That in the assassination of Abraham Lincoln, President of the United States, we have lost our best friend and warmest advocate—that the dastardly act of the murderer fills us with inexpressible horror and indignation, and that we can give no utterance to the feelings of sorrow and sadness which fill our hearts at this present moment.

And further, That this meeting here convened in the house of God, sends forth to the family of our beloved President (now deceased) our heartfelt condolence and sympathy in this the hour of their deep affliction.

The Bishop made an eloquent and appropriate speech in support of the resolutions, followed by Mr. P. N. Judah,[13] O. M. Stewart,[14]

12. George Lewis Ruffin (1834–1886). A Boston lawyer and judge and Massachusetts state legislator, Ruffin was the first black to earn a law degree from Harvard University. Rayford W. Logan and Michael R. Winston (eds.), *Dictionary of American Negro Biography* (New York, 1982), 535; William L. Simmons, *Men of Mark, Eminent, Progressive and Rising* (Cleveland, 1887), 740–43.

13. P. N. Judah (?–?) was possibly a relative of Benjamin Judah, a blacksmith and the largest property owner among black Richmonders before the war. My thanks to Peter Rachleff for the information.

14. O. M. Stewart (?–?) became editor of the *Virginia Star* in the early 1880s. Rachleff, *Black Labor in the South*, 105.

and others. The resolutions were adopted by a unanimous vote, and a motion was made and carried that the proceedings of the meeting be sent to the Richmond *Whig*, the Philadelphia *Recorder*, and the *Anglo-African*, with a request to publish the same. The doxology was then sung and the meeting adjourned.

The editor of the Richmond *Whig*, on receiving the above report, submitted it to General Ord, who returned it with the following endorsement:

"The mayor, the Common Council of Richmond, and a number of citizens of Petersburg, called on the Department commander for permission to hold a meeting of condolence and sympathy on the death of the President, but owing to the peculiar position of affairs here, the meeting was not allowed".

The meeting of the colored people has occurred without any unpleasant circumstances, but not having been authorized by the military commander, it is not deemed proper to publish it here, the city being under military rule. The copy can be sent North and published.

The numerous Secesh of this city are demanding that the loyal blacks shall be excluded from the Capitol Square, while the bands of the colored regiments are giving their tri-weekly serenades in the cool of the afternoon. In fact, the *Times*, conducted by the notorious Pollard,[15] whose name does not appear, has already announced, with considerable chuckling, that this injustice has commenced.

Captain W. H. Hatch, the rebel Commissioner of Exchange, who was captured with others shortly after the surrender of Lee, was arrested yesterday at his residence, on the corner of Leigh and Fourth streets, upon some serious charges of unfair and dishonest dealings with the property and money of our soldiers in rebel prisons. Large quantities of stores which were sent to our suffering troops, and which it now appears never reached their destination, were entrusted to his delivery, and to him has been traced a portion of the complicity which left Union men to starve, while he and others appropriated

15. Edward Alfred Pollard (1831–1872) became co-editor of the Richmond *Examiner* in 1861. A staunch defender of the Confederacy, Pollard despised Davis with a passion and attributed all the South's reverses to the president. Chester made an error when he called Pollard editor of the Richmond *Times*. Wakelyn, *Biographical Dictionary of the Confederacy*, 350–51; J. Cutler Andrews, *The South Reports the Civil War* (1970; rpr. Pittsburgh, 1985), 30–31.

what their relatives and friends at the North had sent to them. Hatch's offence being a serious one, he was confined in Libby, while those of a milder grade are furnished with apartments in Castle Thunder. At the time of the Captain's arrest he was preparing dinner for General Singleton and other Northerners, but was spirited away before the guests arrived. When they came a colored domestic informed them of the involuntary absence of the host, and in her simplicity asked them if they would stay for dinner. They consented to partake of the good things prepared, ate heartily, and after discussing the fate of their host, concluded, late in the afternoon, to see what had become of him.

Hatch's family has, during the war, resided under the old flag in Missouri. After passing the night in Libby in strict confinement, without the privilege of speaking to any one, he was released yesterday morning upon the order of General Ord. The arrest was made by Brigadier General M. R. Patrick, Provost Marshal General.[16]

Mr. E. S. Stewart, who has a kind of a periodical stand in the Spottswood Hotel, was arrested day before yesterday for vending the rebel Marseillaise song. Upon the matter being brought to the notice of General Patrick, he had Stewart escorted to Castle Thunder before his case could be brought to the notice of the higher authorities, who, upon its representation immediately ordered his release. Mr. Stewart is a gentleman of unquestionably loyal instincts.

PETERSBURG, MAY 5, 1865.

THE FIFTH CORPS.

The dull routine of the civil and military administration was relieved yesterday and the day before by the passage through this city of the 25th Corps (colored), under Major General Godfrey Weitzel, followed by the 5th Corps, under Major General Gibbons, and the cavalry under the victorious Sheridan. The negro troops have been camped in the vicinity of this place, but are now gone to a point on the James

16. Marsena Rudolph Patrick (1811–1888). A graduate of West Point and former president of New York State Agricultural College, Patrick fought at Second Bull Run and Antietam. In March, 1865, he was promoted to provost marshal of all armies operating against Richmond. He resigned his post in June over disagreements about how Richmond should be policed. *DAB*, VII, 296–97.

river, about two miles below City Point. There is no remedy so effectual in chilling the warm blood of the South as to put arms in the hands of the negroes. The influence of this element upon the F. F. V.'s —*Fleet-Footed Virginians*—has ever been of a demoralizing tendency upon the relics which may in part explain why it is they are kept so far from these large towns.

The 5th Corps elicited, as it deserves, general commendation for the good order and discipline which it preserved while passing through. The record of the 5th is good, and one of which both officers and men may be justly proud.

SHERIDAN'S CAVALRY.

Sheridan's cavalry was the observed of all observers. The men and horses were in a fine condition.

THE SECOND CORPS.

The 2d Corps has already broken camp at Burkesville, and is moving in this direction. It will pass through the city early this morning, following the 5th.

A BALL.

On last night a ball came off, in good, if not grand style, at the headquarters of Brevet Major General Ferrero. Among the guests were Major General Hartsuff and lady, Brevet Brigadier General McKibbin[17] and lady, Colonel Sewel and lady, Miss Cole, of New York, and Miss Hyle of Philadelphia. The music was furnished by the bands of the 2d Pennsylvania Heavy Artillery and the 10th New York Regiments. The evening was spent in the highest state of enjoyment. The ladies moved like fairies over the floor, and the gentlemen with an ease which the rough experience of martial campaigning had not affected. None but loyalists were present.

17. Gilbert Hunt McKibbin (b. 1837) mustered in as a private, 7th New York Militia, in April, 1861. He was brevetted brigadier general of volunteers in December, 1864. Frederick Phisterer (comp.), *New York in the War of the Rebellion, 1861 to 1865* (5 vols.; New York, 1912), III, 2408, V, 4294.

AMUSING SCENES.

Amusing scenes are daily witnessed at headquarters and at the provost marshal's office, in which former slaveholders are the principal actors. Those which excite the greatest mirth are the demands of the chivalry for an order to make their man Jim or their girl Hannah work for them. Capt. E. O. Brown, A. D. C., on the staff of Gen. Hartsuff, after hearing the complaints, explains, in a very courteous manner, the relationship which this former species of chattle sustains to the chivalry and the community, and winds up with a commendable amount of positiveness, that such requests will not be granted. The rebels, not a little excited, generally want to know if the negroes are to be put upon an equality with them. The Captain, who always preserves his amiability as long as this class keeps within the bounds of propriety, meets these flings by informing the parties that military authorities never discuss their decisions. The gray-coated gentry invariably evaporate.

LADY VISITORS.

The bearing of the Union officers and their lady relatives who are visiting them, towards the rebels in this city, is eminently worthy of the loyalty which they profess. Their conduct, while it is squared by every degree of propriety, evinces a consciousness of that innate respectability and social standing which could not be improved by rebel condescension. The independence of officers and Union ladies, and their manifest indifference to the existence of the chivalry, have the effect of convincing this deluded people that there are some persons from the North who are unwilling to be patronized by disloyalists, and who are the avowed enemies of the Government. Such a dignified course will have great influence.

THE CITY.

The city is very quiet and more orderly than it has been at any period during the rebellion. The patrol duty is well performed, and the citizens are enjoying a degree of security as to their persons and property which they did not experience in Secesh times. Brevet Major

General Ferrero commands the city, and his regulations for the good of all are upon a basis of justice and impartiality.

All citizens are required to be in their houses at ten o'clock, unless they have the proper pass from the authorities authorizing them to remain out later. The difficulties to locomotion after that hour are numerous, and are encountered at every few steps in the attitude of a gentleman in blue, standing at a "ready", commanding you to "halt." After a few questions you are ordered to "advance", and after an inspection of your credentials, if found to be all right, you are permitted to pass until you are halted by the next sentry, which is about a square further off. The same formality is repeated at each halt, which is exceedingly perplexing to civilians, but is absolutely necessary for the security of the city.

RICHMOND, MAY 7, 1865.

Yesterday the people of this city were treated to a display of a part of the martial strength of the nation. The scene was one of congratulation to all loyalists, but inspired different emotions among the rebels. The 5th and 2d Corps of the grand Army of the Potomac, with all their retinue of generals and their staff officers, cavalry and artillery, paraded through the principal streets. To say that the spectacle was a grand one, and that the marching generally was excellent, is but to express what the reader would inevitably imagine. The men all looked well, but in some of the regiments manifested unmistakeable evidences of fatigue.

The three divisions of the 24th Corps, under Foster, Turner, and Devin, were drawn up in line along Main streets, they reached Franklin, thus giving the returning heroes, as they passed by them, a view of the principal part of the city. This corps, having had the advantage of a residence in this city, has provided itself with all those requisites which are necessary to the faultless appearance of soldiers on parade or review. The brushed-up appearance of these troops is an evidence of the good discipline which exists among them.

THE REVIEW.

At nine o'clock, Major General Meade, accompanied by Brigadier Generals Devin, Turner, and Curtis, and their respective staffs, well mounted, passed along Main street, at the head of the column until it reached the city hall, where they dismounted, and taking a position upon the steps, where they were joined by Major General Halleck, Major General Ord, and other general officers, reviewed the army as it passed. The Fifth Corps cheered Generals Halleck and Meade, at first very lively, but as the rear came up, the men were, no doubt, so wearied by the hard marches of the past few days, and exhausted by the rapid gait by which they were brought through the city, that the last of the Fifth and the whole of the Second Corps were physically unable to give expression to that enthusiasm in which soldiers delight to participate.

THE LADIES.

These eminent officers remained on the steps, reviewing the columns, from half-past nine until half-past three before the last of it passed, and though they fronted the capitol grounds, where an abundance of shade would have afforded ample protection to a very large number of the fair ones, the rebel damsels and dames did not make their appearance.

THE DIFFERENT REGIMENTS.

Washington is supposed to be the destination of this army, with a view of being mustered out of service. It may be a matter of interest to their friends to know what regiments are on the way. The 5th Corps, under Major General Griffin,[18] marched by the commanding generals in the following order, the cavalry being in the advance: 14th and 11th Regulars, 10th, 3d, and 50th New York Engineers, 15th New York Engineers, 185th New York, 198th Pennsylvania, 198th New York, 187th New York, 188th New York, 1st Maine, 16th Michigan, 155th Pennsylvania (Zouave), 118th Pennsylvania (Corn Exchange), 83d Pennsylvania, 32d Massachusetts, 8th Delaware, 20th Maine, 91st Pennsylvania, 114th Pennsylvania (Zouaves), 5th New York, 114th New York, 140th New York, 15th New York (heavy artillery), 61st

18. Charles Griffin (1825–1867). A West Point graduate, Griffin was named brigadier general of volunteers in 1862 and commanded a brigade of the V Corps in the Peninsula campaign, Antietam, Fredericksburg, and Chancellorsville. He was put in command of the V Corps in April, 1865. *DAB*, IV, 617–18.

Massachusetts, 8th Maryland, 7th Maryland, 1st Maryland, 4th Maryland, 1st Veteran (210th) Pennsylvania Rifles, 4th Delaware, 3d Delaware, 8th Delaware, 191st Pennsylvania (2d Veteran Reserves), 6th Wisconsin, 7th Wisconsin, 91st New York (heavy artillery), 16th Maine, 107th Pennsylvania, 104th New York, 39th Massachusetts, 97th New York, 11th Pennsylvania, 121st Pennsylvania, 146th Pennsylvania, 147th New York, 24th New York, 95th New York, 88th Pennsylvania, 56th Pennsylvania, and 91st New York. Then came the artillery brigade, under Gen. Wainwright.[19]

Major General Humphreys,[20] commanding the 2d Corps, marched at the head of the column, which was composed as follows: 14th Connecticut, 12th New York, 108th New York, 7th (loyal) Virginia, 4th Ohio, 10th (German) New York, 69th Pennsylvania, 1st Delaware, 20th Massachusetts, 19th Massachusetts, 7th Michigan, 152d New York, 1st Minnesota, 59th New York, 19th Maine, 184th Pennsylvania, 36th Wisconsin, 170th New York, 8th New York Heavy Artillery, 164th New York, 69th New York (Irish), 155th New York, 118th New York (Irish), 4th New York Heavy Artillery. Then followed the artillery under Colonel Hazzard, and the following infantry: 1st Massachusetts Heavy Artillery, 57th Pennsylvania, 141st Pennsylvania, 93d New York, 5th Michigan, behind which a lady was mounted on the back of a horse, probably the daughter of the regiment; 17th Maine, 105th Pennsylvania, 8th New Jersey, 7th New York, 120th New York, 11th New York, 11th Massachusetts, 20th Indiana, 1st Maine Heavy Artillery, 124th New York, 99th Pennsylvania, 73d New York, 86th New York, 40th New York, 110th Pennsylvania, 2d New York Heavy Artillery, 5th New Hampshire, 61st New York, 81st Pennsylvania, 140th Pennsylvania, 26th Michigan, 4th New York Heavy Artillery, 69th New York, 28th Massachusetts, 88th New York, 63d New York, 111th New York, 7th New York (German), 125th New York, 39th New York, 126th New York, 52d New York, 183d Pennsylvania, 116th Pennsylvania, 148th Pennsylvania, 64th New York, 145th Pennsylvania, 53d Pennsylvania.

19. Charles Sheils Wainwright (?–?). Formerly a colonel, 1st New York Artillery, Wainwright was brevetted brigadier general in October, 1864, and was made chief of artillery in the V Corps. Mark Mayo Boatner III, *The Civil War Dictionary* (New York, 1959), 883; *OR*, Ser. I, Vol. XLII, Pt. 3, pp. 449, 462, 483.

20. Andrew Atkinson Humphreys (1810–1883) was Meade's chief of staff until November, 1864, when he left to take command of the II Corps. Henry H. Humphreys, *Andrew Atkinson Humphreys: A Biography* (Philadelphia, 1924), Chap. 15.

TREATMENT OF THE SOLDIERS.

Some idea of the martial grandeur of yesterday may be imagined, by the enumeration of the number of regiments composing the column. With the exception of the cheering of the troops for the generals, no other demonstrations were indulged in, barring one or two instances of ladies along the route waving their handkerchiefs. Some members of the Christian and Sanitary Commissions were on hand supplying the troops with water. Everything passed off quietly; and while the rebels could not but feel mortified at the victorious Army of the Potomac entering Richmond in triumph, which they had claimed to have annihilated, they gave unmistakable evidence of resignation.

APPEARANCE OF THE TROOPS.

With the bands playing, the muskets gleaming, the stars and stripes proudly waving over brave men, the sacred colors which have frequently received their baptism of fire flaunting their tattered remnants, the splendid appearance of the 24th Corps receiving the heroes with appropriate honors, coupled with other parts of the pageantry, combined to make the entry of the army under General Meade yesterday the grandest military display ever witnessed in any city of the Union. If any other evidence was wanting to convince these deluded people of the folly of Secession, it was evident in the manifested power of the Federal Government to vindicate its authority. As the gray cloth gentry looked upon the troops they would remark, one to the other: "We'r not whipped; we'r only outnumbered". It is by such reflection that the chivalry console themselves in their humiliation and disgrace.

THE REWARD FOR JEFF DAVIS.

The reward for Jeff Davis and other conspirators, who plotted the assassination of the late lamented President, has caused great satisfaction among the soldiers and loyal citizens. I have understood from those who accompanied him in his flight, until they were disgusted with his company, that his capture was regarded as almost certain. No event could hardly afford so much satisfaction as the arrest of this arch traitor, and his being brought before the bar of that justice which he has so long outraged for trial.

GENERAL ORD.

The conciliation policy of Gen. Ord to the rebel dignitaries here does not seem, in all cases, to receive the approval of the authorities at Washington. Capt. Hatch, one of the rebel commissioners of exchange, of whose arrest and discharge from Libby I informed you several days ago, has been rearrested, by instructions from the Government, for mal-appropriation of the stores and money belonging to our soldiers while in Southern prisons. Upon an examination of the case, General Ord concluded that Hatch had done nothing worthy of confinement, but higher authorities have taken the liberty to dissent from such judgment, and have ordered his reincarceration in Libby, where he will have abundant opportunities to reflect over the villainy which it appears he has been practicing upon both Union and rebel prisoners.

JUDGE OULD.

Judge Ould, the senior commissioner, has also taken apartments at the hotel de Libby, which, if not as ornamental as those previously occupied by this unfortunate apostate, are exceedingly useful for the purpose for which they are appropriated. When such influential rebels as Ould and Hatch are confined with a view of bringing them to trial, it will have the effect of causing others to realize the extent of their turpitude against the Government, and instead, as they are now doing, muttering defiance against its authority, tremble for the outrages which they have perpetrated upon the constituted authorities who are now in a position to vindicate the majesty of the law.

RICHMOND, MAY 9, 1865.

ARREST OF REBEL DETECTIVES.

Yesterday the provost guard made a descent upon the Spottswood Hotel, and arrested Joseph G. Connor, a detective in the rebel service, who, under Federal rule, has been doing a rushing business in levying black mail, and his comrade, F. W. Roberts,[21] of the English 'suasion. Roberts claims to be in her Majesty's service; that he is unjustly restrained of his liberty, and threatens the military authorities with the growl of the British lion. He has taken rooms in Castle Thunder, while Connor is furnished with accommodations in Libby.

THE SPOTTSWOOD HOTEL.

The Spottswood Hotel is at present the largest place open for the accommodation of the public. It is the resort of the two extremes of society—gentlemen, fashionable loafers, broken-down chivalry, Union officers, rebel chieftains, eminent visitors, thieves, gamblers, and every possible phase of society, are seen thronging in jostling confusion the front and inside of this public house. The post office being under the hotel gives additional life to the animating spectacle that is witnessed throughout the day.

AN INCIDENT.

Among the interesting incidents which are being related in connection with the evacuation of this city, is one which may be worthy of consideration among the medical faculty. A colored girl, whose sight had long been defective, became blind about five months ago, and continued so until the terrible explosion of the magazine in this city, which seemed to shake creation. Recovering herself almost immediately from her fright, she exclaimed, "Mother, I can see". I have conversed with the person, and have been assured by her that her sight since that memorable morning has been wonderfully improved, though her eyes bear evidence of being defective.

21. Possibly F. W. Roberts is a pseudonym for Augustus Charles Hobart Hampden, son of the Earl of Buckinghamshire. Something of a soldier of fortune, Roberts took leave of absence from the British armed forces to conduct gun-running expeditions between Nassau and Wilmington. When his ship, the *Don*, was captured, Roberts had already left his command. The new chief officer did not reveal his identity, and everyone assumed that Roberts had been captured. Northern newspapers trumpeted his capture, only to be embarrassed when the prisoner's true identity was revealed. Ella Lonn, *Foreigners in the Confederacy* (Chapel Hill, 1940), 300–301.

ARREST OF TWO COURIERS.

Nandosan and Barrows, two couriers of the 89th New York, were arrested yesterday for burglariously entering *The Press* Bureau and appropriating some articles to their own use. The property has not been discovered, but sufficient proof has been adduced to deem their incarceration a public benefit.

PHILADELPHIA PRESS BUREAU

RICHMOND, MAY 13, 1865.

AWARDING OF PRIZE MEDALS.

The Secretary of War has awarded beautiful prize medals, for gallant services performed on the memorable 29th of September, 1864, at New Market Heights, to 1st Sergt. Edward Ratcliff,[22] Co. C, 38th U. S. C. T.; Corporal Miles James,[23] Co. B, 36th U. S. C. T.; private James Gardner,[24] Co. I, 36th U. S. C. T.; and private Wm. Barnes,[25] Co. C, 38th U. S. C. T. These testimonials have been received by General Draper, commanding the brigade of which these regiments are a part, and through whom they will be presented to the brave men, who have faithfully earned this acknowledgment from the Government. Major General Weitzel, commanding the Corps, has been chosen to make the presentation speech.

THE NEGRO TROOPS.

The colored corps is now posted near City Point, where it has gone into a camp of instruction. The 36th and 38th Regiments have done

22. Edward Ratcliff (?–?) assumed command after the death of the commanding officer and was the first enlisted man to cross into the enemy's fortifications. George Washington Williams, *A History of the Negro Troops in the War of the Rebellion, 1861–1865* (New York, 1888), 336.

23. Miles James (?–?). A corporal, James was promoted to sergeant after New Market Heights, where he continued to fight even after one of his arms was so badly mutilated that it had to be amputated. Williams, *A History of Negro Troops,* 336.

24. James Gardiner (?–?). A private, Gardiner was promoted to sergeant after New Market Heights, where he rushed the parapets and shot and bayonetted the Rebel officer. Williams, *A History of Negro Troops,* 335.

25. William H. Barnes (?–?). Private Barnes was wounded but continued to fight and was one of the first to enter the Rebels' works. Williams, *A History of Negro Troops,* 336.

good service, and the Government manifests its appreciation of their worth by foreshadowing a policy which is likely to continue all negro troops in the service until their term of enlistment expires.

THE REGULAR OFFICERS.

Those who are lieutenants and captains in the regular army, but who have been brigadiers and major generals in the volunteer service, do not like the idea of coming down from their greatness; and, in order to avoid such a mortification, many officers who heretofore manifested nothing but contempt for negro discipline and valor, and especially for those who commanded them, have signified their willingness to accept positions in the sable military establishment. It is hardly to be expected that the brave war-scarred gentlemen, who have made the negro a soldier under such perilous circumstances, will be mustered out to afford the officers of the regular army commands equal to their rank in the volunteer service. Officers who refused, as they declared, from principle, to enter the colored corps, should not, for the sake of position, be permitted to compromise with their prejudices. There are many persons of the regular army who have commissions in the negro service, who have contributed greatly to its present efficiency, who, as an act of justice to them, and all others engaged in so difficult a task, should be continued as long as they are worthy of the positions.

ESCAPE OF DICK TURNER FROM LIBBY.

It is not without considerable regret that I announce the escape of the notorious Dick Turner[26] from the Libby Prison, on night before last, by breaking or removing one of the iron bars which separated him from the street. This man was one of the under-strappers or keepers of Libby in rebel times, and excelled all the other barbarians in inflicting the most brutal and murderous treatment upon Union prisoners. It is hardly possible for an individual to achieve as much infamy in a similar position as has fallen to the share of Turner. His

26. Dick Turner (?–?). A major, Turner ran Libby Prison and was considered cruel by Union prisoners. He made sure that the inmates had only minimal rations, which consisted of a small square piece of cornbread, usually infested with vermin, and a small piece of bacon. Emory M. Thomas, *The Confederate State of Richmond: A Biography of the Capital* (Austin, 1971), 172.

place of confinement was under ground—his food bread and water, and a sentry was posted before his door to prevent such a misfortune as has taken place. As no guard was in front of the building, on the pavement, it is possible that some assistance was furnished by sympathizing friends from the outside, who afforded him shelter and food. The Libby has recently been used as a camp of distribution, and with the exception of Turner, Judge Ould, and Captain Hatch, the Rebel Commissioners of Exchange, no other persons are confined there.

CASTLE THUNDER.

Castle Thunder is used by the authorities as the military prison, and affords a securer place for criminals than Libby, having been fitted up for that purpose. It is due to the authorities to state that since Dick's escape, a sentry has been posted in front of his place of confinement. He has not been arrested yet, nor is there much likelihood of his recapture where he has so many hiding places among the rebels of Virginia.

ARREST OF HUNTER.

R. M. T. Hunter,[27] ex. U. S. Senator, was arrested a few days since in Essex county, by a guard sent to look him up. It is not known where he is confined or whither he has been sent.

GOVERNOR PIERPONT.

It is now understood that Governor Pierpont[28] will arrive in this city on the 16th inst., when he will immediately locate his Government here.

27. Robert Mercer Taliaferro Hunter (1809–1887). Congressman, Speaker of the House, and senator, Hunter was one of the South's leading spokesmen before the war. During the conflict, he was Davis' secretary of state, and one of Virginia's senators and represented the South at the Hampton Roads Conference. Wakelyn, *Biographical Dictionary of the Confederacy*, 244; Patricia L. Faust (ed.), *Historical Times Illustrated Encyclopedia of the Civil War* (New York, 1986), 376.

28. Francis Harrison Pierpont (1814–1899). A Virginian Unionist and supporter of Lincoln from the western part of the state, Pierpont was elected governor of West Virginia. In 1863 he was wartime governor of the few northern counties of Virginia under the control of Federal forces. *DAB*, VII, 584–85; Faust (ed.), *Historical Times Illustrated Encyclopedia*, 584–85.

PHILADELPHIA PRESS BUREAU

SALE OF GOVERNMENT HORSES AND MULES.

Yesterday a large number of condemned horses and mules, belonging to the Government, were disposed of to the highest bidder. The number of animals sold and the scarcity of the legal-tender combined to afford excellent bargains to those who were prepared for instant settlement. The war has deprived the farmers in Virginia of nearly, if not entirely, all their stock, and the Government is giving them such opportunities to commence anew as are within the ability of the humblest tillers of the soil. Mules and horses were knocked down at very reasonable rates, and the citizens were generally satisfied that they had good bargains. A good deal of private stock was also sold at satisfactory figures.

THE PONTOON BRIDGES.

The pontoon bridges which span the river between this city and Manchester were washed away early yesterday morning by some heavy pieces of timber coming against them, which the sudden rise from the recent heavy rains forced from their moorings on the Richmond shore. Not much, if any, of the bridge was lost. The engineers soon reunited the structure, and uninterrupted communication was had with the village of Manchester. The rapidity with which this breach was repaired is but another evidence of that enterprising spirit in the American army, which has ever been equal to the emergency.

A COMICAL MARRIAGE.

Quite a large concourse of persons were assembled at the Colored Episcopal Church, on Third street, last evening, to witness the marriage of a loving couple. The groom and bride, with a long train of delegated attendants, in all the paraphernalia of fashion, came in carriages, which attracted no little attention as well as created some sensation in the neighborhood. The groom, with a light step, leaped from his seat and assisted out his smiling bride, who had, no doubt, long prayed for that hour. The long retinue of groomsmen and bridesmaids followed the happy pair down the aisles to the altar, where Rev. Mr. Gladman was waiting to perform the ceremony, in the presence of a large concourse of friends and spectators. The minister cleared his throat, arose with solemn countenance, looked complacently upon the couple who stood before him, and asked for the license from the military authorities. The groom immediately replied he had it, and putting his hand quickly into one of his pockets, and then in another, until huge drops of perspiration began to ooze forth, and a gloom of the most unpleasant forebodings began to settle upon the bridal party. All eyes were now turned towards the groom, and every moment they expected to see the magic paper come forth, but, to the utter astonishment of every one, he at length found voice enough to say that he had left the license at home. There was a general murmur of merriment at this intelligence, which the groom pretended not to notice, and started in person for that important document. The interim was spent in laughing over the incident, and on his return every one expected to see a happy issue out of this affliction, but was somewhat startled when he informed the parson that he could not find his license. Amid the suppressed amusement of those assembled, the bridal party were obliged to return to their carriages and their homes, with many regrets that the military authorities require the observance of certain restrictions. General orders No. 4 contains the following extract pertaining to matrimony:

GENERAL ORDER No. 4.

V. No marriage license will be issued until the parties desiring to be married take the oath of allegiance to the United States, and no clergyman, magistrate, or other person, authorized by State laws to perform the marriage ceremony, will officiate in such capacity until he himself and the parties contracting matrimony have taken the prescribed oath of allegiance.

VI. Any person acting in violation of these orders will be arrested, and a full account of the case reported to these headquarters.

By order of Major General Halleck:

J. C. KELTON, A. A. G.

A DISLOYALIST ARRESTED.

John G. Watkins, an inhabitant of Powhatan county, yesterday avowed the most disloyal sentiments. The renegade was soon arrested by the provost guard, whose authority he was a little disinclined to respect, but a couple of persuaders in the form of six-shooters, had a most excellent effect in convincing Watkins that discretion is the better part of valor. He was lodged in Castle Thunder, where better men for a nobler cause have suffered and died.

A BALL.

A public ball is announced to come off next Wednesday evening, 17th inst., under such military protection as will insure good order. A pleasant time and a large crowd are anticipated. Tickets are selling at two dollars each.

CONDITION OF THE POST OFFICE.

The post office here has not yet got into regular working order. At present it is but very little more than an army concern. The mails, with the exception of those for Washington, are all sent to Fortress Monroe, where they remain for twenty-four hours before they are forwarded North. It is to be hoped that Dr. Sharp, the new postmaster, will soon be able to put this office in regular running order, so as to insure the prompt and early forwarding of the mails to all points of the North. Dr. Sharp is a native of Cumberland county, Pennsylvania, though recently he hails from Missouri.

ARREST OF A UNION SCOUT.

Chas. A. Phelps, who has been a Union scout, was detected some time ago in several cases of horse-stealing, and sent to Castle Thunder. He escaped several days ago, but on yesterday morning was rearrested and sent to his old quarters. His operations were chiefly in this city.

CHAPTER 10

Early Reconstruction

PHILADELPHIA PRESS BUREAU

RECEPTION OF THE NEWS OF DAVIS' CAPTURE.

No day in the week has been more eventful than Sunday during the recent war. If battles were not always fought on that holy day, the intelligence of them was generally received, and not unfrequently announced, from the pulpit during divine service. In the absence of reliable intelligence, alarmists would choose it as the most desirable to retail their fears, and often it was deemed proper to set afloat sensational rumors. Ever since we have been in Richmond the quiet of the Sabbath has been disturbed by intelligence of a thrilling and an exciting character. On the first Sabbath after occupation we received the inspiring news that Lee had surrendered, on the second the sad tidings of the assassination of the lamented President was communicated to the people, and on yesterday the loyal people were more than delighted by the information that Jeff Davis and his fugitive followers had all been captured in Georgia. It is unnecessary to say that every Union soldier rejoiced when he heard the joyful news that this arch traitor had really been hunted down and handed over for trial by those laws whose majesty he has so long insulted. The news was regarded at first as too good to be true, but when it was realized the exultation of loyal hearts was evident in their frequent congratulations over the event, and in the gratification which it afforded them to communicate the good news.

FEELING OF THE REBELS IN REGARD TO THE CAPTURE.

The rebels here are much mortified over the misfortune of Davis, and express regrets that he did not make his escape. These are the generations who alone seem to say a good word in his favor; all other classes, regarding him as the cause of all their sufferings, the war, and its attending miseries, have for some time been praying that he might be captured by our forces and handed over to that justice which he has so long outraged by wholesale slaughters of men upon land and innumerable piracies at sea. In the arrest of Davis the high-born and high-titled "graybacks" imagine they see their own doom fore-shadowed. They believe that if the late President were alive that even this great chieftain would receive his clemency, but from Mr. Johnson they expect no mercy.

MISCELLANEOUS SCRAPS OF NEWS.

Major General Wright, commanding the 6th Corps, which is still on duty in Virginia, and Hon. George W. McLellan, one of the Assistant Postmaster Generals, are in town.

The National Bank of Virginia, which has got its arrangements in working order, will commence business to-day in the custom house, with S. T. Sult, late of the banking house of Ford, Sult, & Co., New York, as president, and J. B. Morton, of this city, as cashier.

The General Baptist Association of Virginia is to be convened on the 1st of June. This denomination is quite numerous in this State.

The Richmond College, which, during the rebellion, has been used as a hospital for Louisiana rebels, is about to be reopened for instruction. Before the war the college boasted of a faculty of six professors and a tutor, and had graduated twelve classes.

PHILADELPHIA PRESS BUREAU

RICHMOND, MAY 17, 1865.

HOTELS OFFERED FOR RENT AND SALE.

Yesterday an effort was made in a public manner to lease the Exchange Hotel, but no one was to be found with a sufficient amount of cash to undertake the business. The Ballard House is also for sale, but it is hardly probable that any person in Richmond disposed to engage in such an enterprise, has come out of the wreck of ruins with sufficient available financial ability. These hotels are every way superior to the Spottswood, but were obliged to close, during the war, for a want of the amount of patronage necessary to keep them in running order. They are directly opposite each other on Franklin street, and were conducted as one hotel, being connected by a passage running across from the first story. Some enterprising Yankee has an excellent opportunity here to make a grand bargain, or begin a successful business.

DISTINGUISHED PERSONAGES.

Colonel G. H. Hart, one of Governor Pierpont's suite, has arrived. The Governor is expected tomorrow. Hon. John S. Millison, ex-member of Congress from the Norfolk district, is in the city.

James M. Ford, a Richmondite, was arrested by the military yesterday, and sent to Libby upon charges not yet known to the public.

AUCTION SALE OF REBEL UNIFORMS.

At auction, yesterday, rebel uniform jackets were knocked down at ten cents each, by the box full. This may be regarded as an evidence of the respect which the people here have for the colors in which traitors delighted to shoot down patriots. Nothing can be more gratifying than the consciousness which is herein evinced that the hated gray is morally contraband. Rebel officers who have the means got out of it as fast as they can, while boys and negroes may be seen sporting suits of rank with a wonderful unconsciousness of their infamy.

PHILADELPHIA PRESS BUREAU

RICHMOND, MAY 19, 1865.

FEELING OF THE PEOPLE.

The transition of feelings and sentiments is not always as rapid as events. The sudden and complete triumph of the Union army over the rebels found them wrapt up in all the prejudices and hatred towards the national authority which four years of civil strife could possibly engender. The inexorable logic of events is, however, fast dissipating all ideas of slavery, all delusions of State rights, and all dreams of a Southern Confederacy. The people are rapidly recognizing their duty under the restored order of affairs, having become wisely resigned to what they cannot control. Harmony and good feeling seem to pervade the different phases of society, except among that class of most pious and distinguished poor ladies who cannot yet deny themselves the luxury of turning up their noses at the blue coats. They seem to abominate music even to the tune of "Hail Columbia" and the "Star spangled Banner," and do not hesitate to express the most rebellious sentiments to that class of Union officers who are disposed to be patronized by them. But this state of things will soon subside and yield to their more conservative husbands, fathers, and brothers, who are thoroughly disgusted with war, and have at last realized their folly in attempting to destroy the best Government which a common ancestry could have bequeathed to generations for all time. Strange as it may seem, the better class of Southern people generally are of the opinion, and I think they are sincere, that the Government and the Union are now stronger today than ever before.

RECONSTRUCTION OF VIRGINIA.

The reconstruction of the State of Virginia will not, under the circumstances, be very difficult. The people are a little nervous about confiscation, but with great unanimity agree that slavery and rebellion are both consigned to one grave. The exact policy of the new State Government has not been foreshadowed, but it is generally understood among Unionists of the city that all persons who have taken the oath, without reference to their past connection with the rebellion, will be permitted to exercise the right of suffrage. The negroes are not to be included. The loyal men of Virginia, with more magnanimity than the rebels ever thought of extending to them, are industriously engaged in smoothing the way for their misguided brethren to return to the full enjoyment of their political rights.

GOVERNOR PIERPONT.

Whatever may be thought in the North of Governor Pierpont, his coming here is hailed with goodness by the loyal men of the States, while they are satisfied no one has a right to complain until after he has had a trial of exercising his Executive abilities in the reconstruction of this Commonwealth. The intelligence received that he will not arrive until next week is rather a disappointment, as his advent is supposed to be the inauguration of a policy of conciliation. One thing is certain, that a good man, called to the responsible position of Governor of Virginia, has it in his power, at this time, to reorganize the State upon a basis of enduring loyalty, unswerving justice, and compensated industry to that class whose sudden emancipation requires protection for their property and guarantees for their labor.

OPPOSITION TO GOVERNOR PIERPONT.

It cannot be disguised that those who have been the enemies of the Government are much opposed to Governor Pierpont being the Executive of this Commonwealth. They regard it as an act of humiliation that he should be sent from Alexandria to manage the destinies of this great State. They are even unblushing enough to demand, socially of course, that some prominent rebel should have been honored with this mark of honor and confidence. Some of them say that if men are to be sent from the North to fill the offices that the Southern blood will not submit to it.

ARRIVAL OF TROOPS IN MANCHESTER.

Generals Getty's[1] and Rickett's[2] divisions of the 6th Corps have arrived in Manchester. The other division is under General Wheaton,[3]

1. George Washington Getty (1819–1901). Appointed brigadier general of volunteers in 1862, Getty was attached to the Army of the Potomac and fought at Fredericksburg. He was promoted to major in 1864 and was commander of the VI Corps during the Battle of the Wilderness and at Petersburg. *DAB*, IV, 230.

2. James Brewerton Ricketts (1817–1887). A Mexican War veteran, Ricketts was commander of a battery in General McDowell's army at the outbreak of the war. He was wounded and taken prisoner at First Bull Run, and was exchanged in time to fight at Second Bull Run. He was again wounded at Antietam. By early 1864, he was in command of a division that fought in the Wilderness, at Spotsylvania, and at Petersburg. Ricketts fought with Sheridan in the Shenandoah Valley, where he was wounded at Cedar Creek. *DAB*, VIII, 587.

3. Frank Wheaton (1833–1903). A lieutenant in a Rhode Island Infantry regiment that suffered heavy casualties at Bull Run, Wheaton also fought in the Peninsula campaign and at the end of 1862 was promoted to brigadier general of volunteers. By the end of the war, he had attained the rank of brevet major general. *DAB*, X, 38–39.

and is guarding the railroad and other places where their presence is deemed necessary between Richmond and Danville.

THE SALE OF LIQUORS.

The orders of Brigadier General Dent,[4] the military governor, suppressing the sale of liquor, have not been faithfully observed. From some source the supply was more than equal to the demand, and occasionally intoxicated persons have been seen wandering about under its staggering influences. In order to remedy the evil, the authorities have adopted the right of search among the passengers from the North and Norfolk, with a view of stopping the supply. Day before yesterday this rigorous measure was enforced for the first time, and the opening of trunks, boxes, and band-boxes disclosed various amounts of liquor, from a bottle to ten gallons, all of which were confiscated. As long as liquor is as profitable as it is, there will be found means to elude, in many cases, the efforts of the authorities to capture and confiscate it. An individual by the name of Dickerman, was sent to try the realities of Castle Thunder, for vending liquor yesterday against the peace and dignity of the military regulations.

THE MAYOR.

The big black Russian bloodhound which has just arrived at Washington, and, according to the papers, is creating a sensation, is the property of Joseph Mayo, mayor of this city, who surrendered it. He loaned the dog to the rebel authorities to hunt down Union soldiers, and is now trying to resume the functions of his former position, with the consent of the authorities.

BRIGADIER GENERAL F. T. DENT RELIEVED.

Yesterday morning Brig. Gen. F. T. Dent was relieved from duty as military commander of the city of Richmond, by order of Gen. Ord. Gen. Dent will probably leave this morning for Washington, to present the notice of the difficulty before the higher tribunals for their

4. Frederick Tracy Dent (1812–1892) commanded a regiment in the Army of the Potomac and served as Grant's aide-de-camp. He was made military governor of Richmond. *DAB*, III, 242.

adjustment. The city will be included in the district of Henrico, under Brig. Gen. M. R. Patrick, provost marshal general of the Department of Virginia. Gens. Halleck and Patrick are most harmonious in all their intercourse.

A GENERAL ORDER.

The following general order was issued yesterday:

HEADQ'RS MILITARY DIVISION OF THE JAMES
                          RICHMOND, VA., MAY 18, 1865.

General Orders No.—
I. The President's proclamation in regard to former officers of the rebel Government of Virginia does not apply to clerks of record courts, sheriffs, and local magistrates retained in office or appointed under military order. Officers so retained or appointed derive their authority from the de facto military government, and not from their election or appointment under any former government. They are, therefore, directly responsible to the military power for their conduct and the proper performance of their duties.
II. No civil officer will be appointed or retained in office by military authority who has not voluntarily taken the oath of allegiance, or who does not come within the provisions of the amnesty proclamation. As soon as the proper civil officers in any county, city, or town are duly elected or appointed and qualified under the restored civil government, those appointed or retained by military authority will cease to exercise the functions of their office.
By order of Major General Halleck.

                          J. C. KELTON, A. A. G.

PHILADELPHIA PRESS BUREAU
                          RICHMOND, MAY 22, 1865.

ROBBERY IN RICHMOND.

It would be impossible for Sunday to pass without a sensation of some kind. Yesterday morning, about three o'clock, an individual, who gives his name as James Burke, by the aid of a lamp-post, ascended upon a verandah, which afforded easy access through the windows of the second story to several rooms in the Monumental Hotel. He immediately went to the window of the room where Majors Stanton and Fithian, recently arrived paymasters of the army, with plethoric chests of greenbacks, were quartered, and attempted to raise it, which roused the inmates. Finding some difficulty, he passed along to a room in which were several Baltimorians, where he halted for an instant, and then returned to the attack upon the paymasters. This time he was more successful, and raising the window gently, he commenced to crawl in, when one of the majors received him with the contents of a pistol which passed through his abdomen, and the detected criminal fell into the room in the greatest agony, dropping a huge knife which he carried in his hand. The knife corresponded exactly with a scabbard which was found in one of the rooms of the same hotel which was robbed a few nights ago. Burke, who claims to hail from Baltimore, is hardly expected to recover, though immediate surgical treatment was rendered to his condition. Thus far he refuses to disclose the names of any of his confederates in crime, though he admits his acquaintance with several persons whom he declares to be professional scoundrels. Key No. 9 of the Spottswood Hotel, several pawnbrokers' tickets for watches, a number of sutlers' checks, and about one dollar and a half in money, were found upon his person. Several clues have been obtained which will lead to the arrest and punishment of a gang of thieves who for some time have been operating in this city.

The Negro Corps.

That the negro corps, under General Weitzel, has received marching orders is well known throughout their camps, and they are beginning to put on the war-paint with the impression that they are going to Texas. They look forward to the period of embarkation with a great deal of satisfaction.

Promotion.

Major Charles Warren, 11th Connecticut, provost marshal of the Fourth district, was, for meritorious services, day before yesterday, mustered in as lieutenant colonel of his regiment. As an officer in the city, his undeviating courtesy has won for him the esteem of all good citizens, while his exemplary administration of justice has made him the terror of evil-doers.

THE WET SEASON.

We are now experiencing that kind of weather which is known here as the long season in May, which extends almost into the middle of June. Almost daily showers, thunder storms with terrific lightnings, and a cool atmosphere, are the peculiarities of this season. We were favored last night and this morning with much rain, which to the industrious farmer is a source of great satisfaction. There is a rapid rise in the river, and also in the streets in the vicinity of Rocketts.

DICK TURNER, THE RUNAWAY JAILER.

Dick Turner, whose escape from Libby I noticed several days ago, has not been captured yet. It is generally supposed by persons whose imaginations are fruitful that Turner has been summarily disposed of by the authorities for his many acts of cruelty to Union prisoners while he was one of the heartless and brutal keepers of Libby. He may yet be captured and dealt with as his crimes merit. There are many officers and soldiers who were confined under him in rebel times, who have experienced his barbarity, who declare they will shoot him at the first sight.

Brevet Brigadier General H. L. Abbott[5] has been assigned to duty as chief of artillery on the staff of Major General Ord, commanding the Department of Virginia.

PHILADELPHIA PRESS BUREAU

RICHMOND, JUNE 4, 1865.

THE RECONSTRUCTION OF THE STATE.

The grand work of reconstruction in this State is quietly but surely progressing, upon the policy foreshadowed by the General Government, under such favorable circumstances as will insure the most

5. Henry Larcom Abbott (1831–1927), Corps of Engineers, and formerly of the 1st Connecticut Heavy Artillery, was in control of the heavy mortar, called "the Dictator," which was used very effectively against Petersburg. Francis Trevelyan Miller (ed.), *The Photographic History of the Civil War* (10 vols.; New York, 1957), V, 51; Mark Mayo Boatner III, *The Civil War Dictionary* (New York, 1959), 1.

harmonious results. The advent of Gov. Pierpont has been most auspicious, and will tend to relieve the people from many embarrassments, and to the development of the purposes of the authorities towards those who have been identified with the interests of the rebellion. The Governor entertains for many of this class a great deal of sympathy, without doing any violence to his loyalty as a patriot, or any injustice to the principles of freedom. The Union men in Virginia could not have been more fortunate in having such a sterling Executive; the rebels could not have had a more compassionate Governor, or the negroes a better friend, than Francis Harrison Pierpont, out of this Commonwealth. He is a plain, matter-of-fact person, with a strong compound of common sense, of quick perception, and of uncommon research. With dignity and ease he blends the most respectful attention to the simplest wants of the humblest brokendown specimen of Southern chivalry. All are received with true republican dignity, their complaints listened to or their questions answered with as much promptness and interest as if they were persons of rank, and the flimsy nature of their visits, matters of business.

THE 25TH CORPS.

The 25th Corps (colored) is, with the exception of one or two regiments, on board of the transports, many of which have left City Point for Texas. Major General Weitzel has not yet embarked, nor will he until all his troops are under way.

THE CURIOSITY TO VISIT THE CITY.

This city is the object of mingled curiosity and interest. Persons are attracted here to see Richmond, which, but for the relation it sustained to the late dreams of a Southern confederacy, would have been unknown, except as the great breeding mart of human bondage. This class of persons is generally repaid for their time lost and money spent in witnessing a State restored to freedom and the national authority; in observing the elements which, under proper influences, would develop themselves into the highest state of civilization, and the gradual return to consciousness of these unfortunate people, who have been allured from loyalty by the phantom of States' rights.

ADVENTURERS.

But there is another class of persons who are justly termed adventurers, who are flocking here, who come under the hallucination that Richmond presents a splendid opportunity to acquire fortunes. This place, during the war, has been the receptacle of all the refugees who could reach it from every part of the South. This large class of consumers tended to impoverish the city, and which has been continued without any cessation. The Southern people, blinded by the sophistry of their leaders, have invested all their money in the rebel bonds; and today many of them, living in their own mansions, are reaping the bitter fruits of their folly in a variety of mortifying ways, but none is so humiliating to their pride as the reflection that absolute want is evident where Virginia hospitality shown in all the genial relationship of conventionality.

CONDITION OF THE CITY AND STATE.

Without enumerating the influences which have paralyzed many important branches of industry, it is only necessary to add that Richmond and Virginia, without the aid of Northern capital and enterprise, will be unable to recover from the ruins and stagnation, in which treason has plunged them, in ten years to come. The most of the F. F. V.'s are without any but rebel currency; and the conduct of the business men to our Northern merchants, on the breaking out of the rebellion, has seriously impaired their credit. Many of the latter class are not only in want, but being too proud to solicit rations from the Government, accept food from their colored acquaintances, who delicately administer to their wants in a manner so as not to offend their sensibilities. Such being the poverty of the better class, the others must indeed be in an unfortunate condition.

PROFITABLE BUSINESS.

There are certain kinds of business which will thrive while the army is in Virginia, but which will drag heavily along when their success depends upon the support of those who are reduced to poverty by aiding the rebellion. Pawnbroking and mortgaging promise to be the most substantial pursuits in which persons can engage.

Farming.

It will be some time before the farming interests will do little more than support the families which cultivate them. The former manner of tilling the soil being at an end, it will require some time before the oppressed and the oppressor can adopt such harmonious regulations as will be equally satisfactory. Radical changes always require time to adapt themselves to the circumstances of individuals, and in this case no small amount of civilization is necessary.

General Hints.

From these general hints, gratuitously given for the benefit of adventurers, it must be obvious that the chances for fortunes here are rather limited among the chivalry. A trip of this character to Richmond invariably ends in disappointment to every calenlating speculator, while those who blindly rush into pursuits will soon realize the folly of their undertaking. One thing is certain, that the rebels here hate the Yankee with no abatement, and will not patronize them if they can be accommodated by those of similar sympathy. All the stores not burnt down are in possession of the rebels, who are going North to replenish their goods. There has been such a rush for places of business, that rents have ascended to the dazzling heights which was demanded in rebel trash. In some cases, landlords are requiring their tenants to pay fifty dollars in greenbacks per month, when only twenty-five dollars in Jeff Davis' shinplasters were necessary for a vending establishment.

The Demand for Places of Business.

In view of the demand for places of business, owners of property are trying to annul the contracts which they have made with their tenants previous to our occupation of the city, and are much chagrined that they cannot do so, or charge the high figure in greenbacks which the numerous applicants are willing to give. It might be well for those adventurers who come to Richmond not to be too sanguine that they will be fortunate enough to enter the few channels which promise success.

RICHMOND, JUNE, **1865.**

Gov. Pierpont is being daily visited by delegations of citizens from the Valley, along the Blue Ridge, and some beyond the Allegheny Mountains—by individuals who have held prominent places of distrust in the State and Confederate Governments; by officers of rank, who are included in the excepted class of the amnesty proclamation; by civilians who have remained true to their country— all of whom recognize the inevitable conclusion that slavery is ended; that secession was a delusion, and that State rights is a theoretical idea, which can never be reduced to practice.

IMPRESSION UPON THE GOVERNOR.

These respective delegations have made a decided impression upon the Governor as to the truthfulness of their utterances and the sincerity of their resignation. He has conversed freely and frankly with the people in all conditions of society, soliciting their opinions as to the return of the national authority, which have been given in such a spirit of candid submission to the old flag, as to leave no doubt of their sincerity. The Governor is so impressed with the bearing and deportment of the people of Virginia, as to express the opinion that they accept the triumph of the Union arms with a degree of cheerfulness which he did not anticipate. The original Secessionists, having assured him that their Government has taken the wings of a very early morning for an indefinite flight, have no compunctions in renouncing all allegiance to an authority which has passed away, or philosophically giving up all faith in rebel bonds. This class magnani- mously admits that there is nothing in State sovereignty as originally held by them, and that Virginia must, in accordance with the decision from which there is no appeal, be reconstructed upon the basis of freedom.

THE CONDITION OF THE NEGRO.

A large number of visiting gentlemen are extremely solicitous about the condition, and, not unfrequently, the status of the negro. Some state that their former slaves have remained with them, and are equally, if not more faithful in their labor, under the inspiration of remuneration; while others complain that their property, which has always had a fugacious aspect, has unceremoniously deserted them, and are seeking employment with other persons. The farmers are now trying the advantages of free labor upon as economical a basis as possible, giving to each laborer ten dollars per month and rations. Not a few of the chivalry have declared, with a good deal of pride, that their negroes positively declined to leave them, but are determined to remain.

Change in Rebel Feeling.

All classes of persons who have called upon the Governor have announced, with a great deal of unanimity, that they were heartily rejoiced to be back in the old Union again as citizens of a grand and great country; many of them were rebels from the beginning.

How the Chivalry Now Feel.

The chivalry have now no hesitation in associating the Davis Government with fraud, starvation, destitution, and all manner of iniquities. They have no hesitation now in informing the Governor that the rebellion commenced in that spirit, and was ended with those disgraceful results which have added additional infamy to the crime of treason. It is only since the triumphs of the Union army that they have professed to experience any relief from these great wrongs, under the sanction of usurped authority.

Confiscation and Reorganization.

The governor is importuned more upon the subject of confiscation than any other. The rebels are extremely nervous upon this point, which consumes more of the Executive time and receives more of his attention than any question which is now under consideration in the reconstruction. There seems to be such a general conscientiousness of guilt among the chivalry as to render them incapable of understanding or applying the proclamations of the President on the subject of reorganizing the State. The Governor has done much to repress the solicitude of those most culpable, and explain the proclamations of the President to their satisfaction. Many of these broken-down chivalry are relieved of much anxiety after these interviews, who return to their former homes with the Executive comfort so considerately given, to communicate the good news, which has the effect of stimulating an extra curl of the lips and noses of the fair ones at the Yankee officers as they pass by their residence, since they have a hope that their property will not be confiscated, or in any way involved by the act. The Governor deems the question of political suffrage the most difficult to settle in the reorganization of the State. The Government, of which he is the chief Executive, has designated, in order to exercise the right of suffrage, that the individual must be white; must take the oath to support the restored government of Virginia; that they have not done anything to support the rebellion since 1864. Along the valley of Virginia and the border there is a very considerable number of men who can conscientiously take the prescribed oath. Then, of course, there are other parts of the State in which everybody has been engaged, one way or the other, against the national authority. The people in some localities were poor and without clothing, food, and other necessaries of life, which had to be supplied by the rebel authorities to a certain extent. General Lee not unfrequently made his appeals directly to the people for sustenance and supplies for his army, which they could not refuse, as they were connected by other ties than political destiny with the ragamuffin followers of the rebel chieftain. The instincts of humanity, without any sympathy with the rebellion, might have dictated such a course, and, in some cases, very probably did. This support—for it can be regarded in no other light—has been rendered to a much greater extent since 1864 than at any previous period. The necessities of the case have required it. Some were willing contributors to the rebellion in this respect, while others yielded to the force of circumstances.

WHO ARE DISFRANCHISED?

It is very obvious to the Governor that a large class of persons cannot take the oath, and are, by the restored government of Virginia, disfranchised. He has ascertained, after consulting with the most intelligent persons, that, in organizing some of the counties, there are not qualified constituents enough to fill the county offices, and that hardly one-twentieth of the people could take the oath and become voters. The Governor thinks that, under the circumstances, there is great danger of what he terms the honorable and truthful men refusing to take the oath, while those who care nothing for the privilege of voting may indifferently avail themselves of the opportunity.

The Governor is of the opinion that, while many of the soldiers, who were in the rebel service against their inclination, and from force of circumstances, the policy of excluding their officers, who can exert an influence upon those who served under them, will be productive of great evils. The disfranchised officers would create, he thinks, a great deal of sympathy, which would enable them to control votes which might be used for improper ends, while the bane of proscription rested upon them. The Governor regrets this, since the soldiers and a large number of politicians, whom he deems to be every way inferior to the excluded class, can under the law become qualified voters. He deeply sympathizes with the political disabilities of the chivalry, who have stirred up the very depths of his compassion. He is even now considering whether it is best to restore them to their former political rights or forever disgrace them.

What Governor Pierpont Says.

In speaking upon this subject yesterday, Governor Pierpont remarked that he would sooner cast his lot among the proscribed class, under all the penalties of the authorities, than to be identified with the Copperheads of Ohio, Indiana, Pennsylvania, New York, or Boston, who had the desire to injure the country, but did not possess the courage to enter the field in support of their treason.

The above is neither speculation nor conjecture, but may be relied upon as correct in every particular.

PHILADELPHIA PRESS BUREAU

RICHMOND, JUNE 11, 1865.

John Minor Botts on Reconstruction.

Wishing to be as fully informed as possible, upon the present aspect of reconstruction, I called yesterday on the Hon. John Minor Botts,[6]

6. John Minor Botts (?–?), a representative from Virginia, was imprisoned in 1862 for refusing to support the Confederacy. He headed the Republican Union party, which met in Alexandria in May, 1866, and, among other things, adopted a qualified suffrage

who is at present in this city, at the solicitation of Governor Pierpont, to assist in the reorganization of the State. Mr. Botts says that the people of Virginia would have had no objection to have received Mr. Pierpont as Provisional Governor, but that there is a decided disinclination to acknowledge him as the Executive of this Commonwealth. He thinks it would be unjust to force the Alexandria Constitution,[7] formed in a Convention of only eleven members, and adopted by four or five hundred votes, upon the people of this State. He says, as he honestly opposed the Lecompton Constitution[8] being forced upon the people of Kansas, he cannot consistently ask the people of Virginia to submit without protest to the Alexandria Constitution. Mr. Botts quotes Charles Sumner with much emphasis, in referring to that gentleman's speech, in which he declared that those who presented their credentials to be admitted to the United States Senate were elected by nothing more than a town council.

THE ABOLITION OF SLAVERY.

This eminent gentleman also thinks that the disorganization of labor, by immediate emancipation, is a source of much disquietude. The people would have preferred to have had a voice in what so nearly affects them. They do not like the idea of accepting a fundamental law with whose provision they are unacquainted, and of

---

for both races, in spite of Botts's opposition to the enfranchisement of blacks. Alrutheus Taylor, *The Negro in the Reconstruction of Virginia* (1926; rpr. New York, 1969), 24; Emory M. Thomas, *The Confederate State of Richmond: A Biography of the Capital* (Austin, 1971), 82.

7. A meeting of fifteen delegates from twelve counties convened in Alexandria, the seat of the restored government under Union control, in February, 1864, to revise the state constitution. The new constitution, among other things, proposed to disfranchise those who held civil or military offices in the Confederacy, to insist on a pledge of allegiance to the Union for all voters, and to abolish slavery, though it permitted county courts to apprentice black children. Taylor, *The Negro in the Reconstruction of Virginia,* 8.

8. A convention consisting of representatives from nineteen of the state's thirty-four counties, chosen by less than one-fourth of the eligible electorate, met in 1857 in Lecompton, Kansas, and adopted a proslavery constitution for the state. The constitution's ratification was boycotted by opponents of slavery; in fact, the entire election was a fraud. Congress forced President Buchanan, who pushed for Kansas' admission under the constitution, to demand that the constitution be submitted to a popular referendum. It was roundly defeated in August, 1858. J. G. Randall and David Donald, *The Civil War and Reconstruction* (Boston, 1969), 115–17.

whose spirit they are uninformed. He frankly admits that the antislavery clause is repugnant to the people, yet had they the formation of a new constitution they could be induced, by certain influences, to yield their objections and insert an article abolishing the system.

Mr. Botts has no hesitation in saying that the abolition of slavery was one of the worst measures that the Government has adopted for the slave. He declares that many of the negroes are lazy and worthless, and not in a condition to enjoy freedom; but that if the act had been gradual, they could have been prepared for the position which has been forced upon them. He wants it distinctly understood that he is not in favor of slavery, and that at his death he had intended to make satisfactory provision for his bondsmen. Many of them, however, not knowing of his generous intentions, or, if they did, not caring to wait until that period, mysteriously disappeared, among whom he thinks there are only two or three who are capable of taking care of themselves. They left the women and children with him, whom he cheerfully supports, thankful that it is in his power to do so.

NEGROES REMAINING IN THE SOUTH.

Mr. Botts emphatically declares that the democracy of the people of the South is of that character that they will not permit the negroes to remain in the South in peace as free men. He mentioned the fact of his friendship for the negro in several instances, and spoke of these unfavorable signs, not as expressing his own feelings, but as anticipating unfortunate events. He called attention to the fact that in the Convention of 1850 in this State, to revise the Constitution, when efforts were made to deepen the degradation of the slaves, and to increase the embarrassments and persecutions of the free people of color, he demanded of the representatives of the State what—with the additional weight of legislation, they were about to burden the negroes—they wished to accomplish. When he was answered that if it were deemed necessary, they would be driven into the Chesapeake. His liberality with reference to the negro has frequently been the cause and made the occasion for the most violent vituperation from his political opponents in Virginia, who seriously questioned his fidelity to Southern institutions.

An Important Order.

The uniforms of treason, so offensive to Union men, are declared contraband by the following order, which will be promulgated through the daily papers tomorrow morning, to the astonishment of the rebels:

HEADQUARTERS DEPARTM'T OF VIRGINIA, ARMY OF THE JAMES

RICHMOND, VA., JUNE 10, 1865.

General Order, No. 70—A sufficient time having elapsed since the surrender of the forces late in rebellion with the United States for all who were of such forces to procure other apparel than their uniform,

It is hereby ordered. That no person after June 15, 1865, appear in public in this department wearing any insignia of rank or military service worn by officers or men of the late rebel army.

Where plain buttons cannot be procured, those formerly used can be covered with cloth.

Any person violating this order will be liable to arrest.

By command of Major General E. D. O. Ord,
Edw. W. Smith, Asst. Adjt. General.

Judge Ould and Captain Hatch, rebel commissioners of exchange, still occupy their well-ventilated apartments at the Hotel de Libby. Matters of private interest have demanded their presence elsewhere, but the pressing nature of the invitation to remain, to attend to public affairs, are perfectly irresistible. It is generally supposed that the investigations which are now going on will restore Judge Ould to his liberty. Hatch is believed to be capable of robbing our prisoners. Dishonest practices having been discovered in the bureau, it was deemed necessary to arrest the chief, as well as his subordinate, which will account for the Judge's detention.

PHILADELPHIA PRESS BUREAU

RICHMOND, JUNE 12, 1865.

The Military Rule of the City.

It can no longer be disguised that the military rule of this city has been squared, as far as possible, in accordance with the feelings of the rebels, until it has culminated in the reinstatement of one of the greatest secessionists as mayor of this city, and the reappointment of his rebellious police. Without any evidence of repentance, and with nothing to recommend them but the oath of allegiance—which they have taken with a mental reservation—and with four years of vindictive hate, and hands covered with blood of patriots, the good sense of the American people has been shocked by the elevation to trust and power of this old public sinner and his satellites whose treason in this city before the occupation was regarded as the standard for the Richmond rebels.

Who Reinstated Mayo as Mayor of Richmond?

The reinstatement of Mayo was such an unlooked for act, and such a gross outrage upon the feelings of the Union people of this city, that they are now demanding to know who is guilty of what is very little less than a crime. Gov. Pierpont says he knew nothing about the reinstatement of Mayo, until he saw it in the papers, and that it has been done without his advice, consent, knowledge, or desire. Gen. Patrick positively declares that it is not his work, and that he knew nothing of Mayo's appointment until he reported to him that he was authorized to assume his former functions. The general regards him as an old fogy, literally unqualified for the mayoralty. Gen. Ord has denied his knowledge of this act, and has not hesitated to regret the reinstatement of one whom he considers an incompetent person. Gen. Patrick thinks that Gen. Halleck had nothing to do with it. The governor says it has been done by the military, and the military regard it as an act of the governor. John Minor Botts, representing the Union sentiment of the State, and Charles Palmer of this city, declare it an outrage upon the loyal people. From the aspect of affairs in reference to Mayo, one would suppose that very little harmony or sympathy of feeling existed between the governor and the military authorities. Each is still regarding the other as the author of this piece of iniquity, and will continue to do so until startled by the light of the press. Since the governor has washed his hands of this great wrong and all the generals, with the exception of Halleck—for whom Patrick, to a certain extent, speaks, who has the authority to reinstate Mayo, deny all participation in the humiliation, it would not be inappropriate in the Government at Washington to ascertain who reinstated Mayo as Mayor of Richmond.

A Colored Delegation to Complain to the President.

This morning, Messrs. Fields Cook, Williamson, and Wells[9] leave for Washington, delegated to present a declaration of the wrongs of colored people of this city to the President, and protest against the reinstatement of Mayo.

Reasons for Reinstating Mayo.

The reasons alleged for Joe Mayo's appointment as Mayor are, that this city is in a fearful state; that crime is being daily committed; that the negroes are the guilty parties; that the old rebel police know their resorts; and that much good can be accomplished by their familiarity with the local affairs of the city. The rebels have made the authorities believe that the negroes are the only criminals in the city, and have said that the present insecurity of life and money after night is the logical result of emancipation.

Paroled Rebels are the Criminals.

It has been ascertained, beyond any doubt, that the disgraceful scenes which are of almost nightly occurrence are perpetrated by paroled rebel troops, in the uniform of our soldiers, and not infrequently with blackened faces. Mayo's police, who can be seen on every corner and along every street, in the daytime, sometimes mounted, hunting down loyal negroes, are nowhere to be found in the night, while robberies and almost murder are committed upon the public thoroughfares. While there are some negroes and some Union soldiers who are guilty of many of the crimes perpetrated in this city, the large majority of them are committed by rebel soldiers and citizens whom the misfortunes of war have left in a condition of poverty, either to work or steal if they would escape starvation.

No Pass Considered Better Than Gen. Lee's.

It has been the custom for Mayo's police to arrest all negroes who had not a pass from the provost marshal. The military guard,

9. Richard H. Wells (?–?). A minister, Wells was pastor of the Manchester African Baptist Church and the Ebenezer Baptist Church in Richmond. Taylor, *The Negro in the Reconstruction of Virginia,* 187–88.

previous to their reinstatement, would recognize the passes given by employers to their servants or workmen, but the police, during the last day or two, would not consider them sufficient to protect the blacks from arrest, as many colored persons hired others, and had issued passes to them. Yesterday one of Lee's negro servants was halted by one of the police force, and asked if he had a pass. He replied in the affirmative. "Who is it from?" inquired the rebel policeman. "From General Lee," replied the negro. *"You couldn't have gotten one from a better man,"* was the expressive response of the traitor who holds his office by loyal permission. Of course, Lee's servant was not molested; but if he had been Gen. Grant's, the probabilities are that he would have gone to the city prison.

ADAMS' EXPRESS COMPANY REFUSE TO HIRE REBELS.

Several applications have been made to Adams' Express company by these red-handed rebels, who offered to accept positions for thirty dollars per month, for which the company are now paying loyal gentlemen seventy-five. To the credit of the gentlemen who are conducting this enterprising institution, it must be said that they declined the services of those persons who offered to work for less money than would defray the expenses of their board bills. The company possessed a little too much wisdom to take into its employment men without a character.

THE POST-OFFICE DEPARTMENT WILL NOT EMPLOY REBELS.

Many of the broken-down chivalry have been soliciting positions in the post-offices of this city, with very little success. They even have the assurance to say: "You Yankees can't run the mail South without our assistance and co-operation, and you will be obliged to call upon us to help you", and other equally as refreshing intelligence. The Post-office department has issued instructions to the postmaster here not to employ one of the rebel tribe. As we go marching on, we shall soon learn from the rebel press in this city that this is a violation of the Constitution and the doctrine of States' Rights.

THE WHITES DRAW THE LARGEST AMOUNT OF RATIONS.

The latest classification upon the books of the relief committee is as follows, for the week ending May 22, 1865:

The number of rations distributed to—

White men	950	Negro men	104
White women	3,825	Negro women	1,200
White children	5,085	Negro children	1,840

THE AMOUNT OF RATIONS ISSUED WEEKLY.

Abstract of issues of rations to destitute families for the city of Richmond and surrounding country, by Frederick L. Manning,[10] lieutenant colonel, and president of the Relief Commission, from May 1st to June 12th, 1865:

When Issued	No. of Persons.	No. of Rations.
From May 1st to May 8th	13,764	39,094
From May 8th to May 15th	12,559	59,091
From May 15th to May 22d	12,449	44,602
From May 22d to May 29th	12,458	43,182
From May 29th to June 5th	11,154	39,400
From June 5th to June 11th	10,276	37,896
Total from May 1st to June 12th	72,660	262,765[11]

REFUSE TO WALK UNDER THE FLAG.

There are some of the women who are still so embittered against the Government as to refuse to walk under the flag when they go to procure their rations.

General Ord was invited to dine with Captain Hatch, the rebel commissioner of exchange, who had been guilty of plundering our prisoners, and other acts of villainy, and upon his arrival at the house found the captain spirited away to Libby, and it under guard by the orders of General Patrick, his subordinate. General Ord examined Hatch the next morning, and finding no fault in him, set him at

10. Frederick Lewis Manning (b. 1836) mustered in as a first lieutenant, 148th New York Infantry, in September, 1862, and rose to lieutenant colonel in October, 1864. Frederick Phisterer (comp.), *New York in the War of the Rebellion, 1861 to 1865* (5 vols.; New York, 1912), V, 3727.

11. This seems to be the total given, though the copy is practically illegible.

liberty to complete, if he chose, his arrangements for the dinner which Patrick's bluntness had so unceremoniously postponed. Hatch was, however, rearrested by orders from Washington, and is now in Libby, where he is likely to remain for some time—or in some other place of confinement compatible with his crime.

Just on the eve of closing this letter I learn that Major Gen. Alfred Terry, the hero of Fort Fisher, has arrived in the city and will relieve Generals Halleck and Ord of their commands.

Index